Lord Byron

SELECTED LETTERS AND JOURNALS

"I am not a cautious letter writer
and generally say what comes uppermost at the moment."
BYRON TO MARY SHELLEY, NOVEMBER 14, 1822.

BYRON
From a portrait by
Thomas Phillips, RA, 1814

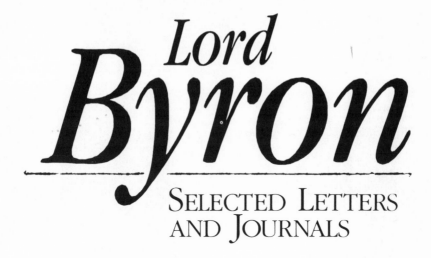

Lord
Byron

SELECTED LETTERS
AND JOURNALS

Edited by Leslie A. Marchand

THE BELKNAP PRESS OF
HARVARD UNIVERSITY PRESS
CAMBRIDGE, MASSACHUSETTS
1982

Printed in the United States of America

Library of Congress Cataloging in Publication Data

Byron, George Gordon Byron, Baron, 1788–1824.
    Lord Byron: selected letters and journals

    Includes index.
    1. Byron, George Gordon Byron, Baron, 1788–1824—
Correspondence. 2. Byron, George Gordon Byron, Baron,
1788–1824—Diaries. 3. Poets, English—19th century—
Biography. I. Marchand, Leslie Alexis, 1900–
II. Title.
PR4381.A385   1982   821'.7 [B]   82-9720
ISBN 0-674-53915-X

CONTENTS

v

For MARION
who knows and likes Byron

EDITORIAL NOTE

The letters in this volume are selected for their general interest and for the qualities which make them among Byron's best and most entertaining. No attempt has been made to choose letters representative of all his various moods and styles, nor to make them tell a complete story of his life, which can be better read in a biography. Since some of the very best and most lively letters were written from Italy, and particularly from Venice, a greater number have been chosen from that period. All letters included are complete and unexpurgated. The text and notes are from the complete edition, but some notes have been added to explain matters which would not otherwise be clear. Selections from the Journals are complete entities in subject matter, or complete sections by date or number, and the Alpine Journal and the Journal written in Cephalonia (Byron's last) are given in their entirety.

The *bons mots* and memorable passages include many from letters and journals which it was impossible to print as a whole in this volume of selections. But they are gems well worth preserving. In the main they are self-contained aphorisms or full statements of the matter in hand, but for the reader who wishes to see them in the context of the whole letter the reference is given after each excerpt.

The biographical summary of Byron given in Appendix I is a brief sequence of events to give the background to the selected letters. Appendix II consists of short biographical sketches of Byron's correspondents in this volume. In every instance the emphasis is on Byron's relations with the subject. Appendix III is a list of the letters included in this volume together with their location in the complete edition.

The letters to Thomas Moore, first published in his *Letters and Journals of Lord Byron* (1830), were printed with many omissions. Moore also made omissions in those of Byron's journals that he transcribed. His omissions are indicated by asterisks. The original manuscripts of these are not known to have survived.

ACKNOWLEDGMENTS

My gratitude is due to all the librarians, booksellers, collectors and friends and strangers who have generously given time and effort to help me gather the vast number of Byron's letters which appeared over the years in the twelve volumes of the Murray–Harvard edition of *Byron's Letters and Journals,* the quintessence of which I have attempted to distil in this one volume.

Above all I am indebted to my friend and publisher John Murray, whose enthusiasm has never flagged and who has contributed more to the grand edition and to this distillation than can easily be recorded. I might add that it is something extraordinary in these days of conglomerate publishing, when little attention can be paid to an author who is not a best seller, to have a "personal publisher". I do believe that he has done as much for me as his ancestor did for Byron. I haven't asked him for red tooth-powder or magnesia or Macassar oil as Byron did of his publisher, but he has served me in ways more pertinent to the business in hand. And unlike his ancestor, who, as Byron complained, was maddeningly delinquent in his correspondence, the 6th John Murray answers letters promptly. I am also grateful to his colleague John Gibbins for his careful reading of copy and proofs and for his helpful suggestions.

Maud Wilcox, Editor-in-Chief at the Harvard University Press, deserves credit for the whole-hearted interest and ardent support she has given this project from its inception.

INTRODUCTION

As successive volumes of Byron's letters have appeared in the Murray–Harvard unexpurgated edition, reviewers and readers in general have been amused, amazed, and impressed with their freshness and vigour, their sparkle and wit and good humour, and their essential honesty and freedom from cant. At a time when letter writing often fell into conventional patterns of polite flattery or serious moralizing, Byron served his correspondents with a hearty dish of "what comes uppermost", and reached depths of truth and realism with teasing wit and tongue-in-cheek cynicism. He told Mary Shelley "I am not a cautious letter writer" and that perhaps accounts in large part for the fact that he is never a dull one.

We see little of the "gloomy egoist" in the letters—of Childe Harold or Manfred, of Conrad or Lara. Most of those moods were siphoned off in his poetry, "the lava of the imagination whose eruption prevents an earthquake". It is true that the persiflage of his letters is often a cover for the deep melancholy and low spirits which frequently obsessed him. He was aware of the character his early *Weltschmerz* poetry had given him with the public and, particularly after his self-exile in Italy, he wanted to counter it. He wrote to Thomas Moore from Venice, asking him to assure Francis Jeffrey, who knew him only through his poetry, "that I was not, and, indeed, am not even *now*, the misanthropical and gloomy gentleman he takes me for, but a facetious companion, well to do with those with whom I am intimate, and as loquacious and laughing as if I were a much cleverer fellow." And when he carried the mood of his letters into his boisterous and satiric poetry such as *Don Juan* and *The Vision of Judgment*, it was difficult for his correspondents to believe that they were sometimes written when he was in the deepest depression. In a letter to Scrope Davies from Venice in 1817 he confessed to being in very low spirits, "which you would not suspect from this buffooning perhaps—if you did not know human nature well enough to be aware that when people are most melancholy they are often most addicted to buffooning." He wrote to Moore from Pisa: "You seem to think that I could not have written the 'Vision,' &c., under the influence of low spirits; but I think you err. A man's poetry is a distinct faculty, or soul, and has no more to do with the every-day individual than the Inspiration with the Pythoness when removed from her tripod."

It is certainly true of his best letters, early and late, that the lightness of touch, the exuberance and zest, often belie his darkest melancholy. One has only to read the letters written while he was composing *Childe Harold* or *Manfred* or *The Corsair* to see how his two selves could co-exist. This is no indictment of the sincerity of the feelings that produced those poems. But to the modern reader the letters show a face and a personality that is generally more congenial to the spirit of our age, even when it is a chameleon face. Byron's is the kind of honesty that eschews consistency. As he said in *Don Juan*, "But if a writer should be quite consistent, / How could he possibly show things existent?" And in his journal he wrote in 1813: "This journal is a relief. When I am tired—as I generally am—out comes this, and down goes everything. But I can't read it over;—and God knows what contradictions it may contain. If I am sincere with myself (but I fear one lies more to one's self than to any one else), every page should confute, refute, and utterly abjure its predecessor." And it is this faithfulness to the mood of the moment that is so refreshing in the letters. Once he has emancipated himself from the need to be consistent, honesty has free play and we are deluged with the most amusing and often profound speculations, sometimes seriously and sometimes with waggish wit. He can be outrageous and still make readers see the underlying truth of his assertions, and the absurdity of their own prejudices. He realized that flippancy had become a habit, but we can hardly be sorry for it. He has the good taste not to belabour his *bons mots* but lets them work singly and often with understatement: "The place is well & quiet & the children only scream in a low voice".

Most of Byron's correspondents knew how to take his levity, but sometimes he felt he should warn them. After making some jesting remarks about Catholicism, he told Moore: "I am afraid that this sounds flippant, but I don't mean it to be so; only my turn of mind is so given to taking things in the absurd point of view, that it breaks out in spite of me every now and then". The twentieth-century reader may find it even more difficult to sift out the serious intent that always lurks in Byron's most extravagant hyperboles. But an extended reading of the letters will give the sympathetic modern man or woman a feeling for his characteristic style and as much tolerance for his wayward opinions and prejudices as one always has for his or her own.

With all his inconsistencies Byron held some firm convictions from which he never deviated. Chief among these, he told Lady Blessington, were his love of liberty and his hatred of cant. And his love of truth was profound. He wrote to Moore concerning his Memoirs: "Over these latter sheets I would leave you a discretionary power; because they contain, perhaps a thing or two which is too sincere for the public. . . . add what you please from your own knowledge; and *above all, contradict* any thing, if I have *mis*-stated; for my first object is the truth, even at my own expense".

What emerges from the letters is a personality, fascinating in its variety and in its genial humanity. No writer of the nineteenth century surpassed Byron in the revelation of his sins and foibles without apologies or hypocritical repentance. And knowing his propensity to exaggerate, we can hardly believe that his sins are cardinal. His tolerant view of the world, his good-humoured cynicism combined with a general benevolence toward human frailty, including his own, disarms all but the most "rigidly righteous".

His style is conversational without being colloquial. Unlike Wordsworth he did not affect the speech of the common man. His letters are full of literary allusions, sometimes playfully distorted to fit his own purposes. He eschewed "fine writing" and preferred quotations from lesser dramatists such as Dibdin's "this tight little island" or Farquhar's "full of pastime and prodigality". His quotations from Shakespeare are not the rhetorical "high flights" but rather some catching phrase from *Much Ado* or *Macbeth* or *Othello*. He plundered Scott and Sheridan and Goldsmith for apt words and lines such as "absurd womankind" from Monckbarns in *The Antiquary*. These he repeated in various contexts to suit the occasion. But his quotations are not literary or bookish, and he moulds them to his own style and uses.

His letters from abroad written during his first pilgrimage to the East belie the world weariness and disillusionment which are the pervading themes of *Childe Harold* composed while he was journeying through some of the most picturesque regions of Albania, Greece, and Turkey. Although he affected to eschew description, his account of his visit to Ali Pasha at Tepelene, written to his mother, overflows with youthful zest for experience and reveals the exhilaration that he felt in novel situations and among strange people. Likewise his bubbling enthusiasm for Sintra and Seville and Cadiz, saved by humorous and cynical touches from too great seriousness, show him to be anything but a blasé traveller.

"I am happy here," he wrote to his friend Hodgson from Lisbon, "because I loves oranges, and talk bad Latin to the monks, who understand it, as it is like their own,—and I goes into society (with my pocket pistols), and I swims in the Tagus all across at once, and I rides on an ass or a mule, and swears Portuguese, and have got a diarrhoea and bites from the mosquitoes. But what of that? Comfort must not be expected by folks that go a pleasuring."

So with his boasting of his swimming the Hellespont, as described to Henry Drury (and to half a dozen other correspondents). "This morning I *swam* from *Sestos* to *Abydos*, the immediate distance is not above a mile but the current renders it hazardous, so much so, that I doubt whether Leander's conjugal powers must not have been exhausted in his passage to Paradise."

Occasionally he grew more serious as when he defended his voyage to his mother: ". . . I am so convinced of the advantages of looking at mankind instead of reading about them, and of the bitter effects of staying at home with all the narrow prejudices of an Islander, that I think there should be a law amongst us to set our young men abroad for a term among the few allies our wars have left us". And to Hodgson he confessed: ". . . I begin to find out that nothing but virtue will do in this damned world. I am tolerably sick of vice which I have tried in its agreeable varieties, and mean on my return to cut all my dissolute acquaintance, leave off wine and 'carnal company', and betake myself to politics and Decorum".

Beset by tragedy (the death of his mother and several close friends) and by money difficulties on his return to England, Byron became earnest again, but his letters are still filled with his irrepressible ebullience. To Hodgson, who tried to console him with conventional religious preachments, he wrote: "As to your immortality, if people are to live, why die? And our carcases, which are to rise again, are they worth raising? I hope, if mine is, that I shall have a better *pair of legs* than I have moved on these two-and-twenty years, or I shall be sadly behind in the squeeze into Paradise". And again, ". . . there is something Pagan in me that I cannot shake off. In short, I deny nothing, but doubt everything".

Byron's sudden fame with the publication of the first two cantos of *Childe Harold* in the spring of 1812 made him a lion of Whig Society. His most important new correspondents were Thomas Moore, the Irish poet, and Lady Melbourne, the mother-in-law of Lady Caroline Lamb in whose web he soon became entangled. In his attempt to extricate himself Byron sought the assistance of Lady Melbourne and she became his most intimate friend and confidante from whom he withheld few secrets about his love affairs. He confided to his diary: "To Lady Melbourne I write with most pleasure—and her answers, so sensible, so *tactique*—I never met with half her talent. If she had been a few years younger, what a fool she would have made of me, had she thought it worth her while,—and I should have lost a valuable and most agreeable *friend*".

Lady Melbourne relayed Byron's first proposal of marriage to her niece Annabella Milbanke. And he shared with her most of the excruciating and sometimes amusing details of his attempt to loosen the tentacles of the madcap Caroline Lamb, his subsequent liaison with Lady Oxford, whose "autumnal charms" enchanted him for some months, and finally his dangerous attachment to his half-sister Augusta Leigh. In an attempt to wean him from that, Lady Melbourne encouraged his flirtation with Lady Frances Webster. Byron's letters to Lady Melbourne giving a day by day account of the progress of that affair, entered upon lightly at first and then growing serious, are among the most amusing of all those he wrote during his years of fame.

He began with some objective and rather cynical observations: "W[ebste]r will be a noble subject for Cuckoldom in three years, though he has managed to impregnate her Ladyship, which consequently can be no very difficult task.—She is certainly very pretty, & if not a dunce, must despise her 'Bud' heartily.—She is not exactly to my taste, but I dare say Dragoons would like her". But after he had been a house guest of the Websters for a few days his interest in her increased and he reported, still with cynical bravado: ". . . one generally *ends* & *begins* with Platonism—& as my proselyte is only twenty—there is time enough to materialize" and shortly after he added a postscript: "This business is growing serious—& I think *Platonism* in some peril". And a few days later: "We have progressively improved into a less spiritual species of tenderness—but the seal is not yet fixed though the wax is preparing for the impression".

But when it came to the crucial point, Byron "spared her", as he told Lady Melbourne. Despite his continuing light account of it, the matter had grown serious for him and, unlike the true Don Juan he was supposed to be, he respected her feelings and her wishes. "I do detest everything which is not perfectly mutual." His bantering style sometimes concealed his true feelings even from such a worldly-wise confidante as Lady Melbourne. He finally wrote to her: ". . . you really *wrong* me too, if you do not suppose that I would sacrifice everything for Ph [Frances Webster]—I hate sentiment—& in consequence my epistolary levity—makes you believe me as hollow & heartless as my letters are light".

He was equally frank and flippant in writing to Lady Melbourne

9

about Annabella Milbanke after her refusal of his suit. "As to Annabella she requires time & all the cardinal virtues, & in the interim I am a little verging towards one who demands neither, & saves me besides the trouble of marrying by being married already." And in another letter he wrote: "I congratulate A[nnabella] & myself on our mutual escape.—That would have been but a *cold collation*, & I prefer hot suppers". But he confessed his continued interest in her. "I am not now in love with her—but I can't at all foresee that I should not be so if it came 'a warm June' (as Falstaff observes) and seriously—I do admire her as a very superior woman a little encumbered with Virtue. . . ."

When Annabella began a correspondence with him, he did not bow to her moral prejudices but stated his position boldly. "Your sweeping sentence 'in the circles where we have met' amuses me much when I recollect some of those who constituted that society—after all bad as it is it has its agremens.—The great object of life is Sensation—to feel that we exist—even though in pain—it is this 'craving void' which drives us to Gaming—to Battle—to Travel—to intemperate but keenly felt pursuits of every description whose principal attraction is the agitation inseparable from their accomplishment." In writing to Lady Melbourne he had called Annabella the "Princess of Parallelograms" because of her interest in mathematics, and added "Her proceedings are quite rectangular, or rather we are two parallel lines prolonged to infinity side by side but never to meet". He would have been happier if he had left the matter there.

After his separation and self-exile, when he was settled in Venice and had achieved calm contentment in the arms of Marianna Segati, "pretty as an antelope", "with great black eyes", his letters achieved new brilliance. With a beyond-the-grave frankness and abandon, he freed himself from the inhibitions of England and wrote as it pleased him. Some of the best letters of this period are those to his publisher, John Murray, to Thomas Moore, to his life-long friend John Cam Hobhouse, and to Douglas Kinnaird, his friend, banker and business agent.

His letters to Murray concern more than the publication of his poems, though that is interesting enough. They are almost a diary of his Italian sojourn and contain many intimate details of his life among the natives, written with a view to their being read by Murray's friends. He wrote to him of the accomplishments of his mistress and ended by saying, "But her great merit is finding out mine—there is nothing so amiable as discernment". His account of his liaison with Margarita Cogni, the "Fornarina" or baker's wife, is even more revealing, and is a masterpiece of character portrayal of that "gentle tigress", "fit to breed gladiators from".

He wrote with equal frankness to Moore both of literary and personal matters. "I verily believe that nor you, nor any man of poetical temperament, can avoid a strong passion of some kind. It is the poetry of life. What should I have known or written, had I been a quiet, mercantile politician, or a lord in waiting? A man must travel, and turmoil, or there is no existence." Responding to Moore's praise of the third canto of *Childe Harold*, he wrote: "I am glad you like it; it is a fine indistinct piece of poetical desolation, and my favourite. I was half mad during the time of its composition, between metaphysics, mountains, lakes, love unextinguishable, thoughts unutterable, and the nightmare of my own delinquencies. I should, many a good day, have blown my brains out, but for the recollection that it would have given pleasure to my mother-in-law; and, even *then*, if I could have been certain to haunt her. . . ." It was to Moore that he addressed his fine lyric:

So we'll go no more a roving
So late into the night. . . .

And to him he confessed his ambition to be something more than a writer. "If I live ten years longer, you will see, however, that it is not over with me—I don't mean in literature, for that is nothing; and it may seem odd enough to say, I do not think it my vocation. But you will see that I will do something or other—the times and fortune permitting . . ." When Moore wrote that he always felt about his art "as the French husband did when he found a man making love to his (the Frenchman's) wife:—'Comment, Monsieur,—sans y être obligé!'" Byron replied: "I feel exactly as you do about our 'art', but it comes over me in a kind of rage every now and then, like * * * *. and then, if I don't write to empty my mind, I go mad. As to that regular, uninterrupted love of writing, which you describe in your friend, I do not understand it. I feel it as a torture, which I must get rid of, but never as a pleasure. On the contrary, I think composition a great pain."

Yet when he found his forte in *Don Juan*, a medium which permitted him to give vent to his every mood and thought with an unrestrained freedom he had never known before, he wrote with gusto, and he defended the poem against the fears of his friends (who thought that it would damage his reputation because of its plain speaking in matters of sex, religion, and politics) and against the public reaction to it.

At first, not knowing how it would be received, he wrote lightly of

11

it, saying that his purpose was to make it "a little quietly facetious upon everything", and that his only aim was "to giggle and make giggle". But later when he realized its possibilities as a free expression of the truth of life as he saw it, he changed his tone: "D[on] Juan will be known by and bye for what it is intended," he wrote to Murray, "a *Satire* on *abuses* of the present states of Society—and not an eulogy of vice—it may be now and then voluptuous—I can't help that—Ariosto is worse—Smollett . . . ten times worse—and Fielding no better. No girl will ever be seduced by reading D. J.—no—no—she will go to Little's poems & Rousseau's romans for that—or even to the immaculate De Stael—they will encourage her & not the Don—who laughs at that—and—and—most other things". Of the Countess Guiccioli's objections to the poem, he wrote: "The truth is that it is TOO TRUE— and the women hate every thing which strips off the tinsel of *Sentiment*". "You sha'n't make Canticles of my Cantos", he protested. "The poem will please if it is lively—if it is stupid it will fail—but I will have none of your damned cutting and slashing." "Come what may", he wrote again, "I will never flatter the million's canting in any shape. . . ." And when Murray and others urged him to write some "great work" which would better employ his talents, he replied: "you have so many '*divine*' poems—is it nothing to have written a *Human* one? without any of your worn out machinery".

To Hobhouse and Kinnaird he wrote most frankly and facetiously, for that was the language of their conversation in the Regency society they had known. He spiced his business correspondence with Kinnaird with humorous allusions to his growing love of money. In acquiescing temporarily and reluctantly in the judgment of his friends that he should not publish *Don Juan*, he protested: "This acquiescence is some thousands of pounds out of my pocket—the very thought of which brings tears into my eyes—I have imbibed such a love for money that I keep some Sequins in a drawer to count, & cry over them once a week". And later when he was hoarding money for an expedition to South America or Greece, he wrote: ". . . my most extravagant passions have pretty well subsided—as it is time that they should on the verge of thirty five.——I always looked to about thirty as the barrier of any real or fierce delight in the passions—and determined to work them out in the younger ore and better veins of the Mine—and I flatter myself (perhaps) that I have pretty well done so—and now the dross is coming—and I loves lucre—for one must love something."

His last attachment, the Countess Teresa Guiccioli, whom he met in Venice and followed to Ravenna, roused in him a deep passion and a genuine love which rather surprised him after his round of Carnival philandering in Venice, when he had resolved to "go no more a roving/ So late into the night". His Italian letters to her were at first more passionate than any he had ever written in English without any of the objective detachment and humour which he managed to keep in reserve in his previous love affairs. In consequence they are somewhat mannered and filled with lovers' clichés. It is true that his letters about her to his friends display his normal flippancy (she was "fair as sunrise, and warm as noon"), but that, if one understands his moods and modes of expression, casts no doubt on the sincerity of his attachment. Later, when his passion had cooled to a conjugal fondness, he could be playful and teasing in his letters to her. Before many months had passed he could write: "I kiss you more often than I have ever kissed you—and this (if memory does not deceive me) should be a fine number of times, counting from the beginning". And in 1821 he could tell his sister, "I can say that without being so *furiously* in love as at first—I am more attached to her—than I thought it possible to be to any woman after three years".

Byron's letters from Greece, when he went there to help the Greeks in their war for independence, are more sober and business like, but his old facetiousness breaks through occasionally, as when he tells John Bowring, secretary of the London Greek Committee, "The Supplies of the Committee are some useful—and all excellent in their kind—but occasionally hardly *practical* enough—in the present state of Greece—for instance the Mathematical instruments are thrown away —none of the Greeks know a problem from a poker—we must conquer first and plan afterwards.—The use of the trumpets too may be doubted—unless Constantinople were Jericho. . . ."

There was a marvellous directness in his assessment of the Greeks and their cause. In one of his last letters from Greece he told Bowring: "I shall continue to pursue my former plan of stating to the Committee things as they *really* are—I am an enemy to Cant of all kinds but it will be seen in time—who are or are not the firmest friends of the Greek cause—or who will stick by them the longest—the Lempriere dictionary quotation Gentlemen—or those who neither dissemble their faults nor their virtues".

Byron's journals furnish a fine supplement to the letters. It is hard to say whether they are more self-revealing, although there are many passages of self-analysis and speculation that delve more deeply into his psyche and elaborate his view of the world without the levities and *bons mots* which he felt impelled to use as embellishment for his observations in his correspondence. His 1813–14 journal is sprinkled, it is true, with the kind of aphorisms that enliven his letters. "I never set myself seriously to wishing without attaining it—and repenting." "I will *not* be the slave of *any* appetite." "All are inclined to believe what they covet, from a lottery-ticket up to a passport to Paradise." But more of it is filled with sober reflections about his own life and the life around him. Lord Holland's friend Allen had lent him "a quantity of Burns's unpublished, and never-to-be-published Letters. They are full of oaths and obscene songs. What an antithetical mind!—tenderness, roughness—delicacy, coarseness—sentiment, sensuality—soaring and grovelling, dirt and deity—all mixed up in that one compound of inspired clay! It seems strange; a true voluptuary will never abandon his mind to the grossness of reality. It is by exalting the earthly, the material, the *physique* of our pleasures, by veiling these ideas, by forgetting them altogether, or, at least, never naming them hardly to one's self, that we alone can prevent them from disgusting."

Self-confessions abound: "There is something to me very softening in the presence of a woman, some strange influence, even if one is not in love with them,—which I cannot at all account for, having no very high opinion of the sex. But yet,—I always feel in better humour with myself and every thing else, if there is a woman within ken". Byron was still the social lion, yet most of the parties he attended bored him. "Last night, *party* at Lansdowne-house. To-night, *party* at Lady Charlotte Greville's—deplorable waste of time, and something of temper. Nothing imparted—nothing acquired—talking without ideas —if any thing like *thought* in my mind, it was not on the subjects on which we were gabbling. Heigho!—and in this way half London pass what is called life."

He reflected on his own writing and the reception of it. "If I valued fame, I should flatter received opinions, which have gathered strength by time, and will yet wear longer than any living works to the contrary. But, for the soul of me, I cannot and will not give the lie to my own thoughts and doubts, come what may. If I am fool, it is, at least, a doubting one; and I envy no one the certainty of his self-approved wisdom." And he was stirred by world events. He devoted several paragraphs to the revolution in Holland and more to the fall of Napoleon, setting down in sober prose what he said less well in his "Ode To Napoleon Buonaparte".

His Alpine Journal is a detailed narrative of his journey through the Bernese Alps with Hobhouse in September, 1816, from which he drew the background for *Manfred*. The scenery seduced him into some unwonted picturesque description: "The torrent is in shape curving over the rock—like the *tail* of a white horse streaming in the wind—such as might be conceived would be that of the '*pale* horse' on which *Death* is mounted in the Apocalypse. It is neither mist nor water but a something between both—it's immense height (nine hundred feet) gives it a wave—a curve—a spreading here—a condensation there—wonderful—& indescribable". The mood is of immense exhilaration mingled with melancholy. ". . . . heard the Avalanches falling every five minutes nearly—as if God was pelting the Devil from Heaven with snow balls." At the Grindelwald he saw a "very fine Glacier—like a *frozen hurricane* . . . the whole of the day as fine in point of weather—as the day on which Paradise was made.—Passed *whole woods of withered pines—all withered*—trunks stripped and barkless—branches lifeless—done by a single winter—their appearance reminded me of me & my family".

His Ravenna Journal, written at a time of imminent revolution in which Byron was deeply involved with the Carbonari, is filled with his record of reading and writing (he composed one drama and planned another while waiting for the sound of musketry), of riding in the pine woods, and visiting the Countess Guiccioli and her family. Mingled with this are occasional sober thoughts. "It has been said that the immortality of the soul is a 'grand peut-être'—but still it is a *grand* one. Every body clings to it—the stupidest, and dullest, and wickedest of human bipeds is still persuaded that he is immortal." The thought of a free Italy, "the very *poetry* of politics" lifted his spirits, but he was obsessed with fits of despondency. "I presume that I shall end . . . like Swift—'dying at top'. I confess I do not contemplate this with so much horror as he apparently did for some years before it happened. But Swift had hardly *begun life* at the very period (thirty-three) when I feel quite an *old sort* of feel. Oh! there is an organ playing in the street —a waltz, too! I must leave off to listen. They are playing a waltz which I have heard ten thousand times at the balls in London, between 1812 and 1815."

The "Detached Thoughts", a curious journal of reminiscences of his childhood and years of fame in London, written while he was waiting to join the Countess Guiccioli in Pisa, is full of random thoughts dashed off like sparks from his active mind. He wished that he had studied languages with more attention, but he was easily distracted, as he confessed readily. "I set in zealously for the Armenian and Arabic—but I fell in love with some absurd womankind both times before I had overcome the Characters and at Malta & Venice left the profitable Orientalists for—for—(no matter what—) notwithstanding that my master the Padre Pasquale Aucher . . . assured me 'that the terrestrial Paradise had been certainly in *Armenia*'—I went seeking it —God knows where—did I find it?—Umph!—Now & then—for a minute or two." His speculations about immortality take a peculiar turn, quasi scientific, metaphysical, and humanitarian rather than religious. ". . . that the *Mind* is *eternal*—seems as possible as that the body is not so. . . . A *material* resurrection seems strange and even absurd except for purposes of punishment—and all punishment which is to *revenge* rather than *correct*—must be *morally wrong*—and when the *World is at an end*—what moral or warning purpose *can* eternal tortures answer? . . . I cannot help thinking that the *menace* of Hell makes as many devils as the severe penal codes of inhuman humanity make villains."

Byron's last journal, written in Cephalonia before he sailed for Missolonghi, records his frank thoughts about the Greeks and speculates with more hope than he felt later on his possible part in the emancipation of the Greeks from their own internal dissensions as well as from the Turks. ". . . after all one should not despair, though all the foreigners that I have hitherto met with amongst the Greeks are going or gone back disgusted. Whoever goes into Greece at the present should do it as Mrs. Fry went into Newgate—not in expectation of meeting with any especial indication of existing probity, but in the hope that time and better treatment will reclaim the present burglarious and larcenous tendencies which have followed this General Gaol delivery."

The letters and journals together give a vivid impression of a fascinating character, who with all his faults, and they were many, insinuates himself into the sympathies of a reader by his transparent humanity. Speaking of his literary reputation, he wrote: "My great comfort is, that the temporary celebrity I have wrung from the world has been in the very teeth of all opinions and prejudices. I have flattered no ruling powers; I have never concealed a single thought that tempted me".

BYRON'S LETTERS AND JOURNALS

Dear Sir.—Your advice was good but I have not determined whether I shall follow it, this place is the *Devil*, or at least his principal residence, they call it the University, but any other appellation would have suited it much better, for Study is the last pursuit of the Society; the Master[1] eats, drinks, and Sleeps, the Fellows *drink, dispute* and *pun,* the *employments* of the under Graduates you will probably conjecture without my description. I sit down to write with a head confused with dissipation, which though I hate, I cannot avoid. I have only supped at home 3 times since my arrival, and my table is constantly covered with invitations, after all I am the most *steady* man in the College, nor have I got into *many* Scrapes, and none of consequence. Whenever you appoint a day my Servant shall come up for Oateater, and as the Time of paying my bill now approaches the remaining £50 will be very *agreeable*. You need not make any deduction as I shall want most of it, I will settle with you for the Saddle and accoutrements *next* quarter. The Upholsterer's bill will not be sent in yet, as my Rooms are to be papered and painted at Xmas, when I will procure them; No Furniture has been got except what was absolutely necessary, including some decanters and wine Glasses. Your Cook certainly deceived you, as I know my Servant was in Town 5 days, and she stated 4. I have yet had no reason to distrust him, but we will examine the affair when I come to Town, when I intend Lodging at Mrs. Massingberds.[2] My Mother and I have quarrelled, which I bear with the *patience* of a philosopher, custom reconciles one to every thing. In the hope that Mrs. H. and the *Battalion* are in good Health I remain Sir & &

BYRON

Sir—After the contents of your epistle you will probably be less

---

[1] William Lort Mansel was Master of Trinity from 1798 until his death in 1820. He was a wit and was noted for his epigrams, but he was a strict disciplinarian.

[2] Elizabeth Massingberd was a widow with a daughter who lived at 16 Piccadilly. In 1802 Mrs. Byron had taken rooms with her, and Byron spent part of the summer there. Thereafter he frequently rented a room from her when he was in London, and later she and her daughter stood security for him with usurers.

surprised at my answer, than I have been at many points of yours;[1] never was I more astonished than at the perusal, for I confess I expected very different Treatment.—Your *indirect* charge of Dissipation does not affect me, nor do I fear the strictest enquiry into my conduct, neither here nor at *Harrow* have I disgraced myself, the "Metropolis" & the "Cloisters" are alike unconscious of my debauchery, and on the plains of *merry Sherwood*, I have experienced *Misery* alone; in July I visited them for the *last* Time. Mrs. Byron & myself are now totally separated, injured by her, I sought refuge with Strangers, too late I see my error, for how was kindness to be expected from *others*, when denied by a *parent*. In you Sir I imagined I had found an Instructor, for your advice I thank you; the Hospitality of yourself & Mrs. H. on many occasions, I shall always gratefully remember, for I am not of opinion, that even present injustice can cancel past obligations. Before I proceed it will be necessary to say a few words concerning Mrs. Byron; you hinted a probability of her appearance at Trinity; the instant I hear of her arrival, I quit Cambridge, though *Rustication* or *Expulsion* be the consequence, many a weary week of *torment* have I passed with her, nor have I forgot the insulting *Epithets* with which, *myself*, my *Sister*, my *Father*, & my *Family* have been repeatedly reviled. To return to you, Sir, though I feel obliged by your hospitality &&; in the present instance, I have been completely deceived. When I came down to College and even previous to that period, I stipulated that not only my Furniture but even my Gowns & Books, should be paid for, that I might set out, free from *Debt*; now, with all the *Sang Froid* of your profession, you tell me, that not only, I shall not be permitted to repair my Rooms (which was at first agreed to) but that I shall not even be indemnified for my present expence. In one word hear my determination. I will *never* pay for them out of my allowance, and the Disgrace will not attach to me, but to *those* by whom I have been deceived. Still, Sir, not even the Shadow of dishonour shall reflect upon *my* name, for I will see that the Bills are discharged, whether by you or not is to me indifferent, so that the men I [emp]loy are not the victims of my Imprudence or your duplicity. I have ordered nothing extravagant, every man in College is allowed to fit up his rooms, mine are secured to me during my residence which will probably be some time, and in

---

[1] Byron misunderstood Hanson's statement about the allowance from the Court of Chancery for his furniture. What he had said was that the sum was not yet available, not that Byron would have to pay the bill out of his general allowance. Byron was mollified by Hanson's explanation in his next letter.

rendering them decent, I am more praiseworthy than culpable.—
The money I requested was but a secondary consideration, as a
Lawyer you were not obliged to advance it till due, as a *Friend* the
request might have been complied with, when it is required at Xmas,
I shall expect the demand will be answered. In the course of my Letter
I perhaps have expressed more asperity than I intended, it is my
nature to feel warmly, nor shall any consideration of interest or Fear
ever deter me from giving vent to my Sentiments when injured
whether by a Sovereign or a subject. I remain & &

BYRON

[TO THE REV. JOHN BECHER]   *Dorant's. February 26th. 1808*

My dear Becher,—Just rising from my Bed, having been up till six
at a Masquerade, I find your Letter, and in the midst of this dissipated
Chaos it is no small pleasure to discover I have some *distant* friends in
their Senses, though mine are rather out of repair.—Indeed, I am
worse than ever, to give you some idea of my late life, I have this
moment received a prescription from Pearson, not for any *complaint*
but from *debility*, and literally *too much Love.*—You know my devotion
to woman, but indeed Southwell was much mistaken in conceiving my
adorations were paid to any Shrine there, no, my Paphian Goddesses
are elsewhere, and I have sacrificed at their altar rather too liberally.—
In fact, my blue eyed Caroline,[1] who is only sixteen, has been lately so
charming, that though we are both in perfect health, we are at present
commanded to *repose*, being nearly worn out.—So much for Venus,
now for Apollo,—I am happy you still retain your predilection, and
that the public allow me some share of praise, I am of so much importance, that a most violent attack is preparing for me in the next
number of the Edinburgh Review,[2] this I have from the authority of a
friend who has seen the proof and manuscript of the Critique, you know
the System of the Edinburgh Gentlemen is universal attack, they praise
none, and neither the public or the author expects praise from them,
it is however something to be noticed, as they profess to pass judgment

[1] The blue-eyed Caroline has not been identified, but it is probable that some
verses he wrote three days before this letter were addressed to her in a tone that
shows that Byron's sentiments are not always to be judged by the seeming callous-
ness of his letters. See "Song", *Poetry*, I, 262–63.

[2] The January number of the *Edinburgh Review*, which appeared in late February, contained the cutting and sarcastic review by Henry Brougham of Byron's
Hours of Idleness.

21

only on works requiring the public attention.—You will see this when it comes out, it is I understand of the most unmerciful description, but I am aware of it, and I hope *you* will not be hurt by its severity.—Tell *Mrs. Byron* not to be out of humour with them, and to prepare her mind for the greatest hostility on their part, it will do no injury however, and I trust her mind will not be ruffled.—They defeat their object by indiscriminate abuse, and they never praise except the partizans of Ld. Holland & Co.³——It is nothing to be abused, when Southey, Moore, Lauderdale, Strangford, and Payne Knight share the same fate.—I am sorry, but C— Recollections must be suppressed during this edition, I have altered at your Suggestion the *obnoxious allusions* in the 6th Stanza of my last ode.—And now, Becher I must return my best acknowledgments for the interest you have taken in me and my poetical Bantlings, and I shall ever be proud to show how much I esteem the *advice* and the *Adviser*.—Believe me

most truly yours
BYRON

[TO HENRY DRURY]   *Falmouth June 25th. 1809*

My dear Drury,—We sail tomorrow in the Lisbon packet having been detained till now by the lack of wind and other necessaries, these being at last procured, by this time tomorrow evening we shall be embarked on the vide vorld of vaters vor all the vorld like Robinson Crusoe.— — — —The Malta vessel not sailing for some weeks we have determined to go by way of Lisbon, and as my servants term it to see "that there *Portingale*" thence to Cadiz and Gibraltar and so on our old route to Malta and Constantinople, if so be that Capt. Kidd our gallant or rather gallows commander understands plain sailing and Mercator, and takes us on our voyage all according to the Chart. — — —Will you tell Dr. Butler that I have taken the treasure of a servant Friese the native of Prussia Proper into my service from his recommendation.— —He has been all among the worshippers of Fire in Persia and has seen Persepolis and all that.—Hobhouse has made woundy preparations for a book at his return, 100 pens two gallons

<hr>

³ Byron assumed that the *Edinburgh Review* praised only Whigs such as Lord Holland, leader of the Moderate Whigs in the House of Lords. And in fact many of its reviews were politically inspired, just as were those of the Tory *Quarterly Review*. But as a member of the Cambridge Whig Club, Byron felt it unjust that he should be attacked by a Whig periodical. He brought it on himself, however, by the "lordly" tone of his preface, made worse by juvenile and mawkish humility.

Japan Ink, and several vols best blank is no bad provision for a discerning Public.—I have laid down my pen, but have promised to contribute a chapter on the state of morals, and a further treatise on the same to be entituled "Sodomy simplified or Paederasty proved to be praiseworthy from ancient authors and modern practice."—Hobhouse further hopes to indemnify himself in Turkey for a life of exemplary chastity at home by letting out his "fair bodye" to the whole Divan.— Pray buy his missellingany[1] as the Printer's Devil calls it, I suppose 'tis in print by this time. Providence has interposed in our favour with a fair wind to carry us out of its reach, or he would have hired a Faquir to translate it into the Turcoman Lingo.— —

> "The Cock is crowing
> "I must be going
> "And can no more

Ghost of Gaffer Thumb[2]
Adieu believe me yours as in duty bound
BYRON

turn over

P.S.—We have been sadly fleabitten at Falmouth.— —

[TO FRANCIS HODGSON]   *Lisbon, July 16th, 1809*

Thus far have we pursued our route, and seen all sorts of marvellous sights, palaces, convents, &c.—which, being to be heard in my friend Hobhouse's forthcoming Book of Travels, I shall not anticipate by smuggling any account whatsoever to you in a private and clandestine manner. I must just observe that the village of Cintra in Estramadura is the most beautiful, perhaps in the world. * * *

I am very happy here, because I loves oranges, and talk bad Latin to the monks, who understand it, as it is like their own,—and I goes

---

[1] Hobhouse's *Imitations and Translations*, commonly referred to by his friends as his "Miscellany", was sent to the printer before he left England with Byron, who had contributed nine poems to the volume. Hobhouse's friend Matthews called it his "missellingany".

[2] Byron was quoting from an adaptation by Kane O'Hara of Fielding's burlesque. *The Tragedy of Tragedies: or the Life and Death of Tom Thumb the Great* as played at the Theatre Royal Haymarket, in 1805.

into society (with my pocket-pistols),[1] and I swims in the Tagus all across at once,[2] and I rides on an ass or a mule, and swears Portuguese, and have got a diarrhœa and bites from the mosquitoes. But what of that? Comfort must not be expected by folks that go a pleasuring. * * *

When the Portuguese are pertinacious, I say, "Carracho!"—the great oath of the grandees, that very well supplies the place of "Damme,"—and, when dissatisfied with my neighbor, I pronounce him "Ambra di merdo." With these two phrases, and a third, "Avra Bouro," which signifieth "Get an ass," I am universally understood to be a person of degree and a master of languages. How merrily we lives that travellers be!—if we had food and raiment. But, in sober sadness, any thing is better than England, and I am infinitely amused with my pilgrimage as far as it has gone.

To-morrow we start to ride post near 400 miles as far as Gibraltar, where we embark for Melita [Malta?] and Byzantium. A letter to Malta will find me, or to be forwarded, if I am absent. Pray embrace the Drury and Dwyer[3] and all the Ephesians[4] you encounter. I am writing with Butler's donative pencil,[5] which makes my bad hand worse. Excuse illegibility. * * *

Hodgson! send me the news, and the deaths and defeats and capital crimes and the misfortunes of one's friends; and let us hear of literary matters, and the controversies and the criticisms. All this will be pleasant—"Suave mari magno," &c.[6] Talking of that, I have been seasick, and sick of the sea. Adieu. Yours faithfully, &c.

---

[1] In a note to *Childe Harold* (*Poetry*, II, 86) Byron says that his carriage was stopped by some ruffians while he was on his way to the theatre in Lisbon. Hobhouse confirmed this in his diary of July 19, 1809: "Attacked in street by four men".

[2] Only a few days after he arrived in Portugal Byron swam "from old Lisbon to Belem Castle, and having to contend with a tide and counter current, the wind blowing freshly, was but little less than two hours in crossing the river". (Hobhouse, *Journey*, II, 808.) Hobhouse called the feat "a more perilous, but less celebrated passage", than Byron's later swimming of the Hellespont.

[3] Unidentified; perhaps a younger master at Harrow.

[4] An Elizabethan slang term meaning boon companions or good fellows. (See *II Henry IV*, II, ii, 136; and *Merry Wives of Windsor*, IV, v, 17.)

[5] Dr. George Butler, Headmaster of Harrow, had presented Byron with a gold pen before his departure. See May 3, 1810, to Drury.

[6] "Suave, mari magno turbantibus aequora ventis. . . ." (Lucretius, *De Rerum Natura*, II, 1.) The full passage in translation reads: "Pleasant it is, when over a great sea the winds trouble the waters, to gaze from shore upon another's great tribulation; not because any man's troubles are a delectable joy, but because to perceive you are free of them yourself is pleasant."

Dear Mother,—I have been so much occupied since my departure from England that till I could address you a little at length, I have forborn writing altogether.—As I have now passed through Portugal & a considerable part of Spain, & have leisure at this place I shall endeavour to give you a short detail of my movements.—We sailed from Falmouth on the 2d. of July, reached Lisbon after a very favourable passage of four days and a half, and took up our abode for a time in that city.—It has been often described without being worthy of description, for, except the view from the Tagus which is beautiful, and some fine churches & convents it contains little but filthy streets & more filthy inhabitants.—To make amends for this the village of Cintra about fifteen miles from the capitol is perhaps in every respect the most delightful in Europe, it contains beauties of every description natural & artificial, Palaces and gardens rising in the midst of rocks, cataracts, and precipices, convents on stupendous heights a distant view of the sea and the Tagus, and besides (though that is a secondary consideration) is remarkable as the scene of Sir H[ew] D[alrymple]'s convention.[1]—It unites in itself all the wildness of the Western Highlands with the verdure of the South of France. Near this place about 10 miles to the right is the palace of Mafra[2] the boast of Portugal, as it might be of any country, in point of magnificence without elegance, there is a convent annexed, the monks who possess large revenues are courteous enough, & understand Latin, so that we had a long conversation, they have a large Library & asked [me?] if the *English* had *any books* in their country.— —I sent my baggage & part of the servants by sea to Gibraltar, and travelled on horseback from Aldea Gallega (the first stage from Lisbon which is only accessible by water) to Seville (one of the most famous cities in Spain where the Government called the Junta is now held) the distance to Seville is nearly four hundred miles & to Cadiz about 90 further

---

[1] The Convention of Cintra (Sintra), which was negotiated by Sir Hew Dalrymple with Junot, the French Commander in Portugal on August 30, 1808, allowed the French to withdraw from the country with their arms and artillery. The Convention, though it bore the name of Cintra, was mainly negotiated near Torres Vedras, and was signed in Lisbon.

[2] The huge monastery at Mafra (the façade is over 800 feet in length) was completed in 1730. It was built lavishly for Joao V by the architect John Frederic Ludwig of Ratisbon. One of the most striking features is the grisaille rococo library.

towards the Coast.—I had orders from the Government & every possible accommodation on the road, as an English nobleman in an English uniform is a very respectable personage in Spain at present. The horses are remarkably good, and the roads (I assure you upon my honour for you will hardly believe it) very far superior to the best British roads, without the smallest toll or turnpike, you will suppose this when I rode post to Seville in four days, through this parching country in the midst of summer, without fatigue or annoyance.—

Seville is a beautiful town, though the streets are narrow they are clean, we lodged in the house of two Spanish unmarried ladies, who possess *six* houses in Seville, and gave me a curious specimen of Spanish manners.—They are women of character, and the eldest a fine woman, the youngest pretty but not so good a figure as Donna Josepha, the freedom of women which is general here astonished me not a little, and in the course of further observation I find that reserve is not the characteristic of the Spanish belles, who are in general very handsome, with large black eyes, and very fine forms.—The eldest honoured your *unworthy* son with very particular attention, embracing him with great tenderness at parting (I was there but 3 days) after cutting off a lock of his hair, & presenting him with one of her own about three feet in length, which I send, and beg you will retain till my return.[3]— Her last words were "Adio tu hermoso! me gusto mucho" "Adieu, you pretty fellow you please me much."—She offered a share of her apartment which my *virtue* induced me to decline, she laughed and said I had some English "Amante," (lover) and added that she was going to be married to an officer in the Spanish army.—I left Seville and rode on to Cadiz! through a beautiful country, at Xeres where the Sherry we drink is made I met a great merchant a Mr. Gordon of Scotland, who was extremely polite and favoured me with the Inspection of his vaults & cellars, so that I quaffed at the Fountain head.—Cadiz, sweet Cadiz! is the most delightful town I ever beheld, very different from our English cities in every respect except cleanliness (and it is as clean as London) but still beautiful and full of the finest women in Spain, the Cadiz belles being the Lancashire witches of their land.—Just as I was introduced and began to like the grandees I was forced to leave it for this cursed place, but before I return to England I will visit it again.—The night before I left it, I sat in the box at the opera with Admiral Cordova's family, he is the commander whom Ld. St.

---

[3] The lock of hair given Byron by Donna Josepha is still preserved among the Byron relics by John Murray.

Vincent defeated in 1797, and has an aged wife and a fine daughter.——
— —Signorita Cordova the girl is very pretty in the Spanish style, in my opinion by no means inferior to the English in charms, and certainly superior in fascination.—Long black hair, dark languishing eyes, *clear* olive complexions, and forms more graceful in motion than can be conceived by an Englishman used to the drowsy listless air of his countrywomen, added to the most becoming dress & at the same time the most decent in the world, render a Spanish beauty irresistible. I beg leave to observe that Intrigue here is the business of life, when a woman marries she throws off all restraint, but I believe their conduct is chaste enough before.—If you make a proposal which in England would bring a box on the ear from the meekest of virgins, to a Spanish girl, she thanks you for the honour you intend her, and replies "wait till I am married, & I shall be too happy."—This is literally & strictly true.—Miss C[ordova] & her little brother understood a little French, and after regretting my ignorance of the Spanish she proposed to become my preceptress in that language; I could only reply by a low bow, and express my regret that I quitted Cadiz too soon to permit me to make the progress which would doubtless attend my studies under so charming a directress; I was standing at the back of the box which resembles our opera boxes (the theatre is large and finely decorated, the music admirable) in the manner which Englishmen generally adopt for fear of incommoding the ladies in front, when this fair Spaniard dispossessed an old women (an aunt or a duenna) of her chair, and commanded me to be seated next herself, at a tolerable distance from her mamma.—At the close of the performance I withdrew and was lounging with a party of men in the passage, when "en passant" the Lady turned round and called me, & I had the honour of attending her to the Admiral's mansion.—I have an invitation on my return to Cadiz which I shall accept, if I repass through the country on my way from Asia.—I have met Sir John Carr Knight errant at Seville & Cadiz, he is a pleasant man.—I like the Spaniards much, you have heard of the battle near Madrid,[4] & in England they will call it a victory, a pretty victory! two hundred officers and 5000 men killed all English, and the French in as great force as ever.—I should have joined the army but we have no time to lose before we get up the Mediterranean & Archipelago,—I am going over to Africa tomorrow, it is only six miles from this Fortress.—My next stage is Cagliari in

[4] The battle of Talavera, July 27 and 28, 1809. Sir Arthur Wellesley defeated Marshal Victor with tremendous loss of British soldiers.

Sardinia where I shall be presented to his S[ardinian] Majesty, I have a most superb uniform as a court dress, indispensable in travelling.—

August 13th

I have not yet been to Africa, the wind is contrary, but I dined yesterday at Algesiras with Lady Westmoreland [*sic*] where I met General Castanos[5] the celebrated Spanish leader in the late & present war, today I dine with him, he has offered me letters to Tetuan in Barbary for the principal Moors, & I am to have the house for a few days of one of their great men, which was intended for Lady W[estmorland],[6] whose health will not permit her to cross the Straits.—

August 15th

I could not dine with Castanos yesterday, but this afternoon I had that honour, he is pleasant, & for aught I know to the contrary, clever, —I cannot go to Barbary, the Malta packet sails tomorrow & myself in it, Admiral Purvis with whom I dined at Cadiz gave me a passage in a frigate to Gibraltar, but we have no ship of war destined for Malta at present, the Packets sail fast & have good accommodations, you shall hear from me on our route, Joe Murray delivers this, I have sent him & the boy back, pray shew the lad any kindness as he is my great favourite, I would have taken him on ⟨but you *know boys* are not *safe* amongst the Turks.—⟩ Say this to his father, who may otherwise think he has behaved ill.—[I hope] This will find you well, believe me yours ever sincerely—

BYRON

P.S.—So Ld. Grey is married to a rustic,[7] well done! if I wed I will bring you home a sultana with half a score cities for a dowry, and reconcile you to an Ottoman daughter in law with a bushel of pearls not larger than ostrich eggs or smaller than Walnuts.— —

[5] General Francisco Janier de Castaños, Duke of Baylen, won a significant victory over the French General Dupont at Baylen in 1808.

[6] Jane Saunders married, as his second wife, the 10th Earl of Westmorland. Byron saw her frequently during his years of fame in London. It was at her house that Lady Caroline Lamb first declined to be introduced to Byron because there were too many women about him.

[7] Lord Grey de Ruthyn, a young man of 23, had leased Newstead Abbey for the period of Byron's minority. In 1809 Lord Grey married Anna Maria, daughter of William Kellam, of Warwick.

My dear Mother,—I have now been some time in Turkey: this place is on the coast but I have traversed the interior of the province of Albania on a visit to the Pacha.—I left Malta in the Spider a brig of war on the 21st. of Septr. & arrived in eight days at Prevesa.—I thence have been about 150 miles as far as Tepaleen his highness's country palace where I staid three days.—The name of the Pacha is Ali,[1] & he is considered a man of the first abilities, he governs the whole of Albania (the ancient Illyricum) Epirus, & part of Macedonia, his Son *Velly* Pacha[2] to whom he has given me letters governs the Morea & he has great influence in Egypt, in short he is one of the most powerful men in the Ottoman empire.—When I reached Yanina the capital after a journey of three days over the mountains through a country of the most picturesque beauty, I found that Ali Pacha was with his army in Illyricum besieging Ibraham Pacha in the castle of Berat.—He had heard that an Englishman of rank was in his dominions & had left orders in Yanina with the Commandant to provide a house & supply me with every kind of necessary, *gratis*, & though I have been allowed to make presents to the slaves &c. I have not been permitted to pay for a single article of household consumption.—I rode out on the viziers horses & saw the palaces of himself & grandsons, they are splendid but too much ornamented with silk & gold.—I then went over the mountains through Zitza a village with a Greek monastery (where I slept on my return) in the most beautiful Situation (always excepting Cintra in Portugal) I ever beheld.[3]—In nine days I reached Tepaleen,

[1] Ali Pasha (Byron regularly spelled it Pacha) (1741–1822) was born at Tepelene in Albania about 75 miles north of Janina, his new capital in the Epirus. When Byron arrived, he had made himself despotic ruler of the whole of what is now modern Greece as far south as the Gulf of Corinth, and of parts of Albania. He had subdued or driven out by treachery the Suliotes, who long defied him, and he used rivals to his advantage, including the French and English in the Ionian Islands. By cunning, treachery, and the use of bandits as soldiers when it suited him, he had raised himself from a petty leader of robber bands to a ruler more powerful in his own domains than the Sultan himself, to whom, as ruler of the Ottoman Empire, he nominally paid tribute and homage. He was short and fat and had a long white beard, and looked benign. But stories of his barbaric cruelty to enemies were well known. Byron used Ali in some measure for a model for Giaffir in *The Bride of Abydos* and for the pirate father of Haidée in *Don Juan*: "the mildest mannered man/That ever scuttled ship or cut a throat".

[2] Veli Pasha, Ali's second son, was master of the Morea (Peloponnesus). Both father and son had a penchant for young boys, and Veli exceeded even his father in treachery, cruelty and lasciviousness.

[3] Byron wrote glowingly of Zitza (Zitsa) in *Childe Harold* (II, 48–52). The monastery, with its magnificent view, still remains, but it is now deserted. On

our Journey was much prolonged by the torrents that had fallen from the mountains & intersected the roads. I shall never forget the singular scene on entering Tepaleen at five in the afternoon as the Sun was going down, it brought to my recollection (with some change of *dress* however) Scott's description of Branksome Castle in his lay, & the feudal system.—The Albanians in their dresses (the most magnificent in the world, consisting of a long *white kilt*, gold worked cloak, crimson velvet gold laced jacket & waistcoat, silver mounted pistols & daggers,) the Tartars with their high caps, the Turks in their vast pelisses & turbans, the soldiers & black slaves with the horses, the former stretched in groupes in an immense open gallery in front of the palace, the latter placed in a kind of cloister below it, two hundred steeds ready caparisoned to move in a moment, couriers entering or passing out with dispatches, the kettle drums beating, boys calling the hour from the minaret of the mosque, altogether, with the singular appearance of the building itself, formed a new & delightful spectacle to a stranger.—I was conducted to a very handsome apartment & my health enquired after by the vizier's secretary "a la mode de Turque." —The next day I was introduced to Ali Pacha, I was dressed in a full suit of Staff uniform with a very magnificent sabre &c.— —The Vizier received me in a large room paved with marble, a fountain was playing in the centre, the apartment was surrounded by scarlet Ottomans, he received me *standing*, a wonderful compliment from a Mussulman, & made me sit down on his right hand.—I have a Greek interpreter for general use, but a Physician of Ali's named [Secularío?] who understands Latin acted for me on this occasion.—His first question was why at so early an age I left my country? (the Turks have no idea of travelling for amusement) he then said the English Minister Capt. Leake[4] had told him I was of a great family, & desired his respects to my mother, which I now in the name of Ali Pacha present to you. He said he was certain I was a man of birth because I had small ears, curling hair, & little white hands, and expressed himself pleased with my appearance & garb.—He told me to consider him as a father

---

the outer wall is a plaque in Greek recording Byron's visit and quoting two lines from *Childe Harold*:

Monastic Zitza! from thy shady brow,
Thou small, but favoured spot of holy ground!

[4] William Martin Leake (1777–1860), a Captain in the British army and British Resident at the court of Ali Pasha, residing at Prevesa and Janina, had been in British service of a semi-diplomatic nature in Constantinople, Egypt and European Turkey since 1800. His travel books and topographical studies of the Near East, published later, brought him fame.

whilst I was in Turkey, & said he looked on me as his son.—Indeed he treated me like a child, sending me almonds & sugared sherbet, fruit & sweetmeats 20 times a day.—He begged me to visit him often, and at night when he was more at leisure—I then after coffee & pipes retired for the first time. I saw him thrice afterwards.—It is singular that the Turks who have no hereditary dignities & few great families except the Sultan's pay so much respect to birth, for I found my pedigree more regarded than even my title.—His Highness is 60 years old, very fat & not tall, but with a fine face, light blue eyes & a white beard, his manner is very kind & at the same time he possesses that dignity which I find universal amongst the Turks.— —He has the appearance of any thing but his real character, for he is a remorseless tyrant, guilty of the most horrible cruelties, very brave & so good a general, that they call him the Mahometan Buonaparte.—Napoleon has twice offered to make him King of Epirus, but he prefers the English interest & abhors the French as he himself told me, he is of so much consequence that he is much courted by both, the Albanians being the most warlike subjects of the Sultan, though Ali is only nominally dependent on the Porte. He has been a mighty warrior, but is as barbarous as he is successful, roasting rebels &c. &c.—Bonaparte sent him a snuffbox with his picture[;] he said the snuffbox was very well, but the picture he could excuse, as he neither liked *it* nor the *original*.—His ideas of judging of a man's birth from ears, hands &c. were curious enough.—To me he was indeed a father, giving me letters, guards, & every possible accommodation.—Our next conversations were of war & travelling, politics & England.—He called my Albanian soldier who attends me, and told him to protect me at all hazards.—His name is Viscillie[5] & like all the Albanians he is brave, rigidly honest, & faithful, but they are cruel though not treacherous, & have several vices, but no meannesses.—They are perhaps the most beautiful race in point of countenance in the world, their women are sometimes handsome also, but they are treated like slaves, *beaten* & in short complete beasts of burthen, they plough, dig & sow, I found them carrying wood & actually repairing the highways, the men are

[5] Byron elsewhere spells his name Vascillie and Basili. He was an Albanian soldier assigned to Byron by Ali Pasha as guide and guard. Byron became attached to him and kept him on as a servant until he left Greece in May 1811. In a note to *Childe Harold* he says that Basili, who was an Albanian Christian, "had a great veneration for the church [Greek Orthodox], mixed with the highest contempt of churchmen, whom he cuffed upon occasion in a most heterodox manner. Yet he never passed a church without crossing himself." When his inconsistency was pointed out, he replied: "Our church is holy, our priests are thieves." (*Poetry*, II, 175–76.)

all soldiers, & war & the chase their sole occupations, the women are the labourers, which after all is no great hardship in so delightful a climate, yesterday the 11th. Nov. I bathed in the sea, today It is so hot that I am writing in a shady room of the English Consul's with three doors wide open no fire or even *fireplace* in the house except for culinary purposes.—The Albanians [11 lines crossed out][6] Today I saw the remains of the town of *Actium* near which Anthony lost the world in a small bay where two frigates could hardly manoeuvre, a broken wall is the sole remnant.—On another part of the gulph stand the ruins of Nicopolis built by Augustus in honour of his victory.— — — Last night I was at a Greek marriage, but this & 1000 things more I have neither time or *space* to describe.—I am going tomorrow with a guard of fifty men to Patras in the Morea, & thence to Athens where I shall winter.—Two days ago I was nearly lost in a Turkish ship of war owing to the ignorance of the captain & crew though the storm was not violent.—Fletcher yelled after his wife, the Greeks called on all the Saints, the Mussulmen on Alla, the Captain burst into tears & ran below deck telling us to call on God, the sails were split, the main-yard shivered, the wind blowing fresh, the night setting in, & all our chance was to make Corfu which is in possession of the French, or (as Fletcher *pathetically* termed it) "a *watery* grave."—I did what I could to console Fletcher but finding him incorrigible wrapped myself up in my Albanian capote (an immense cloak) & lay down on deck to wait the worst, I have learnt to philosophize on my travels, & if I had not, complaint was useless.—Luckily the wind abated & only drove us on the coast of Suli on the main land where we landed & proceeded by the help of the natives to Prevesa again; but I shall not trust Turkish Sailors in future, though the Pacha had ordered one of his own galleots to take me to Patras, I am therefore going as far as Missolonghi by land & there have only to cross a small gulph to get to Patras.—Fletcher's next epistle will be full of marvels, we were one night lost for *nine* hours in the mountains in a *thunder* storm, & since nearly wrecked, in both cases Fletcher was sorely bewildered, from apprehensions of famine & banditti in the first, & drowning in the second instance.—His eyes were a little hurt by the lightning or crying (I dont know which) but are now recovered.—When you write address to me at Mr. *Strané's*[7] English Consul, Patras, Morea.— — —

[6] This deleted passage seems to be an account of a page of Ali Pasha or his son, "who loved an Albanian girl" and there seems to have been a struggle to save her honour from Ali Pasha's son.

[7] Strané had been on the *Spider*, which brought Byron and Hobhouse from Malta

I could tell you I know not how many incidents that I think would amuse you, but they crowd on my mind as much as would swell my paper, & I can neither arrange them in the one, or put them down on the other, except in the greatest confusion & in my usual horrible hand.—I like the Albanians much, they are not all Turks, some tribes are Christians, but their religion makes little difference in their manner or conduct; they are esteemed the best troops in the Turkish service.—I lived on my route two days at once, & three days again in a Barrack at Salora, & never found soldiers so tolerable, though I have been in the garrisons of Gibraltar & Malta & seen Spanish, French, Sicilian & British troops in abundance, I have had nothing stolen, & was always welcome to their provision & milk.—Not a week ago, an Albanian chief (every village has its chief who is called Primate) after helping us out of the Turkish Galley in her distress, feeding us & lodging my suite consisting of Fletcher, a Greek, Two Albanians, a Greek Priest and my companion Mr. Hobhouse, refused any compensation but a written paper stating that I was well received, & when I pressed him to accept a few sequins, "no, he replied, I wish you to love me, not to pay me." These were his words.—It is astonishing how far money goes in this country, while I was in the capital, I had nothing to pay by the vizier's order, but since, though I have generally had sixteen horses & generally 6 or 7 men, the expence has not been *half* as much as staying only 3 weeks in Malta, though Sir A. Ball[8] the governor gave me a house for nothing, & I had only *one servant.*—By the bye I expect Hanson to remit regularly, for I am not about to stay in this province for ever, let him write to me at Mr. Strané's, English Consul, Patras.— —The fact is, the fertility of the plains are wonderful, & specie is scarce, which makes this remarkable cheapness.—I am now going to Athens to study modern Greek which differs much from the ancient though radically similar.—I have no desire to return to England, nor shall I unless compelled by absolute want & Hanson's neglect, but I shall not enter Asia for a year or two as I have much to see in Greece & I may perhaps cross into Africa at least the Ægyptian part.—Fletcher like all Englishmen is very much dissatisfied, though a little reconciled to the Turks by a present of 80 piastres from the

to Patras and Prevesa. Hobhouse described him as "a good kind man very ugly". (Diary, Sept. 26, 1809.)

[8] Admiral Sir Alexander Ball (1757–1809) had fought with Nelson, and was successful in blockading and forcing the capitulation of Malta in 1800. He was knighted for his feat and sent as governor of the island. S. T. Coleridge served as his secretary from May 1804 to October 1805. Ball died in 1809, shortly after Byron's stay at Malta.

vizier, which if you consider every thing & the value of specie here is nearly worth ten guineas English.—He has suffered nothing but from *cold*, heat, & vermin which those who lie in cottages & cross mountains in a wild country must undergo, & of which I have equally partaken with himself, but he is not valiant, & is afraid of robbers & tempests.—I have no one to be remembered to in England, & wish to hear nothing from it but that you are well, & a letter or two on business from Hanson, whom you may tell to write.— —I will write when I can, & beg you to believe me,

yr affect. Son
BYRON

P.S.—I have some very "magnifique" Albanian dresses the only expensive articles in this country they cost 50 guineas each & have so much gold they would cost in England two hundred.[9]—I have been introduced to Hussein Bey,[10] & Mahmout Pacha[11] both little boys grandchildren of Ali at Yanina. They are totally unlike our lads, have painted complexions like rouged dowagers, large black eyes & features perfectly regular. They are the prettiest little animals I ever saw, & are broken into the court ceremonies already, the Turkish salute is a slight inclination of the head with the hand on the breast, intimates always kiss, Mahmout is ten years old & hopes to see me again, we are friends without understanding each other, like many other folks, though from a different cause;—he has given me a letter to his father in the Morea, to whom I have also letters from Ali *Pacha*.—

[TO HENRY DRURY]   *Salsette frigate. May 3d. 1810*
in the Dardanelles off Abydos

My dear Drury,—When I left England nearly a year ago you requested me to write to you.—I will do so.—I have crossed Portugal, traversed the South of Spain, visited Sardinia, Sicily, Malta, and thence passed into Turkey where I am still wandering.—I first landed in Albania the ancient Epirus where we penetrated as far as Mount

[9] One of these Albanian dresses, the one which Byron wore when he sat for a portrait to Thomas Phillips, is now in the possession of the Rt. Hon. the Marquess of Lansdowne, descendant of Miss Mercer Elphinstone, to whom Byron gave the costume for a masquerade.
[10] Son of Mouctar Pasha, Ali's oldest son.
[11] Mahmout was the son of Veli Pasha.

Tomerit,[1] excellently treated by the Chief Ali Pacha, and after journeying through Illyria, Chaonia, &ctr, crossed the Gulph of Actium with a guard of 50 Albanians and passed the Achelous in our route through Acarnania and Ætolia.—We stopped a short time in the Morea, crossed the gulph of Lepanto and landed at the foot of Parnassus, saw all that Delphi retains and so on to Thebes and Athens at which last we remained ten weeks.—His majesty's ship Pylades brought us to Smyrna but not before we had topographised Attica including of course Marathon, and the Sunian Promontory.—From Smyrna to the Troad which we visited when at anchor for a fortnight off the Tomb of Antilochus, was our next stage, and now we are in the Dardanelles waiting for a wind to proceed to Constantinople.—This morning I *swam* from *Sestos* to *Abydos*, the immediate distance is not above a mile but the current renders it hazardous, so much so, that I doubt whether Leander's conjugal powers must not have been exhausted in his passage to Paradise.[2]—I attempted it a week ago and failed owing to the North wind and the wonderful rapidity of the tide, though I have been from my childhood a strong swimmer, but this morning being calmer I succeeded and crossed the "broad Hellespont" in an hour and ten minutes.— —Well, my dear Sir, I have left my home and seen part of Africa & Asia and a tolerable portion of Europe.—I have been with Generals, and Admirals, Princes and Pachas, Governors and Ungovernables, but I have not time or paper to expatiate. I wish to let you know that I live with a friendly remembrance of you and a hope to meet you again, and if I do this as shortly as possible, attribute it to any-thing but forgetfulness.—Greece ancient and modern you know too well to require description. Albania indeed I have seen more of than any Englishman (but a Mr. Leake) for it is a country rarely visited from the savage character of the natives, though abounding in more natural beauties than the classical regions of Greece, which however are still eminently beautiful, particularly Delphi, and Cape Colonna in Attica.—Yet these are nothing to parts of Illyria, and Epirus, where places without a name, and rivers not laid down in maps, may one day when more known be justly esteemed superior subjects for the pencil, and the pen, than the dry ditch of the Ilissus, and the bogs of Bœotia.—The Troad is a fine field for conjecture and Snipe-shooting,

[1] Byron described in *Childe Harold* (II, 55) the sun setting behind Mount Tomerit as he descended to Tepelene in Albania.

[2] Leander, according to the Greek legend, swam every night across the Hellespont from Abydos to visit Hero, the priestess of Aphrodite, in Sestos. One night he perished in the crossing, and Hero threw herself into the sea.

and a good sportsman and an ingenious scholar may exercise their feet and faculties to great advantage upon the spot, or if they prefer riding lose their way (as I did) in a cursed quagmire of the Scamander who wriggles about as if the Dardan virgins still offered their wonted tribute. The only vestige of Troy, or her destroyers, are the barrows supposed to contain the carcases of Achilles[,] Antilochus, Ajax &c. but Mt. Ida is still in high feather, though the Shepherds are nowadays not much like Ganymede.—But why should I say more of these things? are they not written in the *Boke* of Gell?[3] and has not Hobby got a journal? I keep none as I have renounced scribbling.—I see not much difference between ourselves & the Turks, save that we have foreskins and they none, that they have long dresses and we short, and that we talk much and they little.—In England the vices in fashion are whoring & drinking, in Turkey, Sodomy & smoking, we prefer a girl and a bottle, they a pipe and pathic.—They are sensible people, Ali Pacha told me he was sure I was a man of rank because I had *small ears* and hands and *curling hair*.—By the bye, I speak the Romaic or Modern Greek tolerably, it does not differ from the ancient dialects so much as you would conceive, but the pronunciation is diametrically opposite, of verse except in rhyme they have no idea.—I like the Greeks, who are plausible rascals, with all the Turkish vices without their courage. —However some are brave and all are beautiful, very much resembling the busts of Alcibiades, the women not quite so handsome.—I can swear in Turkish, but except one horrible oath, and *"pimp"* and "bread" and "water" I have got no great vocabulary in that language.—They are extremely polite to strangers of any rank properly protected, and as I have got 2 servants and two soldiers we get on with great eclât. We have been occasionally in danger of thieves & once of shipwreck but always escaped.—At Malta I fell in love with a married woman and challenged an aid du camp of Genl. Oakes[4] (a

[3] Sir William Gell had published *The Topography of Troy* in 1804, and *Itinerary in Greece* in 1808. Byron had referred to Gell in *English Bards and Scotch Reviewers*, "Of Dardan tours let Dilettanti tell,/ I leave topography to coxcomb Gell," but having met him before going to press, he changed the phrase to "classic Gell". But after having seen the Troad, Byron changed it again for a fifth edition (never published in his lifetime) to "rapid Gell", and added the note: "Rapid, indeed! He topographised and typographised King Priam's dominions in three days!"

[4] General Sir Hildebrand Oakes (1754–1822), after serving in the Egyptian campaign with Sir John Moore, was appointed in 1808 to command the troops at Malta with the local rank of Lt. General. After the death of Sir Alexander Ball, the Governor of Malta, he became Civil and Military Commissioner of the island until the arrival of his successor, Sir Thomas Maitland in 1813. The Aide-de-camp who aroused Byron's ire was Captain Cary.

rude fellow who grinned at something, I never rightly knew what,) but he explained and apologised, and the lady embarked for Cadiz, & so I escaped murder and adultery.—Of Spain I sent some account to our Hodgson, but I have subsequently written to no one save notes to relations and lawyers to keep them out of my premises.—I mean to give up all connection on my return with many of my best friends as I supposed them, and to snarl all my life, but I hope to have one good humoured laugh with you, and to embrace Dwyer and pledge Hodgson, before I commence Cynicism.—Tell Dr. Butler I am now writing with the gold pen he gave me before I left England, which is the reason my scrawl is more unentelligible [*sic*] than usual.—I have been at Athens and seen plenty of those reeds for scribbling, some of which he refused to bestow upon me because topographer Gell had brought them from Attica.— —But I will not describe, no, you must be satisfied with simple detail till my return, and then we will unfold the floodgates of Colloquoy.—I am in a 36 gun frigate going up to fetch Bob Adair from Constantinople, who will have the honour to carry this letter.— And so Hobby's *boke* is out,[5] with some sentimental singsong of mine own to fill up, and how does it take? eh! and where the devil is the 2d Edition of my Satire with additions? and my name on the title page? and more lines tagged to the end with a new exordium and what not, hot from my anvil before I cleared the Channel?—The Mediterranean and the Atlantic roll between me and Criticism, and the thunders of the Hyberborean Review[6] are deafened by the roar of the Hellespont.— Remember me to Claridge if not translated to College, and present to Hodgson assurances of my high consideration.—Now, you will ask, what shall I do next? and I answer I do not know, I may return in a few months, but I have intents and projects after visiting Constantinople, Hobhouse however will probably be back in September.—On the 2d. of July we have left Albion one year, "oblitus meorum, obliviscendus et illis," I was sick of my own country, and not much prepossessed in favour of any other, but I drag on "my chain" without "lengthening it at each remove".[7]—I am like the jolly miller caring for nobody and not cared for. All countries are much the same in my eyes, I smoke and stare at mountains, and twirl my mustachios very independently, I miss no comforts, and the Musquïtoes that rack the morbid frame of Hobhouse, have luckily for me little effect on mine

[5] Hobhouse's book was *Imitations and Translations* (1809) which contained nine poems by Byron.

[6] The *Edinburgh Review* which had ridiculed *Hours of Idleness*.

[7] Goldsmith, *The Traveller*, line 10.

because I live more temperately.—I omitted Ephesus in my Catalogue, which I visited during my sojourn at Smyrna,—but the temple has almost perished, and St. Paul need not trouble himself to epistolize the present brood of Ephesians who have converted a large church built entirely of marble into a Mosque, and I dont know that the edifice looks the worse for it.—My paper is full and my ink ebbing, Good Afternoon!—If you address to me at Malta, the letter will be forwarded wherever I may be.—Hobhouse greets you, he pines for his poetry, at least some tidings of it.—I almost forgot to tell you that I am dying for love of three Greek Girls at Athens, sisters, two of whom have promised to accompany me to England, I lived in the same house, Teresa, Mariana, and Kattinka, are the names of these divinities all of them under 15.[8]—your ταπεῖνοτατοσ δουλοσ[9]

BYRON

[TO SIR ROBERT ADAIR]   *Pera July 4th. 1810*

Sir,—I regret that your Excellency should have deemed me or my concerns of sufficient importance to give you a thought beyond the moment when they were forced (perhaps unreasonably) on your attention.—On all occasions of this kind one of the parties must be wrong, at present it has fallen to my lot, your authorities (particularly the *German*) are too many for me.[1]—I shall therefore make what atonement I can by cheerfully following not only your excellency "but your servant or your maid your ox or your ass, or any thing that is yours."—I have to apologize for not availing myself of your Excellency['s] kind invitation and hospitable intentions in my favour, but the fact is, that I am never very well adapted for or very happy in society, and I happen at this time from some particular circumstances to be even less so than usual.[2] Your excellency will I

---

[8] The Macri sisters, daughters of Byron's Athens landlady, Mrs. Tarsia Macri, widow of a former British Vice-Consul. The youngest, Teresa, then only 12, Byron celebrated in his poem to the "Maid of Athens".

[9] "most humble servant" in Greek.

[1] The Austrian Internuncio, the authority on diplomatic etiquette, assured Byron that the Turks did not acknowledge precedence of rank in the procession. Byron had been invited to attend the ceremony of farewell for the British Ambassador, Sir Robert Adair, and was piqued by the fact that he would not be given a place commensurate with his rank as a Lord.

[2] Byron was oppressed at the time by news from England. His financial affairs were in the worst state imaginable. Brothers, the Nottingham upholsterer, had presented his bill for £1,600 for furnishing the rooms at Newstead and threatened

trust attribute my omissions to the *right* cause rather than disrespect in your

truly obliged & very obedient humble servant
BYRON

[TO SCROPE BERDMORE DAVIES] *Patras, Morea. July 31st. 1810*

My dear Davies,—Lord Sligo, who travelled with me a few days ago from Athens to Corinth, informs me that previous to his departure he saw you in London.—Though I do not think you have used me very well in not writing after my very frequent requests to that effect, I shall not give you an opportunity of recriminating, but fill this sheet to remind you of my existence and assure you of my regard, which you may accept without scruple, as, God knows, it is no very valuable present.—As I do suppose that before this time my agents have released you from every responsibility,[1] I shall say nothing on that head, excepting, that if they have not, it is proper I should know it immediately, that I may return for that purpose.——Since I left England, I have rambled through Portugal, the South of Spain, touched at Sardinia, Sicily, and Malta, been in the most interesting parts of Turkey in Europe, seen the Troad and Ephesus, Smyrna, &c. in Asia, *swam* on the 3d. of May from *Sestos* to Abydos, and finally sojourned at Constantinople, where I saw the Sultan and visited the interior of the Mosques, went into the Black Sea, and got rid of Hobhouse. I determined after one years purgatory to part with that amiable soul, for though I like him, and always shall, though I give him almost as much credit for his good qualities as he does himself, there is something in his manner &c. in short he will never be any thing but the *"Sow's Ear"*.——I am also perfectly aware that I have nothing to recommend me as a Companion, which is an additional reason for voyaging alone.—Besides, I feel happier, I feel free. "I can go and I can fly" "freely to the Green Earths end"[2] and at present I believe myself to be as comfortable as I ever shall be, and certainly as I

---

an execution. Hanson, his attorney and business agent was desperately trying to placate Byron's creditors, who had bills totalling £10,000, and was only able to pay the £3,000 due to usurers.

[1] Actually Byron did not repay Davies until 1814, when the debt with interest had mounted to more than £6,000. He was able to do so only after receiving an advance from Thomas Claughton, who had contracted to purchase Newstead.

[2] Milton, *Comus*, line 1014: "Quickly to the green earth's end."

ever have been.—My apparatus for "*flying*" consists of a Tartar, two Albanian soldiers, a Dragoman, and Fletcher, besides sundry sumpter horses, a Tent, beds and Canteen.—I have moreover a young Greek in my suite for the purpose of keeping up and increasing my knowledge of the modern dialect, in which I can swear fluently, and talk tolerably. —I am almost a Denizen of Athens, residing there principally when not on the highway.—My next increment from hence is to visit the Pacha at Tripolitza, and so on to headquarters.—

Hobhouse will arrive in England before this, to him I refer you for all marvels, he is bursting to communicate, hear him for pity's sake.— He is also in search of tidings after that bitter "miscellany", of which we hear nothing, Seaton to be sure compared him in a letter to Dryden, and somebody else (a Welch physician I believe) to Pope, and this is all that Hobby has yet got by his book.—I see by the papers 15th May my Satire is in a third Edition, if I cared much about the matter, I should say this was poor work, but at present the Thermometer is *125!!* and I keep myself as cool as possible.—In these parts is my Lord of Sligo with a most innavigable ship, which pertinaciously rejects the addresses of Libs, Notus, and Auster,[3] talking of ships induces me to inform you that in November last, we were in peril by sea in a Galliot of the Pacha of Albania, masts by the board, sails split, captain crying, crew below, wind blowing, Fletcher groaning, Hobhouse despairing, and myself with my upper garments ready thrown open, to swim to a spar in case of accidents; but it pleased the Gods to land us safe on the coast of Suli.—My plans are very uncertain, I may return soon, or perhaps not for another year.—Whenever I do come back it will please me to see you in good plight, I think of you frequently, and whenever Hobhouse unlawfully passed off any of your *good things* as his own, I immediately asserted your claim in all cabins of Ships of war, at tables of Admirals and Generals, Consuls and Ambassadors, so that he has not pilfered a single pun with impunity.—I tell you with great sincerity that I know no person, whom I shall meet with more cordiality.—Address to me at Malta, whence my letters are forwarded to the Levant.—When I was at Malta last,—I fell in love with a married woman, and challenged an officer,[4] but the Lady was chaste, and the gentleman explanatory, and thus I broke no commandments.—I desire to be remembered to no one, I have no friends any where, and my acquaintances are I do suppose either incarcerated or made immortal

---

[3] South and west winds.
[4] See Sept. 15, 1812, to Lady Melbourne.

in the Peninsula of Spain.—I lost five guineas by the demise of H. Parker.[5]—Believe me

yours most truly
BYRON

P.S.—I believe I have already described my suite, six and myself, as Mr. Wordsworth has it "we are seven".—Tell Mr. E. Ellice[6] that Adair has a letter for him from me to be left at Brookes's.—Adio! I place my name in *modern* Greek on the direction of this letter for your edification.—

[TO JOHN CAM HOBHOUSE]   *Tripolitza. August 16th. 1810*

Dear Hobhouse,—I am on the rack of setting off for Argos amidst the usual creaking swearing loading and neighing of sixteen horses and as many men [serving us? servingers?] included.—You have probably received one letter dated Patras and I send this at a venture. —Velly Pacha received me even better than his Father did, though he is to join the Sultan, and the city is full of troops and confusion, which as he said, prevents him from paying proper attention.—He has given me a very pretty horse and a most particular invitation to meet him at Larissa, which last is singular enough as he recommended a different route to Ld. Sligo who asked leave to accompany him to the Danube. —I asked no such thing, but on his enquiring where I meant to go, and receiving for answer that I was about to return to Albania for the purpose of penetrating higher up the country, he replied, "no you must not take that route, but go round by Larissa where I shall remain some time on my way. I will send to Athens, and you shall join me, we will eat and drink well, and go a hunting."—He said he wished all the old men (specifying under that epithet *North, Forresti,*[1] and *Stranè*) to go to his father, but the young ones to come to him, to use his own expression "vecchio con vecchio, Giovane con Giovane."—He honored me with the appellations of his *friend* and *brother,* and hoped that we should be on good terms not for a few days but for Life.—All this is very well, but he has an awkward manner of throwing his arm round

---

[5] Unidentified.

[6] Edward Ellice (1781–1863) married the widow of Byron's cousin, Captain George Bettesworth.

[1] Byron met George Forresti at Malta. He was later (1810) British Resident at Janina. He was a Greek by birth, but with a Western education.

one's waist, and squeezing one's hand in *public*, which is a high compliment, but very much embarrasses *"ingenuous youth"*.—The first time I saw him he received me *standing*, accompanied me at my departure to the door of the audience chamber, and told me I was a παλικαρι[2] and an εὔμορφω παιδι[3]—He asked if I did not think it very proper that as *young* men (he has a *beard* down to his middle) we should live together, with a variety of other sayings, which made Stranè stare, and puzzled me in my replies.—He was very facetious with Andreas and Viscillie,[4] and recommended that my Albanians' heads should be cut off if they behaved ill.—I shall write to you from Larissa, and inform you of our proceedings in that city.—In the mean time I sojourn at Athens.——

I have sent Eustathius back to his home, he plagued my soul out with his whims, and is besides subject to *epileptic* fits (tell *M*[atthews] this) which made him a perplexing companion, in *other* matters he was very tolerable, I mean as to his *learning*, being well versed in the Ellenics.— You remember Nicolo[5] at Athens Lusieri's wife's brother.—Give my *compliments* to *Matthews* from whom I expect a congratulatory letter. ——I have a thousand anecdotes for him and you, but at present Τι να καμω?[6] I have neither time nor space, but in the words of Dawes, "I have things in store."—I have scribbled thus much, where shall I send it, why to Malta or Paternoster Row. Hobby you wretch how is the Miscellany? that damned and damnable work, "what has the learned world said to your paradoxes? I hope you did not forget the importance of Monogamy."[7]—Stranè has just arrived with bags of piastres, so that I must conclude by the usual phrase of

yours &c. &c.
BYRON

P.S.—You knew young Bossari at Yanina, he is a piece of Ali Pacha's!! well did Horace write "Nil Admirari"

---

[2] brave young man.

[3] beautiful boy.

[4] Andreas Zantachi and Viscillie (Vascillie) were Byron's Greek and Albanian servants.

[5] Nicolo Giraud, a boy in his teens, had attached himself to Byron before he went to Constantinople, and became his companion-dragoman on his second excursion to the Morea in September.

[6] Τι να καμω? [Τι να κανω? = What to do?]

[7] Goldsmith, *Vicar of Wakefield*, Chap. 20.

My dear Hodgson—As I have just escaped from a physician and a fever which confined me five days to bed, you wont expect much "allegrezza" in the ensuing letter.—In this place there is an indigenous distemper, which, when the wind blows from the Gulph of Corinth (as it does five months out of six) attacks great and small, and makes woeful work with visitors.—Here be also two physicians, one of whom trusts to his Genius (never having studied) the other to a campaign of eighteen months against the sick of Otranto, which he made in his youth with great effect.—When I was seized with my disorder, I protested against both these assassins, but what can a helpless, feverish, toasted and watered poor wretch do? in spite of my teeth & tongue, the English Consul, my Tartar, Albanians, Dragoman forced a physician upon me, and in three days vomited and glystered me to the last gasp. —In this state I made my epitaph, take it,

> Youth, Nature, and relenting Jove
> To keep my *lamp in* strongly strove,
> But *Romanelli* was so stout
> He beat all three—and *blew* it *out*.—

But Nature and Jove being piqued at my doubts, did in fact at last beat Romanelli, and here I am well but weakly, at your service.—Since I left Constantinople I have made a tour of the Morea, and visited Vely Pacha who paid me great honours and gave me a pretty stallion.— Hobhouse is doubtless in England before even the date of this letter, he bears a dispatch from me to your Bardship.—He writes to me from Malta, and is desperate of his Miscellany, but has other plots against the public, and requests my journal if I keep one, I have none or he should have it, but I have replied in a consolatory and exhortatory epistle, wherein I do recommend him to turn his hand to prose, which must go down or the Devil's in't, at the same time praying him to abate three and sixpence in the price of his next boke, seeing that half a guinea is a price not to be given for any thing save an opera ticket.— As for England, it is long since I have heard from it, every one at all connected with my concerns, is asleep, and you are my only correspondent, agents excepted.—I have really no friends in the world, though all my old school companions are gone forth into the world, and walk about in monstrous disguises, in the garb of Guardsmen, lawyers, parsons, fine gentlemen, and such other masquerade dresses. —So I have shaken hands and cut with all these busy people, none of whom write to me, indeed I asked it not, and here I am a poor traveller and heathenish philosopher, who hath perambulated the greatest part of the Levant, and seen a great quantity of very improveable land and sea, and after all am no better than when I set out, Lord help me.—I have been out fifteen months this very day and I believe my concerns will draw me to England soon, but of this I will apprise you regularly from Malta. On all points Hobhouse will inform you if you are curious as to our adventures.—I have seen some old English papers up to the 15th. of May, I see the "Lady of the Lake" advertised[;] of course it is in his old ballad style, and pretty, after all Scott is the best of them.— The end of all scribblement is to amuse, and he certainly succeeds there, I long to read his new Romance.—And how does Sir Edgar?[1] and your friend Bland?[2] I suppose you are involved in some literary squabble, the only way is to despise all brothers of the quill, I suppose you wont allow me to be an author, but I contemn you all, you dogs! I do.—You dont know Dallas, do you? he had a farce ready for the stage before I left England, and asked me for a prologue, which I promised, but sailed in such a hurry I never penned a couplet.—I am afraid to ask after his drama for fear it should be damned, Lord forgive me for using such a word, but the pit, Sir, you know the pit, they will do those things in spite of merit.—[3] I remember this farce from a curious circumstance; when Drury Lane was burnt to the Ground,[4] by which accident Sheridan and his Son lost the few remaining shillings they were worth, what doth my friend D— do? why, before the fire was out, he writes a note to Tom Sheridan[5] the Manager of this combustible concern, to enquire whether this *farce* was not converted into fuel with about two thousand other unactable manuscripts which of course were in great peril if not actually consumed.—Now was not this characteristic? the ruling passions of Pope are nothing to it.—Whilst the poor distracted manager was bewailing the loss of a building only worth 300 000 £, together with some twenty thousand pounds worth of rags and tinsel in the tiring rooms, Bluebeard's elephants and *all*

[1] *Sir Edgar* was Hodgson's novel.

[2] An assistant master at Harrow while Byron was there, a friend of Hodgson, Drury, and other friends of Byron.

[3] Dallas's farce was acted at the Lyceum, by the Drury Lane Company, in November, 1809. The prologue, which Byron did not write, was written by Walter Rodwell Wright, author of *Horae Ionicae*.

[4] Drury Lane was twice destroyed by fire, first in 1791 and again in 1809.

[5] Thomas Sheridan (1775–1817) was assisting his father Richard Brinsley Sheridan as manager of Drury Lane when it burned in 1809.

that;[6] in comes a note from a scorching author requiring at his hands two acts and odd scenes of a farce!!!—Dear H. remind Drury that I am his wellwisher, and let Scrope Davies be well affected towards me.—I look forward to meeting you at Newstead and renewing our old Champagne evenings with all the Glee of anticipation.—I have written by every opportunity, and expect responses as regular as those of the liturgy, and somewhat longer.—As it is impossible for a man in his senses to hope for happy days, let us at least look forward to merry ones which come nearest to the other in appearance if not in reality, and in such expectations I remain yours very affectly.

BYRON

[TO FRANCIS HODGSON]   *Athens—January 20th. 1811*

My dear Hodgson,—In most of your letters, that is to say *two* the only ones I have received of yours, you complain of my silence, this complaint I presume to be removed by this time, as I have written frequently, but more particularly by H. who is of course long ago landed, and will amply gratify any further curiosity you may have beyond the limits of a letter.——I also wrote by the Black John, which however was taken off Algiers with the Capt. Moses Kennedy & several bags of long letters, but especially Hobhouse's intimates have to regret the capture of some enormous packets, which cost a world of pains at Constantinople in the Troad & elsewhere, as I can witness, & unless the French government publish them, I am afraid we have little chance of recovering these inestimable manuscripts.—But then to make amends he himself followed close on the heels of his letters (by the bye I fear *heels* of letters is a very incorrect metaphor) and will tell the world all how & about it, unless he also has been boarded & taken off Algiers.——Talking of taking, I was nearly taken myself six weeks ago by some Mainnote pirates (Lacedemonians & be damned to them) at Cape Colonna, but being well armed, & attended, the varlets were afraid, or they might have bagged us all with a little skirmishing.—I am still in Athens making little tours to Marathon, Sunium, the top of Hymettus, & the Morea occasionally to diversify the season.—My Grand Giro finished with Constantinople & I shall not (I think) go further Eastward, but I am sure of nothing so little as my own intentions, and if I receive cash & comfortable news from

[6] *Bluebeard, or Female Curiosity,* by George Colman the Younger was being acted at Drury Lane in January, 1809. The elephants were made of wickerwork.

home I shant trouble your foggy Island for amusement.—I am studying modern Greek with a Master, and my current tongue is Levant Italian, which I gabble perforce, my late dragoman spoke bad Latin, but having dismissed him, I am left to my resources which consist in tolerably fluent Lingua Franca, middling Romaic (modern Greek) and some variety of Ottoman oaths of great service with a stumbling horse, or a stupid servant.—I lately sent to England my only remaining Englishman with some papers about money matters, and am left d'ye see all by myself in these outlandish parts, and I don't find it *never* the *worser* for friends and servants that is to say fellow countrymen in those capacities are troublesome fellow travellers.—I have a variety of acquaintance, French, Danes, Germans Greek Italian & Turkish, and have contracted an alliance with Dr. Bronstedt of Copenhagen a pretty philosopher as you'd wish to see.[1]—Besides I am on good terms with some of my countrymen here, Messrs Grahame & Haygarth,[2] & I have in pay a Bavarian Baron named "Lynch" (pronounce it Lyn*k*) who limns landscapes for the lucre of gain.[3]—Here also are Messrs Fiott, Cockerell & Foster[4] all of whom I know, and they are all vastly amiable & accomplished.—I am living in the Capuchin Convent, Hymettus before me, the Acropolis behind, the temple of Jove to my right, the Stadium in front, the town to the left, eh, Sir, there's a situation, there's your picturesque! nothing like that, Sir, in Lunnun, no not even the Mansion House. And I feed upon Woodcocks & red Mullet every day, & I have three horses (one a present from the Pacha of the Morea) and I ride to Piraeus, & Phalerum & Munychia,[5] which

[1] Peter Oluf Brønsted (1780–1842) was an archaeologist from the University of Copenhagen.

[2] Sandford Graham (1788–1852), whom Byron had known at Trinity College, was one of the English travellers in Athens during the winter of 1810–11. He was in Byron's party on the visit to Sounion described in this letter. Graham was later a member of Parliament and a Fellow of the Society of Antiquaries.

[3] Jacob Linckh (1787–1841), a native of Cannstatt, had studied art in Rome before coming to Greece in September, 1810. He joined Cockerell, Foster, and Haller in the excavations of the site of the temple on Ægina in 1811.

[4] John Fiott (1783–1866), a graduate of St. John's College, Cambridge, toured the Near East (1807–1810) as a "travelling Bachelor" of his College, collecting antiquities. He later gained eminence as a collector and man of science.

Charles Robert Cockerell (1788–1863), an architect who later achieved renown, was starting on a course of professional studies by exploring the architectural antiquities of Greece. He spent the winter of 1810–11 in Athens where he saw much of Byron. With other explorers he discovered the Ægina Marbles.

John Foster (1787?–1840), a Liverpool architect, met Cockerell in 1810 in Constantinople and continued his travels and research with him in Greece.

[5] Now called Turcolimano.

however dont look quite so magnificent after the harbours of Cadiz, Lisbon, Constantinople & Gibralter not forgetting Malta. I wish to be sure I had a few books, one's own works for instance, any damned nonsense on a long Evening.—I had a straggling number of the E[dinburgh] Review given me by a compassionate Capt. of a frigate lately, it contains the reply to the Oxonian pamphlet, on the Strabonic controversy, the reviewer seems to be in a perilous passion & heaves out a deal of Slack-jaw as the Sailors call it.—You know to direct to Malta, whence my letters are or ought to be forwarded.—In two days I shall be twenty three, and on the 2d. above a year and a half out of England.—I suppose you & Drury sometimes drink one's health on a speechday, & I trust we shall meet merrily, and make a tour some summer to Wales or Scotland, it will be a great relaxation to me jaunting once more in a Chay.—I need not write at length as Hobby is brimful of remarks, and it would be cruel to curtail him of a syllable.— Tell him I have written to him frequently, as indeed I have to yourself and also to Drury & others, but this is a plaguy distance for a single sheet.—

Yours always
BYRON—

["FOUR OR FIVE REASONS IN FAVOUR OF A CHANGE"]

B. Malta, May 22d. 1811

1st At twenty three the best of life is over and its bitters double. 2ndly I have seen mankind in various Countries and find them equally despicable, if anything the Balance is rather in favour of the Turks. 3dly I am sick at heart.

> "Me jam nec *faemina* . . .
> Nec *Spes animi credula mutui*
> Nec *certare* juvat *Mero*.[1]

4thly A man who is lame of one leg is in a state of bodily inferiority which increases with years and must render his old age more peevish

---

[1] Byron was quoting from memory and somewhat inaccurately Horace's first ode of the fourth book ("To Venus"):

> Nor maid nor youth delights me now,
> Nor credulous dream of heart's exchange, nor hours
> of challenged wine-bout, nor the brow
> Girt with a wreath of freshly gathered flowers.

& intolerable. Besides in another existence I expect to have *two* if not *four* legs by way of compensation.

5thly I grow selfish & misanthropical, something like the "jolly Miller" "I care for nobody no not I and Nobody cares for me."

6thly My affairs at home and abroad are gloomy enough.

7thly I have outlived all my appetites and most of my vanities aye even the vanity of authorship.[2]

[TO HENRY DRURY]   *Volage Frigate off Ushant. July 7th. 1811*

My dear Drury,—After two years absence (on the 2d.) & some odd days I am approaching your Country, the day of our arrival you will see by the outside date of my letter, at present we are becalmed comfortably close to Brest Harbour;—I have never been so near it since I left Duck Puddle.[1]—The enclosed letter is from a friend of yours Surgeon Tucker whom I met with in Greece, & so on to Malta, where he administered to me for three complaints viz. a *Gonorrhea* a *Tertian fever*, & the *Hemorrhoides, all* of which I literally had at once, though he assured me the *morbid* action of only one of these distempers could act at a time, which was a great comfort, though they relieved one another as regularly as Sentinels, & very nearly sent me back to Acheron, my old acquaintance which I left fine & flowing in Albania.— —We left Malta 34 days ago, & (except the Gut of Gibraltar which we passed with an Easterly wind as easy as an oil Glyster) we have had a tedious passage on't.—You have never written, this comes of Matrimony, Hodgson has,—so you see the Balance of Friendship is on the Batchelor's side.—I am at present well, that is, I have only two out of the three aforesaid complaints, & these I hope to be cured of, as they say one's Native fogs are vastly salubrious.— — —You will either see or hear from or of me soon after the receipt of this, as I pass through town to repair my irreparable affairs, & thence I must go to Nott's & raise rents, & to Lanc's, & sell collieries, & back to London, & pay debts, for it seems I shall neither have coals or comfort till I go down to Rochdale in person. I have brought home some marbles for Hobhouse;—& for myself, "Four ancient Athenian Skulls["][2] dug out

---

[2] This memorandum to himself should be considered as a journal entry rather than a letter.

[1] The swimming pool at Harrow.

[2] The Athenian skulls were later given to Walter Scott.

48

of Sarcophagi, a "phial of Attic Hemlock,"[3] ["]four live Tortoises" a Greyhound (died on the passage) two live Greek Servants one an *Athenian*, t'other a *Yaniote*, who can speak nothing but Romaic & Italian, & *myself*, as Moses in the "Vicar of Wakefield" says *slily*,[4] & I may say it too for I have as little cause to boast of my expedition as he of his to the Fair.—I wrote to you from the Cyanean Rocks, to tell you I had swum from Sestos to Abydos, have you received my letter?— — Hobhouse went to England to fish up his Miscellany, which foundered (so he tells me) in the Gulph of Lethe, I dare say it capsized with the vile goods of his contributory friends, for his own share was very portable.—However I hope he will either weigh up or set sail with a fresh Cargo, & a luckier vessel. Hodgson I suppose is four deep by this time, what would he give? to have seen like me the *real Parnassus*, where I robbed the Bishop of Chrisso of a book of Geography,[5] but this I only call plagiarism, as it was done within an hour's ride of Delphi.— —

Believe me yrs. ever
BYRON

[TO AUGUSTA LEIGH] *Newstead Abbey. August 21st. 1811*

My dear Sister,—I ought to have answered your letter before, but when did I ever do anything that I ought?—I am losing my relatives & you are adding to the number of yours, but which is best God knows; —besides poor Mrs. Byron I have been deprived by death of two most particular friends within little more than a month, but as all observations on such subjects are superfluous & unavailing, I leave the dead to their rest, & return to the dull business of life, which however presents nothing very pleasant to me either in prospect or retrospection.— — —I hear you have been increasing his Majesty's Subjects, which in these times of War & tribulation is really patriotic, notwithstanding Malthus tells us that were it not for Battle, Murder, & Sudden death, we should be overstocked, I think we have latterly had a redundance of these national benefits, & therefore I give you all credit for your matronly behaviour.— —I believe you know that for upwards of two years I have been rambling round the Archipelago, & am returned just in time to know that I might as well have staid away

[3] Later given to John Murray.
[4] *Vicar of Wakefield*, Chapter XII.
[5] *Ancient and Modern Geography*, (Venice, 1728) by Meletius of Janina (1661–1714). Meletius was Archbishop of Athens, 1703–14.

for any good I ever have done, or am likely to do at home, & so, as soon as I have somewhat *repaired* my *irreparable* affairs I shall een go abroad again, for I am heartily sick of your climate & every thing it *rains* upon, always save & except *yourself* as in *duty bound.*—I should be glad to see you here (as I think you have never seen the place) if you could make it convenient. Murray[1] is still like a Rock, & will probably outlast some six Lords Byron though in his 75th. Autumn.—
—I took him with me to Portugal, & sent him round by sea to Gibraltar whilst I rode through the Interior of Spain which was then (1809) accessible.— —You say you have much to communicate to me, let us have it by all means, as I am utterly at a loss to guess; whatever it may be it will meet with due attention. Your trusty & well beloved cousin F. Howard[2] is married to a Miss Somebody, I wish him joy on your account, & on his own, though speaking generally I do not affect that Brood.— —By the bye *I* shall marry if I can find any thing inclined to barter money for rank, within six months; after which I shall return to my friends the Turks.—In the interim I am Dear Madam

[Signature cut out.]

Newstead Abbey August 30th. 1811

My dear Augusta,—The embarrassments you mention in your last letter I never heard of before, but that disease is epidemic in our family.[1]——Neither have I been apprised of any of the changes at which you hint, indeed how should I? on the borders of the Black Sea, we heard only of the Russians.—So you have much to tell, & all will be novelty.— —I don't know what Scrope Davies meant by telling you I liked Children, I abominate the sight of them so much that I have always had the greatest respect for the character of *Herod.*— —But as my house here is large enough for us all, we should go on very well, & I need not tell you that I long to see *you.*— —I really do not perceive any thing so formidable in a Journey hither of two days, but all this comes of Matrimony, you have a Nurse & all the &cas. of a family. Well, I must marry to repair the ravages of myself & prodigal ancestry, but if I am ever so unfortunate as to be presented with an Heir, instead of a *Rattle*, he shall be provided with a *Gag.*— — —I

---

[1] Joe Murray, an old servant at Newstead, formerly in the employ of the 5th Lord Byron.

[2] The Hon. Frederick Howard, third son of Lord Carlisle.

[1] Augusta and her gambling husband were always in financial difficulties.

shall perhaps be able to accept D[avies]'s invitation to Cambridge, but I fear my stay in Lancashire will be prolonged, I proceed there in the 2d. week of Septr. to arrange my coal concerns, & then if I can't persuade some wealthy dowdy to ennoble the dirty puddle of her mercantile Blood,—why—I shall leave England & all it's clouds for the East again,—I am very sick of it already.——Joe[2] has been getting well of a disease that would have killed a troop of horse, he promises to bear away the palm of longevity from old Parr.[3]—As you wont come, you will write, I long to hear all these unutterable things, being utterly unable to guess at any of them, unless they concern *your* relative the Thane of Carlisle,[4]—though I had great hopes we had done with him.—I have little to add that you do not already know, and being quite alone, have no great variety of incident to gossip with, I am but rarely pestered with visitors, & the few I have I get rid of as soon as possible.— —I will now take leave of you in the Jargon of 1794. "Health & *Fraternity!*"

Yrs. always
B.—

[TO AUGUSTA LEIGH]   *Newstead Abbey. Sept. 2d. 1811*

My dear Augusta,—I wrote you a vastly dutiful letter since my answer to your second epistle, & I now write you a third for which you have to thank Silence & Solitude.—Mr. Hanson comes hither on the 14th. & I am going to Rochdale on business, but that need not prevent you from coming here, you will find Joe, & the house & the cellar & all therein very much at your Service.—As to a Lady B.—

---

[2] Joe Murray, servant at Newstead.

[3] Thomas Parr, whose longevity was celebrated by John Taylor, the "water-poet". He was said to have been born in 1483 and to have lived until 1635, though there is no confirmation of his birth date.

[4] Frederick Howard, fifth Earl of Carlisle (1748–1825) was distantly related to Byron through the marriage in 1742 of his father, the fourth Earl, to the Hon. Isabella Byron, daughter of the fourth Lord Byron and sister to Byron's grandfather. Through the intervention of John Hanson Lord Carlisle agreed in 1799 to act as the young Lord Byron's guardian, consulting with Hanson on his education and using his influence to get Mrs. Byron a provision of £300 from the Civil List. But Mrs. Byron's temper and tantrums soon alienated him, and Byron himself was shy of asking favours of him. Augusta, who was friendly with the Carlisles and lived with them part of the time, tried with not too great success to bring them together. But a reconciliation became impossible after Byron became incensed by Carlisle's failure to assist him in the formalities of his entrance into the House of Lords and Byron's caustic lines on him in *English bards and Scotch Reviewers.*

when I discover one rich enough to suit me & foolish enough to have me, I will give her leave to make me miserable if she can.—Money is the magnet, as to Women, one is as well as another, the older the better, we have then a chance of getting her to Heaven.—So, your Spouse does not like brats better than myself; now those who beget them have no right to find fault, but *I* may rail with great propriety.— My "Satire!"—I am glad it made you laugh for Somebody told me in Greece that you was angry, & I was sorry, as you were perhaps the only person whom I did *not* want to *make angry*.— — —But how you will make *me laugh* I don't know, for it is a vastly *serious* subject to me I assure you, therefore take care, or I shall hitch *you* into the next Edition to make up our family party.—Nothing so fretful, so despicable as a Scribbler. see what *I* am, & what a parcel of Scoundrels I have brought about my ears, & what language I have been obliged to treat them with to deal with them in their own way;—all this comes of Authorship, but now I am in for it, & shall be at war with Grubstreet, till I find some better amusement.— —You will write to me your Intentions & may almost depend on my being at Cambridge in October.— You say you mean to be &c. in the *Autumn*; I should be glad to know what you call the present Season, it would be Winter in every other Country which I have seen.— —If we meet in Octr. we will travel in my *Vis*.—& can have a cage for the children & a Cart for the Nurse.— Or perhaps we can forward them by the Canal.— —Do let us know all about it, your *"bright thought"* is a little clouded like the Moon in this preposterous climate.—Good even, Child.—

yrs. ever

B —

[TO FRANCIS HODGSON]   *Newstead Abbey, September 3, 1811*

My dear Hodgson,—I will have nothing to do with your immortality; we are miserable enough in this life, without the absurdity of speculating upon another. If men are to live, why die at all? and if they die, why disturb the sweet and sound sleep that "knows no waking"? "Post mortem nihil est, ipsaque Mors nihil . . . quæris quo jaceas post obitum loco? Quo *non* Nata jacent".[1]

---

[1] Seneca *Troades*, 397ff. "There is nothing after death, and death itself is nothing. You seek the place where one lies after death? Where those unborn lie."

As to revealed religion, Christ came to save men; but a good Pagan will go to heaven, and a bad Nazarene to hell; "Argal" (I argue like the gravedigger) why are not all men Christians? or why are any? If mankind may be saved who never heard or dreamt, at Timbuctoo, Otaheite, Terra Incognita, &c., of Galilee and its Prophet, Christianity is of no avail, if they cannot be saved without, why are not all orthodox? It is a little hard to send a man preaching to Judæa, and leave the rest of the world—Negers and what not—*dark* as their complexions, without a ray of light for so many years to lead them on high; and who will believe that God will damn men for not knowing what they were never taught? I hope I am sincere; I was so at least on a bed of sickness in a far distant country, when I had neither friend, nor comforter, nor hope, to sustain me. I looked to death as a relief from pain, without a wish for an after-life, but a confidence that the God who punishes in this existence had left that last asylum for the weary.

Ὄν ὁ θεὸς ἀγαπάει ἀποθνήσκει νέος.[2]

I am no Platonist, I am nothing at all; but I would sooner be a Paulician, Manichean, Spinozist, Gentile, Pyrrhonian, Zoroastrian, than one of the seventy-two villainous sects who are tearing each other to pieces for the love of the Lord and hatred of each other. Talk of Galileeism? Show me the effects—are you better, wiser, kinder by your precepts? I will bring you ten Mussulmans shall shame you in all good-will towards men, prayer to God, and duty to their neighbours. And is there a Talapoin,[3] or a Bonze, who is not superior to a fox-hunting curate? But I will say no more on this endless theme; let me live, well if possible, and die without pain. The rest is with God, who assuredly, had He *come* or *sent*, would have made Himself manifest to nations, and intelligible to all.

I shall rejoice to see you. My present intention is to accept Scrope Davies's invitation; and then, if you accept mine, we shall meet *here* and *there*. Did you know poor Matthews? I shall miss him much at Cambridge.[4]

---

[2] Whom the Gods love dies young.

[3] A word used in the seventeenth century to designate the Buddhist monks of Ceylon and the Indo-Chinese countries. Byron may have taken it from Voltaire. (Dial. XXII, *André des Couches a Siam.*)

[4] Charles Skinner Matthews, a close friend of Hobhouse and Byron, was drowned in the river Cam at Cambridge in August.

My dear Hodgson.—I thank you for your song, or, rather, your two songs—your new song on love, and your *old song* on *religion*. I admire the *first* sincerely, and in turn call upon you to *admire* the following on Anacreon Moore's new operatic farce,[1] or farcical opera—call it which you will:—

> Good plays are scarce,
> So Moore writes farce;
>   Is fame like his so brittle?
> We knew before
> That "Little's" Moore,[2]
>   But now '*tis Moore* that's *Little*.

I won't dispute with you on the arcana of your new calling; they are bagatelles, like the King of Poland's rosary. One remark and I have done: the basis of your religion is *injustice*; the *Son of God*, the *pure*, the *immaculate*, the *innocent*, is sacrificed for the *guilty*. This proves *His* heroism; but no more does away with *man's* guilt than a schoolboy's volunteering to be flogged for another would exculpate the dunce from negligence, or preserve him from the rod. You degrade the Creator, in the first place, by making Him a begetter of children; and in the next you convert Him into a tyrant over an immaculate and injured Being, who is sent into existence to suffer death for the benefit of some millions of scoundrels, who, after all, seem as likely to be damned as ever. As to miracles, I agree with Hume that it is more probable men should *lie* or be *deceived*, than that things out of the course of nature should so happen. Mahomet wrought miracles, Brothers the prophet had *proselytes*,[3] and so would Breslaw the conjurer,[4] had he lived in the time of Tiberius.

Besides, I trust that God is not a *Jew*, but the God of all mankind; and, as you allow that a virtuous Gentile may be saved, you do away the necessity of being a Jew or a Christian.

I do not believe in any revealed religion, because no religion is revealed; and if it pleases the Church to damn me for not allowing a

---

[1] Thomas Moore's *M.P., or The Bluestocking* was played at the Lyceum on September 9, 1811, but was not a success and was withdrawn.

[2] Moore published his early erotic poems under the pseudonym of Thomas Little.

[3] Richard Brothers (1757–1824) believed that in the year 1795 he was to be revealed as Prince of the Hebrews and ruler of the world, but he was arrested and confined as a lunatic.

[4] See *Breslaw's Last Legacy; or, the Magical Companion*, 1784.

nonentity, I throw myself on the mercy of the *"Great First Cause, least understood,"* who must do what is most proper; though I conceive He never made anything to be tortured in another life, whatever it may in this. I will neither read *pro* nor *con*. God would have made His will known without books, considering how very few could read them when Jesus of Nazareth lived, had it been His pleasure to ratify any peculiar mode of worship. As to your immortality, if people are to live, why die? And our carcases, which are to rise again, are they worth raising? I hope, if mine is, that I shall have a better *pair of legs* than I have moved on these two-and-twenty years, or I shall be sadly behind in the squeeze into Paradise. Did you ever read "Malthus on Population?" If he be right, war and pestilence are our best friends, to save us from being eaten alive, in this "best of all possible worlds."[5]

I will write, read, and think no more; indeed, I do not wish to shock your prejudices by saying all I do think. Let us make the most of life, and leave dreams to Emanuel Swedenborg.

Now to dreams of another genus—poesies. I like your song much; but I will say no more, for fear you should think I wanted to coax you into approbation of my past, present, or future acrostics. I shall not be at Cambridge before the middle of October; but, when I go, I should certes like to see you there before you are dubbed a deacon. Write to me, and I will rejoin.

Yours ever,
BYRON

[TO JOHN CAM HOBHOUSE]   *8 St. James's Street. Novr. 16th. 1811*

My dear H.—That is a most *impudent* simile & incorrect, for the *"vomit"* came to the *"dog"* & not the *"dog"* to the *"vomit"* & if you will teach me how to spit in any body's face without offence, I will shake off these gentlemen with the greatest good-will, however I have never *called* on either, so am not to blame for the slightest degree of good manners.— —I send you Demo's[1] traduzione, & make the most of it, you must orthographize it in both languages as you will perceive. Why have you omitted the earthquake in the night at Libochabo? I will give up the *flatulent* Secretary, but do let us have the Terramoto.— I dine today with Ward to meet the Lord knows whom.—Moore & I

---

[5] *Candide*, Chapter XXX.
[1] Demetrius Zograffo, Byron's Greek servant, was translating Greek passages for Hobhouse's travel book.

are on the best of terms, I answered his letters in an explanatory way, but of course conceded nothing in the shape of an apology, indeed his own letters were an odd mixture of complaint, & a desire of amicable discussion.[2]—Rogers said his behaviour was rather Irish, & that mine was candid & manly, I hope it was at *least* the latter.—I consulted Scrope before I sent off my letter, but now the matter is completely adjusted, as R[ogers] said "honourably" to Both. Sotheby, whom I abused in my last, improves, his face is rather against him, & his manner abrupt & dogmatic, but I believe him to be much more amiable than I thought him.—Rogers is a most excellent & unassuming Soul, & Moore an Epitome of all that's delightful, I asked them & Hodgson to dinner. H[odgson] of course was drunk & Sensibilitous.— —Bland (the *Revd*) has been *challenging* an officer of Dragoons, about a *whore*, & my assistance being required, I interfered in time to prevent him from losing his *life* or his *Living*.—The man is mad, Sir, mad, frightful as a Mandrake, & lean as a rutting Stag, & all about a bitch not worth a Bank token.—She is a common Strumpet as his Antagonist assured me, yet he means to marry her, Hodgson meant to marry her, the officer meant to marry her, her first Seducer (seventeen years ago) meant to marry her, and all this is owing to the *Comet!*— —During Bland's absence, H[odgso]n was her Dragon, & left his own Oyster wench to offer her his hand, which she *refused*.—Bland comes home in Hysterics, finds her in keeping (not by H[odgso]n however) & loses his wits.— Hodgson gets drunk & cries, & he & Bland (who have been berhyming each other as you know these six past Olympiads) are now the Antipodes of each other.—I saw this *wonder*, & set her down at seven shilling's worth.— —Here is gossip for you! as you know some of the parties.—As to self, I am ill with a cough, Demo has tumbled down stairs, scalded his leg, been kicked by a horse, hurt his kidneys, got a terrible "catchcold" (as he calls it) & now suffers under these accumulated mischances.—Fletcher is fat & facetious.—

yrs. ever

Μπαιρῶν

[2] Moore had sent Byron a letter on January 1, 1810, while Byron was abroad, which his friend Hodgson had held, sensing it to be a challenge. Moore had taken offence at some derisive lines in Byron's *English Bards and Scotch Reviewers* referring to a farcical duel between him and Francis Jeffrey, editor of the *Edinburgh Review*. Though aimed at Jeffrey, the gibe had put Moore in a ridiculous light. On Byron's return Moore renewed the challenge in milder terms asking for an explanation. When Moore was satisfied that Byron meant to ridicule Jeffrey rather than him, they met at the home of Samuel Rogers, the banker poet, and became fast friends.

My Lord,—With my best thanks I have the honour to return the Notts letter to your Lordship.—I have read it with attention, but do not think I shall venture to avail myself of it's contents, as my view of the question differs in some measure from Mr. Coldham's.—I hope I do not wrong him, but *his* objections to ye. bill appear to me to be founded on certain apprehensions that he & his coadjutors might be mistaken for the *"original advisers"* (to quote him) of the measure.— —For my own part, I consider the manufacturers[1] as a much injured body of men sacrificed to ye. views of certain individuals who have enriched themselves by those practices which have deprived the frame workers of employment.—For instance;—by the adoption of a certain kind of frame 1 man performs ye. work of 7—6 are thus thrown out of business.—But it is to be observed that ye. work thus done is far inferior in quality, hardly marketable at home, & hurried over with a view to exportation.—Surely, my Lord, however we may rejoice in any improvement in ye. arts which may be beneficial to mankind; we must not allow mankind to be sacrificed to improvements in Mechanism. The maintenance & well doing of ye. industrious poor is an object of greater consequence to ye. community than ye. enrichment of a few monopolists by any improvement in ye. implements of trade, which deprives ye workman of his bread, & renders ye. labourer "unworthy of his hire."—My own motive for opposing ye. bill is founded on it's palpable injustice, & it's certain inefficacy.—[2] —I have seen the state of these miserable men, & it is a disgrace to a civilized country.—Their excesses may be condemned, but cannot be subject of wonder.— The effect of ye. present bill would be to drive them into actual rebellion.—The few words I shall venture to offer on Thursday will be founded upon these opinions formed from my own observations on ye. spot.—By previous enquiry I am convinced these men would have been restored to employment & ye. county to tranquillity.—It is perhaps not yet too late & is surely worth the trial. It can never be too late to employ force in such circumstances.— —I believe your Lordship does not coincide with me entirely on this subject, & most cheerfully & sincerely shall I submit to your superior judgment & experience, & take some other line of argument against ye. bill, or be silent altogether, should you deem it more adviseable.— —Condemning, as

---

[1] *i.e.* factory workers.

[2] This is the line of argument in Byron's maiden speech in the House of Lords on February 27, 1812, against the Bill making frame-breaking a capital offence.

every one must condemn the conduct of these wretches, I believe in ye. existence of grievances which call rather for pity than punishment.——I have ye honour to be with great respect, my Lord, yr. Lordship's

most obedt. & obliged Servt.

BYRON

P.S.—I am a little apprehensive that your Lordship will think me too lenient towards these men, & *half a framebreaker myself.*

[TO LADY CAROLINE LAMB]   *Sy. Even [April, 1812?]*

I never supposed you artful, we are *all* selfish, nature did that for us, but even when you attempt deceit occasionally, you cannot maintain it, which is all the better, want of success will curb the tendency.— — Every word you utter, every line you write proves you to be either *sincere* or a *fool*, now as I know you are not the one I must believe you the other. I never knew a woman with greater or more pleasing talents, *general* as in a woman they should be, something of every thing, & too much of nothing, but these are unfortunately coupled with a total want of common conduct.—For instance the *note* to your *page*, do you suppose I delivered it? or did you mean that I should? I did not of course.—Then your heart—my poor Caro, what a little volcano! that pours *lava* through your veins, & yet I cannot wish it a bit colder, to make a *marble slab* of, as you sometimes see (to understand my foolish metaphor) brought in vases tables &c. from Vesuvius when hardened after an eruption.—To drop my detestable tropes & figures you know I have always thought you the cleverest most agreeable, absurd, amiable, perplexing, dangerous fascinating little being that lives now or ought to have lived 2000 years ago.— —I wont talk to you of beauty, I am no judge, but our *beauties* cease to be so when near you, and therefore you have either some or something better. And now, Caro, this nonsense is the first & last compliment (if it be such) I ever paid you, you have often reproached me as wanting in that respect, but *others* will make up the deficiency.—Come to Ly. Grey's,[1] at least do not let me keep you away.—All that you so often *say*, I *feel*, can more be said or felt?— —This same prudence is tiresome enough but one *must* maintain it, or what can we do to be saved?—Keep to it.—

[1] Wife of the second Earl Grey, one of the leading Whig statesmen.

[written on cover]

If you write at all, write as usual—but do as you please, only as I never see you — Basta!

[TO LADY CAROLINE LAMB]   *May 1st. 1812*

My dear Lady Caroline,—I have read over the few poems of Miss Milbank[1] with attention.—They display fancy, feeling, & a little practice would very soon induce facility of expression.—Though I have an abhorrence of Blank verse, I like the lines on Dermody[2] so much that I wish they were in rhyme.—The lines in the cave at Seaham[3] have a turn of thought which I cannot sufficiently commend & here I am at least candid as my own opinions differ upon such subjects.—The first stanza is very good indeed, & the others with a few slight alterations might be rendered equally excellent.—The last are smooth & pretty.—But these are all, has she no others?— —She certainly is a very extraordinary girl, who would imagine so much strength & variety of thought under that placid countenance?— —It is not necessary for Miss M. to be an authoress, indeed I do not think publishing at all creditable either to men or women, and (though you will not believe me) very often feel ashamed of it myself, but I have no hesitation in saying that she has talents, which were it proper or requisite to indulge, would have led to distinction.—A friend of mine (fifty years old & an author but not *Rogers*)[4] has just been here, as there is no name to the M.S.S. I shewed them to him, & he was much more enthusiastic in his praises than I have been.—He thinks them beautiful; I shall content myself with observing that they are better much better than anything of Miss M's protegee Blacket.[5] You will say as much of this to Miss M. as you think proper.—I say all this very sincerely, I have no desire to be better acquainted with Miss Milbank, she is too good for a fallen spirit to know or wish to know, & I should like her more if she were less perfect.—

Believe me yrs. ever most truly

B

[1] Annabella Milbanke, cousin of Caroline's husband, William Lamb. See biographical sketch in Appendix.

[2] Thomas Dermody, a precocious Irish poet who died young. His posthumous *Harp of Erin* was published in 1806; his collected poems in 1807.

[3] The Milbanke home near Durham.

[4] Probably Dallas.

[5] Joseph Blacket (1786–1810), the cobbler-poet, was patronized by a number of people, including Miss Milbanke.

My dear Ly. M.—"If I were looking in your face entre les deux yeux" I know not whether I should find "frankness or truth"—but certainly something which looks quite as well if not better than either, & whatever it may be I would not have it changed for any other expression; as it has defied Time, no wonder it should perplex *me*.— "*Manage* her"!¹—it is impossible—& as to friendship—no—it must be broken off at once, & all I have left is to take some step which will make her hate me effectually, for she must be in extremes.—What you state however is to be dreaded, besides—she presumes upon the weakness & affection of all about her, and the very confidence & kindness which would break or reclaim a good heart, merely lead her own farther from deserving them.—Were this but secure, you would find yourself mistaken in me; I speak from experience; except in one solitary instance, three months have ever cured me, take an example.— In the autumn of 1809 in the Mediterranean I was seized with an *everlasting* passion considerably more violent on my part than this has ever been—² every thing was settled—& *we* (the *we's* of that day) were to set off for the Friuli; but lo! the Peace spoilt every thing, by putting this in possession of the French, & some particular occurrences in the interim determined me to go on to Constantinople.—However we were to meet next year at a certain time, though I told my amica there was no time like the present, & that I could not answer for the future.—She trusted to her power, & I at the moment had certainly much greater doubts of her than myself.—A year sped & on my return downwards, I found at Smyrna & Athens dispatches, requiring the performance of this "bon billet qu'a la Chatre" & telling me that one of us had returned to the spot on purpose.—But things had altered as I foresaw, & I proceeded very leisurely, not arriving till some months after, pretty sure that in the interim my Idol was in no want of Worshippers.—But she *was* there, & we met—at the Palace & the Governor³ (ye. most accomodating of all possible chief Magistrates) was kind enough to leave us to come to the most diabolical of explanations.—It was in the Dogdays, during a Sirocco—(I almost perspire now with the thoughts of it) during the intervals of an inter-

---

¹ This was written when Byron was trying to terminate his liaison with Lady Caroline Lamb, who continued to plague him.

² This is an account, long after the event, of Byron's love affair at Malta with Mrs. Spencer Smith.

³ Major-General Hildebrand Oakes was then "His Majesty's Commissioner for the Affairs of Malta".

mittent fever (my love had also intermitted with my malady) and I certainly feared the Ague & my Passion would both return in full force.—I however got the better of both, & she sailed up the Adriatic & I down to the Straits.— —I had certes a great deal to contend against, for the Lady (who was a *select* friend of the Queen of Naples) had something to gain in a few points, & nothing to lose in *reputation*, & was a woman perfectly mistress of herself & every art of intrigue personal or political, not at all in love, but very able to persuade me that she was so, & sure that I should make a most *convenient* & complaisant fellow traveller.— —She is now I am told writing her Memoirs at Vienna, in which I shall cut a very indifferent figure; & nothing survives of this most ambrosial amour, which made me on one occasion risk my life, & on another almost drove me mad, but a few Duke of York*ish* letters, & certain baubles which I dare swear by this time have decorated the hands of half Hungary, & all Bohemia.—Cosi finiva la Musica.—

[TO LADY MELBOURNE]   *Septr. 25th. 1812*

My dear Ly. M.—It would answer no purpose to write a syllable on any subject whatever & neither accelerate nor retard what we wish to prevent, she must be left to Chance; conjugal affection and the Kilkenny Theatricals are equally in your favour—for my part it is an accursed business *towards* nor *from* which I shall not move a single step; if she throws herself upon me "cosi finiva" if not, the sooner it is over the better—from this moment I have done with it, only before she returns allow me to know that I may act accordingly;[1] but there will be nothing to fear before that time, as if a woman & a selfish woman also, would not fill up the vacancy with the first comer?—As to Annabella she requires time & all the cardinal virtues, & in the interim I am a little verging towards one who demands neither, & saves me besides the trouble of marrying by being married already.— —She besides does not speak English, & to me nothing but Italian, a great point, for from certain coincidences the very sound of that language is Music to me, & she has black eyes & *not* a very white skin, & reminds me of many in the Archipelago I wished to forget, & makes me forget what I ought

[1] In order to break up Caroline Lamb's liaison with Byron, her mother, Lady Bessborough, and Caroline's husband, William Lamb, took her to Ireland. On his side, Byron was trying, with the aid of Lady Melbourne, to escape her clutches, but Caroline would not release him easily.

to remember, all which are against me.—I only wish she did not swallow so much supper, chicken wings—sweetbreads,—custards —peaches & *Port* wine—a woman should never be seen eating or drinking, unless it be *lobster sallad* & *Champagne*, the only truly feminine & becoming viands.—I recollect imploring one Lady not to eat more than a fowl at a sitting without effect, & have never yet made a single proselyte to Pythagoras.—Now a word to yourself—a much more pleasing topic than any of the preceding.—I have no very high opinion of your sex, but when I do see a woman superior not only to all her own but to most of ours I worship her in proportion as I despise the rest.—And when I know that men of the first judgment & the most distinguished abilities have entertained & do entertain an opinion which my own humble observation without any great effort of discernment has enabled me to confirm on the same subject, you will not blame me for following the example of my elders & betters & admiring you certainly as much as you ever were admired.— My only regret is that the very awkward circumstances in which we are placed prevents & will prevent the improvement of an acquaintance which I now almost regret having made—but recollect whatever happens that the loss of it must give me more pain than even the *precious* [*previous?*] *acquisition* (& this is saying *much*) which will occasion that loss. Ld. Jersey has reinvited me to M[iddleton] for the 4 Octr. & I will be there if possible, in the mean time whatever step you take to break off this affair has my full concurrence— but *what* you wished me to write would be a little too indifferent; and *that* now would be an insult, & I am much more unwilling to hurt her feelings now than ever, (not from the mere apprehension of a disclosure in her wrath) but I have always felt that one who has given up much, has a claim upon *me* (at least—whatever she deserve from others) for every respect that she may not feel her own degradation, & this is the reason that I have not written at all lately, lest some expression might be misconstrued by her.—When the Lady herself begins the quarrel & adopts a new "Cortejo" then my Conscience is comforted.—She has not written to me for some days, which is either a very bad or very good omen.—

yrs. ever

I observe that C[aroline] in her late epistles, lays peculiar stress upon her powers of attraction, upon W[illiam]'s attachment &c. & by way of enhancing the extreme value of her regards, tells me, that she

"could make any one in love with her" an amiable accomplishment—
but unfortunately a little too general to be valuable, for was there
ever yet a woman, not absolutely disgusting, who could not say or do
the same thing? any woman can *make* a man in *love* with her, show me
her who can *keep* him so?—*You* perhaps *can* show me such a woman
but I have not seen her for these—*three weeks.*—

[TO LADY MELBOURNE]   *Octr. 18th. 1812*

   My dear Lady M.— —Of A[nnabella] I have little to add, but I do
not regret what has passed;[1] the report alluded to had hurt her feelings.
& she has now regained her tranquillity by the refutation to her own
satisfaction without disturbing mine.—This was but fair—and was
not unexpected by me, all things considered perhaps it could not have
been better.—I think of her nearly as I did, the specimen you send me
is more favourable to her talents than her discernment,[2] & much *too
indulgent* to the subject she has chosen, in some points the resemblance
is very exact, but you have not sent me the whole (I imagine) by the
abruptness of both beginning & end.—I am glad that your opinion
coincides with mine on the subject of her abilities & her excellent
qualities, in both these points she is singularly fortunate.—Still there
is something of the *woman* about her; her *preferring* that the letter to
you should be sent forward to *me per esempio* appears as if though she
would not encourage, she was not disgusted with being admired.—I
also may hazard a conjecture that an *answer* addressed to *herself* might
not have been displeasing, but of this you are the best judge from actual
observation.—I cannot however see the necessity of it's being forwarded unless I was either to admire the composition or reply to ye.
contents.—*One* I certainly do, the other would merely lead to mutual
compliments very sincere but somewhat tedious.—By the bye, what
two famous letters *your own* are, I never saw such traits of discernment, observation of character, knowledge of your *own sex.* & *sly
concealment* of your *knowledge* of the *foibles* of *ours*, than in these
epistles, & so that I preserve you *always* as a friend & *sometimes* as a
correspondent (the oftener the better) believe me my dear Ly. M. I
shall regret nothing but—the week we passed at Middleton till I can

   [1] Partly to escape from Caroline Lamb, Byron had made a tentative proposal of
marriage to her cousin-in-law Annabella Milbanke, through her aunt Lady
Melbourne. Annabella politely refused but wanted to remain his friend.
   [2] This was probably Annabella's "Character" of Byron which she had written on
October 8th, but had not finished.

enjoy such another.—Now for C[aroline]—your name was never mentioned or hinted at—the passage was nearly as follows—"I know from the *best* authority, your *own*, that your time has passed in a very different manner, nor do I object to it, amuse yourself, but leave me *quiet*, what would you have?—I go nowhere, I see no one, I mix with no society—I write when it is proper—these perpetual causeless caprices are equally selfish & absurd." &c. &c. & so on in answer to her description of her *lonely lovelorn condition*!!! much in the same sever*er* style.—And now this must end, if she persists I will leave the country, I shall enter into no explanations, write no epistles softening or reverse; nor will I meet her if it can be avoided, & certainly never but in society, the sooner she is apprized of this the better, but with one so totally devoid of all conduct it is difficult to decide.—I have no objection to her knowing what passed about A[nnabella]—if it would have any good effect, nor do I wish it to be concealed, even from others or the world in general, my vanity will not be piqued by it's development, & though It was not accepted I am not at all ashamed of my admiration of the amiable *Mathematician.*—I did not reproach C[aroline] for *"her behaviour"* but the *misrepresentation* of it, & her suspicions of mine; why tell me she was *dying* instead of *dancing* when I had much rather hear she was acting, as she in fact acted? viz—like any other person in good health, tolerable society & high spirits.— —
In short I am not her lover, & would rather not be her friend, though I never can nor will be her enemy.—If it can be ended let it be without any interference, I will have nothing more to do with it, her letters (all but one about *Ld. Clare*[3] unanswered & the answer to *that* strictly confined to his concerns except a hint on vanity at the close) are filled with the most ridiculous egotism, *"how* the Duke's mob observed her, *how* the boys followed her, the women caressed & the men admired, & *how* many lovers were all sacrificed to this brilliant fit of constancy.["]
—who wants it forsooth or expects it after sixteen?— —Can't she take example from me, do I embarrass myself about A[nnabella]?—or the fifty B. C. D. E. F. G. H's &c. &c. that have preceded her in cruelty or kindness (the *latter* always the greatest plague) not I, & really sans phrase I think *my loss* is the *most considerable.*— —I hear Ly. Holland is ill I hope *not seriously.*— Ld. O[xford] went today, & I am still here with some idea of proceeding either to Herefordshire or to Ld. Harrowby's, & one notion of being obliged to go to London to

[3] Lord Clare was in Ireland at the time. Caroline, knowing him to be a close friend of Byron, tried later to have him get a portrait of her former lover for her. See *Notes and Queries,* 1967, Vol. 14 (Vol. 212 of the continued series), pp. 297–99.

meet my Agent.—Pray let me hear from you; I am so provoked at the thought that our *acquaintance* may be interrupted by the old phantasy. —I had & have twenty thousand things to say & I trust as many to hear, but somehow our conversations never come to a clear conclusion. —I thank you again for your efforts with my Princess of Parallelograms, who has puzzled you more than the Hypothenuse; in her character she has not forgotten *"Mathematics"* wherein I used to praise her cunning.—Her proceedings are quite rectangular, or rather we are two parallel lines prolonged to infinity side by side but never to meet. —Say what you please for or of me, & I will mean it.—Good Even my dear Ly. M.—ever yrs most affectionately

B

[TO LADY MELBOURNE]   *Septr. 5th. 1813*

Dear Lady Melbourne—I return you the plan of A[nnabella]'s spouse elect of which I shall say nothing because I do not understand it[1]—though I dare say it is exactly what it ought to be.—Neither do I know why I am writing this note as I mean to call on you—unless it be to try your "new patent pens" which delight me infinitely with their colours—I have pitched upon a yellow one to begin with— Very likely you will be out—& I must return you the annexed epistles—I would rather have seen your answer—she seems to have been spoiled—not as children usually are—but systematically Clarissa Harlowed into an awkward kind of correctness—with a dependence upon her own infallibility which will or may lead her into some egregious blunder—I don't mean the usual error of young gentlewomen—but she will find exactly what she wants—& then discover that it is much more dignified than entertaining.—[two pages torn away] . . . in town—. . . .

[TO ANNABELLA MILBANKE]   *Septr 6th 1813*

Agreed—I will write to you occasionally & you shall answer at your leisure & discretion.—You must have deemed me very vain & selfish to imagine that your candour could offend—I see nothing that "could hurt my feelings" in your correspondence—you told me you

[1] Annabella Milbanke had sent her aunt a statement of her requirements for a husband, which Lady Melbourne sent on to Byron.

declined me as a lover but wished to retain me as a friend—now as one may meet with a good deal of what is called love in this best of all possible worlds—& very rarely with friendship I could not find fault —upon calculation at least.—I am afraid my first letter was written during some of those moments which have induced your belief in my *general despondency*—now in common I believe with most of mankind— I have in the course of a very useless & ill regulated life encountered events which have left a deep *impression*—perhaps something at the time recalled *this* so forcibly as to make it apparent in my answer— but I am not conscious of any habitual or at least long continued pressure on my spirits.—On the contrary—with the exception of an occasional spasm—I look upon myself as a very facetious personage— & may safely appeal to most of my acquaintance (Ly. M. for instance) in proof of my assertion.—Nobody laughs more—& though your friend Joanna Baillie says somewhere that "Laughter is the *child* of Misery" yet I don't believe her—(unless indeed in a hysteric)— though I think it is sometimes the *Parent*.—Nothing would do me more honour than the acquaintance of that Lady—who does not possess a more enthusiastic admirer than myself—she is our only dramatist since Otway & Southerne—I don't except Home[1]—With all my presumed prejudice against your sex or rather the perversion of manners & principle in many which you admit in some circles— I think the worst woman that ever existed would have made a *man* of very passable reputation—they are all better than us—& their faults such as they are must originate with ourselves.—Your sweeping sentence "in the circles where we have met" amuses me much when I recollect some of those who constituted that society—after all bad as it is it has it's agremens.—The great object of life is Sensation—to feel that we exist—even though in pain—it is this "craving void"[2] which drives us to Gaming—to Battle—to Travel—to intemperate but keenly felt pursuits of every description whose principal attraction is the agitation inseparable from their accomplishment.——I am but an awkward dissembler—as my friend you will bear with my faults— I shall have the less constraint in what I say to you—firstly because I may derive some benefit from your observations—& next because I am very sure *you* can never be perverted by any paradoxes of mine.— You have said a good deal & very well too—on the subject of

[1] John Home (1722–1808) made his first success as a dramatist in Edinburgh with the historical drama *Douglas*.

[2] Pope, *Eloisa to Abelard*, line 94.

Benevolence *systematically* exerted—two lines of Pope will explain mine (if I have any) and that of half mankind—

> 'Perhaps Prosperity becalmed his breast
> 'Perhaps the Wind just shifted from ye. East.[3]—

By the bye you are a *bard* also—have you quite given up that pursuit? —is your friend Pratt[4] one of your critics?—or merely one of your "systematic benevolents? ["] You were very kind to poor Blackett which he requited by falling in love rather presumptuously to be sure[5] like Metastasio with the Empress Maria Theresa.—When you can spare an instant I shall of course be delighted to hear from or of you—but do not let me encroach a moment on better avocations— Adieu

ever yrs.
B

[TO LADY MELBOURNE]   *Aston Hall Rotherham—Septr. 21st. 1813*

My dear Ly. M[elbourn]e—My stay at Cambridge was very short— but feeling feverish & restless in town I flew off & here I am on a visit to my friend Webster now married—& (according to ye. Duke of Buckingham's curse—) "settled in ye. country."—His bride Lady Frances is a pretty pleasing woman—but in delicate health & I fear going—if not gone—into a decline—Stanhope & his wife[1]—pretty & pleasant too but not at all consumptive—left us today—leaving only ye. family—another single gentleman & your slave.—The sister Ly. Catherine is here too—& looks very pale from a *cross* in her love for Lord Bury (Ld. Alb[emarl]e's son)[2] in short we are a society of happy wives & unfortunate maidens.—The place is very well & quiet & the children only scream in a low voice—so that I am not much disturbed & shall stay a few days in tolerable repose.—W[ebster] don't want sense nor good nature but both are occasionally obscured by his suspicions & absurdities of all descriptions—he is passionately fond of

[3] Pope, *Moral Essays*, I, 111–112.
[4] Samuel Jackson Pratt was the patron of the cobbler-poet Joseph Blacket, who was also patronized by Miss Milbanke.
[5] This is a rather interesting revelation if true: that Blacket should have become romantically interested in his patroness.
[1] Philip Henry (Stanhope), 4th Earl Stanhope (1781–1855) married in 1803 Catherine Lucy, daughter of the 1st Baron Carrington.
[2] Lord Bury was the 2nd son of the 4th Earl of Albemarle. The Earl's heir, Augustus Frederick, styled Viscount Bury, died in 1804, when the title passed to the second son.

having his wife admired—& at the same time jealous to jaundice of every thing & every body—I have hit upon the medium of praising her to him perpetually behind her back—& never looking at her before his face—as for her I believe she is disposed to be very faithful—& I don't think any one now here is inclined to put her to the test.— W[ebster] himself is with all his jealousy & admiration a little tired— he has been lately at Newstead—& wants to go again—I suspected this sudden penchant & soon discovered that a foolish nymph of the Abbey—about whom fortunately I care not—was the attraction—now if I wanted to make mischief—I could extract much good perplexity from a proper management of such events—but I am grown so good or so indolent—that I shall not avail myself of so pleasant an opportunity of tormenting mine host—though he deserves it for poaching.—I believe he has hitherto been unsuccessful—or rather it is too astonishing to be believed.—He proposed to me with great gravity to carry him over there—& I replied with equal candour that *he* might set out when he pleased but that I should remain here to take care of his household in the interim—a proposition which I thought very much to the purpose—but which did not seem at all to his satisfaction—by way of opiate he preached me a sermon on his wife's good qualities concluding by an assertion that in all moral & mortal qualities she was very like "*Christ*!!!["] I think the virgin Mary would have been a more appropriate typification—but it was the first comparison of the kind I ever heard & made me laugh till he was angry—& then I got out of humour too—which pacified him & shortened his panegyric—Ld. Petersham³ is coming here in a day or two—who will certainly flirt furiously with Ly. F[rances]—& I shall have some comic Iagoism with our little Othello—I should have no chance with his Desdemona myself—but a more lively & better dressed & formed personage might in an innocent way—for I really believe the girl is a very good well disposed wife & will do very well if she lives & he himself don't tease her into some dislike of her lawful owner.———I passed through Hatfield the night of your *ball*—suppose we had jostled at a turn-pike!!—At Bugden I blundered on a Bishop—the Bishop put me in mind of ye Government—the Government of the Governed—& the governed of their *indifference* towards their governors which you must have remarked as to all *parties*—these reflections expectorated as

³ Charles Stanhope, later (1829), 4th Earl of Harrington, was styled Lord Petersham. He was Lord of the Bedchamber in 1812, and was apparently a ladies' man. He was also a notorious dandy, who had a famous collection of snuff boxes.

follows—you know I *never* send you my scribblings & when you read these you will wish I never may.—

> Tis said—*Indifference* marks the present time
> Then hear the reason—though 'tis told in rhyme—
> A King who *can't*—a Prince of Wales who *don't*—
> Patriots who *shan't*—Ministers who *won't*—
> What matters who are *in* or *out* of place
> The *Mad*—the *Bad*—the *Useless*—or the *Base?*

---

you may read the 2d. couplet *so* if you like—

> "A King who *cannot*—& a Prince who don't—
> Patriots who *would not*—ministers who won't—"

I am asked to stay for the Doncaster races but I am not in plight—& am a miserable beau at the best of times—so I shall even return to town or elsewhere—and in the mean time ever am

yrs. dear Ly. M[elbourn]e
B

P.S.—If you write address to B[enne]t Street, were I once gone—I should not wish my letters to travel *here* after me for fear of *accidents*.————There is a delightful epitaph on Voltaire in Grimm—I read it coming down—the French I should probably misspell so take it only in bad English—"Here lies the spoilt child of *the/a* world which he spoiled."[4]—It is good short & true.———

My dear Lady Melbourne—I sent you a long letter from Aston last week which I hope has been received at *Brocket.*—The Doncaster races (as I *foretold* you) drove me to town but I have an invitation to go down again this week upon which I am pondering—I had reasons of my own some bad & others good for not accompanying the party to

---

[4] Byron had been reading the lengthy review of Baron de Grimm's *Correspondance Littéraire, Philosophique et Critique* which was the leading article in the *Edinburgh Review* for July, 1813. This epitaph, ascribed to Lady Lausanne, is quoted from Grimm on page 274 of the *Edinburgh*: "Ci gît l'enfant gaté du monde qu'il gata."

D[oncaste]r[1]—my time was passed pleasantly enough—& as innocently at *Aston*—as during the *"week"* of immaculate memory last autumn at Middleton.—If you received my letter you will remember my sketch of the *Astonian* family—when I return I shall complete it— at present I doubt about the colours—I have been observing & have made out one conclusion which is that my friend W[ebster] will run his head against a wall of his own building.—There are a Count & Countess—somebody—(I forget the name of the exiles)—the last of whom made a desperate attack on W. at Ld. Waterpark's[2] a few weeks ago—& W. in gratitude invited them to his house—there I suppose they now are—(they had not arrived when I set out) to me it appears from W's own narrative—that he will be detected & bullied by the husband into some infernal compromise—& I told him as much—but like *others* of our acquaintance he is deaf as an adder.—I have known him several years & really wish him well—for which reason I overlooked his interference in some concerns of my own where he had no business—perhaps because also they had ceased to interest me—(for we are all selfish & I no more trust myself than others with a good motive) but be that as it may—I wish he would not indulge in such freaks—for which *he* can have no excuse—& the example will turn out none of the best for Ly. F[ann]y.—She seems pretty & intelligent—as far as I observed which was very little—I had & have other things to reflect upon.—Your opinion of ye. Giaour or rather ye. *additions* honours me highly—you who know how my thoughts were occupied when these last were written—will perhaps perceive in parts a coincidence in my own state of mind with that of my hero[3]—if so you will give me credit for feeling—though on the other hand I lose in your esteem.—I have tried & hardly too to vanquish my demon—but to very little purpose—for a resource that seldom failed me before—did in this instance—I mean *transferring* my regards to another—of which I had a very fair & not *discouraging* opportunity at one time—I willingly would—but the feeling that it was an effort spoiled all again—& *here* I am—*what* I am you know already.[4]—As I have never been accustomed to parade my thoughts before you in a larmoyante strain I shall

---

[1] Byron was pondering going to see Augusta again.

[2] Richard Cavendish, 2nd Baron Waterpark (in the Irish Peerage).

[3] Byron was aware that Lady Melbourne knew enough of his present quandaries to read the meaning of some of his additions to *The Giaour*.

[4] Byron knew that Lady Melbourne would be disappointed that he had not transferred his regards to Lady Frances Webster or another as an escape from his more dangerous attachment to Augusta.

not begin now.—The epistles of your mathematician (*A* would now be ambiguous)[5] continue—& the last concludes with a repetition of a desire that none but Papa & Mamma should know it—why *you* should not seems to me quite ludicrous & is now past praying for—but—observe—here is the strictest of St. Ursula's 11000 what do you call 'ems?[6]—a wit—a moralist—& religionist—enters into a clandestine correspondence with a personage generally presumed a great Roué—& drags her aged parents into this secret treaty—it is I believe not usual for single ladies to risk such brilliant adventures—but this comes of *infallibility*—not that she ever says anything that might not be said by the Town cryer—still it is imprudent—if I were rascal enough to take an unfair advantage.—Alas! poor human nature—here is your niece writing—& doing a foolish thing—*I lecturing* Webster!—& forgetting the tremendous "beam in my own eye" no—I *do* feel but cannot pluck it out.—These various absurdities & inconsistencies may amuse you—but there is a fate in such small as well as great concerns or how came Moreau by his loss of legs?[7] I saw an extract from his last letter to his wife (in M.S. not published) he says—that *"Coquin de Bonaparte est toujours heureux!"* Good night.

ever yrs.
B

[TO LADY MELBOURNE]   *Octr. 8th. 1813*

My dear Ly. M[elbourn]e—I have volumes—but neither time nor space—I have already trusted too deeply to hesitate now—besides for certain reasons you will not be sorry to hear that I am anything but what I was.—Well then—to begin—& first a word of mine host—he has lately been talking *at* rather than *to* me before the party (with the exception of the women) in a tone—which as I never use it myself I am not particularly disposed to tolerate in others—what *he* may do with impunity—it seems—but not suffer—till at last I told him that

---

[5] Since Byron in his letters to Lady Melbourne used the initial A. to refer to Augusta, he had to find some other way of referring to Annabella Milbanke. He sometimes referred to "your A" (Annabella), and "my A." (Augusta).

[6] A reference to the legend of St. Ursula and her 11,000 virgins. Byron saw their supposed bones in Cologne in his passage up the Rhine in 1816, and he gave a couplet to them in *Don Juan* (Canto X, stanza 62):
Eleven thousand maiden heads of bone./The greatest number flesh hath ever known.

[7] Jean Victor Marie Moreau, French general under Napoleon, was mortally wounded at the battle of Dresden. Both his legs were amputated in an attempt to save his life, but he died a few days later.

the whole of his argument involved the interesting contradiction that "he might love where he liked but that no one else might like what he ever thought proper to love" a doctrine which as the learned Partridge observed[1]—contains a "non sequitur" from which I for one begged leave as a general proposition to dissent.—This nearly produced a scene—with me as well as another guest who seemed to admire my sophistry the most of the two—& as it was after dinner & debating time—might have ended in more than wineshed—but that the Devil for some wise purpose of his own thought proper to restore good humour—which has not as yet been further infringed.————In these last few days I have had a good deal of conversation with an amiable persion—whom (as we deal in *letters*—& initials only) we will denominate *Ph.*[Frances]—well—these things are dull in detail—take it once—I have made love—& if I am to believe mere *words* (for there we have hitherto stopped) it is returned.—I must tell you the place of declaration however—a billiard room!—I did not as C[aroline] says "kneel in the middle of the room" but like Corporal Trim to the Nun— "I made a speech"[2]—which as you might not listen to it with the same patience—I shall not transcribe.—We were before on very amiable terms—& I remembered being asked an odd question—"how a woman who liked a man could inform him of it—when he did not perceive it"—I also observed that we went on with our game (of billiards) without *counting* the *hazards*—& supposed that—as mine certainly were not—the thoughts of the other party also were not exactly occupied by what was our ostensible pursuit.—Not quite though pretty well satisfied with my progress—I took a very imprudent step—with pen & paper—in tender & tolerably turned *prose* periods (no *poetry* even when in earnest) here were risks certainly— first how to convey—then how it would be received—it was received however & deposited not very far from the heart which I wished it to reach—when who should enter the room but the person who ought at that moment to have been in the Red sea if Satan had any civility—but

[1] Partridge, the learned schoolmaster in Fielding's *Tom Jones*, replied to the sergeant who said, ". . . every man who curses the cloth would curse the king if he durst," "Excuse me there, Mr. Sergeant, that's a *non sequitur*." (Book IX, Chapter 6.)

[2] Corporal Trim, in telling his story of how the Beguine roused his passions by rubbing his wounded knee, ended by saying "I seized her hand—" and Uncle Toby interposed, "And then thou clapped'st it to thy lips, Trim, . . . and madest a speech." Tristram commented: "Whether the corporal's amour terminated precisely in the way my uncle Toby described it is immaterial . . ." (Sterne, *Tristram Shandy*, Book VIII, Chapter 22.) Byron may have wanted Lady Melbourne to think the same.

she kept her countenance & the paper—& I my composure as well as I could.—It was a risk—& *all* had been lost by failure—but then recollect—how much more I had to gain by the reception—if not declined—& how much one always hazards to obtain anything worth having.—My billet prospered—it did more—it even (I am this moment interrupted by the *Marito*—& write this before him—he has brought me a political pamphlet in M.S. to decypher & applaud—I shall content myself with the last—Oh—he is gone again)—my billet produced an *answer*—a very unequivocal one too—but a little too much about virtue—& indulgence of attachment in some sort of etherial process in which the soul is principally concerned—which I don't very well understand—being a bad metaphysician—but one generally *ends* & *begins* with Platonism—& as my proselyte is only twenty—there is time enough to materialize—I hope nevertheless this spiritual system won't last long—& at any rate must make the experiment.—I remember my last case was the reverse—as Major O'Flaherty recommends "we fought first & explained afterwards."—This is the present state of things—much mutual profession—a good deal of melancholy— which I am sorry to say was remarked by "the Moor" & as much love as could well be made considering the time place & circumstances.——— I need not say that the folly & petulance of —— [Webster] have tended to all this—if a man is not contented with a pretty woman & not only runs after any little country girl he meets with but absolutely boasts of it—he must not be surprised if others admire that which he knows not how to value—besides he literally provoked & goaded me into it—by something not unlike bullying—*indirect* to be sure—but tolerably obvious—"he *would* do this—& he would do that—if any man["] &c. &c.—& *he* thought that every woman "was *his* lawful prize nevertheless["]—Oons! who is this strange monopolist?—it is odd enough but on other subjects he is like other people but on this he seems infatuated—if he had been rational—& not prated of his pursuits —I should have gone on very well—as I did at Middleton—even now I shan't quarrel with him—if I can help it—but one or two of his speeches has blackened the blood about my heart—& curdled the milk of kindness—if put to the proof—I shall behave like other people I presume.—I have heard from A[nnabella]—but her letter to me is *melancholy*—about her old friend Miss M[ontgomer]y's[3] departure &c.

---

[3] Mary Millicent Montgomery, an invalid, had been Annabella's friend from girlhood. Her brother, Hugh Montgomery, was one of Annabella's early suitors, as she later confessed to Byron.

—&c.—I wonder who will have her at last—her letter to you is *gay*—
you say—that to me must have been written at the same time—the
little demure Nonjuror!————I wrote to C[aroline] the other day—
for I was afraid she might repeat the last year's epistle—& make it
circular among my friends.———Good evening—I am now going to
billiards.—

P.S. 6 o'clock—This business is growing serious—& I think *Platonism* in some peril—There has been very nearly a scene—almost an
hysteric & really without cause for I was conducting myself with (to me)
very irksome decorum—her *expressions* astonish me—so young & cold
as she appeared—but these professions must end as usual—& *would*—
I think—*now*—had "l'occasion" been *not* wanting—had any one come
in during the *tears* & consequent consolation all had been spoiled—we
must be more cautious or less larmoyante.———

P.S. second—10 o'clock—I write to you just escaped from Claret &
vociferation—on G–d knows what paper—my Landlord is a rare
gentleman—he has just proposed to me a bet "that *he* for a certain sum
wins any given *woman*—against any given *homme* including *all friends*
present['']—which I declined with becoming deference to him & the
rest of the company—is not this at this moment a perfect comedy?—
I forgot to mention that on his entrance yesterday during the letter
scene—it reminded me so much of an awkward passage in "the Way to
keep him"[4] between Lovemore—Sir Bashful—& my Lady—that embarrassing as it was I could hardly help laughing—I hear his voice in
the passage—he wants me to go to a ball at Sheffield—& is talking to
me as I write—Good Night. I am in the act of praising his pamphlet.—
I don't half like your story of *Corinne*—some day I will tell you why—
If I can—but at present—Good Night.

[TO LADY MELBOURNE]   *Newstead Abbey Octr. 10th. 1813*
My dear Ly. M[elbourn]e—I write to you from the melancholy
mansion of my fathers—where I am dull as the longest deceased of my
progenitors—I hate reflection on irrevocable things & won't now turn
sentimentalist. W[ebster] alone accompanied me here (I return

---

[4] *The Way to Keep Him*, a comedy by Arthur Murphy (1760). The "awkward
passage" occurs in Act V, scene 1, when Lovemore's love letter to another woman
is discovered to his wife.

tomorrow to Aston) he is now sitting opposite—& between us are Red & white Champ[agn]e—Burgundy—two sorts of Claret—& lighter vintages—the relics of my youthful cellar which is yet in formidable number & famous order—but I leave the wine to him—& prefer conversing soberly with you.—Ah! if you knew what a quiet Mussulman life (except in wine) I led here for a few years—but no matter.—Yesterday I sent you a long letter & must now recur to the same subject which is uppermost in my thoughts.—I am as much astonished but I hope not so much mistaken as Lord Ogleby[1] at the denouement or rather commencement of the last week—it has changed my views—my wishes—my hopes—my everything—& will furnish you with additional proof of my weakness.—Mine guest (late host) has just been congratulating himself on possessing a partner without *passion*—I don't know—& cannot yet speak with certainty— but I never yet saw more decisive preliminary symptoms.————As I am apt to take people at their word—on receiving my answer—that whatever the weakness of her heart might be—I should never derive further proof of it than the confession—instead of pressing the point— I told her that I was willing to be hers on her own terms & should never attempt to infringe upon the conditions—I said this without pique—& believing her perfectly in earnest for the time—but in the midst of our mutual professions or to use her own expression "more than mutual" she burst into an agony of crying—& at such a time & in such a place as rendered such a scene particularly perilous to both— her sister in the next room—& —— [Webster] not far off—of course I said & did almost everything proper on the occasion—& fortunately we restored sunshine in time to prevent anyone from perceiving the cloud that had darkened our horizon.—She says—she is convinced that my own declaration was produced solely because I perceived her previous penchant—which by the bye—as I think I said to you before— I neither perceived nor expected—I really did not suspect her of a predilection for anyone—& even now in public with the exception of those little indirect yet mutually understood—I don't know how & it is unnecessary to name or describe them—her conduct is as coldly correct as her still—fair—Mrs. L[amb] like aspect.—She however managed to give me a note—& to receive another & a ring before —— [Webster]'s very face—& yet she is a thorough devotee—& takes prayers morning and evening—besides being measured for a new bible once a quarter.— The only alarming thing—is that —— [Webster] complains of her

[1] Lord Ogleby is a superannuated peer who affects the manners of a youth in *The Clandestine Marriage* by Garrick and the elder Colman.

aversion from being beneficial to population & posterity—if this is an invariable maxim—I shall lose my labour.—Be this as it may—she *owns* to more—than I ever heard from any woman within the time—& I shan't take —— [Webster]'s word any more for her feelings than I did for that celestial comparison which I once mentioned.—I think her eye—her change of colour—& the trembling of her hand—& above all her devotion tell a different tale.—Good night—we return tomorrow —& now I drink your health—you are my only correspondent & I believe friend—

ever yrs.

B

[TO LADY MELBOURNE]   *Newstead Abbey—Octr. 17th. 1813*

My dear Ly. M[elbourn]e—The whole party are here—and now to my narrative.—But first I must tell you that I am rather unwell owing to a folly of last night—About midnight after deep and drowsy potations I took it into my head to empty my *skull cup* which holds rather better than a bottle of Claret at *one draught*—and nearly died the death of Alexander—which I shall be content to do when I have achieved his conquests—I had just sense enough left to feel that I was not fit to join the ladies—& went to bed—where my Valet tells me that I was first convulsed & afterwards so motionless that he thought "Good Night to Marmion."—I don't know how I came to do so very silly a thing— but I believe my guests were boasting—& "company villainous company hath been the spoil of me" I detest drinking in general—& beg your pardon for this excess—I *can't* do so any more.——To my theme—you were right—I have been a little too sanguine—as to the *conclusion*—but hear.—One day left entirely to ourselves was nearly fatal—another such *victory* & with Pyrrhus we were lost———it came to this—"I am entirely at your *mercy*—I own it—I give myself up to you—I am not *cold*—whatever I seem to others—but I know that I cannot bear the reflection hereafter—do not imagine that these are mere words—I tell you the truth—now act as you will—["] was I wrong?—I spared her.—There was a something so very peculiar in her manner—a kind of mild decision—no scene—not even a struggle— but still I know not what that convinced me she was serious—it was not the mere *"No"* which one has heard forty times before—& always with the same accent—but the *tone*—and the aspect—yet I sacrificed much—the hour *two* in the morning——away—the Devil whispering that it was mere *verbiage* &c.—& yet I know not whether I can regret it—she seems so very thankful for my forbearance—a proof at least that she was not playing merely the usual decorous reluctance which is sometimes so tiresome on these occasions.———You ask if I am prepared to go "all lengths" if you mean by "all lengths" any thing including duel or divorce—I answer *yes*—I love her—if I did not and much too—I should have been more *selfish* on the occasion before mentioned—I have offered to go away with her—& her answer whether sincere or not is "that on *my account* she declines it"—in the mean time we are all as wretched as possible—*he* scolding on *account* of *unaccountable* melancholy—the sister very suspicious but rather amused—the friend very suspicious too but (why I know not) not at all amused—il Marito something like Lord Chesterfield in De Grammont[1]—putting on a martial physignomy—prating with his worthy ally—swearing at servants—sermonizing both sisters—& buying sheep—but never quitting her side now—so that we are in despair—*I* very feverish—restless—and silent—as indeed seems to be the *tacit* agreement of every one else—in short I can foresee nothing—it may end in nothing—but here are half a dozen persons very much occupied—& two if not three in great perplexity—& as far as I can judge—so we must continue.———She *don't* & *won't* live with him—& they have been so far separate for a long time—therefore—I have nothing to answer for on that point—poor thing—she is either the most *artful* or *artless* of her age (20) I ever encountered—she *owns* to so much—and perpetually says—"rather than you should be *angry*"—or—"rather than you should like anyone else I will do whatever you please" ["]I won't speak to this that or the other if you dislike it—["] & throws or seems to throw herself so entirely upon my direction in every respect—that it disarms me quite—but I am really wretched with the perpetual conflict with myself.—Her health is so very delicate —she is so thin & pale—& seems to have lost her appetite so entirely —that I doubt her being much longer—this is also her own opinion— but these fancies are common to all who are not very happy———if she were once my wife or likely to be so—a warm climate should be the first resort nevertheless for her recovery.—The most perplexing—& yet I can't prevail on myself to give it up—is the *caressing* system—in her it appears perfectly childish—and I do think innocent—but it really puzzles all the Scipio about me to confine myself to the laudable

---

[1] The 2nd Earl of Chesterfield (1633–1713) is pictured in the *Memoirs* of the Comte de Gramont as being tortured by an insane and ridiculous jealousy of his second wife, whom he married in 1660.

portion of these endearments.————What a cursed situation I have thrust myself into—Potiphar (it used to be O[xford]'s name) putting some stupid question to me the other day—I told him that I rather admired the *sister*—& what does he? but tell *her* this & his *wife* too— who a little too hastily asked him "if he was *mad*"? which put him to demonstration that a man ought not to be asked if he was mad—for relating that a friend thought his wife's sister a pretty woman—upon this topic he held forth with great fervour for a customary period—I wish he had a quinsey.————Tell Ly. H[olland] that Clarke is the name—& Craven Street (No. forgotten) the residence—may be heard of at Trin. Coll.—excellent man—able physician—shot a friend in a duel (about his sister) & I believe killed him professionally afterwards— Ly. H[olland] may have him for self or friends—I don't know where I am going—my mind is a chaos—I always am setting all upon single stakes—& this is one—your story of the Frenchman is Matta in Grammont & the Marquis[2]—Heigh ho!—Good Night—address to *Aston.*—

ever yrs.
B

P.S.—My stay is quite uncertain—a moment may overturn every thing—but you shall hear—happen what may—nothing or something.

[TO ANNABELLA MILBANKE]   *Novr. 10th. 1813*

A variety of circumstances & movements from place to place—none of which would be very amusing in detail—nor indeed pleasing to any one who (I may flatter myself) is my friend have hitherto prevented me from answering your two last letters—but if my daily self-reproach for the omission can be any atonement—I hope it may prove as satis- factory an apology to you—as it has been a "compunctious visiting" to myself.————Your opinion of my "reasoning powers" is so exactly my own—that you will not wonder if I avoid a controversy with so skilful a casuist—particularly on a subject where I am certain to get the worst of it in this world—and perhaps incur a warmer confuta-

---

[2] Charles de Bourdeille, Comte de Matta (1614–1674), was a celebrated wit. The story to which Byron refers, as recounted in Gramont's *Memoirs*, concerns the gallantries of Gramont and Matta at the Court of Turin with Mlle. de Saint- Germain and Mme. de Sénantes. The story might have been pertinent to Byron's remarks on Webster because of the brash self-confidence of Matta as a lover and gallant.

tion in the next.—But I shall be most happy to hear your observations on the subject—or on any subject—if anybody could do me much *good* —probably you might—as by all accounts you are mistress of the practice as well as theory of that benevolent science (which I take to be better than even your *Mathematics*) at all events it is *my* fault if I derive no benefit from your remarks.—I agree with you quite upon Mathematics too—and must be content to admire them at an incomprehensible distance—always adding them to the catalogue of my regrets—I know that two and two make four—& should be glad to prove it too if I could—though I must say if by any sort of process I could convert 2 & 2 into *five* it would give me much greater pleasure.— The only part I remember which gave me much delight were those theorems (is that the word?) in which after ringing the changes upon— A—B—& C—D. &c. I at last came to "which is absurd—which is impossible" and at this point I have always arrived & I fear always shall through life—very fortunate if I can continue to stop there. ———I perceive by part of your last letter—that you are still a little inclined to believe me a very gloomy personage—those who pass so much of their time entirely alone cannot be always in very high spirits —yet I don't know—though I certainly do enjoy society to a certain extent I never passed two hours in mixed company in my life—without wishing myself out of it again—still I look upon myself as a facetious companion—well respected by all the Wits—at whose jests I readily laugh—& whose repartees I take care never to incur by any kind of contest—for which I feel as little qualified as I do for the more solid pursuit of demonstration.—I am happy so far in the *intimate* acquaintance of two or three men with whom for ten years of my life I have never had one word of difference—and what is rather strange—their opinions religious moral & political are diametrically opposite to mine— so that when I say "difference" I mean of course *serious* dispute—coolness—quarrel—or whatever people call it—now for a person who began life with that endless source of squabble—satire—I may in this respect think myself fortunate.—My reflections upon this subject qualify me to sympathize with you very sincerely in the departure of your friend Miss Montgomery—the more so—as notwithstanding many instances of the contrary I believe the friendship of *good* women —more sincere than that of men—& certainly more tender—at least I never heard of a male intimacy that spoilt a man's dinner—after the age of fifteen—which was that when I began to think myself a mighty fine gentleman & to feel ashamed of liking anybody better than one'- self. I have been scribbling another poem—as it is called—Turkish as before—for I can't empty my head of the East—and horrible enough—though not so sombre quite as ye. Giaour (that unpronounceable name) and for the sake of intelligibility it is *not* a fragment.—The scene is on the Hellespont—a favourite sejour of mine—and if you will accept it—I will send you a copy—there are some Mussulman words in it which I inflict upon you in revenge for your "Mathematical ["] & other superiority.————When shall you be in town?—by the bye—you won't take *fright* when we meet will you? & imagine that I am about to add to your thousand and one pretendants?—I have taken exquisite care to prevent the possibility of that[1]—though less likely than ever to become a Benedick—indeed I have not seen (with one exception) for many years a Beatrice——and she will not be troubled to assume the part.—I think we understand each other perfectly—& may talk to each other occasionally without exciting speculation—the worst that can be said—is—that I *would*—& you *wont*—and in this respect *you* can hardly be the sufferer—and I am very sure I *shant*.—If I find my heart less philosophic on the subject than I at present believe it—I shall keep out of the way—but I *now* think it is well shielded—at least it has got a new suit of armour—and certainly it stood in need of it.—I have heard a rumour of another added to your list of unacceptables—and I am sorry for him—as I know that he has talent—& his pedigree ensures him wit & good humour.[2]—You make sad havock among "us youth" it is lucky that Me. de Staël has published her Anti-suicide at so killing a time—*November* too!—I have not read it—for fear that the love of contradiction might lead me to a practical confutation.—Do you know her? I don't ask if you have *heard* her? her tongue is "the perpetual motion."—

ever yrs.

B

P.S. Nov. 17th.—The enclosed was written a week ago & has lain in my desk ever since—I have had forty thousand plagues to make me forget not *you* but *it*—and now I might as well burn it—but let it go & pray forgive ye. scrawl & the Scribe

ever yrs.

B

[1] Annabella was probably not much pleased at Byron's hint that he had formed another attachment.

[2] It appears that one of Annabella's suitors was Stratford Canning (later Lord Stratford de Redcliffe). His biographer says: "An additional cause of [his] depression [in 1814] was his failure to win the hand of Annabella Milbanke . . ." (*The Life of Stratford Canning*, by E. F. Malcolm-Smith, London, 1933, p. 49.)

[in another hand?] If you favour me with an answer—any letter addressed here will reach me wherever I may be—I have a little cousin Eliza Byron coming—no—going to some school at Stockton—will you notice her? it is the prettiest little blackeyed girl of Paradise—& but 7 years old.—

[TO ANNABELLA MILBANKE]   *Novr. 29th. 1813*

No one can *as*sume or *pre*sume less than you do though very few with whom I am acquainted possess half your claims to that "Superiority" which you are so fearful of affecting—nor can I recollect one expression since the commencement of our correspondence which has in any respect diminished my opinion of your talents—my respect for your virtues.—My only reason for avoiding the discussion of *sacred* topics—was the sense of my own ignorance & the fear of saying something that might displease—but I *have listened* & will listen to you with not merely patience but pleasure.—When we meet—if we do meet—in Spring—you will find me ready to acquiesce in all your notions upon the point merely personal between ourselves—you will act according to circumstances—it would be premature in us both to anticipate reflections which may never be made—& if made at all—are certainly unfounded.—You wrong yourself very much in supposing that "the charm" has been broken by our nearer acquaintance—on ye. contrary —that very intercourse convinces me of the value of what I have lost— or rather never found—but I will not deny that circumstances have occurred to render it more supportable.[1]——You will think me very capricious & apt at sudden fancies—it is true I could not exist without some object of attachment—but I have shewn that I am not quite a slave to impulse—no man of tolerable situation in life who was quite without self command could have reached the age of 26 (which I shall be—I grieve to speak it—in January) without marrying & in all probability foolishly.—But however weak—(it may merit a harsher term) in my disposition to attach myself—(and as society is now much the same in this as in all other European countries—it were difficult to avoid it) in my search for the "ideal" the being to whom I would commit the whole happiness of my future life—I have never yet seen but two approaching to the likeness—the first I was too young to

1 Thinking that Annabella was attached to another, Byron was again hinting at an attachment of his own in order to make her more comfortable in their "friendship". (See Nov. 10, 1813, to Annabella, note 2) But Annabella was already regretting that she had let him think that her heart was engaged elsewhere.

have a prospect of obtaining—& subsequent events have proved that my expectations might not have been fulfilled had I ever proposed to & secured my early idol[2]—the *second*—the *only* woman to whom I ever seriously pretended as a wife—had disposed of her heart already —and I think it too late to look for a third.—I shall take ye. world as I find it—& I have seen it much the same in most climates—(a little more fiery perhaps in Greece & Asia—for there they are a strange mixture of languid habits & stormy passions) but I have no confidence & look for no constancy in affections founded in caprice—& preserved (if preserved) by accident—& lucky conformity of disposition without any fixed principles.—How far this may be my case at present—I know not—& have not had time to ascertain—I can only say that I never was cured of loving any one but by the conduct—by the change —or the violence of the object herself—and till I see reason for distrust I shall flatter myself as heretofore—& perhaps with as little cause as ever.———I owe you some apology for this disquisition— but the singularity of *our* situation led me to dwell on this topic—& your friendship will excuse it.—I am anxious to be candid with you though I fear sometimes I am betrayed into impertinence.—They say that a man never *forgives* a woman who stands in the relation which you do towards me—but to *forgive*—we must first be offended—& I think I cannot recall—even a moment of pique at the past to my memory—I have but *2 friends* of your sex—yourself & Ly. Melbourne—as different in years as in disposition—& yet I do not know which I prefer —believe me a better-*hearted* woman does not exist—and in talent I never saw her excelled & hardly equalled—her kindness to me has been uniform—and I fear severely & ungratefully tried at times on my part—but as it cannot be so again—at least in the same manner—I shall make what atonement I can—if a regard which my own inclination leads me to cultivate—can make any amends for my trespasses on her patience.———The word *patience* reminds me of ye. book I am to send you—it shall be ordered to Seaham tomorrow.—I shall be most happy to see any thing of your writing—of what I have already seen you once heard my favourable & sincere opinion.—I by no means rank poetry or poets high in the scale of intellect—this may look like Affectation—but it is my real opinion—it is the lava of the imagination whose eruption prevents an earth-quake—they say Poets never or rarely go *mad*—Cowper & Collins are instances to the contrary—(but Cowper was no poet)—it is however to be remarked that they rarely

[2] Mary Chaworth.

do—but are generally so near it—that I cannot help thinking rhyme is so far useful in anticipating & preventing the disorder.—I prefer the talents of *action*—of war—or the Senate—or even of Science—to all the speculations of these mere dreamers of another existence (I don't mean *religiously* but *fancifully*) and spectators of this.——Apathy—disgust—& perhaps incapacity have rendered me now a mere spectator—but I have occasionally mixed in the active & tumultuous departments of existence—& on these alone my *recollection* rests with any satisfaction—though not the *best* parts of it.—I wish to know your Joanna[3]—& shall be very glad of the opportunity—never mind *ma cousine*[4] I thought Stockton had been your Post town & nearer Seaham. —Mr. Ward & I have talked (I fear it will be only talk as things look undecided in that quarter) of an excursion to Holland—if so—I shall be able to compare a Dutch canal with the Bosphorus.—I never saw a Revolution transacting[5]—or at least completed—but I arrived just after the last Turkish one—& the *effects* were visible—& had all the grandeur of desolation in their aspect——Streets in ashes—immense barracks (of a very fine construction) in ruins—and above all Sultan Selim's favourite gardens round them in all the wildness of luxurient neglect—his fountains waterless—& his kiosks defaced but still glittering in their decay.—They lie between the city & Buyukderé on the hills above the Bosphorus—& the way to them is through a plain with the prettiest name in the world—"the Valley of Sweet Waters".[6] —But I am sending a volume not a letter.

ever yrs. most truly
B

---

[3] Joanna Baillie, who was a friend of Annabella and her family.

[4] His cousin Eliza.

[5] Holland, which had been a kingdom of France since 1806, was incorporated with the French Empire in 1810. On Nov. 15, 1813, the people of Amsterdam revolted, raised the Orange colours, and expelled the French. They were joined by other provinces, and on Nov. 21 they sent a delegation to London to ask the Prince of Orange to lead the movement for independence. He landed in Holland on Nov. 30. To see "a Revolution transacting" was one of Byron's motives for wanting to go to Holland.

[6] One of Byron's favourite rides while he was in Constantinople was to "the Valley of Sweet Waters". Büyükdere is a village on the Bosphorus, at the head of its largest bay, which gives a first view of the Black Sea.

JOURNAL

November 14, 1813—April 19, 1814

If this had been begun ten years ago, and faithfully kept!!!—heigho! there are too many things I wish never to have remembered, as it is. Well,—I have had my share of what are called the pleasures of this life, and have seen more of the European and Asiatic world than I have made a good use of. They say "virtue is its own reward,"—it certainly should be paid well for its trouble. At five-and-twenty, when the better part of life is over, one should be *something*;—and what am I? nothing but five-and-twenty—and the odd months. What have I seen? the same man all over the world,—ay, and woman too. Give *me* a Mussulman who never asks questions, and a she of the same race who saves one the trouble of putting them. But for this same plague—yellow fever—and Newstead delay, I should have been by this time a second time close to the Euxine. If I can overcome the last, I don't so much mind your pestilence; and, at any rate, the spring shall see me there,— provided I neither marry myself nor unmarry any one else in the interval. I wish one was—I don't know what I wish. It is odd I never set myself seriously to wishing without attaining it—and repenting. I begin to believe with the good old Magi, that one should only pray for the nation and not for the individual;—but, on my principle, this would not be very patriotic.

.   .   .   .   .

Two nights ago I saw the tigers sup at Exeter 'Change. Except Veli Pacha's lion in the Morea,—who followed the Arab keeper like a dog,—the fondness of the hyæna for her keeper amused me most. Such a conversazione!—There was a "hippopotamus," like Lord L[iverpoo]l in the face; and the "Ursine Sloth" hath [had] the very voice and manner of my valet—but the tiger talked too much. The elephant took and gave me my money again—took off my hat—opened a door— *trunked* a whip—and behaved so well, that I wish he was my butler. The handsomest animal on earth is one of the panthers; but the poor antelopes were dead. I should hate to see one *here*:—the sight of the *camel* made me pine again for Asia Minor. "Oh quando te aspiciam?"

* * * * * * * * * * * * * * *

Went last night with Lewis to see the first of Antony and Cleopatra.[1] It was admirably got up and well acted—a salad of Shakespeare and Dryden. Cleopatra strikes me as the epitome of her sex—fond, lively, sad, tender, teasing, humble, haughty, beautiful, the devil!—coquettish to the last, as well with the "asp" as with Anthony. After doing all she can to persuade him that—but why do they abuse him for cutting off that poltroon Cicero's head? Did not Tully tell Brutus it was a pity to have spared Antony? and did he not speak the Philippics? and are not *"words things?"*[2] and such *"words"* very pestilent *"things"* too? If he had had a hundred heads, they deserved (from Antony) a rostrum (his was stuck up there) apiece—though, after all, he might as well have pardoned him, for the credit of the thing. But to resume— Cleopatra, after securing him, says, "yet go"—"it is your interest," etc.—how like the sex! and the questions about Octavia—it is woman all over.

To-day received Lord Jersey's invitation to Middleton—to travel sixty miles to meet Madame * * [De Staël]! I once travelled three thousand to get among silent people; and this same lady writes octavos, and *talks* folios. I have read her books—like most of them, and delight in the last; so I won't hear it, as well as read.

* * * * * * * * * * * * * * *

Read Burns to-day. What would he have been, if a patrician? We should have had more polish—less force—just as much verse, but no immortality—a divorce and a duel or two, the which had he survived, as his potations must have been less spirituous, he might have lived as long as Sheridan, and outlived as much as poor Brinsley. What a wreck is that man! and all from bad pilotage; for no one had ever better gales, though now and then a little too squally. Poor dear Sherry! [Sheridan] I shall never forget the day he and Rogers and Moore and I passed together; when *he* talked, and *we* listened, without one yawn, from six till one in the morning.

. . . . .

[1] In the revival of *Antony and Cleopatra* at Covent Garden, Nov. 15, 1813, additions were made from Dryden's *All for Love or the World Well Lost*.

[2] It is interesting to see how phrases stored in Byron's memory found their way into his poetry:

> But words are things, and a small drop of ink,
> Falling like dew, upon a thought, produces
> That which makes thousands, perhaps millions, think.
>
> *Don Juan*, 3, 88.

Byron elsewhere ascribed the phrase "words are things" to Mirabeau.

I wish I could settle to reading again,—my life is monotonous, and yet desultory. I take up books, and fling them down again. I began a comedy and burnt it because the scene ran into *reality*;—a novel, for the same reason. In rhyme, I can keep more away from facts; but the thought always runs through, through . . . yes, yes, through. I have had a letter from Lady Melbourne—the best friend I ever had in my life, and the cleverest of women.

.   .   .   .   .

I have begun, or had begun, a song, and flung it into the fire. It was in remembrance of Mary Duff, my first of flames, before most people begin to burn. I wonder what the devil is the matter with me! I can do nothing, and—fortunately there is nothing to do. It has lately been in my power to make two persons (and their connexions) comfortable, *pro tempore*, and one happy, *ex tempore*,[3]—I rejoice in the last particularly, as it is an excellent man. I wish there had been more inconvenience and less gratification to my self-love in it, for then there had been more merit. We are all selfish—and I believe, ye gods of Epicurus! I believe in Rochefoucault about *men*, and in Lucretius (not Busby's translation) about yourselves. Your bard has made you very *nonchalant* and blest; but as he has excused *us* from damnation, I don't envy you your blessedness *much*—a little, to be sure. I remember, last year, * * [Lady Oxford] said to me, at * * [Eywood]. "Have we not passed our last month like the gods of Lucretius?" And so we had.

.   .   .   .   .

Mr. Murray has offered me one thousand guineas for the "Giaour" and the "Bride of Abydos." I won't—it is too much, though I am strongly tempted, merely for the *say* of it. No bad price for a fortnight's (a week each) what?—the gods know—it was intended to be called Poetry.

I have dined regularly to-day, for the first time since Sunday last— this being Sabbath, too. All the rest, tea and dry biscuits—six *per diem*. I wish to God I had not dined now!—It kills me with heaviness, stupor, and horrible dreams;—and yet it was but a pint of bucellas, and fish. Meat I never touch,—nor much vegetable diet. I wish I were in the country, to take exercise,—instead of being obliged to *cool* by

[3] Byron had given £3,000 to Augusta to extricate her from the debts of her husband, and had given enough to Hodgson to clear him of his father's debts so that he could marry.

abstinence, in lieu of it. I should not so much mind a little accession of flesh,—my bones can well bear it. But the worst is, the devil always came with it,—till I starve him out,—and I will *not* be the slave of *any* appetite. If I do err, it shall be my heart, at least, that heralds the way. Oh my head—how it aches?—the horrors of digestion! I wonder how Buonaparte's dinner agrees with him?

.   .   .   .   .

Nov. 22d. 1813

Rogers is silent,—and, it is said, severe. When he does talk, he talks well; and, on all subjects of taste, his delicacy of expression is pure as his poetry. If you enter his house—his drawing-room—his library—you of yourself say, this is not the dwelling of a common mind. There is not a gem, a coin, a book thrown aside on his chimney-piece, his sofa, his table, that does not bespeak an almost fastidious elegance in the possessor. But this very delicacy must be the misery of his existence. Oh the jarrings his disposition must have encountered through life!

Southey, I have not seen much of. His appearance is *Epic*; and he is the only existing entire man of letters. All the others have some pursuits annexed to their authorship. His manners are mild, but not those of a man of the world, and his talents of the first order. His prose is perfect. Of his poetry there are various opinions: there is, perhaps, too much of it for the present generation; posterity will probably select. He has *passages* equal to any thing. At present, he has a *party*, but no *public*—except for his prose writings. The life of Nelson is beautiful.

.   .   .   .   .

M[oor]e has a peculiarity of talent, or rather talents,—poetry, music, voice, all his own; and an expression in each, which never was, nor will be, possessed by another. But he is capable of still higher flights in poetry. By the by, what humour, what—every thing, in the "Post-Bag!" There is nothing M[oor]e may not do, if he will but seriously set about it. In society, he is gentlemanly, gentle, and, altogether more pleasing than any individual with whom I am acquainted. For his honour, principle, and independence, his conduct to * * * * speaks "trumpet-tongued." He has but one fault—and that one I daily regret —he is not *here*.

.   .   .   .   .

If I had any views in this country, they would probably be parliamentary. But I have no ambition; at least, if any, it would be "aut Caesar aut nihil." My hopes are limited to the arrangement of my affairs, and settling either in Italy or the East (rather the last), and drinking deep of the languages and literature of both. Past events have unnerved me; and all I can now do is to make life an amusement, and look on, while others play. After all—even the highest game of crowns and sceptres, what is it? *Vide* Napoleon's last twelvemonth. It has completely upset my system of fatalism. I thought, if crushed, he would have fallen, when *"fractus illabitur orbis,"*[4] and not have been pared away to gradual insignificance;—that all this was not a mere *jeu* of the gods, but a prelude to greater changes and mightier events. But Men never advance beyond a certain point;—and here we are, retrograding to the dull, stupid old system,—balance of Europe— poising straws upon king's noses, instead of wringing them off! Give me a republic, or a despotism of one, rather than the mixed government of one, two, three. A republic!—look in the history of the Earth— Rome, Greece, Venice, France, Holland, America, our short (*eheu!*) Commonwealth, and compare it with what they did under masters. The Asiatics are not qualified to be republicans, but they have the liberty of demolishing despots, which is the next thing to it. To be the first man—not the Dictator—not the Sylla, but the Washington or the Aristides—the leader in talent and truth—is next to the Divinity! Franklin, Penn, and, next to these, either Brutus or Cassius —even Mirabeau—or St. Just. I shall never be any thing, or rather always be nothing. The most I can hope is, that some will say, "He might, perhaps, if he would."

.   .   .   .   .

Thursday, 26th November

I have been thinking lately a good deal of Mary Duff. How very odd that I should have been so utterly, devotedly fond of that girl, at an age when I could neither feel passion, nor know the meaning of the word. And the effect! My mother used always to rally me about this childish amour; and, at last, many years after, when I was sixteen, she told me one day, "Oh, Byron, I have had a letter from Edinburgh, from Miss Abercromby, and your old sweetheart Mary Duff is

---

[4] Horace, *Odes*, III, iii, 7: "If wide Creation broke".

married to a Mr. Coe."[5] And what was my answer? I really cannot explain or account for my feelings at that moment; but they nearly threw me into convulsions, and alarmed my mother so much, that after I grew better, she generally avoided the subject—to *me*—and contented herself with telling it to all her acquaintance. Now, what could this be? I had never seen her since her mother's faux pas at Aberdeen had been the cause of her removal to her grandmother's at Banff; we were both the merest children. I had and have been attached fifty times since that period; yet I recollect all we said to each other, all our caresses, her features, my restlessness, sleeplessness, my tormenting my mother's maid to write for me to her, which she at last did, to quiet me. Poor Nancy thought I was wild, and, as I could not write for myself, became my secretary. I remember, too, our walks, and the happiness of sitting by Mary, in the children's apartment, at their house not far from Plainstones at Aberdeen, while her lesser sister Helen played with the doll, and we sat gravely making love, in our way.

How the deuce did all this occur so early? where could it originate? I certainly had no sexual ideas for years afterwards; and yet my misery, my love for that girl were so violent, that I sometimes doubt if I have ever been really attached since. Be that as it may, hearing of her marriage several years after was like a thunder-stroke—it nearly choked me—to the horror of my mother and the astonishment and almost incredulity of every body. And it is a phenomenon in my existence (for I was not eight years old) which has puzzled, and will puzzle me to the latest hour of it; and lately, I know not why, the *recollection* (*not* the attachment) has recurred as forcibly as ever. I wonder if she can have the least remembrance of it or me? or remember her pitying sister Helen for not having an admirer too? How very pretty is the perfect image of her in my memory—her brown, dark hair, and hazel eyes; her very dress! I should be quite grieved to see *her now*; the reality, however beautiful, would destroy, or at least confuse, the features of the lovely Peri which then existed in her, and still lives in my imagination, at the distance of more than sixteen years. I am now twenty-five and odd months . . . .

I think my mother told the circumstances (on my hearing of her marriage) to the Parkynses, and certainly to the Pigot family, and probably mentioned it in her answer to Miss A[bercromby], who was well acquainted with my childish *penchant*, and had sent the news on purpose for *me*,—and thanks to her!

[5] Mary Duff married Robert Cockburn, a wine merchant of Edinburgh and London.

Next to the beginning, the conclusion has often occupied my reflections, in the way of investigation. That the facts are thus, others know
as well as I, and my memory yet tells me so, in more than a whisper.
But, the more I reflect, the more I am bewildered to assign any cause
for this precocity of affection.

.   .   .   .   .

Saturday, 27th (I believe—or rather am in *doubt*,
which is the ne plus ultra of mortal faith.)
Redde the Edinburgh Review of Rogers.[6] He is ranked highly—but
where he should be. There is a summary view ot us all—*Moore* and *me*
among the rest; and both (the *first* justly) praised—though, by
implication (justly again) placed beneath our memorable friend.
Mackintosh is the writer, and also of the critique on the Staël.[7] His
grand essay on Burke, I hear, is for the next number. But I know
nothing of the Edinburgh, or of any other Review, but from rumour;
and I have long ceased—indeed, I could not, in justice, complain of any,
even though I were to rate poetry, in general, and my rhymes in
particular, more highly than I really do. To withdraw *myself* from
myself (oh that cursed selfishness!) has ever been my sole, my entire,
my sincere motive in scribbling at all; and publishing is also the
continuance of the same object, by the action it affords to the mind,
which else recoils upon itself. If I valued fame, I should flatter received
opinions, which have gathered strength by time, and will yet wear
longer than any living works to the contrary. But, for the soul of me,
I cannot and will not give the lie to my own thoughts and doubts, come
what may. If I am a fool, it is, at least, a doubting one; and I envy no
one the certainty of his self-approved wisdom.

All are inclined to believe what they covet, from a lottery-ticket
up to a passport to Paradise,—in which, from description, I see
nothing very tempting. My restlessness tells me I have something
within that "passeth show." It is for Him, who made it, to prolong

---

[6] The review of Rogers's *Poems* including Fragments of a Poem called the
Voyage of Columbus in the *Edinburgh Review* of October, 1813, paid some compliments to Byron and Moore without naming them. Commenting on the stanzas in
Childe Harold inspired by Greece, the critic wrote: "Full of enthusiasm for those
perfect forms of heroism and liberty, which his imagination had placed in the
recesses of antiquity, he gave vent to his impatience of the imperfections of living
men and real institutions, in an original strain of sublime satire, which clothes
moral anger in imagery of an almost horrible grandeur . . . ."

[7] The critique on De Staël followed the one on Rogers in the *Edinburgh Review*,
of October, 1813.

that spark of celestial fire which illuminates, yet burns, this frail tenement; but I see no such horror in a "dreamless sleep," and I have no conception of any existence which duration would not render tiresome. How else "fell the angels," even according to your creed? They were immortal, heavenly, and happy, as their *apostate Abdiel* is now by his treachery. Time must decide; and eternity won't be the less agreeable or more horrible because one did not expect it. In the mean time, I am grateful for some good, and tolerably patient under certain evils—grace à Dieu et mon bon tempérament.

.　　.　　.　　.　　.

Sunday, 28th. Monday, 29th. Tuesday, 30th.

Sunday, a very handsome note from Mackintosh, who is a rare instance of the union of very transcendent talent and great good-nature. To-day (Tuesday) a very pretty billet from M. la Baronne de Staël Holstein. She is pleased to be much pleased with my mention of her and her last work in my notes.[8] I spoke as I thought. Her works are my delight, and so is she herself, for—half an hour. I don't like her politics—at least, her *having changed* them; had she been *qualis ab incepto*, it were nothing. But she is a woman by herself, and has done more than all the rest of them together, intellectually;—she ought to have been a man. She *flatters* me very prettily in her note;—but I *know* it. The reason that adulation is not displeasing is, that, though untrue, it shows one to be of consequence enough, in one way or other, to induce people to lie, to make us their friend:—that is their concern.

* * is, I hear, thriving on the repute of a *pun* (which was *mine* at Mackintosh's dinner some time back), on Ward, who was asking, "how much it would take to *re-whig* him?" I answered that, probably, he "must first, before he was *re-whigged*, be re-*warded*." This foolish quibble, before the Staël and Mackintosh, and a number of conversationers, has been mouthed about, and at last settled on the head of * *, where long may it remain!

.　　.　　.　　.　　.

Yesterday, a very pretty letter from Annabella, which I answered. What an odd situation and friendship is ours!—without one spark of

8 *The Bride of Abydos*, Canto I, stanza 6. In a note Byron wrote: "For an eloquent passage in the latest work of the first female writer of this, perhaps of any, age, on the analogy . . . between 'painting and music', see vol. iii, cap. 10, *De L'Allemagne*."

love on either side, and produced by circumstances which in general lead to coldness on one side, and aversion on the other. She is a very superior woman, and very little spoiled, which is strange in an heiress —a girl of twenty—a peeress that is to be, in her own right—an only child, and a *savante*, who has always had her own way. She is a poetess—a mathematician—a metaphysician, and yet, withal, very kind, generous, and gentle, with very little pretension. Any other head would be turned with half her acquisitions, and a tenth of her advantages.

.   .   .   .   .

Wednesday, December 1st, 1813.

To-day responded to La Baronne de Staël Holstein, and sent to Leigh Hunt (an acquisition to my acquaintance—through Moore—of last summer) a copy of the two Turkish tales. Hunt is an extraordinary character, and not exactly of the present age. He reminds me more of the Pym and Hampden times—much talent, great independence of spirit, and an austere, yet not repulsive, aspect. If he goes on *qualis ab incepto*, I know few men who will deserve more praise or obtain it. I must go and see him again;—the rapid succession of adventure, since last summer, added to some serious uneasiness and business, have interrupted our acquaintance; but he is a man worth knowing; and though, for his own sake, I wish him out of prison, I like to study character in such situations. He has been unshaken, and will continue so. I don't think him deeply versed in life;—he is the bigot of virtue (not religion), and enamoured of the beauty of that "empty name", as the last breath of Brutus pronounced, and every day proves it. He is, perhaps, a little opinionated, as all men who are the *centre* of *circles*, wide or narrow—the Sir Oracles, in whose name two or three are gathered together—must be, and as even Johnson was; but, withal, a valuable man, and less vain than success and even the consciousness of preferring "the right to the expedient" might excuse.

.   .   .   .   .

Monday, Dec. 6th.

This journal is a relief. When I am tired—as I generally am—out comes this, and down goes every thing. But I can't read it over; —and God knows what contradictions it may contain. If I am sincere with myself (but I fear one lies more to one's self than to any one else), every page should confute, refute, and utterly abjure its predecessor.

.   .   .   .   .

Went to bed, and slept dreamlessly, but not refreshingly. Awoke, and up an hour before being called; but dawdled three hours in dressing. When one subtracts from life infancy (which is vegetation),—sleep, eating, and swilling—buttoning and unbuttoning—how much remains of downright existence? The summer of a dormouse. * * * * *

．　　　．　　　．　　　．　　　．

Monday, December 13, 1813.

Allen (Lord Holland's Allen[9]—the best informed and one of the ablest men I know—a perfect Magliabecchi[10]—a devourer, a Helluo of books, and an observer of men,) has lent me a quantity of Burns's unpublished, and never-to-be-published, Letters. They are full of oaths and obscene songs. What an antithetical mind!—tenderness, roughness—delicacy, coarseness—sentiment, sensuality—soaring and grovelling, dirt and deity—all mixed up in that one compound of inspired clay!

It seems strange; a true voluptuary will never abandon his mind to the grossness of reality. It is by exalting the earthly, the material, the *physique* of our pleasures, by veiling these ideas, by forgetting them altogether, or, at least, never naming them hardly to one's self, that we alone can prevent them from disgusting.

．　　　．　　　．　　　．　　　．

December 17, 18.

Lord Holland told me a curious piece of sentimentality in Sheridan. The other night we were all delivering our respective and various opinions on him and other *hommes marquans*, and mine was this. "Whatever Sheridan has done or chosen to do has been, *par excellence*, always the *best* of its kind. He has written the *best* comedy (School for Scandal) the *best* drama (in my mind, far before that St. Giles's lampoon, the Beggar's Opera), the best farce (the *Critic*—it is only too good for a farce), and the best Address (Monologue on Garrick), and, to crown all, delivered the very best Oration (the famous Begum Speech) ever conceived or heard in this country." Somebody told S. this the next day, and on hearing it he burst into tears!

．　　　．　　　．　　　．　　　．

[9] John Allen, M.D. (1771–1843) accompanied Lord Holland to Spain and later lived at Holland House, where he contributed to the brilliance of the Holland House circle. He wrote numerous articles for the *Edinburgh Review* and the one on Fox in the *Encyclopaedia Britannica*.

[10] Antonio Magliabecchi (1633–1714), Librarian to the Grand Duke of Tuscany, to whom he bequeathed his collection of 30,000 volumes. He had a reputation for learning and was said to be able to direct an enquirer to any book in the world.

Went to my box at Covent-garden to-night; and my delicacy felt a little shocked at seeing S * * *'s mistress (who, to my certain knowledge, was actually educated, from her birth, for her profession) sitting with her mother, "a three-piled b – – d, b – – d-Major to the army," in a private box opposite. I felt rather indignant; but, casting my eyes round the house, in the next box to me, and the next, and the next, were the most distinguished old and young Babylonians of quality;— so I burst out a laughing. It was really odd; Lady * * *divorced*—Lady * * and her daughter, Lady * *, both *divorceable*—Mrs. * *, in the next, the *like*, and still nearer * * * * * *! What an assemblage to *me*, who know all their histories. It was as if the house had been divided between your public and your *understood* courteseans;—but the Intriguantes much outnumbered the regular mercenaries. On the other side were only Pauline and *her* mother, and, next box to her, three of inferior note. Now, where lay the difference between *her* and *mamma*, and Lady * *[11] and daughter? except that the two last may enter Carleton and any *other house*, and the two first are limited to the opera and b – – -house. How I do delight in observing life as it really is!— and myself, after all, the worst of any. But no matter—I must avoid egotism, which, just now, would be no vanity.

.   .   .   .   .

January 16, 1814.

As for me, by the blessing of indifference, I have simplified my politics into an utter detestation of all existing governments; and, as it is the shortest and most agreeable and summary feeling imaginable, the first moment of an universal republic would convert me into an advocate for single and uncontradicted despotism. The fact is, riches are power, and poverty is slavery all over the earth, and one sort of establishment is no better, nor worse, for a *people* than another. I shall adhere to my party, because it would not be honourable to act otherwise; but, as to *opinions*, I don't think politics *worth* an *opinion*. *Conduct* is another thing:—if you begin with a party, go on with them. I have no consistency, except in politics; and *that* probably arises from my indifference on the subject altogether.

.   .   .   .   .

---

[11] Moore's note says these names indicated by asterisks were left blank in the original manuscript of the journal.

Is there any thing beyond?—*who* knows? *He* that can't tell. Who tells that there *is*? He who don't know. And when shall he know? perhaps, when he don't expect, and, generally when he don't wish it. In this last respect, however, all are not alike: it depends a good deal upon education,—something upon nerves and habits—but most upon digestion.

·   ·   ·   ·   ·

Sunday, February 27th.

There is something to me very softening in the presence of a woman,—some strange influence, even if one is not in love with them,—which I cannot at all account for, having no very high opinion of the sex. But yet,—I always feel in better humour with myself and every thing else, if there is a woman within ken. Even Mrs. Mule, my firelighter,—the most ancient and withered of her kind,—and (except to myself) not the best-tempered—always makes me laugh,— no difficult task when I am "i the vein".

·   ·   ·   ·   ·

Sunday, March 20th.

I remember, in riding from Chrisso to Castri (Delphos), along the sides of Parnassus, I saw six eagles in the air. It is uncommon to see so many together; and it was the number—not the species, which is common enough—that excited my attention.

The last bird I ever fired at was an *eaglet*, on the shore of the Gulf of Lepanto, near Vostitza. It was only wounded, and I tried to save it, the eye was so bright; but it pined, and died in a few days; and I never did since, and never will, attempt the death of another bird. I wonder what put these two things into my head just now? I have been reading Sismondi, and there is nothing there that could induce the recollection.

·   ·   ·   ·   ·

Albany, March 28.

This night got into my new apartments, rented of Lord Althorpe,[12] on a lease of seven years. Spacious, and room for my books and

[12] In 1804 Albany House, which had been the residence of the Duke of York and Albany, was converted into bachelor chambers. Byron took over the lease of number 2 in the original building that had been occupied by John Charles Spencer, Viscount Althorp (later 3rd Earl Spencer), who was getting married.

sabres. *In* the *house*, too, another advantage. The last few days, or whole week, have been very abstemious, regular in exercise, and yet very *un*well.

Yesterday, dined *tête-a-tête* at the Cocoa with Scrope Davies—sat from six till midnight—drank between us one bottle of champagne and six of claret, neither of which wines ever affect me. Offered to take Scrope home in my carriage; but he was tipsy and pious, and I was obliged to leave him on his knees praying to I know not what purpose or pagod. No headache, nor sickness, that night nor to-day. Got up, if any thing, earlier than usual—sparred with Jackson *ad sudorem*, and have been much better in health than for many days. I have heard nothing more from Scrope. Yesterday paid him four thousand eight hundred pounds, a debt of some standing, and which I wished to have paid before. My mind is much relieved by the removal of that *debit*.[13]

.   .   .   .   .

April 10th.

I do not know that I am happiest when alone; but this I am sure of, that I never am long in the society even of *her* I love, (God knows too well, and the Devil probably too,) without a yearning for the company of my lamp and my utterly confused and tumbled-over library. Even in the day, I send away my carriage oftener than I use or abuse it. *Per esempio,*—I have not stirred out of these rooms for these four days past: but I have sparred for exercise (windows open) with Jackson an hour daily, to attenuate and keep up the ethereal part of me. The more violent the fatigue, the better my spirits for the rest of the day; and then, my evenings have that calm nothingness of languor, which I most delight in. To-day I have boxed one hour—written an ode to Napoleon Buonaparte—copied it—eaten six biscuits—drunk four bottles of soda water—redde away the rest of my time—besides giving poor * * a world of advice about this mistress of his, who is plaguing him into a phthisic and intolerable tediousness. I am a pretty fellow truly to lecture about "the sect." No matter, my counsels are all thrown away.

---

[13] Byron had paid the remainder of his debt to Scrope Davies, who apparently had borrowed from usurers to furnish cash for Byron's first trip abroad in 1809.

My dear Ly. M[elbourn]e.—I do not see how you could well have said less—and that I am not angry may be proved by my saying a word more on ye. subject.—You are quite mistaken however as to *her*[1]— and it must be from some misrepresentation of mine that you throw the blame so completely on the side least deserving and least able to bear it—I dare say I made the best of my own story as one always does from natural selfishness without intending it—but it was not her fault—but my own *folly* (give it what name may suit it better) and her weakness—for—the intentions of both were very different and for some time adhered to—& when *not* it was entirely my own— in short I know no name for my own conduct.—Pray do not speak so harshly of her to me—the cause of all————I wrote to you yesterday on other subjects and particularly C[aroline]———As to *manner*— mine is the same to anyone I know or like—and I am almost sure less marked to her than to *you*—besides any constraint or reserve would appear much more extraordinary than the reverse—until something more than manner is ascertainable.—Nevertheless I heartily wish Me. de Stael at the Devil—with her observations—I am certain I did not see her—and she might as well have had something else to do with her eyes than to observe people at so respectful a distance.———So "*Ph* [Frances Webster] is out of my thoughts"—in the first place if she were out of them—she had probably not found a place in my words—and in the next—she has no *claim*—if people will stop at the first tense of the verb "aimer" they must not be surprised if one finishes the conjugation with somebody else.—"How soon I get the better of"—in the name of St. Francis and his wife of Snow[2]—and Pygmalion & his statue what was there here to get the better of?—a few kisses for which she was no worse—and I no better.——Had the event been different—so would my subsequent resolutions & feelings —for I am neither ungrateful—nor at all disposed to be disappointed— on the contrary I do firmly believe—that I have often only begun to *love*—at the very time I have heard people say that some dispositions become indifferent.————Besides—her fool of a husband—and my own recent good resolutions—and a mixture of different piques and mental stimulants together with something not unlike encouragement on her part—led me into that foolish business—out of which the way

[1] Augusta Leigh.

[2] The legend that St. Francis dampened his passions with a wife of snow was one which Byron referred to again in *Don Juan* (6: 17).

is quite easy—and I really do not see that I have much to reproach my-self with on her account—if you think differently pray say so.—As to Mrs. C[haworth-Musters] I will go[3]—but I don't see any good that can result from it—certainly none to me—but I have no right to con-sider myself.—When I say this I merely allude to uncomfortable *feelings*—for there is neither chance nor fear of anything else—for she is a very good girl—and I am too much dispirited to rise even to admiration.—I do verily believe—*you* hope otherwise—as a means of *improving* me—but I am sunk in my own estimation—and care of course very little for that of others.———As to *Ph*—she will end as all women in her situation do—it is impossible she can *care* about a man who acted so weakly as I did with regard to herself.———What a fool I am—I have been interrupted by a visitor who is just gone—& have been laughing this half hour at a thousand absurdities as if I had nothing serious to think about.—

yrs. ever
B

P.S.—Another epistle from M[ary Chaworth-Musters]—my answer must be under cover to "dear friend" who is doing or suffering a folly—what can *she Miss R[adford]* be about?[4]—the only thing that could make it look ill—is *mystery*—I wrote to her and *franked*—thinking there was no need of concealment—and indeed conceiving the affectation of it an impertinence.—but she desires me not—and I obey—I suspect *R[adford]* of wishing to make a scene between *him* & *me* out of dislike to both—but that shall not prevent me from going a moment—I shall leave town on Sunday.———

[page missing?] pantomime—I don't think I laughed once save in soliloquy for ten days—which *you* who know me won't believe (every one else thinks me the most gloomy of existences) we used to sit & look at one another—except in *duetto* & then even our serious nonsense was not fluent—to be sure our gestures were rather more sensible—the most amusing part was the interchange of notes—for we sat up all night scribbling to each other—& came down like Ghosts in the morning—I shall never forget the quiet manner in which she would pass her epistles in a music book—or any book—looking in——[Webster]'s face with great tranquillity the whole time—& taking mine in the

---

[3] Byron's frustrated childhood love for Mary Chaworth lingered long in his memory, but now that she was married and separated from her husband, she wanted to see him. He, however, was reluctant to risk the disillusionment of a meeting and postponed and never made the visit.

[4] Mary described her as a "near and dear relative".

same way—once she offered one as I was leading her to dinner at N[ewstead]—all the servants before—& W[ebster] & sister close behind—to take it was impossible—and how she was to retain it without *pockets*—was equally perplexing—I had the cover of a letter from Claughton in mine—and gave it to her saying "there is the Frank for Ly. Water[ford?] you asked for" she returned it with the note beneath with—"it is dated wrong—alter it tomorrow" and W[ebster] complaining that women did nothing but scribble— wondered how people could have the patience to frank & alter franks— and then happily digressed to the day of the month—fish sauce—good wine—& bad weather.——Your "matrimonial ladder" wants but one more descending step—"*d—nation*" I wonder how the *carpenter* omitted it—it amused me much.—I wish I were married—I don't care about beauty nor *subsequent* virtue—nor much about fortune—I have made up my mind to share the decorations of my betters—but I should like—let me see—liveliness—gentleness—cleanliness—& something of comeliness—& *my own* first born—was ever man more moderate? what do you think of my "Bachelor's wife"? What a letter have I written"

[TO JAMES HOGG[1]] *Albany, March 24,* [*1814*]

Dear Sir,—I have been out of town, otherwise your letter should have been answered sooner. When a letter contains a request, the said request generally figures towards the *finale,* and so does yours, my good friend. In answering perhaps the other way is the better: so not to make many words about a trifle, (which any thing of mine must be,) you shall have a touch of my quality for your first Number—and if you print that, you shall have more of the same stuff for the successors. Send me a few of your proofs, and I will set forthwith about something, that I at least hope may suit your purposes. So much for the Poetic Mirror,[2] which may easily be, God knows, entitled to hang higher than the prose one.

You seem to be a plain spoken man, Mr. Hogg, and I really do not like you the worse for it. I can't write verses, and yet you want a bit of

---

[1] James Hogg, the Ettrick Shepherd.

[2] Hogg had planned a volume consisting of contributions from contemporary poets but finally wrote clever parodies of Wordsworth, Byron, Southey, Coleridge, Wilson, Scott, and himself, and published them with an ingenious preface in 1816 as "The Poetic Mirror, or the Living Bards of Great Britain."

my poetry for your book. It is for you to reconcile yourself with your-self.—You shall have the *verses*.

You are mistaken, my good fellow, in thinking that I (or, indeed, that any living verse-writer—for we shall sink *poets*) can write as well as Milton. Milton's Paradise Lost is, as a whole, a heavy concern; but the two first books of it are the very finest poetry that has ever been produced in this world—at least since the flood—for I make little doubt Abel was a fine pastoral poet, and Cain a fine bloody poet, and so forth; but we, now-a-days, even we, (you and *I*, *i.e.*) know no more of their poetry than the *brutum vulgus*—I beg pardon, the swinish multitude, do of Wordsworth and Pye. Poetry must always exist, like drink, where there is a demand for it. And Cain's may have been the brandy of the Antedeluvians, and Abel's the small [?] still.

Shakespeare's name, you may depend on it, stands absurdly too high and will go down. He had no invention as to stories, none whatever. He took all his plots from old novels, and threw their stories into a dramatic shape, at as little expense of thought as you or I could turn his plays back again into prose tales. That he threw over whatever he did write some flashes of genius, nobody can deny: but this was all. Suppose any one to have the *dramatic* handling for the first time of such ready-made stories as Lear, Macbeth, &c. and he would be a sad fellow, indeed, if he did not make something very grand of them. [As] for his historical plays, properly historical, I mean, they were mere re-dressings of former plays on the same subjects, and in twenty cases out of twenty-one, the finest, the very finest things, are taken all but *verbatim* out of the old affairs. You think, no doubt, that *A horse, a horse, my kingdom for a horse!* is Shakespeare's. Not a syllable of it. You will find it all in the old nameless dramatist. Could not one take up Tom Jones and improve it, without being a greater genius than Fielding? I, for my part, think Shakespeare's plays might be improved, and the public seem, and have seemed for to think so too, for not one of his is or ever has been acted as he wrote it; and what the pit applauded three hundred years past, is five times out of ten not Shakespeare's, but Cibber's.

Stick you to Walter Scott, my good friend, and do not talk any more stuff about his not being willing to give you real advice, if you really will ask for real advice. You love Southey, forsooth—I am sure Southey loves nobody but himself, however. I hate these talkers one and all, body and soul. They are a set of the most despicable impostors —that is my opinion of them. They know nothing of the world; and what is poetry, but the reflection of the world? What sympathy have this people with the spirit of this stirring age? They are no more able to understand the least of it, than your *lass*—nay, I beg her pardon, *she* may very probably have intense sympathy with both its spirit, (I mean the whisky,) and its body (I mean the bard.) They are mere old wives. Look at their beastly vulgarity, when they wish to be homely; and their exquisite stuff, when they clap on sail, and aim at fancy. Coleridge is the best of the trio—but bad is the best. Southey should have been a parish-clerk, and Wordsworth a man-midwife—both in darkness. I doubt if either of them ever got drunk, and I am of the old creed of Homer the wine-bibber. Indeed I think you and Burns have derived a great advantage from this, that being poets, and drinkers of wine, you have had a new potation to rely upon. Your whisky has made you original. I have always thought it a fine liquor. I back you against beer at all events, gill to gallon.

By the bye, you are a fine hand to cut up the minor matters of verse-writing; you indeed think harmony the all-in-all. My dear sir, you may depend upon it, you never had *name* yet, without making it rhyme to *theme*. I overlook all that sort of thing, however, and so must you, in your turn, pass over my real or supposed ruggedness. The fact is, that I have a theory on the subject, but that I have not time at present for explaining it. The first time all the poets of the age meet— it must be in London, glorious London is the place, after all—we shall, if you please, have a small trial of skill. You shall write seventeen odes for me, anything from Miltonian blank down to Phillupian [sic] namby, and I a similar number for you, and let a jury of good men and true be the judges between us. I name Scott for foreman—Tom Campbell may be admitted, and Mrs. Baillie, (though it be not exactly a matron case.) You may name the other nine worthies yourself. We shall, at all events, have a dinner upon the occasion, and I stipulate for a small importation of the peat reek.

Dear sir, believe me sincerely yours,
BYRON

I delivered "Mamma's message" with anatomical precision—the *knee* was the refractory limb—was it not? injured I presume at prayers —for I cannot conjecture by what other possible attitude a female knee could become so perverse.—Having given an account of my embassy— I enclose you a note which will only repeat what you already know—— but to obviate a possible *Pharisaical* charge—I must observe that the first part of her epistle[1] alludes to an answer of mine—in which talking about that eternal Liturgy—I said that I had no great opinion one way or the other—assuredly no decided unbelief—and that the *clamour* had wrung from me many of the objectionable passages—in the pure quintessence of the spirit of contradiction &c &c.—She talks of "talking" on these same metaphysics—to shorten the conversation I shall propose the Litany—"from the crafts & *assau*—" ay—that will do very well—what comes next—"Deliver us"—an't it?—Seriously—if she imagines that I particularly delight in canvassing the creed of St. Athanasius—or prattling of rhyme—I think she will be mistaken—but *you know* best—I don't suspect myself of often talking about poets or clergymen—of rhyme or the rubrick—but very likely I am wrong—for assuredly no one knows *it*self—and for aught I know—I may for these last 2 years have inflicted upon you a world of theology—and the greater part of Walker's rhyming dictionary.————I don't know what to say or do about going—sometimes I wish it—at other times I think it foolish—as assuredly my design will be imputed to a motive—which by the bye—if once fairly there is very likely to come into my head—and *failing* to put me into no very good humour with myself—I am not now in love with her—but I can't at all foresee that I should not be so if it came "a warm June" (as Falstaff observes) and seriously—I do admire her as a very superior woman a little encumbered with Virtue—though perhaps your opinion & mine from the laughing turn of "our philosophy" may be less exalted upon her merits than that of the more zealous—though in fact less benevolent advocates of charity schools & Lying in Hospitals.——By the close of her note you will perceive that she has been "frowning" occasionally and has written some pretty lines upon it to a friend (he or she is not said) as for rhyme I am naturally no fair judge & can like it no better than a Grocer does figs.[2]————I am quite irresolute—and undecided—if I were sure of *myself* (not of her) I would go—but I am not—& never can be—and what is still worse I have no judgement—& less common sense than an infant—this is *not affected humility*—with *you* I have no affectation—with the world I have a part to play—to be diffident there is to wear a drag-chain—and luckily I do so thoroughly despise half the people in it—that my insolence is almost natural.—I enclose you also a letter written some time ago and of which I do not remember the precise contents—most likely they contradict every

[1] Annabella Milbanke's letter.
[2] Fielding says of Parson Barnabas (*Joseph Andrews*, Book I, chapter 17) that he "loved sermons no better than a grocer doth figs."

syllable of this—no matter.—Don't plague yourself to write—we shall meet at Mrs. Hope's³ I trust—

ever yrs.

B

My dear Lady M[elbourn]e.—*You*—or rather *I* have done *my A*—[Augusta] much injustice—the expression which you recollect as objectionable meant only "loving" in the *senseless* sense of that wide word—and—it must be some selfish stupidity of mine in telling my own story—but really & truly—as I hope mercy & happiness for her—by that God who made me for my own misery—& not much for the good of others—*she* was not to blame—one thousandth part in comparison—she was not aware of her own peril—till it was too late—and I can only account for her subsequent *"abandon"* by an observation which I think is not unjust—that women are much more *attached* than men—if they are treated with any thing like fairness or tenderness.

——————As for *your* A—[Annabella] I don't know what to make of her—I enclose her last but one——and *my* A's last but one—from which you may form your own conclusions on *both*—I think you must allow *mine*—to be a very extraordinary person in point of *talent*—but I won't say more—only do not allow your good nature to lean to my side of *this* question—on all others I shall be glad to avail myself of your partiality.—Now for *common* life.—There *is* a party at Lady J[ersey]'s on Monday and on Wednesday—I am asked to both—and excused myself out of Tuesday's dinner because I want to see Kean in Richard again—pray *why* did you say—I am getting into a *scrape* with R's moiety?¹—one must talk to somebody—I always give you the preference when you are disposed to listen—and when you seem fidgetted as you do now & then—(and no wonder—for latterly I do but repeat—) I turn to anyone and she was the first that I stumbled upon—as for anything more—I have not even advanced to the tip of her little finger—and never shall—unless she gives it.—You won't believe me—& won't care if you do—but I really believe that I have more true regard and affection for yourself than for any other existence—as for my A— my feelings towards her—are a mixture of good

---

³ The wife of Thomas Hope, the author of *Anastasius* (1819), and collector and patron of sculpture. Mrs. Hope was a well known hostess in Whig society during the Regency.

¹ Lady Rancliffe?

& diabolical—I hardly know one passion which has not some share in them—but I won't run into the subject.—Your Niece has committed herself perhaps—but it can be of no consequence—if I pursued & succeeded in that quarter—of course I must give up all other pursuits—and the fact is that my wife if she had common sense would have more power over me—than any other whatsoever—for my heart always alights upon the nearest *perch*—if it is withdrawn—it goes God knows where—but one must like something.—

ever yrs.

B

[TO HENRIETTA D'USSIÈRES[1]]   *June 8th. 1814*

Excepting your compliments (which are only excusable because you don't know me) you write like a clever woman for which reason I hope you *look* as *un*like one as possible—I never knew but one of your country—Me. de Stael—and she is frightful as a precipice.—As it seems impracticable my visiting you—cannot you contrive to visit me? telling me the time previously that I may be in ye. way—and if this same interview leads to the "leap into the Serpentine" you mention—we can take the jump together—and shall be very good company—for I swim like a Duck—(one of the few things I can do well) and you say that your Sire taught you the same useful acquirement.—I like your education of all things—it in some degree resembles my own—for the first ten years of my life were passed much amongst mountains—and I had also a tender and peremptory parent who indulged me sometimes with holidays and now and then with a box on the ear.—If you will become acquainted with me—I will promise not to make love to you unless you like it—and even if I did there is no occasion for you to receive more of it than you please:—you must however do me two favours—the first is not to mistake me for *S*[2]— who is an excellent man—but to whom I have not the honour to bear the smallest (I won't say *slightest* for he has the circumference of an Alderman) resemblance—and the next is to recollect that as "no man is a hero to his Valet" so I am a hero to no person whatsoever—and not treat me with such outrageous respect and awe—which makes me

---

[1] Henrietta D'Ussières was one of the many women who wrote to Byron after he achieved fame. She apparently wrote him several letters before he replied. A number of her epistles are published in *To Lord Byron* by George Paston and Peter Quennell (1939), pp. 121–141.

[2] Unidentified.

feel as if I was in a strait waistcoat.—you shall be a *heroine* however if you prefer it and I will be and am

yr. very humble Sert.

B

P.S.—"Surprized" oh! no!—I am surprized at nothing—except at your taking so much trouble about one who is not worth it.———You say—what would "my servants think?" 1stly. they seldom think at all—2dly. they are generally out of the way—particularly when most wanted—3dly. *I* do not know you—and I humbly imagine that they are no wiser than their Master.—

[TO ANNABELLA MILBANKE]   *Newstead Abbey. Septr. 7th. 1814*

It is Porson's letter to Travis[1] to which you allude and—if I recollect rightly—one of his remarks (the highest praise to be passed on an Historian) is—that amidst the immensity of reading through which he had tracked Gibbon—not *one* of his *authorities* was misquoted or perverted even unto a syllable—perhaps I am wrong in giving this as from P's preface—for years have elapsed since I saw it—but of the fact as P's opinion—and no one could be a better judge—I am certain.—Porson was slowly extinguishing—while I was a Cantab—I have seen him often—but not in "his happier hour" for to him that of "social pleasure" could not be so termed—he was always—that is daily—intoxicated to brutality ———I hate to think of it—for he was a perfect wonder in powers and attainments.———Newstead is mine again—for the present—Mr. C[laughton] after many delays in completion—relinquished his purchase———I am sorry for it—he has lost a considerable sum in forfeiture by his temporary inability or imprudence—but he has evinced a desire to resume or renew his contract with greater punctuality—& in justice to him—though against the advice of lawyers—and the regrets of relations—I shall not hesitate to give him an opportunity of making good his agreement—but I shall expect—indeed I will not endure such trifling for the future. ——I am much amused with *your* "sovereign good" being placed in *repose*—I need not remind you that this was the very essence of the Epicurean philosophy—and that both the Gods (who concerned them-

---

[1] Richard Porson's most widely read work was his *Letters* to Archdeacon Travis on a disputed passage in the Bible, *I John*, V, 7: "For there are three that bear record in heaven, the Father, the Word, and the Holy Ghost: and these three are one."

selves with nothing on earth) and the Disciples of the illustrious idler the founder of that once popular sect—defined the *"Tò Καλον"* to consist in literally doing nothing—and that all agitation was incompatible with pleasure.—The truth possibly is that these materialists are so far right—but to enjoy repose we must be weary—and it is to "the heavy laden" that the invitation to "rest" speaks most eloquent music.————You accuse yourself of "apparent inconsistencies"— to me they have not appeared—on the contrary—your consistency has been the most *formidable* Apparition I have encountered—there seem to be no grounds for complaint on one side nor vindication on the other—and as to explanations—*they* are always a puzzle. After one or two letters which lately passed between us—and to which—I must request your pardon for recurring—we—at least *I* (to speak for myself) could hardly have met without some embarrassment—possibly on both sides—certainly on one—this has been avoided—and so far is a subject of congratulation.——Your letters are generally answered on the day of their arrival so that it can't be very "irksome to me to write soon."——On my return to London which will not take place immediately I shall have great pleasure in forwarding the book offered in my last.—The "Agricola"[2] is beautiful—it is a pity that there are so many objections to a like perusal of Suetonius also; whose portraits are but too faithful even in their coarsest features.————You must be partial to Sallust—but after all there are none like Tacitus & him you have.——

ever yours

B

[TO ANNABELLA MILBANKE]   *Newstead Abbey. Septr. 9th 1814*

You were good enough in your last to say that I might write "soon"—but you did not add *often*—I have therefore to apologize for again intruding on your time—to say nothing of patience.—There is something I wish to say—and as I may not see you for some—perhaps for a long time—I will endeavour to say it at once.———A few weeks ago you asked me a question—which I answered—I have now one to propose—to which if improper—I need not add that your declining to reply to it will be sufficient reproof.—It is this.—Are the "objections" —to which you alluded—insuperable?—or is there any line or change of conduct which could possibly remove them?—I am well aware that

[2] *De Vita et Moribus Iulii Agricolae* by Tacitus.

all such changes are more easy in theory than practice—but at the same time there are few things I would not attempt to obtain your good opinion—at all events I would willingly know the worst—still I neither wish you to promise or pledge yourself to anything—but merely to learn a *possibility* which would not leave you the less a free agent.————When I believed you attached—I had nothing to urge—indeed I have little now—except that having heard from yourself that your affections are not engaged—my importunities may appear not quite so selfish however unsuccessful—It is not without a struggle that I address you once more on this subject—yet I am not very consistent—for it was to avoid troubling you upon it that I finally determined to remain an absent friend rather than become a tiresome guest—if I offend it is better at a distance.————With the rest of my sentiments you are already acquainted—if I do not repeat them it is to avoid—or at least not increase your displeasure.—[1]

ever yrs. most truly
B

[TO ANNABELLA MILBANKE]   *Newstead Abbey. Septr. 19th. 1814*

I wrote to you yesterday—not very intelligibly I fear—and to your father in a more embarrassed manner than I could have wished—but the fact is that I am even now apprehensive of having misunderstood you and of appearing presumptuous when I am only happy—in the hope that you will not repent having made me more so than I ever thought to have been again.————Perhaps in some points our dispositions are not so contrasted as at times you have supposed—but even if they were—I am not sure that a perfect sameness of character (a kind of impossibility by the bye) would ensure the happiness of two human beings any more than an union of tempers and pursuits of very dissimilar qualities.—Our *pursuits* at least I think are not unlike—you have no great passion for the *world* as it is called—and both have those intellectual resources which are the best—if not the only preventatives of ennui of oneself or others;—*my* habits I trust are not very anti-domestic—I have no pleasure in what is named Conviviality—nor is Gaming nor Hunting my vice or my amusement—and with regard to other and perhaps far more objectionable faults & levities of former

---

[1] This was Byron's tentative proposal, which Annabella took for a real one and replied in haste to accept him. "I am and have long been pledged to myself to make your happiness my first object in life."

conduct—I know that I cannot exculpate myself to my own satisfaction—far less to yours—yet there have been circumstances which would prove that although "sinning" I have also been "sinned against." —I have long stood alone in life—and my disposition though I think not unaffectionate—was yet never calculated to acquire the friendships which are often *born* to others—the few that chance or circumstances have presented I have been fortunate enough to preserve—& some whom I could little have hoped to number amongst them.——————I wont go on with this Egotism—will you write to me soon?—I shall be in London on Thursday I think—I do not answer oftener than is least irksome—but permit me to address you occasionally till I can see you —which I wish so much—and yet I feel more tremblingly alive to that meeting than I quite like to own to myself—when your letter arrived my sister was sitting near me and grew frightened at the effect of it's contents—which was even painful for a moment—not a long one—nor am I often so shaken.—I have written—yet hardly a word that I intended to say—except that you must pardon me for repeating so soon how entirely I am

yr. attached & sincere
BYRON

P.S.—Do not forget me to your father & mother—whom I hope to call mine.—

[TO LADY MELBOURNE]   *Novr. 13th. 1814*

My dear Lady Mel[bourn]e.—I delivered your letters—but have only mentioned ye receipt of your *last* to myself.—————Do you know I have great doubts—if this will be a marriage now.[1]—her disposition is the very reverse of *our* imaginings—she is overrun with fine feelings—scruples about herself & *her* disposition (I suppose in fact she means mine) and to crown all is taken ill once every 3 days with I know not what—but the day before and the day after she seems well—looks & eats well & is cheerful & confiding & in short like any other person in good health & spirits.—A few days ago she made one *scene*—not altogether out of C[aroline]'s style—it was too long & too trifling in fact for me to transcribe—but it did me no good——in

---

[1] Byron was on his first visit to his fiancée whom he had met only briefly in London in 1812 at the home of her aunt, Lady Melbourne.

the article of conversation however she has improved with a ven-geance—but I don't much admire these same agitations upon slight occasions.—I don't know—but I think it by no means impossible you will see me in town soon—I can only interpret these things one way—& merely wait to be certain to make my obeisances and "exit singly." I hear of nothing but "feeling" from morning till night—except from Sir Ralph with whom I go on to admiration—Ly. M[ilbanke] too is pretty well—but I am never sure of A[nnabella]—for a moment—the least word—and you know I rattle on through thick & thin (always however avoiding anything I think can offend her favourite notions) if only to prevent me from yawning—the least word—or alteration of tone—has some inference drawn from it—sometimes we are too much alike—& then again too unlike—this comes of *system*—& squaring her notions to the Devil knows what—for my part I have lately had recourse to the eloquence of *action* (which Demosthenes calls the first part of oratory) & find it succeeds very well & makes her very quiet which gives me some hopes of the efficacy of the "calming process" so renowned in *"our* philosophy."—In fact and entre nous it is really amusing—she is like a child in that respect—and quite *caressable* into kindness and good humour—though I don't think her temper *bad* at any time—but very *self*-tormenting—and anxious—and romantic. —————In short—it is impossible to foresee how this will end *now*—anymore than 2 years ago—if there is a break—it shall be *her* doing not mine.—

ever yrs. most truly

B

[TO ANNABELLA MILBANKE]　　　　　*Boroughbridge—Novr. 16th. 1814*

My Heart—We are thus far separated—but after all one mile is as bad as a thousand—which is a great consolation to one who must travel six hundred before he meets you again.——If it will give you any satisfaction—I am as comfortless as a pilgrim with peas in his shoes—and as cold as Charity—Chastity or any other Virtue.—On my way to Castle Eden I waylaid the Post—& found letters from Hanson—which I annex for the amusement of Lady Milbanke who having a passion for business will be glad to see any thing that looks like it.—I expect to reach Newstead tomorrow & Augusta the day after.—Present to our parents as much of my love as you like to part with—& dispose of the rest as you please.—ever thine

P.S.—I will begin my next with what I meant to be the postscript of this.—

[TO JOHN CAM HOBHOUSE]   *Seaham—January 26th. 1815*

My dear H[obhous]e—Your packet hath been perused and firstly I am lost in wonder & obligation at your good nature in taking so much trouble with Spooney[1] and my damnable concerns—I would leave to your choice our "Counsellors at law" as Mrs. Heidelberg calls them—a—Templeman[2]—I think stands first on your list—so prithee fix on him—or whom you please—but do *you fix*—for you know *I* never could.— *N[ewstead] must* be sold—without delay—and even at a loss—*out* of *debt* must be my first object—and the sooner the better.—My debts can hardly be less than thirty thousand—there is *six thousand* charged on N[ewstead] to a Mr. Sawbridge—a *thousand*—to Mrs. B[yron] at Nott[ingha]m—a *Jew debt* of which the interest must be more than the principal—& of which H[anson] must get an amount from *Thomas*—another Jew debt—six *hundred* prin[cipa]l—and no interest (as I have kept that down) to a man in New Street—I forget his name but shall know on half year's day—a good deal still before majority—in which the "old women"[3] of former celebrity were concerned—but *one* is defunct—and the debt itself may wait my convenance—since it is not in my name—and indeed the interest has pretty well paid principal & all being transcendantly usurious,—a good deal of tradesmen &c. &c.—You know I have paid off *Scrope* that is 6000 & more—nearly 3000 to *Hans*. Carvel[4]—then I lent rather more than £1600 to Hodgson—£1000 to "bold" Webster—and nearly 3000 to George L[eigh] or rather to Augusta—the *last* sums

---

[1] Spooney was a cant term in "flash" language for a foolish pretending fellow. Byron from this time used the appellation for Hanson in writing to Hobhouse, particularly when he was irritated with his attorney and business agent.

[2] Giles Templeman, Solicitor.

[3] Mrs. Elizabeth Massingberd, Byron's landlady in London during his youth, and her daughter acted for him as agents for securing loans from usurers.

[4] "Hans Carvel", a fabliau verse tale by Matthew Prior, in which the hero is a coarse fellow. The underscoring of *Hans* indicates that Byron referred to Hanson who had borrowed £2,800 to buy some property.

I never *wish* to see again—and others I *may wish*—I have W[ebster]'s bond which is worth a damn or two—but from Hodg[son] I neither asked nor wanted security—but there was 150 lent at Hastings to the same Hod[gson] which was punctually *promised* to be paid in six weeks—and has been paid with the usual punctuality—viz—not at all. —I think I have now accounted for a good deal of Clau[ghton]'s disbursements—the rest was swallowed up by duns—necessities— luxuries—fooleries—jewelleries—"whores and fiddlers".—As for expectations, don't talk to me of "expects" (as Mr Lofty says to Croaker of *"suspects"*)[5] the Baronet is eternal—the Viscount immortal—and my Lady (*senior*) without end.—They grow more healthy every day and I verily believe Sir R[alph] Ly. M[ilbanke] and Lord W[entworth] are at this moment cutting a fresh set of teeth and unless they go off by the usual fever attendant on such children as don't use the "American soothing syrup" that they will live to have them all drawn again.—

[displaced sheet perhaps belonging here]

"The Melodies"—damn the melodies—I have other tunes—or rather tones—to think of—but—Murray *can't* have them, or *shan't*— or I shall have Kin[nair]d and Braham upon me.——Take the *box* any night or all nights week after *next*—only send to Lady Melbourne—to tell her of your intention for the night or nights—as I have long ago left her paramount during my absence.—

ever d[ea]r H. thine

B

[TO JAMES WEDDERBURN WEBSTER]

Piccadilly Terrace.—Sept. 4th. 1815

My dear W.—Certainly—if Lady Frances [Webster] has no objection—& you are disposed to be so complimentary—I cannot but be accordant with your wish;—I give you joy of the event & hope the name will be fortunate.[1]—Lady B. is very well & expects to lie in in December.—I wish a boy of course—they are less trouble in every point of view—both in education & after life.—

You are misinformed—I am writing nothing—nor even dreaming of repeating that folly—& as to Lady B. she has too much good sense

---

[5] In Goldsmith's *Good Natured Man* Lofty says to Croaker: ". . . and talk to me of suspects!"

[1] Apparently Webster asked permission to name an expected child after Byron.

to be a scribbler—your informant is therefore more facetious than accurate.————

A word to you of Lady [Caroline Lamb]—I speak from experience—*keep clear of her*—(I do not mean as a woman—that is all fair) she is a villainous intriguante—in every sense of the word——mad & malignant—capable of all & every mischief—above all—guard your *connections* from her society——with all her apparent absurdity there is an indefatigable & active spirit of meanness & destruction about her—which delights & often succeeds in inflicting misery—once more—I tell you keep her from all that you value—as for *yourself*—do as you please—no human being but myself knows the thorough baseness of that wretched woman—& now I have done.———

I believe I can guess the "important subject" on which you wish to write—but I would rather decline hearing or speaking of it—for many reasons—the most obvious & proper of which is that however false—it is too delicate for discussion even with your most intimate friends—to copy your own words I "believe nothing I hear" on this point—& advise you to follow the example.———

I write in the greatest hurry—just returned to London——if you answer I will write again—in the interim

Yrs ever

B

[TO JAMES WEDDERBURN WEBSTER]

13 Terrace Pic[cadill]y Sept. 18th 1815

My dear W.—Your letter of the 10th is before me.—Since your last I received a note from Lady Frances [Webster] containing a repetition of your request—which was already answered in my reply to you—I am obliged by her politeness & regret that she should have taken the trouble of which I presume *you* were the occasion.————

With regard to Lady C.[aroline] L.[amb]——I wrote rather hurriedly & probably said more than I intended or than she deserved—but I fear the main points are correct—she is such a mixture of good & bad—of talent and absurdity—in short—an exaggerated woman—that—that—in fact I have no right to abuse her—and did love her very well—till she took abundant pains to cure me of it—& there's an end—You will deliver her the enclosed note from me—if you please—it contains my thanks for a cross of the "Legion of Honour" which she sent me some time ago from Waterloo—I never received it till yesterday.[1]————You may have seen "much" but not enough to know her thoroughly in this time—she is a good study for a couple of years at least.—I will give you one bit of advice which may be of use—she is most *dangerous* when *humblest*—like a Centipede she *crawls & stings.*———

As for *"him"* [William Lamb]—we have not spoken these three years—so that I can hardly answer your question—but he is a handsome man as you see—and a clever man as you may see—of his temper I know nothing—I never heard of any prominent faults that he possesses—and indeed she has enough for both————In short his good qualities are his own—and his misfortune is having her—if the woman was quiet & like the rest of the amatory world it would not so much signify—but no—everything she says—does—or imagines—must be public—which is exceedingly inconvenient in the end however piquant at the beginning.————

And now to the serious part of your epistle—Humph—what the devil can I say?——as your mind is so divided upon the subject—I wonder you should ask me to say anything—it is thrusting poor dear innocent me into the part of Iago—from whom however I shall only take one sentence—

"Long live she so—& long live you to think so!"—
I must repeat however that it is not a topic for discussion———you must know & judge for yourself—and as to the "real opinion of the World" which you wish to hear—you may surely discover that without my turning it's speaking trumpet—one thing you may be sure of—if there is any thing bad you will always as Sheridan says "find some damned good natured friend or other to tell it you"————[2]

---

[1] The Websters and the Lambs were in Paris where the English fashionable world had flocked after the Peace. Lady Caroline and Lady Frances both flirted with the military officers, including Wellington. And Webster, a notorious philanderer, apparently made advances to Lady Caroline.

[2] This may well refer to some suspicions Webster voiced about his wife and Wellington. In the Court of Common Pleas on February 16, 1816, James Wedderburn Webster obtained a judgment of £2000 damages against a Mr. Baldwin for a libel charging Webster's wife Lady Frances and the Duke of Wellington with adultery. Byron was inclined to be sceptical of the virtue of Lady Frances after he had "spared" her, following his flirtation of 1813. It was at this time that he wrote his verses to her beginning "When we two parted". When Moore later met Lady Frances Webster, he recorded in his diary of January 5, 1819, that the conversation was chiefly about Byron "whom she talked of, as if nothing had happened—and (if I may believe Scroope Davies) nothing ever did—but B. certainly gave me to think otherwise, and her letters (which I saw) showed, at least, that she was (or fancied herself) much in love with him—His head was full of her, when he wrote the Bride. . . . I should pronounce her cold-blooded & vain to an excess—& I believe her great ambition is to attract people of celebrity—if so, she must have been gratified

Pray are the Rawdons in Paris?—if they are—I wish you could remember me to Miss R—& tell her that Lady B. has not heard from her since she wrote from Rome.————

If you come to England—you will easily find me—probably in London—

ever yrs. most truly

B

[TO SAMUEL TAYLOR COLERIDGE]

13—Terrace Piccadilly—Oct. 18th. 1815

Dear Sir—Your letter I have just received.—I will willingly do whatever you direct about the volumes in question—the sooner the better— it shall not be for want of endeavour on my part—as a Negociator with the "Trade" (to talk technically) that you are not enabled to do yourself justice.—Last Spring I saw W[alte]r Scott—he repeated to me a considerable portion of an unpublished poem of yours[1]—the wildest & finest I ever heard in that kind of composition—the title he did not mention—but I think the heroine's name was Geraldine—at all events —the "toothless mastiff bitch"—& the "witch Lady"—the descriptions of the hall—the lamp suspended from the image—& more particularly of the *Girl* herself as she went forth in the evening—all took a hold on my imagination which I never shall wish to shake off.—I mention this—not for the sake of boring you with compliments—but as a prelude to the hope that this poem is or is to be in the volumes you are now about to publish.—I do not know that even "Love" or the "Ancient Mariner" are so impressive—& to me there are few things in our tongue beyond these two productions.———W[alte]r Scott is a staunch & sturdy admirer of yours—& with a just appreciation of your capacity—deplored to me the want of inclination & exertion which prevented you from giving full scope to your mind.—I will answer your question as to the "Beggar's [Bush?]"[2]—tomorrow—or next day—I shall see Rae & Dibdin (the acting M[anage]rs) tonight for

---

—as the first Poet [Byron] & first Captain [Wellington] of the age have been among her lovers—the latter liaison was, at all events, not altogether spiritual— at least the character of the man makes such platonism not very probable—her manner to me very flattering & the eyes played off most skillfully—but this is evidently her habit—the fishing always going on, whether whales or sprats are to be caught—"

[1] *Christabel.*

[2] The *Beggar's Bush* was the title of a tragi-comedy by John Fletcher and Philip Massinger.

that purpose.—Oh—your tragedy—I do not wish to hurry you—but I am indeed very anxious to have it under consideration—it is a field in which there are none living to contend against you & in which I should take a pride & pleasure in seeing you compared with the dead—I say this *not* disinterestly but as a *Committee* man[3]—we have nothing even tolerable—except a tragedy of Sotheby's—which shall not interfere with yours—when ready—you can have no idea what trash there is in the four hundred *fallow* dramas now lying on the shelves of D[rury] L[ane]. I never thought so highly of good writers as lately—since I have had an opportunity of comparing them with the bad.—

ever yrs. truly

BYRON

[TO LEIGH HUNT]   *13 Terrace Piccadilly Septr.—Octr. 30th. 1815*

My dear Hunt—Many thanks for your books of which you already know my opinion.[1]—Their external splendour should not disturb you as inappropriate—they have still more within than without.——I take leave to differ from you on Wordsworth as freely as I once agreed with you—at that time I gave him credit for promise which is unfulfilled—I still think his capacity warrants all you say of *it* only—but that his performances since "Lyrical Ballads"—are miserably inadequate to the ability which lurks within him:—there is undoubtedly much natural talent spilt over "the Excursion" but it is rain upon rocks where it stands & stagnates—or rain upon sands where it falls without fertilizing—who can understand him?—let those who do make him intelligible.—Jacob Behman—Swedenborg—& Joanna Southcote are mere types of this Arch-Apostle of mystery & mysticism—but I have done:—no I have not done—for I have two petty & perhaps unworthy objections in small matters to make to him—which with his pretension to accurate observation & fury against Pope's false translation of the "Moonlight scene in Homer" I wonder he should have fallen into—these be they.—He says of Greece in the body of his book—that it is a land of

> "rivers—fertile plains—& sounding shores
> Under a cope of variegated sky"[2]

---

[3] Byron was a member of the Drury Lane sub-committee of management, and was seeking new plays by men of talent for the Theatre.

[1] The revised edition of Hunt's *The Feast of the Poets*.

[2] *Excursion*, Book IV (first edition, 1814).

The rivers are dry half the year—the plains are barren—and the shores *still* & *tideless* as the Mediterranean can make them—the Sky is anything but variegated—being for months & months—but "darkly—deeply—beautifully blue."—The next is in his notes—where he talks of our "Monuments crowded together in the busy &c. of a large town"—as compared with the "still seclusion of a Turkish cemetery in some *remote* place"—this is pure stuff—for *one* monument in our Churchyards—there are *ten* in the Turkish—& so crowded that you cannot walk between them—they are always close to the walks of the towns—that is—merely divided by a path or road—and as to "*remote* places"—men never take the trouble in a barbarous country to carry their dead very far—they must have lived near to where they are buried—there are no cemeteries in "remote places"—except such as have the cypress & the tombstone still left when the olive & the habitation of the living have perished.——These things I was struck with as coming peculiarly in my own way—and in both of these he is wrong—yet I should have noticed neither but for his attack on Pope for a like blunder—and a peevish affectation about him of despising a popularity which he will never obtain.—I write in great haste—& I doubt—*not* much to the purpose—but you have it hot & hot—just as it comes—& so let it go.——By the way—both he & you go too far against Pope's "so when the Moon &c." it is no translation I know—but it is not such *false* description as asserted—I have read it on the spot—there is a burst—and a lightness—and a glow—about the night in the Troad—which makes the "planets vivid"—& the "pole glowing" the moon is—at least the sky is clearness itself—and I know no more appropriate expression for the expansion of such a heaven—over the scene—the plain—the sea—the sky—Ida—the Hellespont—Simois—Scamander—and the isles—than that of a "flood of Glory."——I am getting horribly lengthy—& must stop—to the whole of your letter I say "ditto to Mr. Burke" as the Bristol Candidate cried by way of Electioneering harangue:[3]—you need not speak of morbid feelings—& vexations to me—I have plenty—for which I must blame partly the times—& chiefly myself: but let us forget them—*I* shall be very apt to do so—when I see you next—will you come to the theatre & see our new Management?—you shall cut it up to your heart's content root & branch afterwards if you like—but come & see it?—if not I must come & see you.—

ever yrs very truly & affectly.
BYRON

[3] Henry Cruger, seeking a seat with Burke at Bristol, spoke those words on the

P.S.—Not a word from Moore for these 2 months.—Pray let me have the rest of "Rimini["] you have 2 excellent points in that poem—originality—& Italianism—I will back you as a bard against half the fellows on whom you throw away much good criticism & eulogy—but don't let your bookseller publish in *Quarto* it is the worst size possible for circulation—I say this on Bibliopolical authority—

again—yours ever

ß

[TO THOMAS MOORE] *Terrace, Piccadilly, October 31, 1815*

I have not been able to ascertain precisely the time of duration of the stock market; but I believe it is a good time for selling out, and I hope so. First, because I shall see you; and, next, because I shall receive certain monies on behalf of Lady B[yron], the which will materially conduce to my comfort,—I wanting (as the duns say) "to make up a sum."

Yesterday, I dined out with a largeish party, where were Sheridan and Colman, Harry Harris of C[ovent] G[arden] and his brother, Sir Gilbert Heathcote, D[ougla]s Kinnaird, and others, of note and notoriety. Like other parties of the kind, it was first silent, then talky, then argumentative, then disputatious, then unintelligible, then altogethery, then inarticulate, and then drunk. When we had reached the last step of this glorious ladder, it was difficult to get down again without stumbling;—and, to crown all, Kinnaird and I had to conduct Sheridan down a d————d corkscrew staircase, which had certainly been constructed before the discovery of fermented liquors, and to which no legs, however crooked, could possibly accommodate themselves. We deposited him safe at home, where his man, evidently used to the business, waited to receive him in the hall.

Both he and Colman were, as usual, very good; but I carried away much wine, and the wine had previously carried away my memory; so that all was hiccup and happiness for the last hour or so, and I am not impregnated with any of the conversation. Perhaps you heard of a late answer of Sheridan to the watchman who found him bereft of that "divine particle of air," called reason, * * * * * * * * * * * He, the watchman, found Sherry in the street, fuddled and bewildered, and

hustings, according to Burke's biographers. Apparently they were effective, for both were returned to Parliament.

117

almost insensible. "Who are you, sir?"—no answer. "What's your name?"—a hiccup. "What's your name?"—Answer, in a slow, deliberate, and impassive tone—"Wilberforce!!!"[1] Is not that Sherry all over?—and, to my mind, excellent. Poor fellow, *his* very dregs are better than the "first sprightly runnings" of others.

My paper is full, and I have a grievous headache.

P.S.—Lady B[yron] is in full progress. Next month will bring to light (with the aid of "Juno Lucina, *fer opem*," or rather *opes*,[2] for the last are most wanted), the tenth wonder of the world—Gil Blas being the eighth, and he (my son's father) the ninth.

[TO SIR RALPH NOEL]   *February 2d. 1816*

Sir—I have received your letter.[1]—To the vague & general charge contained in it I must naturally be at a loss how to answer—I shall therefore confine myself to the tangible fact which you are pleased to alledge as one of the motives for your present proposition.—Lady Byron received no "dismissal" from my house in the sense you have attached to the word—she left London by medical advice—she parted from me in apparent—and on my part—real harmony—though at that particular time rather against my inclination for I begged her to remain with the intention of myself accompanying her when some business necessary to be arranged permitted my departure.——It is true—that previous to this period—I had suggested to her the expediency of a temporary residence with her parents:—my reason for this was very simple & shortly stated—viz—the embarrassment of my circumstances & my inability to maintain our present establishment.—The truth of what is thus stated may be easily ascertained by reference to Lady B[yron]—who is Truth itself—if she denies it—I abide by that denial.——My intention of going abroad originated in the same pain-

[1] William Wilberforce (1759–1833), chiefly noted as an anti-slavery advocate, became a strict Evangelical, one of the "Clapham Sect", and was a teetotaller.

[2] According to mythological tradition, Juno Lucina presided over child-birth, and newly born babies were under her protection. ferre opem = to bring aid; opes = means, wealth.

[1] Sir Ralph had written to Byron: ". . . with your opinions it cannot tend to your happiness to continue to live with Lady Byron, and I am yet more forcibly convinced that after her dismissal from your house, and the treatment she experienced whilst in it, those on whose protection she has the strongest natural claims could not feel themselves justified in permitting her return thither." And he proposed that arrangements be made through lawyers for a separation.

ful motive—& was postponed from a regard to her supposed feelings on that subject.——During the last year I have had to contend with distress without—& disease within:—upon the former I have little to say—except that I have endeavoured to remove it by every sacrifice in my power—& the latter I should not mention if I had not recent & professional authority for saying—that the disorder which I have to combat—without much impairing my apparent health—is such as to induce a morbid irritability of temper—which—without recurring to external causes—may have rendered me little less disagreeable to others than I am to myself.——I am however ignorant of any particular ill treatment which your daughter has encountered:—she may have seen me gloomy—& at times violent—but she knows the causes too well to attribute such inequalities of disposition to herself—or even to me—if all things be fairly considered.——And now Sir—not for your satisfaction—for I owe you none—but for my own—& in justice to Lady Byron—it is my duty to say that there is no part of her conduct—character—temper—talents—or disposition—which could in my opinion have been changed for the better—neither in word nor deed—nor (as far as thought can be dived into) thought—can I bring to recollection a fault on her part—& hardly even a failing—She has ever appeared to me as one of the most amiable of beings—& nearer to perfection than I had conceived could belong to Humanity in it's present existence.——Having said thus much—though more in words—less in substance—than I wished to express——I must come to the point—on which subject I must for a few days decline giving a decisive answer. —I will not however detain you longer than I can help—and as it is of some importance to your family as well as mine—and a step which cannot be recalled when taken—you will not attribute my pause to any wish to inflict pain or vexation on you & yours:—although there are parts of your letter—which—I must be permitted to say—arrogate a right which you do not now possess——for the present at least—your daughter is my wife:—she is the mother of my child—& until I have her express sanction of your proceedings—I shall take leave to doubt the propriety of your interference.—This will be soon ascertained—& when it is—I will submit to you my determination—which will depend very materially on hers.——I have the honour to be

yr. most obedt. & very humble Sert.
BYRON

I have received a letter from your father proposing a separation between us—to which I cannot give an answer without being more acquainted with your own thoughts & wishes—& from *yourself*:—to vague & general charges & exaggerated statements from others I can give no reply:——it is to *you* that I look—& with *you*—that I can communicate on this subject,——when I permit the interference of relatives—it will be as a courtesy to them—& not the admission of a right.——I feel naturally at a loss how to address you—ignorant as I am—how far the letter I have received—has received your sanction—& in the circumstances into which this precipitation has forced me—whatever I might say would be liable to misconstruction—I am really ignorant to what part of Sir Ralph's letter alludes—will you explain?——To conclude—I shall eventually abide by your decision—but I request you most earnestly to weigh well the probable consequences—& to pause before you pronounce.——Whatever may occur—it is but justice to you to say—that you are exempt from all fault whatever—& that neither now nor at any time have I the slightest imputation of any description to charge upon you.——I cannot sign myself other than

> yours ever most affectionately
> Bn

Dearest Bell—No answer from you yet—perhaps it is as well—but do recollect—that all is at stake—the present—the future—& even the colouring of the past:—The whole of my errors—or what harsher name you choose to give them—you know—but I loved you—& will not part from you without your *own* most express & *expressed* refusal to return to or receive me.——Only say the word—that you are still mine in your heart—and "Kate!—I will buckler thee against a million"[1]—

> ever yours dearest most
> B

[On cover in Byron's hand] Mrs. Fletcher[2] is requested to deliver the enclosed with her *own hands* to Lady Byron.

---

[1] *The Taming of the Shrew*, Act III, scene 2.

[2] Ann Rood, Annabella's maid, had married Byron's valet Fletcher just before she left London.

All I can say seems useless—and all I could say—might be no less unavailing—yet I still cling to the wreck of my hopes—before they sink forever.——Were you then *never* happy with me?—did you never at any time or times express yourself so?—have no marks of affection—of the warmest & most reciprocal attachment passed between us?—or did in fact hardly a day go down without some such on one side and generally on both?—do not mistake me—[two lines crossed out] I have not denied my state of mind—but you know it's causes—& were those deviations from calmness never followed by acknowledgement & repentance?—was not the last which occurred more particularly so?—& had I not—had we not—the days before & on the day when we parted —every reason to believe that we loved each other—that we were to meet again—were not your letters kind?—had I not acknowledged to you all my faults & follies—& assured you that some had not—& would not be repeated?—I do not require these questions to be answered to me—but to your own heart.——The day before I received your father's letter—I had fixed a day for rejoining you—if I did not write lately—Augusta did—and as you had been my proxy in correspondence with her—so did I imagine—she might be the same for me to you.—Upon your letter to me—this day—I surely may remark— that it's expressions imply a treatment which I am incapable of inflicting—& you of imputing to me—if aware of their latitude—& the extent of the inferences to be drawn from them.—This is not just—— but I have no reproaches—nor the wish to find cause for them.—— Will you see me?—when & where you please—in whose presence you please:—the interview shall pledge you to nothing—& I will say & do nothing to agitate either—it is torture to correspond thus—& there are things to be settled & said which cannot be written.——You say "it is my disposition to deem what I *have worthless*"—did I deem *you* so?—did I ever so express myself to you—or of you—to others?—— You are much changed within these twenty days or you would never have thus poisoned your own better feelings—and trampled upon mine.——

ever yrs. most truly & affectionately
B

My dear H[obhous]e—You will be surprized that we are not more "en avant" and so am I—but Mr. Baxter's[1] wheels and springs have not done their duty—for which I beg that you will abuse him like a pickpocket (that is—*He*—the said *Baxter* being the *pickpocket*) and say that I expect a deduction—having been obliged to come out of the way to this place—which was not in my route—for repairs—which however I hope to have accomplished so as to put us in motion in a day or two.———We passed through Ghent—Antwerp—and Mechlin —& thence diverged here—having seen all the sights—pictures— docks—basins—& having climbed up steeples &c. & so forth———the first thing—after the flatness & fertility of the country which struck me—was the beauty of the towns—Bruges first—where you may tell Douglas Kinnaird—on entering at Sunset—I overtook a crew of beggarly looking gentlemen not unlike Oxberry[2]—headed by a Monarch with a Staff the very facsimile of King Clause in the said D[ouglas] K[innaird]'s revived drama.———We lost our way in the dark—or rather twilight—not far from Ghent—by the stupidity of the postilion (*one* only by the way to 4 horses) which produced an alarm of intended robbery among the uninitiated—whom I could not convince —that four or five well-armed people were not immediately to be plundered and anatomized by a single person fortified with a horse-whip to be sure—but nevertheless a little encumbered with large jack boots—and a tight jacket that did not fit him—The way was found again without loss of life or limb:———I thought the learned Fletcher at least would have known better after our Turkish expeditions—and defiles—and banditti—& guards &c. &c. than to have been so valourously alert without at least a better pretext for his superfluous courage. I don't mean to say that they were *frightened* but they were vastly suspicious without any cause.—At Ghent we stared at pictures —& climbed up a steeple 450 steps in altitude—from which I had a good view & notion of these "paese bassi."———Next day we broke down—by a damned wheel (on which Baxter should be broken) pertinaciously refusing it's stipulated rotation—this becalmed us at Lo-Kristi—(2 leagues from Ghent)—& obliged us to return for repairs—At Lo Kristi I came to anchor in the house of a Flemish Blacksmith (who was ill of a fever for which Dr. Dori[3] physicked him —I dare say he is dead by now) and saw somewhat of Lo-Kristi—

[1] Byron had ordered from Baxter the coachmaker a huge Napoleonic travelling coach before he left England at a cost of £500 (still unpaid).

[2] William Oxberry (1784-1824) was an actor who had made his debut at Covent Garden and was for some time manager of the Olympic Theatre. In 1816 he played the part of Moses in Sheridan's *School for Scandal* at Drury Lane.

[3] Dr. John William Polidori, whom Byron had hired as a personal physician.

Low-country—low life—which regaled us much—besides it being a Sunday—all the world were in their way to Mass—& I had the pleasure of seeing a number of very ordinary women in extraordinary garments:—we found the "Contadini" however very goodnatured & obliging though not at all useful.——At Antwerp we pictured—churched—and steepled again—but the principal Street and *bason* pleased me most—poor dear Bonaparte!!!—and the foundries &c.—as for Rubens—I was glad to see his tomb on account of that ridiculous description (in Smollet's P[eregrine] Pickle) of Pallet's absurdity at his monument—but as for his works—and his superb "tableaux"—he seems to me (who by the way know nothing of the matter) the most glaring—flaring—staring—harlotry imposter that ever passed a trick upon the senses of mankind—it is not nature—it is not art—with the exception of some linen (which hangs over the cross in one of his pictures) which to do it justice looked like a very handsome table cloth —I never saw such an assemblage of florid night-mares as his canvas contains—his portraits seem clothed in pulpit cushions.——On the way to Mechlin—a wheel—& a *spring* too gave way—that is—the one went—& the other would not go—so we came off here to get into dock—I hope we shall sail shortly.———On to Geneva.—Will you have the goodness—to get at my account at Hoares—(my bankers) I believe there must be a balance in my favour—as I did not draw a great deal previously to going:—whatever there may be over the two thousand five hundred—they can send by you to me in a further credit when you come out:—I wish you to enquire (for fear any tricks might be played with my drafts) my bankers books left with you—will show you exactly what I have drawn—and you can let them have the book to make out the remainder of the account. All I have to urge to Hanson—or to our friend Douglas K[innaird]—is to *sell* if possible. ——All kind things to Scrope—and the rest—

ever yrs. most truly & obligedly
B

P.S.—If you hear of my child—let me know any good of her health —& well doing.—Will you bring out πασανιας[4] (Taylor's ditto) when you come—I shall bring to for you at Geneva—don't forget to urge Scrope into our crew—we will buy females and found a colony—provided Scrope does not find those ossified barriers to "the fore-fended place"—which cost him such a siege at Brighthelmstone—write at your leisure—or "ipse veni".——

4 Pausanias's *Description of Greece* was one of the books listed as among Byron's possessions when he died in Missolonghi.

My dearest Augusta—By two opportunities of private conveyance—
I have sent answers to your letter delivered by Mr. H[obhouse].——
S[crope] is on his return to England—& may probably arrive before
this.—He is charged with a few packets of seals—necklaces—balls
&c.—& I know not what—formed of Chrystals—Agates—and other
stones—*all of* & *from Mont Blanc* bought & brought by me on &
from the spot—expressly for you to divide among yourself and the
children—including also your niece Ada, for whom I selected a ball
(of Granite—a soft substance by the way—but the only one there)
wherewithall to roll & play—when she is old enough—and mischievous enough—and moreover a Chrystal necklace—and anything
else you may like to add for her—the Love!——The rest are for you—
& the Nursery—but particularly Georgiana—who has sent me a very
nice letter.—I hope Scrope will carry them all safely—as he promised
——There are seals & all kinds of fooleries—pray—like them—
for they come from a very curious place (nothing like it hardly in all
I ever saw)—to say nothing of the giver.——And so—Lady B[yron]
has been "kind to you" you tell me—"very kind"—umph—it is as
well she should be kind to some of us—and I am glad she has the heart
& the discernment to be still *your* friend—you was ever so to her.—I
heard the other day—that she was very unwell—I was shocked
enough—and sorry enough—God knows—but never mind;—
H[obhouse] tells me however that she is *not* ill—that she *had* been
indisposed—but is better & well to do.—this is a relief.——As for
me I am in good health—& fair—though very unequal—spirits—but
for all that—she—or rather—the Separation—has broken my heart—
I feel as if an Elephant had trodden on it—I am convinced I shall
never get over it—but I try.———I had enough before I ever knew her
and more than enough—but time & agitation had done something for
me; but this last wreck has affected me very differently,—if it were
acutely—it would not signify—but it is not that,—I breathe lead.——
While the storm lasted & you were all pressing & comforting me with
condemnation in Piccadilly—it was bad enough—& violent enough—
but it is worse now.—I have neither strength nor spirits—nor inclination to carry me through anything which will clear my brain or
lighten my heart.—I mean to cross the Alps at the end of this month—
and go—God knows where—by Dalmatia—up to the Arnauts again—
if nothing better can be done;—I have still a world before me—this—
or the next.——H[obhouse] has told me all the strange stories in

circulation of me & mine;—*not* true,—I have been in some danger on the lake—(near Meillerie) but nothing to speak of; and as to all these "mistresses"—Lord help me—I have had but one.—Now—don't scold—but what could I do?—a foolish girl[1]—in spite of all I could say or do—would come after me—or rather went before me—for I found her here—and I have had all the plague possible to persuade her to go back again—but at last she went.—Now—dearest—I do most truly tell thee—that I could not help this—that I did all I could to prevent it—& have at last put an end to it.—I am not in love—nor have any love left for any,—but I could not exactly play the Stoic with a woman—who had scrambled eight hundred miles to unphilosophize me—besides I had been regaled of late with so many "two courses and a *desert*" (Alas!) of aversion—that I was fain to take a little love (if pressed particularly) by way of novelty.——And now you know all that I know of that matter—& it is over. Pray—write—I have heard nothing since your last—at least a month or five weeks ago.——
I go out very little—except into the *air*—and on journeys—and on the water—and to Coppet—where Me. de Stael has been particularly kind & friendly towards me—& (I hear) fought battles without number in my very indifferent cause.—It has (they say) made quite as much noise on this as the other side of "La Manche"—Heaven knows why—but I seem destined to set people by the ears.——Don't hate me—but believe me ever

yrs. most affectly.

B

ALPINE JOURNAL

[TO AUGUSTA LEIGH]   *Clarens. Septr. 18th. 1816*

Yesterday September 17th. 1816—I set out (with H[obhouse]) on an excursion of some days to the Mountains.—I shall keep a short journal of each day's progress for my Sister Augusta—

Sept. 17th.—

Rose at 5.—left Diodati about seven—in one of the country carriages— (a Charaban)—our servants on horseback—weather very fine—the Lake calm and clear—Mont Blanc—and the Aiguille of Argentière

---

[1] Claire Clairmont, who had forced herself on Byron's attention just before he left England, and who pursued him to Geneva where she introduced him to Shelley and Mary Godwin, her half-sister.

both very distinct—the borders of the Lake beautiful—reached Lausanne before Sunset—stopped & slept at Ouchy.—H[obhouse] went to dine with a Mr. Okeden—I remained at our Caravansera (though invited to the house of H's friend—too lazy or tired—or something else to go) and wrote a letter to Augusta—Went to bed at nine—sheets damp—swore and stripped them off & flung them— Heaven knows where—wrapt myself up in the blankets—and slept like a Child of a month's existence—till 5 o Clock of

Septr. 18th.

Called by Berger (my Courier who acts as Valet for a day or two—the learned Fletcher being left in charge of Chattels at Diodati) got up— H[obhouse] walked on before—a mile from Lausanne—the road over-flowed by the lake—got on horseback & rode—till within a mile of Vevey—the Colt young but went very well—overtook H. & resumed the carriage which is an open one—stopped at Vevey two hours (the second time I have visited it) walked to the Church—view from the Churchyard superb—within it General Ludlow (the Regicide's) monument—black marble—long inscription—Latin—but simple— particularly the latter part—in which his wife (Margaret de Thomas) records her long—her tried—and unshaken affection—he was an Exile *two and thirty years*—one of the King's (Charles's) Judges—a fine fellow.—I remember reading his memoirs in January 1815 (at Halnaby—) the first part of them very amusing—the latter less so,— I little thought at the time of their perusal by me of seeing his tomb— near him Broughton (who read King Charles's sentence to Charles Stuart)—is buried with a *queer* and rather *canting*—but still a Republican epitaph——Ludlow's house shown—it retains still his inscription "Omne Solum forte patria"—Walked down to the Lake side—servants—Carriage—saddle horses—all set off and left us plantés la by some mistake—and we walked on after them towards Clarens—H[*obhouse*] ran on before and overtook them at last —arrived the second time (1st time was by water) at Clarens beautiful Clarens!—went to Chillon through Scenery worthy of I know not whom—went over the Castle of Chillon again—on our return met an English party in a carriage—a lady in it fast asleep!— fast asleep in the most anti-narcotic spot in the world—excellent—I remember at Chamouni—in the very eyes of Mont Blanc—hearing another woman—English also—exclaim to her party—"did you ever see any thing more *rural*"—as if it was Highgate or Hampstead—or Brompton—or Hayes.—"*Rural*" quotha!—Rocks—pines—torrents—

Glaciers—Clouds—and Summits of eternal snow far above them—and "*Rural!*" I did not know the thus exclaiming fair one—but she was a—very good kind of a woman.——After a slight & short dinner—we visited the Chateau de Clarens—an English woman has rented it recently—(it was not let when I saw it first) the roses are gone with their Summer—the family out—but the servants desired us to walk over the interior—saw on the table of the saloon—Blair's sermons—and somebody else's (I forgot who's—) sermons—and a set of noisy children—saw all worth seeing and then descended to the "Bosquet de Julie" &c. &c.—our Guide full of *Rousseau*—whom he is eternally confounding with *St. Preux*—and mixing the man and the book—on the steps of a cottage in the village—I saw a young *paysanne*—beautiful as Julie herself—went again as far as Chillon to revisit the little torrent from the hill behind it—Sunset—reflected in the lake—have to get up at 5 tomorrow to cross the mountains on horseback—carriage to be sent round—lodged at my old Cottage—hospitable & comfortable—tired with a longish ride—on the Colt—and the subsequent jolting of the Charaban—and my scramble in the hot sun—shall go to bed—thinking of you dearest Augusta.——Mem.—The Corporal who showed the wonders of Chillon was as drunk as Blucher[1]—and (to my mind) as great a man.—He was *deaf* also—and thinking every one else so—roared out the legends of the Castle so fearfully that H[obhouse] got out of humour—however we saw all things from the Gallows to the Dungeon (the *Potence* & the *Cachets*) and returned to Clarens with more freedom than belonged to the 15th. Century.——At Clarens—the only book (except the Bible) a translation of "*Cecilia*" (Miss Burney's *Cecilia*) and the owner of the Cottage had also called her dog (a fat Pug *ten* years old—and hideous as *Tip*)[2] after Cecilia's (or rather Delville's) dog—Fidde—

Septr. 19th.

Rose at 5—ordered the carriage round.—Crossed the mountains to Montbovon on horseback—and on Mules—and by dint of scrambling on foot also,—the whole route beautiful as a *Dream* and now to me almost as indistinct,—I am so tired—for though healthy I have not the strength I possessed but a few years ago.—At Mont Davant we breakfasted—afterwards on a steep ascent—dismounted—tumbled down & cut a finger open—the baggage also got loose and fell down a ravine, till stopped by a large tree—swore—recovered baggage—

---

[1] Byron had observed, or been told of, the drunkenness of Blücher when he visited England during "the summer of the Sovereigns", in 1814.

[2] Tip was Augusta's dog.

horse tired & dropping—mounted Mule—at the approach of the summit of Dent Jamant—dismounted again with H. & all the party.— Arrived at a lake in the very nipple of the bosom of the Mountain.— left our quadrupeds with a Shepherd—& ascended further—came to some snow in patches—upon which my forehead's perspiration fell like rain making the same dints as in a sieve—the chill of the wind & the snow turned me giddy—but I scrambled on & upwards— *H.* went to the highest *pinnacle*—I did not—but paused within a few yards (at an opening of the Cliff)—in coming down the Guide tumbled three times—I fell a laughing & tumbled too—the descent luckily soft though steep & slippery—H. also fell—but nobody hurt. The whole of the Mountain superb—the shepherd on a very steep & high cliff playing upon his *pipe*—very different from Arcadia—(where I saw the pastors with a long Musquet instead of a Crook—and pistols in their Girdles)—our Swiss Shepherd's pipe was sweet—& his time agreeable—saw a cow strayed—told that they often break their necks on & over the crags—descended to Montbovon—pretty scraggy village with a wild river—and a wooden bridge.—H. went to fish—caught one—our carriage not come—our horses—mules &c. knocked up— ourselves fatigued—(but so much the better—I shall sleep). The view from the highest point of today's journey comprized on one side the greatest part of Lake Leman—on the other—the valleys & mountains of the Canton Fribourg—and an immense plain with the Lakes of Neufchatel & Morat—and all which the borders of these and of the Lake of Geneva inherit—we had both sides of the Jura before us in one point of view, with Alps in plenty.—In passing a ravine—the Guide recommended strenuously a quickening of pace—as the stones fall with great rapidity & occasional damage—the advice is excellent—but like most good advice impracticable—the road being so rough in this precise point—that neither mules nor mankind—nor horses—can make any violent progress.—Passed without any fractures or menace thereof.—The music of the Cows' bells (for their wealth like the Patriarchs is cattle) in the pastures (which reach to a height far above any mountains in Britain—) and the Shepherds' shouting to us from crag to crag & playing on their reeds where the steeps appeared almost inaccessible, with the surrounding scenery—realized all that I have ever heard or imagined of a pastoral existence—much more so than Greece or Asia Minor—for there we are a little too much of the sabre & musquet order—and if there is a Crook in one hand, you are sure to see a gun in the other—but this was pure and unmixed—solitary— savage and patriarchal—the effect I cannot describe—as we went they

played the "Ranz des Vaches" and other airs by way of farewell.—
I have lately repeopled my mind with Nature.

Septr. 20th.

Up at 6—off at 8—the whole of this days journey at an average of
between from two thousand seven hundred to three thousand feet
above the level of the Sea. This valley the longest—narrowest—&
considered one of the finest of the Alps——little traversed by
travellers—saw the Bridge of La Roche—the bed of the river very
low & deep between immense rocks & rapid as anger—a man & mule
said to have tumbled over without damage—(the mule was lucky
at any rate—unless I knew the *man* I should be loth to pronounce *him*
fortunate).—The people looked free & happy and *rich* (which last
implies neither of the former) the cows superb—a Bull nearly leapt
into the Charaban—"agreeable companion in a postchaise"—Goats &
Sheep very thriving—a mountain with enormous Glaciers to the right
—the Kletsgerberg—further on—the Hockthorn—nice names—so
soft—Hockthorn I believe very lofty & craggy—patched with snow
only—no Glaciers on it—but some good epaulettes of clouds.—Past
the boundaries—out of Vaud—& into Bern Canton—French
exchanged for a bad German—the district famous for Cheese—
liberty—property—& no taxes.—H. went to fish—caught none—
strolled to river—saw a boy [and] a kid—kid followed him like a dog
—kid could not get over a fence & bleated piteously—tried myself to
help kid—but nearly overset both self & kid into the river.—Arrived
here about six in the evening—nine o clock—going to bed—H. in
next room—knocked his head against the door—and exclaimed of
course against doors—not tired today—but hope to sleep nevertheless
—women gabbling below—read a French translation of Schiller—
Good Night—Dearest Augusta.——

Septr. 21st.

Off early—the valley of Simmenthal as before—entrance to the plain
of Thoun very narrow—high rocks—wooded to the top—river—new
mountains—with fine Glaciers—Lake of Thoun—extensive plain
with a girdle of Alps—walked down to the Chateau de Schadau—
view along the lake—crossed the river in a boat rowed by women—
women [went?] right for the first time in my recollection.—Thoun a
pretty town—the whole day's journey Alpine & proud.—

Septr. 22d.

Left Thoun in a boat which carried us the length of the lake in three hours—the lake small—but the banks fine—rocks down to the water's edge.—Landed at Neuhause—passed Interlachen—entered upon a range of scenes beyond all description—or previous conception.— Passed a rock—inscription—2 brothers—one murdered the other— just the place fit for it.—After a variety of windings came to an enormous rock—Girl with fruit—very pretty—blue eyes—good teeth—very fair—long but good features—reminded me of Fy. bought some of her pears—and patted her upon the cheek—the expression of her face very mild—but good—and not at all coquettish. —Arrived at the foot of the Mountain (the Yung-frau—i.e. the Maiden) Glaciers—torrents—one of these torrents *nine hundred feet* in height of visible descent—lodge at the Curate's—set out to see the Valley—heard an Avalanche fall—like thunder—saw Glacier— enormous—Storm came on—thunder—lightning—hail—all in perfection—and beautiful—I was on horseback—Guide wanted to carry my cane—I was going to give it him when I recollected that it was a Swordstick and I thought that the lightning might be attracted towards him—kept it myself—a good deal encumbered with it & my cloak— as it was too heavy for a whip—and the horse was stupid—& stood still every other peal. Got in—not very wet—the Cloak being staunch —H. wet through—H. took refuge in cottage—sent man—umbrella— & cloak (from the Curate's when I arrived—) after him.—Swiss Curate's house—very good indeed—much better than most English Vicarages—it is immediately opposite the torrent I spoke of—the torrent is in shape curving over the rock—like the *tail* of a white horse streaming in the wind—such as it might be conceived would be that of the *"pale* horse" on which *Death* is mounted in the Apocalypse.—It is neither mist nor water but a something between both—it's immense height (nine hundred feet) gives it a wave—a curve—a spreading here—a condensation there—wonderful—& indescribable.—I think upon the whole—that this day has been better than any of this present excursion.—

Septr. 23d.

Before ascending the mountain—went to the torrent (7 in the morning) again—the Sun upon it forming a *rainbow* of the lower part of all colours—but principally purple and gold—the bow moving as you move —I never saw anything like this—it is only in the Sunshine.——Ascended the Wengren [sic] Mountain.——at noon reached a valley near the summit—left the horses—took off my coat & went to the summit— 7000 feet (English feet) above the level of the *sea*—and about 5000 above the valley we left in the morning—on one side our view comprized the *Yung frau* with all her glaciers—then the *Dent d'Argent*—shining like truth—then the *little Giant* (the Kleiner Eiger) & the great Giant (the Grosser Eiger) and last not least—the Wetterhorn. —The height of the Yung frau is 13000 feet above the sea—and 11000 above the valley—she is the highest of this range,—heard the Avalanches falling every five minutes nearly—as if God was pelting the Devil down from Heaven with snow balls—from where we stood on the *Wengren* [sic] Alp—we had all these in view on one side—on the other the clouds rose from the opposite valley curling up perpendicular precipices—like the foam of the Ocean of Hell during a Springtide—it was white & sulphery—and immeasurably deep in appearance—the side we ascended was (of course) not of so precipitous a nature—but on arriving at the summit we looked down the other side upon a boiling sea of cloud—dashing against the crags on which we stood (these crags on one side quite perpendicular);—staid a quarter of an hour—began to descend—quite clear from cloud on that side of the mountain—in passing the masses of snow—I made a snowball & pelted H. with it—got down to our horses again—eat something—remounted—heard the Avalanches still—came to a morass—H. dismounted—H. got well over—I tried to pass my horse over—the horse sunk up [to] the chin—& of course he & I were in the mud together—bemired all over—but not hurt—laughed & rode on.—Arrived at the Grindenwald—dined—mounted again & rode to the higher Glacier—twilight—but distinct—very fine Glacier—like a *frozen hurricane*—Starlight—beautiful—but a devil of a path—never mind—got safe in—a little lightning—but the whole of the day as fine in point of weather—as the day on which Paradise was made.—Passed *whole woods of withered pines*—*all withered*—trunks stripped & barkless—branches lifeless—done by a single winter—their appearance reminded me of me & my family.—

Septr. 24th.

Set out at seven—up at five—passed the black Glacier—the Mountain Wetterhorn on the right—crossed the Scheideck mountain—came to the Rose Glacier—said to be the largest & finest in Switzerland.—*I* think the Bossons Glacier at Chamouni—as fine—H. does not—came to the Reichenback waterfall—two hundred feet high—halted to rest the horses—arrived in the valley of Oberhasli—rain came on—drenched a little—only 4 hours rain however in 8 days—came to Lake of Brientz—then to town of Brientz—changed—H. hurt his head against door.—In the evening four Swiss Peasant Girls of Oberhasli came & sang the airs of their country—two of the voices beautiful—

the tunes also—they sing too that *Tyrolese air* & song which you love—
Augusta—because I love it—& I love because you love it— they are
still singing—Dearest—you do not know how I should have liked
this—were you with me—the airs are so wild & original & at the
same time of great sweetness.——The singing is over—but below
stairs I hear the notes of a Fiddle which bode no good to my nights
rest.—The Lord help us!—I shall go down & see the dancing.—

Septr. 25th.

The whole town of Brientz were apparently gathered together in the
rooms below—pretty music—& excellent Waltzing—none but
peasants—the dancing much better than in England—the English
can't Waltz—never could—nor ever will.—One man with his pipe in
his mouth—but danced as well as the others—some other dances in
pairs—and in fours—and very good.——I went to bed but the
revelry continued below late & early.—Brientz but a village.——
Rose early.—Embarked on the Lake of Brientz.—Rowed by women in
a long boat—one very young & very pretty—seated myself by her—
& began to row also—presently we put to shore & another woman
jumped in—it seems it is the custom here for the boats to be *manned by
women*—for of five men & three women in our bark—all the women
took an oar—and but one man.——Got to Interlachen in three
hours—pretty Lake—not so large as that of Thoun.—Dined at
Interlachen—Girl gave me some flowers—& made me a speech in
German—of which I know nothing—I do not know whether the
speech was pretty but as the woman was—I hope so.—Saw another—
very pretty too—and *tall* which I prefer—I hate short women—for
more reasons than one.—Reembarked on the Lake of Thoun—fell
asleep part of the way—sent our horses round—found people on the
shore blowing up a rock with gunpowder—they blew it up near our
boat—only telling us a minute before—mere stupidity—but they might
have broke our noddles.—Got to Thoun in the Evening—the weather
has been tolerable the whole day—but as the wild part of our tour is
finished, it don't matter to us—in all the desirable part—we have been
most lucky in warmth & clearness of Atmosphere—for which "Praise
we the Lord."——

Septr. 26th.

Being out of the mountains my journal must be as flat as my journey.
——From Thoun to Bern good road—hedges—villages—industry—
prosperity—and all sorts of tokens of insipid civilization.——From
Bern to Fribourg.—Different Canton—Catholics—passed a field of

Battle—Swiss beat the French—in one of the late wars against the French Republic.—Bought a dog—a very ugly dog—but *"tres mechant"*. this was his great recommendation in the owner's eyes & mine—for I mean him to watch the carriage—he hath no tail—& is called "Mutz"—which signifies *"Short-tail"*—he is apparently of the Shepherd dog genus!—The greater part of this tour has been on horse-back—on foot—and on mule;—the Filly (which is one of two young horses I bought of the Baron de Vincy) carried me very well—she is young and as quiet as anything of her sex can be—very goodtempered —and perpetually neighing—when she wants any thing—which is every five minutes—I have called her *Biche*—because her manners are not unlike a little dog's—but she is a very tame—pretty childish quadruped.—

Septr. 28th. [27th.]

Saw the tree planted in honour of the battle of Morat—340 years old— a good deal decayed.—Left Fribourg—but first saw the Cathedral— high tower—overtook the baggage of the Nuns of La Trappe who are removing to Normandy from their late abode in the Canton of Fribourg—afterwards a coach with a quantity of Nuns in it—Nuns old—proceeded along the banks of the Lake of Neufchatel—very pleasing & soft—but not so mountainous—at least the Jura not appearing so—after the Bernese Alps—reached Yverdun in the dusk —a long line of large trees on the border of the lake—fine & sombre— the Auberge nearly full—with a German Princess & suite—got rooms—we hope to reach Diodati the day after tomorrow—and I wish for a letter from you my own dearest Sis—May your sleep be soft and your dreams of me.—I am going to bed—good night.—

Septr. 29th. [28th.]

Passed through a fine & flourishing country—but not mountainous— in the evening reached Aubonne (the entrance & bridge something like that of Durham) which commands by far the fairest view of the Lake of Geneva—twilight—the Moon on the Lake—a grove on the height—and of very noble trees.—Here Tavernier (the Eastern traveller) bought (or built) the Chateau because the site resembled and equalled that of *Erivan* (a frontier city of Persia) here he finished his voyages—and I this little excursion—for I am within a few hours of Diodati—& have little more to see—& no more to say.—In the weather for this tour (of 13 days) I have been very fortunate— fortunate in a companion (Mr. H[obhous]e) fortunate in our pros-pects—and exempt from even the little petty accidents & delays which

133

often render journeys in a less wild country—disappointing.—I was disposed to be pleased—I am a lover of Nature—and an Admirer of Beauty—I can bear fatigue—& welcome privation—and have seen some of the noblest views in the world.—But in all this—the recollections of bitterness—& more especially of recent & more home desolation—which must accompany me through life—have preyed upon me here—and neither the music of the Shepherd—the crashing of the Avalanche—nor the torrent—the mountain—the Glacier—the Forest—nor the Cloud—have for one moment—lightened the weight upon my heart—nor enabled me to lose my own wretched identity in the majesty & the power and the Glory—around—above—& beneath me.—I am past reproaches—and there is a time for all things—I am past the wish of vengeance—and I know of none like for what I have suffered—but the hour will come—when what I feel must be felt—& the——but enough.——To you—dearest Augusta—I send—and *for* you—I have kept this record of what I have seen & felt.—Love me as you are beloved by me.———

My dearest Augusta—I have been at Churches, Theatres, libraries, and picture galleries. The Cathedral is noble, the theatre grand, the library excellent, and the galleries I know nothing about—except as far as liking one picture out of a thousand. What has delighted me most is a manuscript collection (preserved in the Ambrosian library), of original love-letters and verses of Lucretia de Borgia & Cardinal Bembo; and a lock of hair—so long—and fair & beautiful—and the letters so pretty & so loving that it makes one wretched not to have been born sooner to have at least seen her. And pray what do you think is one of her *signatures?*—why this + a Cross—which she says "is to stand for her name &c." Is not this amusing?[1] I suppose you know that she was a famous beauty, & famous for the use she made of it; & that she was the love of this same Cardinal Bembo (besides a story about her papa Pope Alexander & her brother Cæsar Borgia— which some people don't believe—& others do), and that after all she

[1] The cross was a secret love symbol used frequently in Byron's letters to Augusta, and sometimes in hers to him.

ended with being Duchess of Ferrara, and an excellent mother & wife also; so good as to be quite an example. All this may or may not be, but the hair & the letters are so beautiful that I have done nothing but pore over them, & have made the librarian promise me a copy of some of them; and I mean to get some of the hair if I can. The verses are Spanish—the letters Italian—some signed—others with a cross—but all in her own hand-writing.

I am so hurried, & so sleepy, but so anxious to send you even a few lines my dearest Augusta, that you will forgive me troubling you so often; and I shall write again soon; but I have sent you so much lately, that you will have too many perhaps. *A thousand loves* to *you* from *me*—which is very generous for I only ask *one* in return

Ever dearest thine
B

[TO AUGUSTA LEIGH] *Octr. 28th. 1816*

My dearest Augusta—Two days ago I wrote you the enclosed but the arrival of your letter of the 12th. has revived me a little, so pray forgive the apparent *"humeur"* of the other, which I do not tear up—from laziness—and the hurry of the post as I have hardly time to write another at present.

I really do not & cannot understand all the mysteries & alarms in your letters & more particularly in the last. All I know is—that no human power short of destruction—shall prevent me from seeing you when—where—& how—I may please—according to time & circumstance; that you are the only comfort (except the remote possibility of my daughter's being so) left me in prospect in existence, and that I can bear the rest—so that you remain; but anything which is to divide us would drive me quite out of my senses;[1] Miss Milbanke appears in all respects to have been formed for my destruction; I have thus far—as you know—regarded her without feelings of personal bitterness towards her, but if directly or indirectly—but why do I say this?—You

[1] Lady Byron had been menacing Augusta and trying to wring a confession from her about her relations with Byron and had frightened her into a promise that she would not see him again if he returned to England. Augusta could not bring herself to tell Byron this and her letters were full of vague "mysteries and alarms".

135

know she is the cause of all—whether intentionally or not is little to the purpose——You surely do not mean to say that if I come to England in Spring, that you & I shall not meet? If so I will never return to it—though I must for many reasons—business &c &c—But I quit this topic for the present.

My health is good, but I have now & then fits of giddiness, & deafness, which make me think like Swift—that I shall be like him & the *withered* tree he saw—which occasioned the reflection and "die at top" first. My hair is growing grey, & *not* thicker; & my teeth are sometimes *looseish* though still white & sound. Would not one think I was sixty instead of not quite nine & twenty? To talk thus—Never mind—either this must end—or I must end—but I repeat it again & again—*that woman* has destroyed me.

Milan has been made agreeable by much attention and kindness from many of the natives; but the whole tone of Italian society is so different from yours in England; that I have not time to describe it, tho' I am not sure that I do not prefer it. Direct as usual to Geneva— hope the best—& love me the most—as I ever must love you.

B

[TO THOMAS MOORE]   *Venice, November 17th, 1816*

I wrote to you from Verona the other day in my progress hither, which letter I hope you will receive. Some three years ago, or it may be more, I recollect your telling me that you had received a letter from our friend Sam, dated "On board his gondola". *My* gondola is, at this present, waiting for me on the canal; but I prefer writing to you in the house, it being autumn—and rather an English autumn than otherwise. It is my intention to remain at Venice during the winter, probably, as it has always been (next to the East) the greenest island of my imagination. It has not disappointed me; though its evident decay would, perhaps, have that effect upon others. But I have been familiar with ruins too long to dislike desolation. Besides, I have fallen in love, which, next to falling into the canal, (which would be of no use, as I can swim.) is the best or the worst thing I could do. I have got some extremely good apartments in the house of a "Merchant of Venice," who is a good deal occupied with business, and has a wife in her twenty-second year. Marianna (that is her name)[1] is in her appearance altogether like an antelope. She has the large, black, oriental eyes, with that peculiar expression in them which is seen rarely among *Europeans*—even the Italians—and which many of the Turkish women give themselves by tinging the eyelid,—an art not known out of that country, I believe. This expression she has *naturally*,—and something more than this. In short, I cannot describe the effect of this kind of eye,—at least upon me. Her features are regular, and rather aquiline—mouth small—skin clear and soft, with a kind of hectic colour—forehead remarkably good: her hair is of the dark gloss, curl, and colour of Lady J * * 's [Jersey's]: her figure is light and pretty, and she is a famous songstress—scientifically so; her natural voice (in conversation, I mean) is very sweet; and the naiveté of the Venetian dialect is always pleasing in the mouth of a woman.

November 23.

You will perceive that my description, which was proceeding with the minuteness of a passport, has been interrupted for several days. In the meantime *

December 5

Since my former dates, I do not know that I have much to add on the subject, and, luckily, nothing to take away; for I am more pleased than ever with my Venetian, and begin to feel very serious on that point—so much so, that I shall be silent. * * * * * * * * * * * * * *

By way of divertisement, I am studying daily, at an Armenian monastery,[2] the Armenian language. I found that my mind wanted something craggy to break upon; and this—as the most difficult thing I could discover here for an amusement—I have chosen, to torture me into attention. It is a rich language, however, and would amply repay any one the trouble of learning it. I try, and shall go on;—but I answer for nothing, least of all for my intentions or my success. There

[1] Marianna Segati who with her husband, a draper, lived in the Frezzeria, a narrow street just off the Piazza San Marco.

[2] The Armenian Mekhitarist Convent was founded by Peter Mekhitar in 1717. It was on the Island of San Lazzaro near the Lido about two miles from Venice.

are some very curious MSS. in the monastery, as well as books; translations also from Greek originals, now lost, and from Persian and Syriac, &c.; besides works of their own people. Four years ago the French instituted an Armenian professorship. Twenty pupils presented themselves on Monday morning, full of noble ardour, ingenuous youth, and impregnable industry. They persevered, with a courage worthy of the nation and of universal conquest, till Thursday; when *fifteen* of the *twenty* succumbed to the six-and-twentieth letter of the alphabet. It is, to be sure, a Waterloo of an Alphabet[3]—that must be said for them. But it is so like these fellows, to do by it as they did by their sovereigns—abandon both; to parody the old rhymes, "Take a thing and give a thing"—"Take a King and give a King". They are the worst of animals, except their conquerors.

I hear that H[odgso]n is your neighbour, having a living in Derbyshire.[4] You will find him an excellent-hearted fellow, as well as one of the cleverest; a little, perhaps, too much japanned by preferment in the church and the tuition of youth, as well as inoculated with the disease of domestic felicity, besides being over-run with fine feelings about women and *constancy* (that small change of Love, which people exact so rigidly, receive in such counterfeit coin, and repay in baser metal); but, otherwise, a very worthy man, who has lately got a pretty wife, and (I suppose) a child by this time. Pray remember me to him, and say that I know not which to envy most— his neighbourhood, him, or you.

Of Venice I shall say little. You must have seen many descriptions; and they are most of them like. It is a poetical place; and classical, to us, from Shakespeare and Otway. I have not yet sinned against it in verse, nor do I know that I shall do so, having been tuneless since I crossed the Alps, and feeling, as yet, no renewal of the "estro".[5] By the way, I suppose you have seen "Glenarvon".[6] Madame de Stael lent it me to read from Copet last autumn. It seems to me that, if the authoress had written the *truth*, and nothing but the truth—the whole truth—the romance would not only have been more *romantic*, but more entertaining. As for the likeness, the picture can't be good—I

---

[3] The Armenian alphabet has 38 characters.

[4] Francis Hodgson, one of Byron's closest friends in England, was appointed on July 18, 1816, to the living at Bakewell in Derbyshire.

[5] Inspiration, ardour, whim.

[6] Lady Caroline Lamb's novel, in which Byron is the hero-villain.

did not sit long enough. When you have leisure, let me hear from and of you, believing me,

Ever and truly yours most affectionately,

B

P.S.—Oh! *your Poem*—is it out? I hope Longman has paid his thousands: but don't you do as H[orace] T[wiss]'s father did, who, having made money by a quarto tour, became a vinegar merchant; when, lo! his vinegar turned sweet (and be damned to it) and ruined him. My last letter to you (from Verona) was enclosed to Murray— have you got it? Direct to me *here, poste restante*. There are no English here at present. There were several in Switzerland—some women; but, except Lady Dalrymple Hamilton, most of them as ugly as virtue—at least, those I saw.

[TO JOHN MURRAY]   *Venice Novr. 25th. 1816*

Dear Sir—It is some months since I have heard from or of you—I think—*not* since I left Diodati.—From Milan I wrote once or twice;— but have been here some little time—and intend to pass the winter without removing.—I was much pleased with the Lago di Garda & with Verona—particularly the amphitheatre—and a sarcophagus in a Convent garden—which they show as Juliet's—they insist on the *truth* of her history.—Since my arrival at Venice—the Lady of the Austrian Governor[1] told me that between Verona & Vicenza there are still ruins of the Castle of the *Montecchi*—and a chapel once appertaining to the Capulets—Romeo seems to have been of *Vicenza* by the tradition—but I was a good deal surprized to find so firm a faith in Bandello's novel[2]—which seems really to have been founded on a fact.——Venice pleases me as much as I expected—and I expected much—it is one of those places which I know before I see them—and has always haunted me the most—after the East.——I like the gloomy gaiety of their gondolas—and the silence of their canals—I do not even dislike the evident decay of the city—though I regret the singularity of it's vanished costume—however there is much left still; —the Carnival too is coming.——St. Mark's—and indeed Venice—is most alive at night—the theatres are not open till *nine*—and the

---

[1] Countess Goetz.

[2] Matteo Bandello (1450–1562) borrowed the story from Luigi da Porto in whose hands the old story first took on the Shakespearean form.

society is proportionably late—all this is to my taste—but most of your countrymen miss & regret the rattle of hackney coaches—without which they can't sleep.——I have got remarkably good apartments in a private house—I see something of the inhabitants (having had a good many letters to some of them) I have got my gondola—I read a little—& luckily could speak Italian (more fluently though than accurately) long ago;—I am studying out of curiosity the *Venetian* dialect—which is very naive — soft & peculiar—though not at all classical—I go out frequently—and am in very good contentment.——The *Helen* of Canova—(a bust which is in the house of M[adam]e the Countess d'Albrizzi[3] whom I know) is without exception to my mind the most perfectly beautiful of human conceptions—and far beyond my ideas of human execution.—

————

In this beloved marble view
   Above the works & thoughts of Man—
What Nature *could*—but *would not* do—
   And Beauty and Canova *can!*
Beyond Imagination's power—
   Beyond the Bard's defeated art,
With immortality her dower—
   Behold the *Helen* of the *heart!*

————

Talking of the "heart" reminds me that I have fallen in love—which except falling into the Canal—(and that would be useless as I swim) is the best (or worst) thing I could do.——I am therefore in love—fathomless love—but lest you should make some splendid mistake—& envy me the possession of some of those Princesses or Countesses with whose affections your English voyagers are apt to invest them-selves—I beg leave to tell you—that my Goddess is only the wife of a "Merchant of Venice"—but then she is pretty as an Antelope,—is but two & twenty years old—has the large black Oriental eyes—with the Italian countenance—and dark glossy hair of the curl & colour of Lady Jersey's—then she has the voice of a lute—and the song of a Seraph (though not quite so sacred) besides a long postscript of graces—virtues and accomplishments—enough to furnish out a new

[3] The Countess Isabella Teotochi Albrizzi conducted the most celebrated salon, or *conversazione*, in Venice. She was a friend of Canova, the sculptor, Pindemonte, Alfieri, Ugo Foscolo, and most of the literati and artists of the day. She was called the Madame de Staël of Italy.

Chapter for Solomon's song.—But her great merit is finding out mine—there is nothing so amiable as discernment.—Our little arrangement is completed—the usual oaths having been taken—and everything fulfilled according to the "understood relations" of such liaisons. The general race of women appear to be handsome—but in Italy as on almost all the Continent—the highest orders are by no means a well looking generation—and indeed reckoned by their countrymen very much otherwise.—Some are exceptions but most of them as ugly as Virtue herself.—If you write—address to me *here* *Poste Restante*—as I shall probably stay the winter over.—I never see a newspaper & know nothing of England—except in a letter now & then from my Sister.—Of the M.S. sent you I know nothing except that you have received it—& are to publish it &c. &c. but when—where—& how—you leave me to guess—. But it don't much matter.— —I suppose you have a world of works passing through your process for next year—when does Moore's poem appear?—I sent a letter for him addressed to your care the other day.—So—Mr. *Frere* is married —and you tell me in a former letter that he had "nearly forgotten that he was so—"4—he is fortunate.——

yrs ever & very truly
B

[TO DOUGLAS KINNAIRD]   *Venice. Novr. 27th. 1816*

My dear Kinnaird—Before I left Switzerland I answered your last letter & feel a little anxious to know that you have received it—as it was partly on business—that is to say on the disposition of Murray's proposed payment.—I fear there seems little chance of an immediate Sale of Newstead, which is to be wished for many reasons.— H[ob-house] & I have been some time in the North of Italy—& reached Venice about a fortnight ago—where I shall remain probably during the winter.——It is a place which I like—and which I long anticipated that I should like—besides—I have fallen in love—and with a very

---

⁴ Murray had written that Frere "came to see me while at breakfast this morning, and between some stanzas which he was repeating to me of a truly original poem of his own, he said carelessly, 'By the way, about *half-an-hour ago* I was so silly (taking an immense pinch of snuff and priming his nostrils with it) as to get *married*!'" (Samuel Smiles, *A Publisher and his Friends*, I, 366) John Hookham Frere, diplomatist and friend of Canning, had been a contributor of clever satires to the *Anti-Jacobin*, and later his "Whistlecraft" gave Byron a model for the mock-heroic style of *Beppo* and *Don Juan*.

pretty woman—so much so—as to obtain the approbation of the not easily approving H[obhouse]—who is in general rather tardy in his applause of the fairer part of the creation.——She is married—so our arrangement was formed according to the incontinent continental system—which need not be described to you an experienced voyager— and gifted withal with a modest self-confidence—which my bashful nature is not endowed with—but nonetheless I have got the woman— I do not very well know how—but we do exceedingly well together.— She is not two and twenty—with great black Eastern eyes—and a variety of subsidiary charms &c. &c. and amongst her other accomplishments—is a mighty & admirable singer—as most of the Italians are—(though not a public one)—luckily I can speak the language fluently—& luckily (if I did not) we could employ ourselves a little without talking.——I meant to have given up gallivanting altogether —on leaving your country—where I had been totally sickened of that & every thing else—but I know not how it is—my health growing better—& my spirits not worse—the "besoin d'aimer" came back upon my heart again—after all there is nothing like it.——So much for that matter.——I hear you are in a room with Dibdin & Fanny Kelly[1]—& the Devil knows whom—Humph!——I hear also that at the meeting or in the committee—you said that I was coming back in spring—it is probable—& if you have said so I *will* come—for sundry reasons—to see my daughter—my sister—and my friends—(and not least nor last—yourself) to renew my proxy (if Parliament be dissolved) for the Whigs—to see Mr. Waite & Mr. Blake[2]—and the newest play—and the S[ub] committee—and to sell Newstead (if I can) but not to reside in England again—it neither suits me—nor I it—my greatest error was remaining there—that is to say—my greatest error but *one*—my ambition—if ever I had merits—is over— or at least limited—if I could but remain as I now am—I should not merely be happy—but *contented* which in my mind is the strongest & most difficult attainment of the two—for any one who will hazard enough may have moments of happiness.——I have books—a decent establishment—a fine country—a language which I prefer—most of the amusements & conveniences of life—as much of society as I choose to take—and a handsome woman—who is not a bore—and

---

[1] Thomas John Dibdin (1771–1841) was a prolific writer of dramatic productions and songs. After the death of Whitbread, Dibdin and Alexander Rae were appointed joint managers of the theatre. Frances Maria (Fanny) Kelly was a popular actress and singer long associated with Drury Lane.

[2] Waite was a dentist and Blake a fashionable hair-dresser or barber.

does not annoy me with looking like a fool & ⟨pretending⟩ setting up for a sage.—Life has little left for my curiosity—there are few things in it of which I have not had a sight and a share—it would be silly to quarrel with my luck because it did not last—& even that was partly my own fault.———If the present does—I should not fall out with the past:—and if I could but manage to arrange my pecuniary concerns in England—so as to pay my debts—& leave me what would be here a very fair income—(though nothing remarkable at home) you might consider me as posthumous—for I would never willingly dwell in the "tight little Island".[3]———Pray write to me a line or two addressed to Venice—*Poste Restante*—I hope to remain here the winter—remember me to Maria—and believe me yrs. ever & truly & affectly.

B

P.S.—Colonel Finch[4] an English acquaintance of H[obhouse]'s & mine has I believe written to you to complain of his banker (who is also mine) and has with our permission mentioned our names to you as knowing him.—I must however say that *I* have no complaint whatever against (Mr. Siri) the banker—who has on the contrary been remarkably civil & attentive to both H & myself.———Of Col. Finch's row with him I understand nothing—but that he had one.———Pray let me hear from you—& tell me what Murray has done—& if you have received my letter from Geneva in answer to your former one.——

P.S.—If you write to me—pray—do not refer to any *persons* or *events*—except our own *theatrical—political—personal—attorneycal— poetical—& diabolical*—concerns. You see I give a pretty wide range still—but what I wish to put under Quarantine are (*my*) *family events*—& all allusion thereto past—present—or to come.—It is what I have laid an embargo on with all my other friends.—It will be better that the *Author* of these lines[5] (if spoken) be *not* avowed— pray—make it a secret & keep it so.———

[3] Byron was fond of this phrase from a song by Dibdin, "The Snug Little Island", in a musical play called *The British Raft* (1797).

[4] An Englishman living in Italy whom Byron had first met in Milan. Robert Finch, M.A. Balliol College, Oxford, was a parson, traveller, scholar, and antiquary, who assumed the title of Colonel. The Shelleys later met him in Rome and considered him ridiculous and a great bore.

[5] Byron's "Monody" on the death of Sheridan was spoken at Drury Lane without Byron's name as the author and later published thus by Murray.

My dearest Augusta—I have received one letter dated 19th. Novr. I think (or rather earlier by a week or two perhaps) since my arrival in Venice—where it is my intention to remain probably till the Spring. —The place pleases me—I have found some pleasing society—& the romance of the situation—& it's extraordinary appearance—together with all the associations we are accustomed to connect with Venice— have always had a charm for me—even before I arrived here— and I have not been disappointed in what I have seen.——I go every morning to the Armenian Convent (of *friars not nuns*—my child) to study the language—I mean the *Armenian* language—(for as you perhaps know—I am versed in the Italian which I speak with fluency rather than accuracy—) and if you ask me my reason for studying this out of the way language—I can only answer that it is Oriental & difficult—& employs me—which are—as you know my Eastern & difficult way of thinking—reasons sufficient. Then I have fallen in love with a very pretty Venetian of two and twenty—with great black eyes —she is married—and so am I—which is very much to the purpose— we have found & sworn an eternal attachment—which has already lasted a lunar month—& I am more in love than ever—& so is the lady—at least she says so—& seems so,—she does not plague me (which is a wonder—) and I verily believe we are one of the happiest —unlawful couples on this side of the Alps.——She is very handsome —very Italian or rather Venetian—with something more of the Oriental cast of countenance;—accomplished & musical after the manner of her nation—her spouse is a very good kind of man who occupies himself elsewhere—and thus the world goes on here as elsewhere.——This adventure came very opportunely to console me— for I was beginning to be "like Sam Jennings very *unappy*" but at present—at least for a month past—I have been very tranquil—very loving—& have not so much embarrassed myself with the tortures of the last two years—and that virtuous monster Miss Milbanke, who had nearly driven me out of my senses.——Hobhouse has gone to Rome with his brother & sister—but returns here in February:—you will easily suppose that I was not disposed to stir from my present position. I have not heard recently from England & wonder if Murray has published the po's sent to him—& I want to know if you don't think them very fine & all that—Goosey my love—don't they make you "put finger in eye?"—You can have no idea of my thorough wretchedness from the day of my parting from you till nearly a month ago—though I struggled against it with some strength—at present I am better—thank Heaven above—& woman beneath—and will be a very good boy.——Pray remember me to the babes—& tell me of little *Da*—who by the way—is a year old—and a few days over.—— My love to you all—& to Aunt *Sophy*—pray tell *her* in particular that I have consoled myself;——and tell Hodgson that his prophecy is accomplished—he said—you remember—I should be in love with an Italian—so I am.—

ever dearest yrs.

B

P.S.—I forgot to tell you—that the *Demoiselle*—who returned to England from Geneva[1]—went there to produce a new baby B.—who is now about to make his appearance—you wanted to hear some adventures—these are enough I think for one epistle.——Pray address direct to Venice. Poste Restante.

[TO AUGUSTA LEIGH]   *Venice. Decr. 19th. 1816*

My dearest Augusta—I wrote to you a few days ago.—Your letter of the 1st. is arrived—and you have "a *hope*" for me—it seems— what "hope"—child?—my dearest Sis. I remember a methodist preacher who on perceiving a profane grin on the faces of part of his congregation—exclaimed "no *hopes* for *them* as *laughs*"[1] and thus it is —with us—we laugh too much for hopes—and so even let them go—I am sick of sorrow—& must even content myself as well as I can—so here goes—I won't be woeful again if I can help it.—My letter to my moral Clytemnestra required no answer—& I would rather have none —I was wretched enough when I wrote it—& had been so for many a long day & month—at present I am less so—for reasons explained in my late letter (a few days ago) and as I never pretend to *be* what I am not you may tell her if you please that I am recovering—and the reason also if you like it.— I do not agree with you about Ada—there was *equivocation* in the answer—and it shall be settled one way or the other—I wrote to Hanson to take proper steps to prevent such a removal of my daughter—and even the probability of it—you do not

[1] Claire Clairmont.
[1] In a note to *Hints from Horace* (line 382) Byron gave the name of the preacher as John Stickles.

know the woman so well as I do—or you would perceive in her *very negative answer*—that she *does intend* to take Ada with her—if she should go abroad.——I have heard of Murray's squabble with one of his brethren—who is an impudent impostor—and should be trounced. ——You do not say whether the *true po's* are out—I hope you like them.—You are right in saying that I like Venice—it is very much what you would imagine it—but I have no time just now for description;—the Carnival is to begin in a week—and with it the mummery of masking.——I have not been out a great deal—but quite as much as I like—I am going out this evening—in my *cloak* & *Gondola*—there are two nice Mrs. Radcliffe words for you—and then there is the place of St Mark—and conversaziones—and various fooleries—besides many *nau*[ghty]. indeed every body is *nau.* so much so that a lady with only *one lover* is not reckoned to have overstepped the modesty of marriage—that being a regular thing;—some have two—three—and so on to twenty beyond which they don't account—but they generally begin by one.——The husbands of course belong to any body's wives—but their own.——My present beloved—is aged two & twenty—with remarkably fine black eyes—and very regular & pretty features—figure light & pretty—hair dark—a mighty good singer—as they all are—she is married (of course) & has one child—a girl.— Her temper very good—(as you know it had need to be) and lively— she is a Venetian by birth—& was never further from Venice than Milan in her days—her lord is about five years older than me—an exceeding good kind of a man.—That amatory appendage called by us a lover—is here denominated variously—sometimes an "Amoroso" (which is the same thing) and sometimes a Cavaliero servente— which I need not tell you—is a serving Cavalier.——I told my fair one—at setting out—that as to the love and the Cavaliership—I was quite of accord—*but as to the servitude*—it would not suit me at all—so I begged to hear no more about it.—You may easily suppose I should not at all shine in the ceremonious department—so little so—that instead of handing the Lady as in duty bound into the Gondola—I as nearly as possible conveyed her into the Canal—and this at midnight— to be sure it was as dark as pitch—but if you could have seen the gravity with which I was committing her to the waves—thinking all the time of something or other not to the purpose;—I always forget that the streets are canals—and was going to walk her over the water —if the servants & the Gondoliers had not awakened me.——So much for love & all that.——The music here is famous—and there will be a whole tribe of singers & dancers during the Carnival—besides the usual theatres.—The Society here is something like our own—except that the women sit in a semicircle at one end of the room—& the men stand at the other.—I pass my mornings at the Armenian convent studying Armenian. My evenings here & there—tonight I am going to the Countess Albrizzi's—one of the noblesse—I have also been at the Governor's—who is an Austrian—& whose wife the Countess Goetz appeared to me in the little I have seen of her a very amiable & pleasing woman—with remarkably good manners—as many of the German women have.——There are no English here—except birds of passage—who stay a day & then go on to Florence—or Rome.—I mean to remain here till Spring.—When you write address *directly* here—as in your present letter.—

ever dearest yrs.
B

[TO THOMAS MOORE]   *Venice, December 24th, 1816*

I have taken a fit of writing to you, which portends postage—once from Verona—once from Venice, and again from Venice—*thrice* that is. For this you may thank yourself, for I heard that you complained of my silence—so, here goes for garrulity.

I trust that you received my other twain of letters. My "way of life"[1] (or "May of life," which is it, according to the commentators?) —my "way of life" is fallen into great regularity. In the mornings I go over in my gondola to babble Armenian with the friars of the convent of St. Lazarus, and to help one of them in correcting the English of an English and Armenian grammar which he is publishing. In the evenings I do one of many nothings—either at the theatres, or some of the conversaziones, which are like our routs, or rather worse, for the women sit in a semicircle by the lady of the mansion, and the men stand about the room. To be sure, there is one improvement upon ours—instead of lemonade with their ices, they hand about stiff *rum-punch—punch*, by my palate; and this they think *English*. I would not disabuse them of so agreeable an error,—"no, not for Venice".[2]

Last night I was at the Count Governor's, which, of course, comprises the best society, and is very much like other gregarious meetings in every country,—as in ours,—except that, instead of the Bishop of Winchester, you have the Patriarch of Venice, and a motley crew of

[1] *Macbeth*, Act V, scene 3.
[2] *Merchant of Venice*, Act IV, scene 1.

Austrians, Germans, noble Venetians, foreigners and, if you see a quiz, you may be sure he is a Consul. Oh, by the way, I forgot, when I wrote from Verona, to tell you that at Milan I met with a countryman of yours—a Colonel [Fitzgerald], a very excellent, good-natured fellow, who knows and shows all about Milan, and is, as it were, a native there. He is particularly civil to strangers, and this is his history,—at least, an episode of it.

Six-and-twenty years ago, Col. [Fitzgerald], than an ensign, being in Italy, fell in love with the Marchesa [Castiglione], and she with him. The lady must be, at least, twenty years his senior. The war broke out; he returned to England, to serve—not his country, for that's Ireland—but England, which is a different thing; and *she*— heaven knows what she did. In the year 1814, the first annunciation of the Definitive Treaty of Peace (and tyranny) was developed to the astonished Milanese by the arrival of Col. [Fitzgerald], who, flinging himself full length at the feet of Mad. [Castiglione], murmured forth, in half-forgotten Irish Italian, eternal vows of indelible constancy. The lady screamed, and exclaimed, "Who are you?" The Colonel cried, "What! don't you know me? I am so and so," &c., &c., &c.; till, at length, the Marchesa, mounting from reminiscence to reminiscence through the lovers of the intermediate twenty-five years, arrived at last at the recollection of her *povero* sub-lieutenant. She then said, "Was there ever such virtue?" (that was her very word) and, being now a widow, gave him apartments in her palace, reinstated him in all the rights of wrong, and held him up to the admiring world as a miracle of incontinent fidelity, and the unshaken Abdiel of absence.

Methinks this is as pretty a moral tale as any of Marmontel's. Here is another. The same lady, several years ago, made an escapade with a Swede, Count Fersen (the same whom the Stockholm mob quartered and lapidated not very long since), and they arrived at an Osteria on the road to Rome or thereabouts. It was a summer evening, and, while they were at supper, they were suddenly regaled by a symphony of fiddles in an adjacent apartment, so prettily played, that, wishing to hear them more distinctly, the Count rose, and going into the musical society, said, "Gentlemen, I am sure that, as a company of gallant cavaliers, you will be delighted to show your skill to a lady, who feels anxious," &c., &c. The men of harmony were all acquiescence—every instrument was tuned and toned, and, striking up one of their most ambrosial airs, the whole band followed the Count to the lady's apartment. At their head was the first fiddler, who, bowing and fiddling at the same moment, headed his troop and advanced up the room. Death and discord!—it was the Marquis himself, who was on a serenading party in the country, while his spouse had run away from town. The rest may be imagined—but, first of all, the lady tried to persuade him that she was there on purpose to meet him, and had chosen this method for an harmonic surprise. So much for this gossip, which amused me when I heard it, and I send it to you in the hope it may have the like effect. Now we'll return to Venice.

The day after to-morrow (to-morrow being Christmas-day) the Carnival begins. I dine with the Countess Albrizzi and a party, and go to the opera. On that day the Phenix, (not the Insurance Office, but) the theatre of that name, opens: I have got me a box there for the season, for two reasons, one of which is, that the music is remarkably good. The Contessa Albrizzi, of whom I have made mention, is the De Stael of Venice; not young, but a very learned, unaffected, good-natured woman; very polite to strangers, and, I believe not at all dissolute, as most of the women are. She has written very well on the works of Canova, and also a volume of Characters, besides other printed matter. She is of Corfu, but married a dead Venetian—that is, dead since he married.

My flame (my "Donna" whom I spoke of in my former epistle, my Marianna) is still my Marianna, and I her—what she pleases. She is by far the prettiest woman I have seen here, and the most loveable I have met with any where—as well as one of the most singular. I believe I told you the rise and progress of our *liaison* in my former letter. Lest that should not have reached you, I will merely repeat, that she is a Venetian, two-and-twenty years old, married to a merchant well to do in the world, and that she has great black oriental eyes, and all the qualities which her eyes promise. Whether being in love with her has steeled me or not, I do not know; but I have not seen many other women who seem pretty. The nobility, in particular, are a sad-looking race—the gentry rather better. And now, what art *thou* doing?

> What are you doing now,
>   Oh Thomas Moore?
> What are you doing now,
>   Oh Thomas Moore?
> Sighing or suing now,
> Rhyming or wooing now,
> Billing or cooing now,
>   Which, Thomas Moore?

Are you not near the Luddites? By the Lord! if there's a row, but I'll be among ye! How go on the weavers—the breakers of frames—the Lutherans of politics—the reformers?

> As the Liberty lads o'er the sea
> Bought their freedom, and cheaply, with blood,
>> So we, boys, we
>> Will *die* fighting, or *live* free,
> And down with all kings but King Ludd!
>
> When the web that we weave is complete,
> And the shuttle exchanged for the sword,
>> We will fling the winding-sheet
>> O'er the despot at our feet,
> And dye it deep in the gore he has pour'd.
>
> Though black as his heart its hue,
> Since his veins are corrupted to mud,
>> Yet this is the dew
>> Which the tree shall renew
> Of Liberty, planted by Ludd!

There's an amiable *chanson* for you—all impromptu. I have written it principally to shock your neighbour * * [Hodgson?], who is all clergy and loyalty—mirth and innocence—milk and water.

> But the Carnival's coming,
>> Oh Thomas Moore,
> The Carnival's coming,
>> Oh Thomas Moore,
>
> Masking and humming,
> Fifing and drumming,
> Guitarring and strumming,
>> Oh Thomas Moore.

The other night I saw a new play,—and the author. The subject was the sacrifice of Isaac. The play succeeded, and they called for the author—according to continental custom—and he presented himself, a noble Venetian, Mali—or Malapiero, by name. Mala was his name, and *pessima* his production,—at least, I thought so; and I ought to know, having read more or less of five hundred Drury Lane offerings, during my coadjutorship with the sub-and-super Committee.

When does your Poem of Poems come out? I hear that the E[*dinburgh*] R[*eview*] has cut up Coleridge's Christabel, and declared against me for praising it.[3] I praised it, firstly, because I thought well of it; secondly, because Coleridge was in great distress, and after doing what little I could for him in essentials, I thought that the public avowal of my good opinion might help him further, at least with the booksellers. I am very sorry that J[effrey] has attacked him, because, poor fellow, it will hurt him in mind and pocket. As for me, he's welcome—I shall never think less of J[effrey] for any thing he may say against me or mine in future.

I suppose Murray has sent you, or will send (for I do not know whether they are out or no) the poem, or poesies, of mine, of last summer. By the mass! they're sublime—"Ganion Coheriza"[4]—gainsay who dares! Pray, let me hear from you, and of you, and, at least, let me know that you have received these three letters. Direct right *here, poste restante.*

Ever and ever, &c.

P.S.—I heard the other day of a pretty trick of a bookseller, who has published some d[amne]d nonsense, swearing the bastards to me, and saying he gave me five hundred guineas for them. He lies—I never wrote such stuff, never saw the poems, nor the publisher of them, in my life, nor had any communication, directly or indirectly, with the fellow. Pray say as much for me, if need be. I have written to Murray, to make him contradict the imposter.

[TO JOHN MURRAY]   *Venice.—January 2d. 1817*

My dear Sir.—Your letter has arrived.—Pray—in publishing the 3d. Canto—have you *omitted* any passage or passages?—I hope *not*—and indeed wrote to you on my way over the Alps to prevent such an accident—say in your next whether or not the *whole* of the Canto (as sent to you) has been published.————I wrote to you again the other day (*twice* I think—) and shall be glad to hear of the reception of these letters.—To day is the 2d. January—on this day *3* years ago the Corsair's publication is dated I think in my letter to Moore—on this day *two* years I married—"Whom the Lord loveth he chasteneth—blessed be *the* name of the Lord!"—I shan't forget the day in a hurry—& will take care to keep the anniversary before the Evening is over.——It is odd enough that I this day received a letter from you

---

[3] Byron praised *Christabel* in a note to *The Siege of Corinth* (line 522).
[4] The motto of the Macdonalds, chiefs of Clanranald.

announcing the publication of C[hil]d H[arol]d on the day of the date of "the Corsair—and that I also received one from my Sister written on the *10th.* of Decr. my daughter's birth-day (and relative chiefly to my daughter) & arriving on the day of the date of my marriage—this present 2d. [of] January the month of my birth and various other Astrologous matters which I have no time to enumerate.—By the way —you might as well write to Hentsch my Genevese Banker—and enquire whether the *two packets* consigned to his care—were or were not delivered to Mr. St. Aubyn—or if they are still in his keeping.— One contains papers, letters & all the original M.S. of your 3d Canto —as first conceived—& the other—some bones from the field of Morat.——Many thanks for your news—& the good Spirits in which your letter is written.——Venice & I agree very well—but I do not know that I have any thing new to say—except of the last new Opera —which I sent in my last letter.—The Carnival is commencing—and there is a good deal of fun here & there—besides business—for all the world are making up their intrigues for the season—changing—or going on upon a renewed lease.—I am very well off with Marianna who is not at all a person to tire me—firstly because I do not tire of a woman *personally*—but because they are generally bores in their disposition—& secondly—because she is amiable & has a tact which is not always the portion of the fair creation—& 3dly she is very pretty—& 4thly—but there is no occasion for further specification.— I have passed a great deal of my time with her since my arrival at Venice—and never a twenty-four hours—without giving and receiving from one to three (and occasionally an extra or so) pretty unequivocal proofs of mutual good contentment.—So far we have gone on very well—as to the future I never anticipate—"Carpe diem" the past at least is one's own—which is one reason for making sure of the present. ——So much for my proper liaison.—The general state of morals here is much the same as in the Doge's time—a woman is virtuous (according to the code) who limits herself to her husband and one lover—those who have two three or more are a little *wild*;—but it is only those who are indiscriminately diffuse—and form a low connection —such as the Princess of Wales with her Courier (who by the way is made a Knight of Malta) who are considered as overstepping the modesty of marriage.—In Venice—the Nobility have a trick of marrying with dancers or singers—& truth to say—the women of their own order are by no means handsome—but the general race—the women of the 2d & other orders—the wives of the Advocates—mer-chants & proprietors—& untitled gentry are mostly "bel' sangue" and it is with these that the more amatory connections are usually formed —there are also instances of stupendous constancy—I know a woman of fifty who never had but one lover who dying early—she became devout—renouncing all but her husband—she piques herself as may be presumed upon this miraculous fidelity—talking of it occasionally with a species of misplaced morality—which is rather amusing.—There is no convincing a woman here—that she is in the smallest degree deviating from the rule of right or the fitness of things—in having an "Amoroso". The great sin seems to lie in concealing it—or in having more than one—that is—unless such an extension of the prerogative is understood & approved of by the prior claimant.—In my case—I do not know that I had any predecessor—& am pretty sure that there is no participator—& am inclined to think from the youth of the party—& from the frank undisguised way in which every body avows everything in this part of the world—when there is any thing to avow—as well as from some other circumstances—such as the marriage being recent &c &c—that this is the "premier pas"—it does not much signify.———In another sheet I send you some sheets of a grammar English & Armenian for the use of the Armenians—of which I promoted & indeed induced the publication; (it cost me but a thousand francs of French livres) I still pursue my lessons in the language—without any rapid progress—but advancing a little daily— Padre Paschal—with some little help from me as a translator of his Italian into English—is also proceeding in an M.S. grammar for the *English* acquisition of Armenian—which will be printed also when finished.—We want to know if there are any *Armenian types* or letter-press in England—at Oxford—Cambridge or elsewhere?—You know I suppose that many years ago the two Whistons[1] published in England an original text of a history of Armenia with their own Latin trans-lation.—Do these types still exist? & where.—Pray enquire among your learned acquaintance.—When this grammar—(I mean the one now printing) is done will you have any objection to take 40 or fifty copies which will not cost in all above five or ten guineas—& try the curiosity of the learned with the sale of them.—Say yes or no as you like.—I can assure you that they have some very curious books & M.S. chiefly translations from Greek originals now lost.—They are besides a much respected and learned community & the study of their language was taken up with great ardour by some literary Frenchmen in

---

[1] John Whiston (d. 1780), son of William Whiston (1667–1752), a divine whose unorthodox Newtonian views caused the loss of his Cambridge professor-ship. The younger Whiston was a bookseller in Fleet Street.

Buonaparte's time.—I have not done a stitch of poetry since I left Switzerland—& have not at present the *"estro"* upon me—the truth is that you are *afraid* of having a *4th.* Canto *before* September—& of another copyright—but I have at present no thoughts of resuming that poem nor of beginning any other.—If I write—I think of trying prose —but I dread introducing living people or applications which might be made to living people—perhaps one day or other—I may attempt some work of fancy in prose—descriptive of Italian manners & of human passions—but at present I am preoccupied.—As for poesy—mine is the *dream* of my sleeping Passions—when they are awake—I cannot speak their language—only in their Somnambulism.—& Just now they are dormant.———If Mr. G[ifford] wants Carte blanche as to the "Siege of Corinth"—he has it—& may do as he likes with it.—I sent you a letter contradictory of the Cheapside man—(who invented the story you speak of) the other day.—My best respects to Mr. Gifford —& such of my friends as you may see at your house.—I wish you all prosperity & new years gratulation & I am

Yrs ever & truly

B

[TO DOUGLAS KINNAIRD]   *Venice—January 20th. 1817*

My dear Kinnaird—Your letter and its contents (viz. the circulars & indication for £500) are safely arrived—thanks———I have been up all night at the Opera—& at the Ridotto & it's Masquerade—and the devil knows what—so that my head aches a little—but to business.— —My affairs ought to be in a small compass—if Newstead were sold they would be settled without difficulty—and if Newstead & Rochdale both were sold—I should think with ease—but till one or both of these are disposed of—they are in a very unpleasant situation.—It is for this reason I so much urge a sale—even at almost any price.— With regard to Hanson—I know not how to act—& I know not what to think—except that I think he wishes me well—it is certainly not his fault that Claughton could not fulfil the conditions of sale.—— Mr. Riley[1] has reason—but he must really wait till something can be done about the property—if he likes he may proceed against *it,*—but as to the produce of my *brain*—my M. S.—my Night mare is my own personalty—& by the Lord as I have earned the sum—so will I

---

[1] Unidentified. It is apparent that he was one of Byron's creditors.

expend it upon my own proper pleasances—voyagings & what not—
so that I request that you will *not* disburse a ducat save to *me* the
owner.—You do not say a word about the publication itself—from
which I infer that it has failed—if so—you may tell me at once—on
Murray's account rather than on mine—for I am not to be perturbed
by such matters at this time of day—as the fall of the thermometer of a
poetical reputation—but I should be sorry for M[urray] who is a very
good fellow.——However—as with one thing or another—he—
Murray must have cleared on the whole account—dating from the
commencement—I feel less anxious for him than I otherwise should.
—Your quotation from Shakespeare—humph—I believe that it is
applied by Othello to his *wife*—who by the way was *innocent*—the
Moor made a mistake—& so have you.——My desire that Murray
should pay in the agreement will not appear singular—when you
recollect that the time has elapsed within a few days when three
quarters of the whole were to have been disbursed by him.——
Since my departure from England I have not spent (in nine months)
within some hundreds of two thousand pounds so that neither my
pleasures nor my perils—when you consider the ground I have gone
over & that I had a physician (now gone thank heaven) to fee & feed
out of it—a very extravagant silly gentleman he was into the bargain.
——By the way—I should wish to know if Hanson has been able to
collect *any rent* at all (but little it can be in these times) from
N[ewstead]—if he has & there be any balance—it may also come to me
in the shape of circulars—the time is also approaching when—there
will be something due from that magnificent father *at* law of mine—
Sir R[alph] N[oel]—from whom I expect punctuality—& am not
disposed to remit him any of his remaining duties—let him keep to his
time—even in trifles.——You tell me Shelley's wife has drowned
herself—the devil she has—do you mean his *wife*—or his Mistress?—
Mary Godwin?—I hope not the last—I am very sorry to hear of anything which can plague poor Shelley—besides I feel uneasy about
another of his *menage.*—You know—& I believe saw once that odd-
headed girl—who introduced herself to me shortly before I left
England—but you do not know—that I found her with Shelley & her
sister at Geneva—I never loved nor pretended to love her—but a man
is a man—& if a girl of eighteen comes prancing to you at all hours—
there is but one way—the suite of all this is that she was with *child*—
& returned to England to assist in peopling that desolate island.—
Whether this impregnation took place before I left England or since—
I do not know—the (carnal) connection had commenced previously

to my setting out—but by or about this time she has—or is about to produce.—The next question is is the brat *mine?*—I have reason to think so—for I know as much as one can know such a thing—that she had *not lived* with S[helley] during the time of our acquaintance—& that she had a good deal of that same with me.—This comes of "putting it about" (as Jackson calls it) & be damned to it—and thus people come into the world.———So you wish me to come to England— why? for what?—my affairs—I wish they could be settled without—I repeat that your country is no country for me.—I have neither ambition nor taste for your politics—and there is nothing else among you which may not be had better elsewhere.—Besides—Caroline Lamb—& Lady B[yron]—my "Lucy" & my "Polly" have destroyed my *moral* existence amongst you—& I am rather sick of being the theme of their mutual inventions—in ten years I could unteach myself even to your language—& am very sure that—but I have no time nor space for further tirade at present—

ever yrs. very truly
B

P.S.—Pray write soon.——

Venice & I agree very well—in the mornings I study Armenian— & in the evenings I go out sometimes—& indulge in coition always. ——I mentioned my liaison to you in a former letter—it still con- tinues—& probably will—It has however kept me here instead of gadabouting the country.—The Carnival is begun—but the zenith of the masking will not arrive for some weeks.—There is a famous Opera—& several theatres—Catalani is to be here on the 20th— Society is like other foreign society—I see as much of it as I wish—& might see more if I liked it.—

ever yrs. most truly
B

P.S.—My respects to *Madame*—pray answer my letters—& mention anything or everything except my—*family*—I will say— for the other word makes me unwell.——

[TO THOMAS MOORE]   *Venice, February 28th, 1817*

You will, perhaps, complain as much of the frequency of my letters now, as you were wont to do of their rarity. I think this is the fourth within as many moons. I feel anxious to hear from you, even more than usual, because your last indicated that you were unwell. At present, I am on the invalid regimen myself. The Carnival—that is, the latter part of it—and sitting up late o'nights, had knocked me up a little. But it is over,—and it is now Lent, with all its abstinence and Sacred Music.

The mumming closed with a masked ball at the Fenice, where I went, as also to most of the ridottos, etc., etc.; and, though I did not dissipate much upon the whole, yet I find "the sword wearing out the scabbard," though I have but just turned the corner of twenty-nine.

> So we'll go no more a roving
> So late into the night,
> Though the heart be still as loving,
> And the moon be still as bright.
>
> For the sword outwears its sheath,
> And the soul wears out the breast,
> And the heart must pause to breathe,
> And Love itself have rest.
>
> Though the night was made for loving,
> And the day returns too soon,
> Yet we'll go no more a roving
> By the light of the moon.

I have lately had some news of litter*atoor*. as I heard the editor of the Monthly pronounce it once upon a time. I hear that W. W.[1] has been publishing and responding to the attacks of the Quarterly, in the learned Perry's Chronicle. I read his poesies last autumn, and amongst them found an epitaph on his bull-dog, and another on *myself*. But I beg to assure him (like the astrologer Partridge) that I am not only alive now but was alive also at the time he wrote it. * * * * Hobhouse has (I hear, also) expectorated a letter against the Quarterly, addressed to me. I feel awkwardly situated between him and Gifford, both being my friends.

And this is your month of going to press—by the body of Diana! (a Venetian oath,) I feel as anxious—but not fearful for you—as if it were myself coming out in a work of humour, which would, you know, be the antipodes of all my previous publications. I don't think you have any thing to dread but your own reputation. You must keep up

---

[1] Wedderburn Webster.

to that. As you never showed me a line of your work, I do not even know your measure; but you must send me a copy by Murray forthwith, and then you shall hear what I think. I dare say you are in a pucker. Of all authors, you are the only really *modest* one I ever met with,—which would sound oddly enough to those who recollect your morals when you were young—that is, when you were *extremely* young— I don't mean to stigmatise you either with years or morality.

I believe I told you that the E[dinburgh] R[eview] had attacked me, in an article on Coleridge (I have not seen it)—"*Et tu,* Jeffrey?"— "there is nothing but roguery in villanous man."[2] But I absolve him of all attacks, present and future; for I think he had already pushed his clemency in my behoof to the utmost, and I shall always think well of him. I only wonder he did not begin before, as my domestic destruction was a fine opening for all the world, of which all, who could, did well to avail themselves.

If I live ten years longer, you will see, however, that it is not over with me—I don't mean in literature, for that is nothing; and it may seem odd enough to say, I do not think it my vocation. But you will see that I will do something or other—the times and fortune permitting —that, "like the cosmogony, or creation of the world, will puzzle the philosophers of all ages."[3] But I doubt whether my constitution will hold out. I have, at intervals, ex*orc*ised it most devilishly.

I have not yet fixed a time of return, but I think of the spring. I shall have been away a year in April next. You never mention Rogers, nor Hodgson, your clerical neighbour, who has lately got a living near you. Has he also got a child yet?—his desideratum, when I saw him last.
* * * * * * * *
Pray let me hear from you, at your time and leisure, believing me ever and truly and affectionately, &c.

[TO THOMAS MOORE] *Venice, April 11th, 1817*

I shall continue to write to you while the fit is on me, by way of penance upon you for your former complaints of long silence. I dare say you would blush, if you could, for not answering. Next week I set out for Rome. Having seen Constantinople, I should like to look at t'other fellow. Besides, I want to see the Pope, and shall take care to tell him that I vote for the Catholics and no Veto.

[2] *Henry IV, Part I*, Act II, scene 4.
[3] *Vicar of Wakefield*, Chapter XIV.

I sha'n't go to Naples. It is but the second best sea-view, and I have seen the first and third, viz. Constantinople and Lisbon (by the way, the last is but a river-view; however, they reckon it after Stamboul and Naples, and before Genoa), and Vesuvius is silent, and I have passed by Ætna. So I shall e'en return to Venice in July; and if you write, I pray you to address to Venice, which is my head, or rather my *heart*-quarters.

My late physician, Dr. Polidori, is here on his way to England, with the present Lord G[uilford] and the widow of the late earl.[1] Dr. Polidori has, just now, no more patients, because his patients are no more. He had lately three, who are now all dead—one embalmed. Horner and a child of Thomas Hope's are interred at Pisa and Rome. Lord G[uilford] died of an inflammation of the bowels: so they took them out, and sent them (on account of their discrepancies), separately from the carcass, to England. Conceive a man going one way, and his intestines another, and his immortal soul a third!—was there ever such a distribution? One certainly has a soul; but how it came to allow itself to be enclosed in a body is more than I can imagine. I only know if once mine gets out, I'll have a bit of a tussle before I let it get in again to that or any other.

And so poor dear Mr. Maturin's second tragedy has been neglected by the discerning public! [Sotheby] will be d—d glad of this, and d—d without being glad, if ever his own plays come upon "any stage."

I wrote to Rogers the other day, with a message for you. I hope that he flourishes. He is the Tithonus of poetry—immortal already.—You and I must wait for it.

I hear nothing—know nothing. You may easily suppose that the English don't seek me, and I avoid them. To be sure, there are but few or none here, save passengers. Florence and Naples are their Margate and Ramsgate, and much the same sort of company too, by all accounts,—which hurts us among the Italians.

I want to hear of Lalla Rookh—are you out? Death and fiends! why don't you tell me where you are, what you are, and how you are? I shall go to Bologna by Ferrara, instead of Mantua: because I would rather see the cell where they caged Tasso, and where he became mad and * *, than his own MSS. at Modena, or the Mantuan birthplace of that harmonious plagiary and miserable flatterer,[2] whose cursed hexa-

1 Francis North, second son of Lord North, George III's Prime Minister succeeded his elder brother as the 4th Earl of Guilford in 1802. He died in Pisa in 1817, and was succeeded by his younger brother Frederick.
2 Virgil was born near Mantua.

meters were drilled into me at Harrow. I saw Verona and Vicenza on my way here—Padua too.

I go *alone*,—but *alone*, because I mean to return here. I only want to see Rome. I have not the least curiosity about Florence, though I must see it for the sake of the Venus, &c., &c.; and I wish also to see the Fall of Terni, I think to return to Venice by Ravenna and Rimini, of both of which I mean to take notes for Leigh Hunt, who will be glad to hear of the scenery of his Poem. There was a devil of a review of him in the Quarterly, a year ago, which he answered. All answers are imprudent: but to be sure, poetical flesh and blood must have the last word—that's certain. I thought, and think, very highly of his Poem; but I warned him of the row his favourite antique phraseology would bring him into.

You have taken a house at Hornsey: I had much rather you had taken one in the Apennines. If you think of coming out for a summer, or so, tell me, that I may be upon the hover for you.

Ever, &c.

[TO JOHN MURRAY] *Venice May 30th 1817*

Dear Sir—I returned from Rome two days ago—& have received your letter but no sign nor tidings of the parcel sent through Sir—— Stuart[1] which you mention;—after an interval of months a packet of "Tales," &c. found me at Rome—but this is all—& may be all that ever will find me—the post seems to be the only sane conveyance—& *that only for letters.*—From Florence I sent you a poem on Tasso— and from Rome the new third act of "Manfred," & by Dr. Polidori two pictures for my sister. I left Rome & made a rapid journey home. —You will continue to direct here as usual.—Mr. Hobhouse is gone to Naples—I should have run down there too for a week—but for the quantity of English whom I heard of there—I prefer hating them at a distance—unless an Earthquake or a good real eruption of Vesuvius were insured to reconcile me to their vicinity.—I know no other situation except Hell which I should feel inclined to participate with them—as a race—always excepting several individuals.—There were few of them in Rome—& I believe none whom you know—except that old Blue-*bore* Sotheby—who will give a fine account of Italy in which

[1] Sir Charles Stuart (1779–1845) held various diplomatic posts.

he will be greatly assisted by his total ignorance of Italian—& yet this is the translator of Tasso.—The day before I left Rome I saw three robbers guillotined—the ceremony—including the *masqued* priests—the half-naked executioners—the bandaged criminals—the black Christ & his banner—the scaffold—the soldiery—the slow procession —& the quick rattle and heavy fall of the axe—the splash of the blood —& the ghastliness of the exposed heads—is altogether more impressive than the vulgar and ungentlemanly dirty "new drop" & dog-like agony of infliction upon the sufferers of the English sentence. Two of these men—behaved calmly enough—but the first of the three—died with great terror and reluctance—which was very horrible—he would not lie down—then his neck was too large for the aperture—and the priest was obliged to drown his exclamations by still louder exhortations—the head was off before the eye could trace the blow—but from an attempt to draw back the head—notwithstanding it was held forward by the hair—the first head was cut off close to the ears—the other two were taken off more cleanly;—it is better than the Oriental way—& (I should think) than the axe of our ancestors.—The pain seems little —& yet the effect to the spectator—& the preparation to the criminal —is very striking & chilling.—The first turned me quite hot and thirsty—& made me shake so that I could hardly hold the opera-glass (I was close—but was determined to see—as one should see every thing once—with attention) the second and third (which shows how dreadfully soon things grow indifferent) I am ashamed to say had no effect on me—as a horror—though I would have saved them if I could.———It is some time since I heard from you—the *12th April* I believe.—

yrs. ever truly,
B

[TO AUGUSTA LEIGH]   *Venice.—June 3d.–4th. 1817*

Dearest Augusta—I returned home a few days ago from Rome—but wrote to you on the road—at Florence I believe—or Bologna—the last city you know—or do not know—is celebrated for the production of Popes—Cardinals—painters—& sausages—besides a female professor of anatomy—who has left there many models of the art in waxwork—some of them not the most decent.—I have received all your letters—I believe—which are full of woes—as usual—megrims & mysteries—but my sympathies remain in suspense—for—for the life of me I can't make out whether your disorder is a broken heart or the ear-ache—or whether it is *you* that have been ill or the children—or what your melancholy—& mysterious apprehensions tend to—or refer to—whether to Caroline Lamb's novels—Mrs Clermont's[1] evidence—Lady Byron's magnanimity—or any other piece of imposture;—I know nothing of what you are in the doldrums about at present—I should think—all that could affect *you*—must have been over long ago—& as for me—leave me to take care of myself—I may be ill or well—in high or low spirits—in quick or obtuse state of feelings—like every body else—but I can battle my way through—better than your exquisite piece of helplessness G[eorge] L[eigh] or that other poor creature George Byron[2]—who will be finely helped up in a year or two with his new state of life—I should like to know what they would do in my situation—or in any situation—I wish well to your George—who is the best of the two a devilish deal—but as for the other I shan't forget him in a hurry—& if ever I forgive or allow an opportunity to escape of evincing my sense of his conduct (& of more than his) on a certain occasion—write me down—what you will —but do not suppose me asleep—"let them look to their bond"—sooner or later time & Nemesis will give me the ascendant—& then "let them look to their bond." I do not of course allude only to that poor wretch—but to all—to the 3d. & 4th. generations of these accursed Amalekites—& the woman who has been the stumbling block of my—

June 4th. 1817

I left off yesterday at the stumbling block of my Midianite marriage—but having received your letter of the 20th. May—I will be in good humour for the rest of this letter.—I had hoped you would like the miniatures at least one of them—which is in pretty good health—the other is thin enough to be sure—& so was I—& in the ebb of a fever when I sate for it.—By the "man of fashion" I suppose you mean that poor piece of affectation and imitation Wilmot[3]—another disgrace to me & mine—that fellow. I regret not having shot him—which the persuasions of others—& circumstances which at that time would

---

[1] Mary Anne Clermont was Lady Noel's trusted maid, who had been with her at the time of Annabella's birth and after, and then returned as governess and confidante. Byron, probably not wrongly, ascribed to her Lady Byron's intransigence during the separation and afterward.

[2] Byron's cousin and heir who took the part of Lady Byron in the separation dispute.

[3] Robert John Wilmot was Byron's first cousin, being the son of Byron's father's sister Juliana. He was tactless and far from impartial as a mediator in the Byron separation, and later had a hand in the burning of Byron's Memoirs.

have rendered combats presumptions against my cause—prevented.—
I wish you well of your indispositions which I hope are slight—or I
should lose my senses—

yours ever & very truly

B

[TO JOHN MURRAY]
La Mira—Near Venice—August 21st. 1817

Dear Sir—I take you at your word about Mr. Hanson—& will feel
obliged if you will *go* to him—& request Mr. Davies also to visit him
by my desire—& repeat that I trust that neither Mr. Kinnaird's
absence nor mine will prevent his taking all proper steps to accelerate
and promote the sales of Newstead and Rochdale—upon which the
whole of my future personal comfort depends—it is impossible for me
to express how much any delays upon these points would inconvenience
me—& I do not know a greater obligation that can be conferred upon
me than the pressing these things upon Hanson—& making him act
according to my wishes.—I wish you would *speak out* at least to *me* &
tell me what you allude to by your odd way of mentioning him—all
mysteries at such a distance are not merely tormenting—but mischievous—& may be prejudicial to my interests—so pray—expound—
that I may consult with Mr. Kinnaird when he arrives—& remember
that I prefer the most disagreeable certainties to hints & inuendoes—
the devil take every body—I never can get any person to be explicit
about any thing—or any body—& my whole life is past in conjectures
of what people mean—you all talk in the style of Caroline Lamb's
novels.———It is not Mr. St. John—but *Mr. St. Aubyn*, Son of Sir
John St. Aubyn.—*Polidori* knows him—& introduced him to me—he is
of Oxford—& has got my parcel—the Doctor will ferret him out or
ought.—The Parcel contains many letters—some of Madame de
Stael's and other people's—besides M.S.S., &c.—By G—d—if I find
the gentleman & he don't find the parcel—I will say something he
won't like to hear.—You want a "civil and delicate declension"[1] for
the medical tragedy? Take it—

Dear Doctor—I have read your play

Which is a good one in it's way

---

[1] Murray had written to Byron, Aug. 5, 1817: "Polidori has sent me his
tragedy! Do me the kindness to send by return of post a *delicate* declension of it,
which I engage faithfully to copy."

Purges the eyes & moves the bowels
And drenches handkerchiefs like towels
With tears that in a flux of Grief
Afford hysterical relief
To shatter'd nerves & quickened pulses
Which your catastrophe convulses.
I like your moral & machinery
Your plot too has such scope for Scenery!
Your dialogue is apt & smart
The play's concoction full of art—
Your hero raves—your heroine cries
All stab—& every body dies;
In short your tragedy would be
The very thing to hear & see—
And for a piece of publication
If I decline on this occasion
It is not that I am not sensible
To merits in themselves ostensible
But—and I grieve to speak it—plays
Are drugs—mere drugs, Sir, nowadays—
I had a heavy loss by "Manuel"—[2]
Too lucky if it prove not annual—
And Sotheby with his damned "Orestes"
(Which by the way the old Bore's best is,)
Has lain so very long on hand
That I despair of all demand—
I've advertized—but see my books—
Or only watch my Shopman's looks—
Still Ivan—Ina[3] & such lumber
My back shop glut—my shelves encumber.—
There's Byron—too—who once did better
Has sent me—folded in a letter—
A sort of—it's no more a drama[4]
Than Darnley—Ivan—or Kehama[5]—
So altered since last year his pen is—
I think he's lost his wits at Venice—

[2] Maturin's tragedy was produced at Drury Lane March 8, 1817, with Kean in the title role, but it failed. Murray published it as he had Maturin's successfu play Bertram.

[3] Mrs. Wilmot's tragedy.

[4] Manfred.

[5] Darnley and Ivan by Sotheby; Kehama by Southey.

Or drained his brains away as Stallion
To some dark-eyed & warm Italian;
In short—Sir—what with one & t'other
I dare not venture on another—
I write in haste, excuse each blunder
The Coaches through the Street so thunder.
My Room's so full—we've Gifford here
Reading M.S.S.—with Hookham Frere
Pronouncing on the nouns & particles
Of some of our forthcoming articles,
The Quarterly—Ah Sir! if you
Had but the Genius to review—
A smart Critique upon St. Helena
Or if you only would but tell in a
Short compass what—but, to resume
As I was saying—Sir—the Room—
The Room's so full of wits & bards—
Crabbes—Campbells—Crokers—Freres—& Wards,
And others neither bards nor wits;
My humble tenement admits
All persons in the dress of Gent.
From Mr. Hammond[6] to Dog Dent.[7]
A party dines with me today
All clever men who make their way,[8]
They're at this moment in discussion
On poor De Stael's late dissolution—
"Her book they say was in advance—
Pray Heaven! she tell the truth of France,[9]
'Tis said she certainly was married
To Rocca—& had twice miscarried,
No—not miscarried—I opine—
But brought to bed at forty-nine,
Some say she died a Papist—Some
Are of opinion *that's* a Hum—

[6] George Hammond (1763–1853) was a diplomatist and one time Under-Secretary of State for Foreign Affairs. Byron had met him at Murray's.

[7] John Dent, M.P., banker, was nicknamed "Dog Dent" because of his concern for the Dog-tax bill in 1796.

[8] Byron subsequently added two lines here: "Crabbe, Malcolm, Hamilton and Chantrye, / Are all partakers of my pantry."

[9] Madame de Staël's *Considérations sur la Révolution Française* was offered to Murray for £4,000, but before an agreement was reached she died (July 14, 1817). The book was published by Baldwin and Cradock.

I don't know that—the fellow Schlegel[10]
Was very likely to inveigle
A dying person in compunction
To try the extremity of Unction.—
But peace be with her—for a woman
Her talents surely were uncommon.
Her Publisher (& Public too)
The hour of her demise may rue—
For never more within his shop he—
Pray—was not she interred at Coppet?["]
Thus run our time and tongues away—
But to return Sir—to your play—
Sorry—Sir—but I can not deal—
Unless 'twere acted by O'Neill[11]—
My hands are full—my head so busy—
I'm almost dead—& always dizzy—
And so with endless truth & hurry—
Dear Doctor—I am yours

John Murray.

P.S.—I've done the 4th & last Canto—which mounts 133 Stanzas.—
I desire you to name a price—if you don't—*I* will—so I advise you in
time.

yrs.

there will be a good many notes.

[TO JOHN MURRAY]   *Sept 15th. 1817*

Dear Sir—I enclose a sheet for correction if ever you get to another
edition—you will observe that the blunder in printing makes it appear
as if the Chateau was *over* St. Gingo—instead of being on the opposite
shore of the lake over Clarens—so—separate the paragraphs otherwise
my *top*ography will seems as inaccurate as your *typ*ography on this
occasion.[1]——The other day I wrote to convey my proposition with
regard to the 4th & concluding Canto—I have gone over—& extended it to one hundred and fifty stanzas which is almost as long as

[10] August Wilhelm von Schlegel (1767–1845) was a frequenter of Madame de
Staël's salon at Coppet. He and Byron did not like each other. Byron attributed
Schlegel's dislike to the fact that he (Byron) would not flatter him.
[11] Miss Eliza O'Neil was a leading actress at Drury Lane, taking the place of
Mrs. Siddons in tragic parts.
[1] Byron here refers to the third canto of *Childe Harold*.

166

the two first were originally—& longer by itself—than any of the smaller poems except the "Corsair"—Mr. Hobhouse has made some very valuable & accurate notes of considerable length—& you may be sure I will do for the text all that I can to finish with decency.—I look upon C[hild]e Harold as my best—and as I begun—I think of concluding with it—but I make no resolutions on that head—as I broke my former intention with regard to "the Corsair"—however—I fear that I shall never do better—& yet—not being thirty years of age for some moons to come—one ought to be progressive as far as Intellect goes for many a good year—but I have had a devilish deal of wear & tear of mind and body—in my time—besides having published too often & much already. God grant me some judgement! to do what may be most fitting in that & every thing else—for I doubt my own exceedingly.——I have read "Lallah Rookh"—but not with sufficient attention yet—for I ride about—& lounge—& ponder &—two or three other things—so that my reading is very desultory & not so attentive as it used to be.—I am very glad to hear of its popularity—for Moore is a very noble fellow in all respects—& will enjoy it without any of the bad feelings which Success—good or evil—sometimes engenders in the men of rhyme.—Of the poem itself I will tell you my opinion when I have mastered it—I say of the *poem*—for I don't like the *prose* at all—at all—and in the mean time the "Fire-worshippers" is the best and the "Veiled Prophet" the worst, of the volume.——With regard to poetry in general[2] I am convinced the more I think of it—that he and *all* of us—Scott—Southey—Wordsworth—Moore—Campbell—I—are all in the wrong—one as much as another—that we are upon a wrong revolutionary poetical system—or systems—not worth a damn in itself—& from which none but Rogers and Crabbe are free—and that the present & next generations will finally be of this opinion.—I am the more confirmed in this—by having lately gone over some of our Classics—particularly *Pope*—whom I tried in this way— I took Moore's poems & my own & some others—& went over them side by side with Pope's—and I was really astonished (I ought not to have been so) and mortified—at the ineffable distance in point of sense—harmony—effect—and even *Imagination* Passion—& *Invention* —between the little Queen Anne's Man—& us of the lower Empire— depend upon it [it] is all Horace then, and Claudian now among us

2 Murray showed this letter to Gifford who wrote the following note with respect to Byron's critique of modern poets and his judgment of Pope: "There is more good sense, and feeling and judgment in this passage, than in any other I ever read, or Lord Byron wrote." (*LJ*, IV, 169n.)

—and if I had to begin again—I would model myself accordingly—
Crabbe's the man—but he has got a coarse and impracticable subject—
& Rogers the Grandfather of living Poetry—is retired upon half-pay,
(I don't mean as a Banker)—

> Since pretty Miss Jaqueline
> With her nose aquiline

and has done enough—unless he were to do as he did formerly.—

[TO JOHN MURRAY]   *Venice, January 8th. 1818*

1.

My dear Mr. Murray,
You're in a damned hurry
To set up this ultimate Canto,
But (if they don't rob us)
You'll see Mr. Hobhouse
Will bring it safe in his portmanteau.—[1]

2.

For the Journal you hint of.[2]
As ready to print off;
No doubt you do right to commend it
But as yet I have writ off
The devil a bit of
Our "Beppo", when copied—I'll send it.—[3]

3.

In the mean time you've "Gally"[4]
Whose verses all tally,
Perhaps you may say he's a Ninny,

---

[1] Hobhouse left Venice for England on January 8, carrying with him the manuscript of the fourth canto of *Childe Harold*.

[2] Murray had contemplated starting a new periodical of his own, and had suggested that Byron might contribute to it. He finally purchased a half-share in William Blackwood's *Edinburgh Monthly Magazine* (founded in 1817—Murray became half proprietor in August, 1818, but sold his share the following year).

[3] Byron finally copied and sent *Beppo* to Murray on January 19th. It was published on February 28th.

[4] Byron made sport of the Oriental verse tales of Henry Gally Knight.

But if you abashed are
Because of "Alashtar"
He'll piddle another "Phrosine".—

4.

Then you've Sotheby's tour,[5]
No great things to be sure—
You could hardly begin with a less work,
For the pompous rascallion
Who don't speak Italian
Nor French, must have scribbled by guesswork.

5.

No doubt he's a rare man
Without knowing German
Translating his way up Parnassus,
And now still absurder
He meditates Murder
As you'll see in the trash he calls *Tasso's*

6.

But you've others his betters
The real men of letters—
Your Orators—critics—and wits—
And I'll bet that your Journal
(Pray is it diurnal?)
Will pay with your luckiest hits.—

7.

You can make any loss up—
With "Spence"[6] and his Gossip,
A work which must surely succeed,
Then Queen Mary's Epistle-craft,[7]
With the new "Fytte" of "Whistlecraft"[8]
Must make people purchase and read.—

[5] Sotheby's *Farewell to Italy* was published in 1818. Byron started to write a skit on Sotheby's tour. See *LJ*, IV, 452–453.
[6] *Observations, Anecdotes, and Characters of Books and Men*, by the Rev. Joseph Spence, arranged with notes by the late Edmond Malone, 1820.
[7] *The Life of Mary Queen of Scots*, by George Chalmers, 1819.
[8] John Hookham Frere's "Whistlecraft" was first published in 1817 and gave Byron a hint for the style of *Beppo*. Cantos III and IV were published in 1818.

8.

Then you've General Gordon[9]
Who "girded his sword on"
To serve with a Muscovite Master
And help him to polish
A ⟨people⟩ Nation so *owlish*,
They thought shaving their beards a disaster.

9.

For the man *"poor and shrewd"* *
With whom you'd conclude
A Compact without more delay.
Perhaps some such pen is
       *(Vide your letter)
Still extant in Venice,
But ⟨pray⟩ please Sir to mention *your pay?*—

10.

Now tell me some news
Of your friends and the Muse
Of the Bar,—or the Gown—or the House,
From Canning the tall wit
To Wilmot the small wit
Ward's creeping Companion and *Louse.*—

11.

⟨He's⟩ Who's so damnably bit
With fashion and Wit
That ⟨still a⟩ he crawls on the surface like Vermin
But an Insect in both,—
By his Intellect's growth
Of what *size* you may quickly determine.

12.

Now, I'll put out my taper
(I've finished my paper

---

[9] Thomas Gordon (1788–1841) had visited Ali Pasha shortly after Byron was there. Byron must have assumed that Murray was negotiating with him for the publication of a book. Gordon later served with Ipsilanti in the Greek war for independence and wrote a *History of the Greek Revolution* (1832)

For these stanzas you see on the *brink* stand)
There's a whore on my right
For I rhyme best at Night
When a C—t is tied close to *my Inkstand.*

13.

It was Mahomet's notion   (See his life in
That comical motion   Gibbon's abstract)
Increased his "devotion in prayer"—
If that tenet holds good
In a Prophet, it should
In a poet be equally fair.—

14.

For, in rhyme or in love
(Which both come from above)
I'll *stand* with our *"Tommy"* or *"Sammy"* ("Moore" and
   "Rogers")
But the Sopha and lady
Are both of them ready
And so, here's "Good Night to you dammee!"

[TO JOHN MURRAY]   *Venice.—February 20th. 1818*

Dear Sir—I have to thank Mr. Croker[1] for the arrival—& you for the Continents of the Parcel which came last week—much quicker than any before—owing to Mr C[roker]'s kind attention, and the official exterior of the bags, and all safe—except much fraction amongst the Magnesia—of which only two bottles came entire—but it is all very well—and I am accordingly obliged to you.——The books I have read, or rather am reading—pray who may be the Sexagenarian[2]— whose Gossip is very amusing—many of his sketches I recognize— particularly Gifford — Mackintosh — Drummond — Dutens[3] — H. Walpole—Mrs. Inchbald—Opie &c. with the Scotts—Loughborough & most of the divines and lawyers—besides a few shorter hints of

[1] John Wilson Croker, a contributor to Murray's *Quarterly Review*, was a friend of Canning and Secretary to the Admiralty.

[2] *The Sexagenarian, or Recollections of a Literary Life* was a posthumous publication of the Rev. William Beloe (1756–1817), Keeper of Printed Books at the British Museum and editor of *The British Critic.*

[3] Louis Dutens (1730–1812), French writer settled in England, published his *Memoirs of a Traveller* in 1806.

authors—& a few lines about a certain *"Noble Author"*4 charac-
terized as Malignant and Sceptical according to the good old story
"as it was in the beginning—is now—*but not* always shall be"—do
you know such a person Master Murray? eh? and pray of the Booksellers which be you? the dry—the dirty—the honest—the opulent—
the finical—the splendid, or the Coxcomb Bookseller?5—"Stap my
vitals"6—but the author grows scurrilous in his grand Climacteric.
——I remember to have seen Porson at Cambridge in the Hall of our
College—and in private parties—but not frequently—and I never can
recollect him except as drunk or brutal and generally both—I mean in
an Evening for in the hall he dined at the Dean's table—& I at the
Vice-Master's so that I was not near him, and he then & there appeared
sober in his demeanour—nor did I ever hear of excess or outrage—
on his part in public—Commons—college—or Chapel—but I have
seen him in a private party of under-Graduates—many of them
freshmen & strangers—take up a poker to one of them—& heard
him use language as blackguard as his action; I have seen Sheridan
drunk too with all the world, but his intoxication was that of Bacchus—
& Porson's that of Silenus—of all the disgusting brutes—sulky—
abusive—and intolerable—Porson was the most bestial as far as the
few times that I saw him went—which were only at Wm. Bankes's
(the Nubian Discoverer's) rooms—I saw him once go away in a rage
—because nobody knew the name of the "Cobbler of Messina"7
insulting their ignorance with the most vulgar terms of reprobation.—
He was tolerated in this state amongst the young men—for his talents
—as the Turks think a Madman—inspired—& bear with him;—he
used to recite—or rather vomit pages of all languages—& could
hiccup Greek like a Helot—& certainly Sparta never shocked her
children with a grosser exhibition than this Man's intoxication.———I
perceive in the book you sent me a long account of him—of Gilbert
Wakefield's account of him which is very savage[.]8 I cannot judge as I

4 Beloe spoke of "the Noble Author" as "certainly possessed of great intellectual
powers, and a peculiar turn for a certain line of poetry", but his "bad passions so
perpetually insinuate themselves in every thing which he writes, that it is hardly
possible to escape the injury of his venom. . . ." (*Sexagenarian*, II, 230.)
5 Murray was referred to as the "coxcomb" Bookseller (*Sexagenarian*, II, 253).
6 Byron frequently repeated this phrase of Lord Foppington in Vanbrugh's *The
Relapse* (or Sheridan's adaptation of it, *The Trip to Scarborough*).
7 Probably the shoemaker's apprentice mentioned by Juvenal in his 5th satire.
He won wealth and power at the court of Nero by accusing the most distinguished
men of the time and exposing corruption.
8 The Sexagenarian defended Porson from the attacks of Gilbert Wakefield in
his *Correspondence* with Charles James Fox (pp. 99–101).

never saw him sober—except in *Hall* or Combination room—& then I was never near enough to hear—& hardly to see him—of his drunken deportment I can be sure because I saw it.——With the Reviews I have been much entertained—it requires to be as far from England as I am—to relish a periodical paper properly—it is like Soda water in an Italian Summer—but what cruel work you make with Lady Morgan[9]— you should recollect that she is a woman—though to be sure they are now & then very provoking—still as authoresses they can do no great harm—and I think it a pity so much good invective should have been laid out upon her—when there is such a fine field of us Jacobin Gentlemen for you to work upon; it is perhaps as bitter a critique as ever was written—& enough to make sad work for Dr. Morgan— both as a husband and an Apothecary—unless she should say as Pope did—of some attack upon him—"that it is as good for her as a dose of *Hartshorn*".——I heard from Moore lately & was very sorry to be made aware of his domestic loss—thus it is—"Medio de fonte leporum" in the acme of his fame—& of his happiness comes a draw- back as usual.—His letter somehow or other was more than two months on the road—so that I could only answer it the other day.— What you tell me of R⟨ogers⟩ in your last letter is like him—but he had best let *us* that is one of us—if not both—alone—he cannot say that I have not been a sincere & a warm friend to him—till the black drop of his liver oozed through too palpably to be overlooked—now if I once catch him at any of his juggling with me or mine—let him look to it—for—if I spare him—then write me down a goodnatured gentleman; & the more that I have been deceived—the more that I once relied upon him—I don't mean his petty friendship (what is that to me?) but his *good* will—which I really tried to obtain thinking him at first a good fellow—the more will I pay off the balance—and so if he values his quiet—let him look to it—in three months I could restore him to the Catacombs.——Mr. Hoppner—whom I saw this morning—has been made the father of a very fine boy—Mother & Child doing very well indeed.—By this time Hobhouse should be with you—& also certain packets—letters—&c. of mine sent since his departure.——I am not at all well in health within this last eight days;—my remembrances to Gifford & all friends

yrs. [truly?]
B

---

[9] There was a severe critique of Lady Morgan's *France* in the *Quarterly Review*, Vol. XVII, page 260.

P.S.—In the course of a Month or two, Hanson will have probably to send off a Clerk with conveyances to sign—(N[ewstea]d being sold in Novr. last for Ninety four thousand & five hundred pounds) in which case I supplicate supplies of articles as usual—for which desire Mr. Kinnaird to settle from funds in their bank—& deduct from my account with him.—

P.S.—Tomorrow night I am going to see 'Otello" an opera from our "Othello"—and one of Rossini's best, it is said.—It will be curious to see in Venice—the Venetian story itself represented—besides to discover what they will make of Shakespeare in Music.—

[TO THOMAS MOORE]
Palazzo Mocenigo, Canal Grande, Venice, June 1st. 1818

Your letter is almost the only news, as yet, of Canto 4th, and it has by no means settled its fate—at least, does not tell me how the "Poeshie" has been received by the public. But I suspect, no great things,—firstly, from Murray's "horrid stillness;" secondly, from what you say about the stanzas running into each other, which I take *not* to be *yours*, but a notion you have been dinned with among the Blues. The fact is, that the terza rima of the Italians, which always *runs* on and in, may have led me into experiments, and carelessness into conceit—or conceit into carelessness—in either of which events failure will be probable, and my fair woman, "superne," end in a fish;[1] so that Childe Harold will be like the mermaid, my family crest, with the Fourth Canto for a tail thereunto. I won't quarrel with the public, however, for the "Bulgars" are generally right; and if I miss now, I may hit another time:—and so, the "gods give us joy."[2]

You like *Beppo*, that's right. * * * * I have not had the Fudges[3] yet, but live in hopes. I need not say that your successes are mine. By the way, Lydia White[4] is here, and has just borrowed my copy of "Lalla Rookh."

* * * * * * * * * * * * * * * *

Hunt's letter is probably the exact piece of vulgar coxcombry you might expect from his situation. He is a good man, with some poetical

[1] Horace, *Ars Poetica*, line 4: "Desinat in piscem mulier formosa superne". (Paints a woman above, a fish below.)
[2] *As You Like It*, Act III, scene 3.
[3] Moore's *The Fudge Family in Paris* (1818).
[4] Lydia White was a wealthy Irish "blue-stocking" (literary lady) well known for her dinners and conversation parties. She was the "Miss Diddle" in Byron's *The Blues*.

174

elements in his chaos; but spoilt by the Christ-Church Hospital and a Sunday newspaper,—to say nothing of the Surry Jail, which conceited him into a martyr. But he is a good man. When I saw "Rimini" in MSS., I told him that I deemed it good poetry at bottom, disfigured only by a strange style. His answer was, that his style was a system, or *upon system*, or some such cant; and, when a man talks of system, his case is hopeless: so I said no more to him, and very little to any one else.

He believes his trash of vulgar phrases tortured into compound barbarisms to be *old* English; and we may say of it as Aimwell says of Captain Gibbet's regiment, when the Captain calls it an "old corps." —"the *oldest* in Europe, if I may judge by your uniform,"[5] He sent out his "Foliage"[6] by Percy Shelley * * * , and, of all the ineffable Centaurs that were ever begotten by Selflove upon a Night-mare, I think this monstrous Sagittary[7] the most prodigious. *He* (Leigh H.) is an honest Charlatan, who has persuaded himself into a belief of his own impostures, and talks Punch in pure simplicity of heart, taking himself (as poor Fitzgerald said of *him*self in the Morning Post) for *Vates* in both senses, or nonsenses, of the word.[8] Did you look at the translations of his own which he prefers to Pope and Cowper, and says so?[9]—Did you read his skimble-skamble about [Wordsworth] being at the head of his own *profession*, in the *eyes* of *those* who followed it? I thought that Poetry was an *art*, or an *attribute*, and not a *profession*;—but be it one, is that * * * * * at the head of *your* profession in *your* eyes? I'll be curst if he is of *mine*, or ever shall be. He is the only one of us (but of us he is not) whose coronation I would oppose. Let them take Scott, Campbell, Crabbe, or you, or me, or any of the living, and throne him;—but not this new Jacob Behmen, this * * * whose pride might have kept him true, even had his principles turned as perverted as his *soi-disant* poetry.

But Leigh Hunt is a good man, and a good father—see his Odes to all the Masters Hunt;—a good husband—see his Sonnet to Mrs.

---

[5] Farquhar, *The Beaux' Strategem*, Act III, scene 2:
> "Gibbet. A marching Regiment, Sir, an old Corps.
> Aimwell (aside). Very old, if your Coat be Regimental."

[6] Leigh Hunt's *Foliage, or Poems Original and Translated* (1818).

[7] *Troilus and Cressida*, Act V, scene 5: "The dreadful Sagittary appals our numbers".

[8] William Thomas Fitzgerald, who considered himself a kind of poet laureate, was ridiculed by Byron in *English Bards and Scotch Reviewers*.

[9] Hunt said that Cowper's translation of Homer was spoiled by "over-timidity", and he spoke of Pope's "elegant mistake ... called Homer's *Iliad*". (Hunt's *Foliage*, Preface, p. 31).

175

Hunt;—a good friend—see his Epistles to different people;—and a great coxcomb and a very vulgar person in every thing about him. But that's not his fault, but of circumstances.

* * * * * * * * * * * * * * *
* * * * * * * * * * * * * * *

I do not know any good model for a life of Sheridan but that of *Savage*. Recollect, however, that the life of such a man may be made far more amusing than if he had been a Wilberforce;—and this without offending the living, or insulting the dead. The Whigs abuse him; however, he never left them, and such blunderers deserve neither credit nor compassion. As for his creditors,—remember, Sheridan *never had* a shilling, and was thrown, with great powers and passions, into the thick of the world, and placed upon the pinnacle of success, with no other external means to support him in his elevation. Did Fox * * * *pay his* debts?—or did Sheridan take a subscription? Was the Duke of Norfolk's drunkeness more excusable than his? Were his intrigues more notorious than those of all his contemporaries? and is his memory to be blasted, and theirs respected? Don't let yourself be led away by clamour, but compare him with the coalitioner Fox, and the pensioner Burke, as a man of principle, and with ten hundred thousand in personal views, and with none in talent, for he beat them all *out* and *out*. Without means, without connexion, without character, (which might be false at first, and make him mad afterwards from desperation,) he beat them all, in all he ever attempted. But alas poor human nature! Good night—or, rather, morning. It is four, and the dawn gleams over the Grand Canal, and unshadows the Rialto. I must to bed; up all night—but, as George Philpot says, "it's life, though, damme it's life!"[10]

Ever yours,
B

Excuse errors—no time for revision. The post goes out at noon, and I shan't be up then. I will write again soon about your *plan* for a publication.

[TO JOHN CAM HOBHOUSE] *Venice. June 25th. 1818*

Dear Hobhouse—I have received yrs. of the 5th.—& have had no letters from any one else—nor desire any—but *letters* of *Credit*.—

---

[10] Arthur Murphy, *The Citizen*, Act I, scene 2. Young George Philpot says, "Up all night—stripped of nine hundred pounds . . . cruel luck!—damn me, it's life though—this is life."

Since my last I have had another *Swim* against Mingaldo[1]—whom both Scott & I beat hollow—leaving him breathless & five hundred yards behind hand before we got from Lido to the entrance of the Grand Canal.—Scott went from Lido as far as the Rialto—& was then taken into his Gondola—I swam from Lido right to the end of the Grand Canal—including it's whole length—besides that space from Lido to the Canal's entrance (or exit) by the statue of Fortune—near the Palace—and coming out finally at the end opposite Fusina and Maestri—staying in half an hour &—I know not what distance more than the other two—& swimming easy—the whole distance computed by the Venetians at four and a half of Italian miles.—I was in the sea from half past 4—till a quarter past 8—without touching or resting.— I could not be much fatigued having had a *piece* in the forenoon—& taking another in the evening at ten of the Clock—The Scott I mention is not the vice-Consul—but a traveller—who lives much at Venice—like My*sen*.—He got as far as the Rialto swimming well— the Italian—miles behind & knocked up—hallooing for the boat.— Pray—make Murray *pay*—& Spooney[2] pay—& send the Messenger— & with the other things the enclosed *Corn rubbers*.—As you are full of politics I say nothing—except that I wish you more pleasure than such trash could give to me.

yrs. very truly & affectly.

B

P.S.—*The wind & tide were both with me. Corn rubbers two dozen—* recollect *they are light & may come in letters.*—

[TO JAMES WEDDERBURN WEBSTER]   *Venice. Septr. 8th. 1818*

Dear Webster—[12 lines crossed out] It is not agreeable to me to hear that you are still in difficulties—but as every one has to go through a certain portion of sufferance in this world—the earlier it happens perhaps the better—and in all cases one is better able to battle up in one's youth than in the decline of life.——My own worldly affairs have had leisure to improve during my residence abroad—Newstead has been sold—& well sold I am given to under-

---

[1] The Cavalier Angelo Mengaldo (Byron frequently spelled it "Mingaldo") was a former soldier in Napoleon's army who boasted of his swimming exploits, particularly of swimming the Beresina under fire during the retreat from Moscow.

[2] See Jan. 26, 1815, to Hobhouse, note 1.

stand—my debts are in the prospect of being paid—and I have still a large Capital from the residue—besides Rochdale—which ought to sell well—& my reversionary prospects which are considerable in the event of the death of Miss Milbanke's mother.—There is (as is usually said) a great advantage in getting the water between a man and his embarrassments—for things with time and a little prudence insensibly reestablish themselves—and I have spent less money—and had more for it—within the two years and a half since my absence from England —than I have ever done within the same time before—and my literary speculations allowed me to do it more easily—leaving my own property to liquidate some of the claims, till the Sale enables me to discharge the whole;—out of England I have no debts whatever.— —You ask about Venice;—I tell you as before that I do not think *you* would like it—at least few English do—& still fewer remain there— Florence & Naples are their Lazarettoes where they carry the infection of their society—indeed if there were as many of them in Venice as residents—as Lot begged might be permitted to be the Salvation of Sodom,—it would not be my abode a week longer—for the reverse of the proposition I should be sure that they would be the *damnation* of all pleasant or sensible society;—I never see any of them when I can avoid it—& when occasionally they arrive with letters of recommendation—I do what I can for them—if they are sick—and if they are well I return my card for theirs—but little more.——Venice is not an expensive residence—(unless a man chooses it) it has theatres— society—and profligacy rather more than enough—I keep four horses on one of the Islands where there is a beach of some miles along the Adriatic—so that I have daily exercise—I have my Gondola—about fourteen servants including the nurse (for a little girl—a natural daughter of mine) and I reside in one of the Mocenigo palaces on the Grand Canal—the rent of the *whole* house which is very *large* & *furnished* with linen &c. &c. inclusive is two hundred a year—(& I gave more than I need have done) in the two years I have been at Venice—I have spent about *five* thousand pounds—& I needed not have spent one *third* of this—had it not been that I have a passion for women which is expensive in it's variety every where but less so in Venice than in other cities.——You may suppose that in *two years*—with a large establishment—horses—houses—box at the opera—Gondola— journeys—women—and Charity—(for I have not laid out all upon my pleasures—but have bought occasionally a shillings-worth of Salvation) villas in the country—another carriage & horses purchased for the country—books bought &c. &c.—in short every thing I wanted—

178

& *more* than I ought to have wanted—that the sum of five thousand pounds sterling is no great deal—particularly when I tell you that more than half was laid out on the Sex—to be sure I have had plenty for the money—that's certain—I think at least two hundred of one sort or another—perhaps more—for I have not lately kept the recount.——— If you are disposed to come this way—you might live very comfortably—and even splendidly for less than a thousand a year—& find a palace for the rent of one hundred—that is to say—an Italian palace —you know that all houses with a particular front are called so—in short an enormous house,—but as I said—I do not think *you* would like it—or rather that Lady Frances would not—it is not so gay as it has been—and there is a monotony to many people in it's Canals & the comparative silence of it's streets—to me who have been always passionate for Venice—and delight in the dialect & naivete of the people—and the romance of it's old history & institutions & appearance all it's disadvantages are more than compensated by the sight of a single Gondola—The view of the Rialto—of the piazza—& the Chaunt of Tasso (though less frequent than of old) are to me worth all the cities on earth—save Rome & Athens.—Good even

yrs. ever & most truly
B

[TO THOMAS MOORE]   *Venice, September 19th, 1818*

An English newspaper here would be a prodigy, and an opposition one a monster; and except some extracts *from* extracts in the vile, garbled Paris gazettes, nothing of the kind reaches the Veneto-Lombard public, who are perhaps the most oppressed in Europe. My correspondencies with England are mostly on business, and chiefly with my [attorney], who has no very exalted notion, or extensive conception, of an author's attributes; for he once took up an Edinburgh Review, and, looking at it a minute, said to me, "So, I see you have got into the magazine,"—which is the only sentence I ever heard him utter upon literary matters, or the men thereof.

My first news of your Irish Apotheosis has, consequently, been from yourself.[1] But, as it will not be forgotten in a hurry, either by your friends or your enemies, I hope to have it more in detail from some of the former, and, in the mean time, I wish you joy with all my heart.

---

[1] Because of his Irish National songs and his defence of Irish causes, Moore was made much of during his visit to Ireland.

Such a moment must have been a good deal better than Westminster-abbey,—besides being an assurance of *that* one day (many years hence, I trust), into the bargain.

I am sorry to perceive, however, by the close of your letter, that even *you* have not escaped the "surgit amari,"[2] &c., and that your damned deputy has been gathering such "dew from the still *vext* Bermoothes"[3]—or rather *vexatious.* Pray, give me some items of the affair, as you say it is a serious one; and, if it grows more so, you should make a trip over here for a few months, to see how things turn out. I suppose you are a violent admirer of England by your staying so long in it. For my own part, I have passed, between the age of one-and-twenty and thirty, half the intervenient years out of it without regretting any thing, except that I ever returned to it at all, and the gloomy prospect before me of business and parentage obliging me, one day, to return to it again,—at least, for the transaction of affairs, the signing of papers, and inspecting of children.

I have here my natural daughter, by name Allegra,—a pretty little girl enough, and reckoned like papa. Her mamma is English,—but it is a long story, and—there's an end. She is about twenty months old. * * * * * *

I have finished the First Canto (a long one, of about 180 octaves) of a poem in the style and manner of "Beppo," encouraged by the good success of the same.[4] It is called "Don Juan", and is meant to be a little quietly facetious upon every thing. But I doubt whether it is not —at least, as far as it has yet gone—too free for these very modest days. However, I shall try the experiment, anonymously, and if it don't take, it will be discontinued. It is dedicated to S[outhey] in good, simple, savage verse, upon the [Laureate's] politics, and the way he got them. But the bore of copying it out is intolerable; and if I had an amanuensis he would be of no use, as my writing is so difficult to decipher.

---

[2] Lucretius, *De Rerum Natura*, IV, 1133:

"Nequiquam, quoniam medio de fonte leporum
     surgit amari aliquid quod in issis floribus angat"

("All is vanity, since from the very fountain of enchantment rises a drop of bitterness to torment amongst all the flowers.")

[3] *Tempest*, Act I, scene 2. Moore had been appointed in 1803 Registrar to the Admiralty in Bermuda. He left the duties of the office to a deputy whose embezzlement left Moore liable for claims amounting to a thousand guineas.

[4] As usual Byron added stanzas and when it was published the following year the first canto had grown to 222 stanzas.

My poem's Epic, and is meant to be
Divided in twelve books, each book containing,
With love and war, a heavy gale at sea—
A list of ships, and captains, and kings reigning—
New characters, &c. &c.

The above are two [sic] stanzas, which I send you as a brick of my Babel, and by which you can judge of the texture of the structure.

In writing the Life of Sheridan, never mind the angry lies of the humbug whigs. Recollect that he was an Irishman and a clever fellow, and that *we* have had some very pleasant days with him. Don't forget that he was at school at Harrow, where, in my time, we used to show his name—R. B. Sheridan, 1765,—as an honour to the walls. Remember ＊ ＊ ＊ ＊ ＊ ＊

＊ ＊ ＊ ＊ ＊ ＊ ＊ ＊ ＊ ＊ ＊ ＊ ＊ ＊

Depend upon it that there were worse folks going, of that gang, than ever Sheridan was.

What did Parr[5] mean by "haughtiness and coldness?" I listened to him with admiring ignorance, and respectful silence. What more could a talker for fame have?—they don't like to be answered. It was at Payne Knight's[6] I met him, where he gave me more Greek than I could carry away. But I certainly meant to (and *did*) treat him with the most respectful deference.

I wish you a good night, with a Venetian benediction, "Benedetto te, e la terra che ti fara!"—"May you be blessed, and the *earth* which you will *make*" is it not pretty? You would think it still prettier if you had heard it, as I did two hours ago, from the lips of a Venetian girl,[7] with large black eyes, a face like Faustina's, and the figure of a Juno—tall and energetic as a Pythoness, with eyes flashing, and her dark hair streaming in the moonlight—one of those women who may be made any thing. I am sure if I put a poniard into the hand of this one, she would plunge it where I told her,—and into *me*, if I offended her. I like this kind of animal, and am sure that I should have preferred Medea to any woman that ever breathed. You may, perhaps, wonder

---

[5] Samuel Parr (1747–1825), an assistant master at Harrow while Sheridan was there, was visited by Moore, then gathering material for a life of Sheridan. Parr had a reputation as a scholar which was probably inflated. He was called a Whig Dr. Johnson.

[6] Richard Payne Knight (1750–1824), numismatist and writer on ancient art. He was a collector of bronzes which he bequeathed to the British Museum.

[7] Probably Margarita Cogni, See Aug. 1, 1819, to Murray.

that I don't in that case[8] take to my wife. But she is a poor, mawkish, moral Clytemnestra (and no Medea) who likes to be vindictive according to law, and to hew me down as Samuel sawed Agag, religiously. I could have forgiven the dagger or the bowl, any thing, but the deliberate desolation piled upon me, when I stood alone upon my hearth, with my household gods shivered around me, * * * * * * * * Do you suppose I have forgotten or forgiven it? It has comparatively swallowed up in me every other feeling, and I am only a spectator upon earth, till a tenfold opportunity offers. It may come yet. There are others more to be blamed than * * * *, and it is on these that my eyes are fixed unceasingly.

[TO JOHN CAM HOBHOUSE]   *Venice Novr. 11th. 1818*

Dear Hobhouse/—By the favour of Lord Lauderdale[1] (who tells me by the way that you have made some very good speeches—and are to turn out an Orator—*seriously*) I have sent an "Oeuvre" of "Poeshie" which will not arrive probably till some [time] after this letter—though they start together—as the letter is rather the youngest of the two.— It is addressed to you at Mr. Murray's.——I request you to read—& having read—and if possible approved to obtain the largest or (if large be undeserved—) the fairest price from him or any one else.— There are firstly—the first Canto of Don Juan—(in the style of Beppo —and Pulci—forgive me for putting Pulci second it is a slip—"Ego et Rex meus") containing two *hundred Octaves*—and a dedication in verse of a dozen to Bob Southey—bitter as necessary—I mean the dedication; I will tell you why.—The Son of a Bitch on his return from Switzerland two years ago—said that Shelley and I "had formed a League of Incest and practiced our precepts with &c."—he lied like a rascal—for they *were not Sisters—one* being Godwin's daughter by Mary Wollstonecraft—and the other the daughter of the present Mrs. G[odwin] by a *former* husband.—The Attack contains no allusion to the cause—but—some good verses—and all political & poetical.— He lied in another sense—for there was no promiscuous intercourse— my commerce being limited to the carnal knowledge of the Miss

---

[8] The words from here to the end of the sentence come from an unpublished part of Moore's journal.

[1] James Maitland, 8th Earl of Lauderdale (1759–1839). He held various governmental posts, but retired in 1807 and lived much of his life abroad.

C[lairmont]—I had nothing to do with the offspring of Mary Wollstonecraft—which Mary was a former Love of Southey's—which might have taught him to respect the fame of her daughter.—— Besides this *"Pome"* there is "Mazeppa" and an Ode on Venice—the last not very intelligible—and you may omit it if you like—Don Juan—and Mazeppa are perhaps better—you will see.—The Whole consists of between two and three thousand lines—and you can consult Douglas K[innaird] about the price thereof and your own Judgment —& whose else you like about their merits.—As one of the poems is as free as La Fontaine—& bitter in politics—too—the damned Cant and Toryism of the day may make Murray pause—in that case you will take any Bookseller who bids best;—when I say *free*—I mean that freedom—which Ariosto Boiardo and Voltaire—Pulci—Berni—all the best Italian & French—as well as Pope & Prior amongst the English permitted themselves;—but no improper words nor phrases—merely some situations—which are taken from life.—However you will see to all this—when the M. S. S. arrive.——I only request that you & Doug. will see to a fair price—"as the Players have had my Goods too cheap"—if Murray won't—another will.—I name no price—calculate by quantity—and quality—and do you and Doug. pronounce—always recollecting as impartial Judges—that you are my friends—and that he is my Banker.—Spooney arrived here today—but has left in Chancery Lane *all* my *books*—everything in short except a damned— (Something)-SCOPE.[2] I have broke the glass & cut a finger in ramming it together—and the *Cornrubbers* but I have given it him!—I have been blaspheming against Scrope's God—ever since his arrival. ——Only think—he has left every thing—every thing except his legal papers.—You must send off a Man on purpose with them on the receipt of this—I will pay anything within *three hundred pounds* for the expence of their transportation—but pray let them be sent without fail—and by a person on purpose—they are all in Chancery—(I mean the *Lane*—not the Court—for they would not come out of that in a hurry) with young Spooney[3]—extract them—and send a man by Chaise on purpose—never mind expence nor weight—I must have books & Magnesia—particularly "Tales of my Landlord".——I'll be revenged on Spooney—five men died of the Plague the other day—in the Lazaretto—I shall take him to ride at the Lido—he hath a reverend care & fear of his health—I will show him the Lazaretto which is not far off you know—& looks nearer than it is—I will tell him of the five

2 Murray had sent a kaleidoscope.
3 Charles Hanson.

men—I will tell him of my contact with Aglietti in whose presence they died—& who came into my Box at the (St. Benedetto's) Opera the same evening—& shook hands with me;—I will tell him all this —and as he is hypochondriac—perhaps it may kill him.——The Monster left my books—everything—my Magnesia—my tooth powder—&c. &c. and wanted me besides to go to Geneva——but I made him come.—He is a queer fish—the Customs House Officers wanted to examine or have money—he would not pay—they opened every thing.—"Ay—Ay—(said he) look away—*Carts Carts*" that was his phrase for *papers* with a strong English emphasis & accent on the *s* and he actually made them turn over all the Newstead & Rochdale —& Jew—& Chancery papers exclaiming "*Carts Carts*" & came off triumphant with paying a *Centime*—the Officers giving up the matter in despair—finding nothing else—& not being able to translate what they found.——But I have been in a damned passion for all that—for this adventure nearly reconciled me to him.[4]—Pray remember the man & books—and mind & make me a proper paction with Murray or others—I submit the matter to you and Doug.—and you may show the M. S. to Frere and William Rose—and Moore—& whoever you please.—Forgive the Scrawl & the trouble—& write & believe me

ever & truly yrs.
[scrawl for signature]

P.S.—Lord Lauderdale set off today the 12th. Novr.—& means to be in England in about a Month.—

[TO HOBHOUSE AND KINNAIRD]   *Venice January 19th. 1819*

Dear H. and dear K.—I approve and sanction all your legal proceedings with regard to my affairs, and can only repeat my thanks & approbation—if you put off the payments of debts "till *after* Lady Noel's death"—it is well—if till *after* her damnation—better—for

---

[4] The other side of the story is told by Newton Hanson in a manuscript account quoted by Prothero. He said that Murray had left a wagonload of books at Chancery Lane which they could not bring, that Byron was nervous and irritable during their visit, that the reason his father had himself come on the voyage was that he had hoped to effect a reconciliation between Byron and his wife, but that Byron soon dispelled such hopes by a remark on the death of Romilly: "How strange it is that one man will die for the loss of his partner, while another would die if they were compelled to live together." Newton Hanson observed: "Lord Byron could not have been more than 30, but he looked 40. His face had become pale, bloated, and sallow. He had grown very fat, his shoulders broad and round, and the knuckles of his hands were lost in fat." (*LJ*, IV, 266–267n.)

that will last forever—yet I hope not:—for her sake as well as the Creditors'—I am willing to believe in Purgatory.——With regard to the Poeshie—I will have no "cutting & slashing" as Perry calls it— you may omit the stanzas on Castlereagh[1]—indeed it is better—& the two *"Bobs"* at the end of the 3d. stanza of the dedication— which will leave "high" & "adry" good rhymes without any *"double* (or Single) Entendre"[2]—but no more—I appeal—not "to Philip fasting" but to Alexander drunk—I appeal to Murray at his ledger—to the people—in short, Don Juan shall be an entire horse or none.—If the objection be to the indecency, the Age which applauds the "Bath Guide" & Little's poems—& reads Fielding & Smollett still—may bear with that;—if to the poetry—I will take my chance.— I will not give way to all the Cant of Christendom—I have been cloyed with applause & sickened with abuse;—at present—I care for little but the Copyright,—I have imbibed a great love for money—let me have it—if Murray loses this time—he won't the next—he will be cautious—and I shall learn the decline of his customers by his epistolary indications.——But in no case will I submit to have the poem muti- lated.—There is another Canto written—but not copied—in two hundred & odd Stanzas,—if this succeeds—as to the prudery of the present day—what is it? are we more moral than when Prior wrote— is there anything in Don Juan so strong as in Ariosto—or Voltaire— or Chaucer?—Tell Hobhouse—his letter to De Breme has made a great Sensation—and is to be published in the Tuscan & other Gazettes—Count R[izzo][3] came to consult with me about it last Sunday—we think of Tuscany—for Florence and Milan are in literary war—but the Lombard league is headed by Monti[4]—& would make a difficulty of insertion in the Lombard Gazettes—once published in the Pisan—it will find its way through Italy—by translation or reply.—— So Lauderdale has been telling a story!—I suppose this is my reward for presenting him at Countess Benzone's—& shewing him—what attention I could.——Which "piece" does he mean?—since last year

---

1 In the Dedication (to Southey) of *Don Juan* Byron referred to "The intellectual eunuch Castlereagh", but since he published the first two cantos anonymously, he omitted the Dedication.

2 The ribaldry of this couplet caused consternation among Byron's friends in England, to whom the *double entendre* was obvious. In Regency slang "a dry Bob" meant coition without emission.

3 Count Francesco Rizzo-Patarol, a Venetian nobleman in the circle of the Countess Albrizzi.

4 Vincenzo Monti, the Italian poet whom Byron and Hobhouse had met in Milan.

I have run the Gauntlet;—is it the Tarruscelli[5]—the Da Mosti[6]—the Spineda—the Lotti—the Rizzato—the Eleanora—the Carlotta—the Giulietta—the Alvisi—the Zambieri—The Eleanora da Bezzi—(who was the King of Naples' Gioaschino's mistress—at least one of them) the Theresina of Mazzurati—the Glettenheimer—& her Sister—the Luigia & her mother—the Fornaretta—the Santa—the Caligari—the Portiera [Vedova?]—the Bolognese figurante—the Tentora and her sister—cum multis aliis?—some of them are Countesses—& some of them Cobblers wives—some noble—some middling—some low—& all whores—which does the damned old "Ladro—& porco fottuto"[7] mean?—I have had them all & thrice as many to boot since 1817— Since *he* tells a story about me—I will tell one about him;—when he landed at the *Custom house* from *Corfu*—he called for *"Post horses— directly"*—he was told that there were no horses except mine nearer than the Lido—unless he wished for the four bronze Coursers of St. Mark—which were at his Service.—

I am yrs. ever—

Let me have H's Election immediately—I mention it *last* as being what I was least likely to forget.——

P.S.—Whatever Brain-money—you get on my account from Murray—pray remit me—I will never consent to pay away what I *earn*—that is *mine*—& what I get by my brains—I will spend on my b——ks—as long as I have a tester or a testicle remaining.—I shall not live long—& for that Reason—I must live while I can—so—let him disburse—& me receive—"for the Night cometh."———If I had but had twenty thousand a year I should not have been living now— but all men are not born with a silver or Gold Spoon in their mouths. ——My balance—also—my balance—& a Copyright—I have another Canto—too—ready—& then there will be my half year in June— recollect—*I* care for nothing but "monies".—January 20th. 1819.— You say nothing of Mazeppa—did it arrive—with one other—besides that you mention?——

---

[5] Arpalici Taruscelli (variously spelled) was a ballerina at the Venice opera. Byron later recommended her to his friends in London when she followed the troupe there.

[6] Byron had written Hobhouse on Feb. 23, 1818: "a Girl (Whom you don't know—Elena da Mosta—a Gentil Donna) was clapt—& she has clapt me—to be sure it was *gratis*, the first Gonorrhea I have not paid for."

[7] Fottuto = Fr. foutre, an epithet of disgust or disrespect.

My dear Scrope—Yesterday I received through Hobhouse the decision of your Æreopagus or Apollophagus—or Phœbopagus;[1]— and by the same post I growled back my reluctant acquiescence (for the present) of which I have repented ever since—and it is now four & twenty hours.—What I meant to call was a Jury—(not ⟨a Jury⟩ of *Matrons*) and not a Coroner's Inquest.—That Hobhouse the politician & Candidate should pause—I marvel not—his existence just now depends upon "the breath of Occupation"[2]—that Frere the poet and Symposiast of the Coteries should doubt was natural—but that you a man of the world and a wit,—and Douglas Kinnaird—my friend—my Power of Attorney—and banker—should give in to the atrocious cant of the day surprizes me.——The motto "domestica facta" in any case —whether fully published—or simply printed for distribution, must be erased—there is no occasion for a motto at all.[3]—What I meant by "domestica facta" was *"Common life"*—& not one's own adventures— Juan's are no adventures of mine—but some that happened in Italy about seven or eight years ago—to an Italian.—If the bitch Inez resembles any other bitch[4]—that's fair—nature is for the poet & the painter.—The lines on Castlereagh must be omitted[5]—(as I am not now near enough to give him an exchange of shots—)—& also the words *Bob* at the end of the third stanza—which leave "high & dry" decent & pointless rhymes.——

I have finished another canto in 206 stanzas—with less love in it— and a good deal of Shipwreck—for which I have studied the Sea, many narratives—and some experience, at least of Gales of Wind.—If we are to yield to this sort of cant—*Johnson* is an immoral writer—for in his first imitation—*London* he has "cures a Clap"—and again—

---

[1] This might roughly be translated: "your solemn judges or Apollo consumers— or judges of the sun." All of Byron's friends had objected to the publication of *Don Juan* on the grounds that its frankness and its obvious satire on Lady Byron would damage his reputation.

[2] *Corialanus*, Act IV, scene 6: "you that stood so much / Upon the voice of occupation and / The breath of garlic-eaters!"

[3] Byron changed his mind, however, for when the first two cantos were published anonymously on July 15, 1819, they bore the motto: "Difficile est proprie communia dicere. Horace, *Epist. ad Pison.*"

[4] Donna Inez, Don Juan's mother, is in some parts obviously drawn from the character of Lady Byron, but as a fictional character she has many other traits, even some of Byron's mother.

[5] The whole of the "Dedication" containing the lines on "The intellectual eunuch Castlereagh" was omitted because, Byron said, "I won't attack the dog so fiercely without putting my name".

["]——swear

He gropes his breeches with a Monarch's air".—
Surely far grosser—& coarser than anything in Juan.—Consult
"*London*".—I will try what I can do against this disgusting affectation
—and whether I succeed or not—the experiment will be made.——It
is my intention to write a preface stating that the poem is printed
against the opinion of all my friends and of the publisher also,—&
that the whole responsibility is mine—& mine only.——H[obhouse]
talks to me about the woman—& of the thing being forgotten—is it
so?—*I* have *not* forgotten—nor *forgiven*.——And Ellice talks of my
standing *"well & high"*—who cares how I stand—if my standing is to
be shaken by the breath of a bitch—or her infamous Setters on?——If
she was Scylla with all her dogs—I care not—I have swum through
Charybdis already.—I write in haste and in very bad humour—but in
all hurry and in every Mood always

yrs. truly & affectly
B

P.S.—I have written in such haste, as to omit the most essential of
All—"the *Monies*"—I should like to know what is to make me amends
for the *"ducats"* I should have received—fairly & hardly earned—am
I neither to have them nor "my pound of flesh nearest the heart?"—I
will have both.——

[On cover] Take for the Motto "No Hopes for them as laughs"—
Stickles's Sermons.—You will recollect the passage.——

[TO DOUGLAS KINNAIRD]   *Venice. January 27th. 1819*

My dear Douglas—I have received a very clever letter from
Hobhouse against the publication of Don Juan—in which I understand
you have acquiesced (you be damned)—I acquiesce too—but reluctantly.——This acquiescence is some thousands of pounds out of my
pocket—the very thought of which brings tears into my eyes—I
have imbibed such a love for money that I keep some Sequins in a
drawer to count, & cry over them once a week—and if it was not for a
turn for women—(which I hope will be soon worn out)—I think in
time that I should be able not only to clear off but to accumulate.——
God only knows how it rends my heart—to part with the idea of the
sum I should have received from a fair bargain of my recent "poeshie"

the Sequins are the great consideration—as for the applauses of posterity—I would willingly sell the Reversion at a discount—even to Mr. Southey—who seems fond of it—as if people's Grandchildren were to be wiser than their forefathers—although no doubt the simple Chances of change are in favour of the deuce-ace turning up at last—just as in the overturn of a Coach the odds are that your arse will be first out of the window.—I say—that as for fame and all that—it is for such persons as Fortune chooses—and so is money.—And so on account of this damned prudery—and the reviews—and an Outcry and posterity—a Gentleman who has "a proper regard for his fee" is to be curtailed of his "Darics," (I am reading about Greece & Persia) this comes of consulting friends—I will see you all damned—before I consult you again—what do you mean now by giving advice when you are asked for it?—don't you know that it is like asking a man how he does—and that the answer in both cases should always be *"Very well I thank you"?——*

yrs. ever [scrawl]
B

P.S.—Give my love to Frere and tell him—he is right—but I never will forgive him nor any of you.——"My fee—My fee"—"I looked for a suit &c. &c. and you stop my mouth with &c. a whoreson Achitophel—May he be damned like the Glutton."[1]——

[TO JOHN MURRAY]   *Venice April 6 1819*

Dear Sir—The Second Canto of Don Juan was sent on Saturday last by post in 4 packets—two of 4—& two of three sheets each—containing in all two hundred & seventeen stanzas octave measure.—But I will permit no curtailments except those mentioned about Castlereagh & the two "*Bobs*" in the introduction.—You sha'n't make *Canticles* of my Cantos. The poem will please if it is lively—if it is stupid it will fail—but I will have none of your damned cutting & slashing.—If you please you may publish *anonymously*[;] it will perhaps be better;—but I will battle my way against them all—like a Porcupine.—So you and Mr. Foscolo &c. want me to undertake what you call a "great work" an Epic poem I suppose or some such pyramid. —I'll try no such thing—I hate tasks—and then "seven or eight years!" God send us all well this day three months—let alone years—

---

[1] Adapted from *Henry IV*, Part II, Act I, scene 2.

if one's years can't be better employed than in sweating poesy—a man had better be a ditcher.—And works too!—is Childe Harold nothing? you have so many *"divine"* poems, is it nothing to have written a *Human* one? without any of your worn out machinery.—Why—man— I could have spun the thought of the four cantos of that poem into twenty—had I wanted to book-make—& it's passion into as many modern tragedies—since you want *length* you shall have enough of *Juan* for I'll make 50 cantos.—And Foscolo too! why does *he* not do something more than the letters of Ortis—and a tragedy—and pamphlets—he has good fifteen years more at his command than I have—what has he done all that time?—proved his Genius doubtless —but not fixed it's fame—nor done his utmost.—Besides I mean to write my best work in *Italian*—& it will take me nine years more thoroughly to master the language—& then if my fancy exists & I exist too—I will try what I *can* do *really*.—As to the Estimation of the English which you talk of, let them calculate what it is worth—before they insult me with their insolent condescension.—I have not written for their pleasure;—if they are pleased—it is that they chose to be so, —I have never flattered their opinions—nor their pride—nor will I.— Neither will I make "Ladies books" "al dilettar le femine e la plebe"— I have written from the fullness of my mind, from passion—from impulse—from many motives—but not for their "sweet voices."[1]—I know the precise worth of popular applause—for few Scribblers have had more of it—and if I chose to swerve into their paths—I could retain it or resume it—or increase it—but I neither love ye—nor fear ye—and though I buy with ye—and sell with ye—and talk with ye—I will neither eat with ye—drink with ye—nor pray with ye.[2]—They made me without my search a species of popular Idol—they—without reason or judgement beyond the caprice of their Good pleasure—threw down the Image from it's pedestal—it was not broken with the fall— and they would it seems again replace it—but they shall not. You ask about my health—about the beginning of the year—I was in a state of great exhaustion—attended by such debility of Stomach—that nothing remained upon it—and I was obliged to reform my "way of life" which was conducting me from the "yellow leaf" to the Ground with all deliberate speed.—I am better in health and morals—and very much yrs. ever,

[scrawl]

[1] *Coriolanus,* Act II, scene 3.
[2] *Merchant of Venice,* Act I, scene 3.

P.S.—Tell Mrs. Leigh I never had "my Sashes" and I want some tooth-powder—the red—by all or any means.—

[TO JOHN CAM HOBHOUSE]   *Venice April 6. 1819*

My dear Hobhouse—I have not derived from the Scriptures of Rochfoucault that consolation which I expected "in the misfortunes of our best friends".[1]——I had much at heart your gaining the Election[2] —but from "the filthy puddle" into which your Patriotism had run you—I had like Croaker my bodings but like old "Currycomb" you make so "handsome a Corpse"[3]—that my wailing is changed into admiration.—With the Burdettites divided—and the Whigs & Tories united—what else could be expected? If I had guessed at your *opponent*[4] —I would have made one among you Certes—and have f——d Caroline Lamb out of her "two hundred votes" although at the expence of a testicle.——I think I could have neutralized her zeal with a little management—but alas! who could have thought of that Cuckoldy family's ⟨sitting⟩ *standing* for a *member*—I suppose it is the first time that George Lamb ever *stood* for any thing—& William with his "Corni Cazzo da Seno!" (as we Venetians say—it means— Penis *in earnest*—a sad way of swearing) but that you who know them should have to con*cur* with such dogs—well—did I ever—no I never &c. &c. &c.——I have sent my second Canto—but I will have no gelding.——Murray has my order of the day.—Douglas Kinnaird with more than usual politeness writes me vivaciously that Hanson or I willed the *three per cents* instead of the five—as if I could prefer *three* to *five* per Cent!—death & fiends!—and then *he* lifts up his leg against the publication of Don Juan—et "tu *Brute*" (the *e mute* recollect) I shall certainly hitch our dear friend into some d——d story or other —"my dear Mr. Sneer—Mr. Sneer—my dear"———I must write again in a few days—it being now past four in the morning—it is Passion week—& rather dull.—I am dull too for I have fallen in love with a

---

[1] Rochefoucauld's *Maxim*: "There is something in the misfortunes of our best friends which does not always displease us."

[2] Hobhouse lost tne election to the House of Commons from Westminster to George Lamb.

[3] At the end of the first act of Goldsmith's *The Good-Natured Man*, Croaker says: "but come with me, and we shall see something that will give us a great deal of pleasure, I promise you; old Ruggins, the curry-comb maker, lying in state: I am told he makes a very handsome corpse...."

[4] Lady Caroline Lamb electioneered for her brother-in-law George Lamb.

Romagnuola Countess from Ravenna[5]—who is nineteen years old &
has a Count of fifty—whom She seems disposed to qualify the first
year of marriage being just over.—I knew her a little last year at her
starting, but they always wait a year—at least generally.—I met her
first at the Albrizzi's, and this Spring at the Benzone's—and I have
hopes Sir—hopes—but She wants me to come to Ravenna—& then to
Bologna—now this would be all very well for certainties—but for
mere hopes—if She should plant[6] me—and I should make a "fiasco"
never could I show my face on the Piazza.——It is nothing that
Money can do—for the Conte is awfully rich—& would be so even in
England—but he is fifty and odd—has had two wives & children before
this his third—(a pretty fair-haired Girl last year out of a Convent—
now making her second tour of the Venetian Conversazioni—) and
does not seem so jealous this year as he did last—when he stuck close
to her side even at the Governor's.——She is pretty—but has no tact
—answers aloud—when she should whisper—talks of age to old
ladies who want to pass for young—and this blessed night horrified a
correct company at the Benzona's—by calling out to me "Mio Byron"
in an audible key during a dead Silence of pause in the other prattlers,
who stared & whispered [to] their respective Serventi.—One of her
preliminaries is that I must never leave Italy;—I have no desire to
leave it—but I should not like to be frittered down into a regular
Cicisbeo.—What shall I do! I am in love—and tired of promiscuous
concubinage—& have now an opportunity of settling for life.—

[ever yours]

P.S.—We have had a fortnight ago the devil's own row with an
Elephant who broke loose—ate up a fruitshop—killed his keeper—
broke into a Church—and was at last killed by a Cannon Shot brought
from the Arsenal.—I saw him the day he broke open his own house—
he was standing in the *Riva* & his keepers trying to persuade him with
peck-loaves to go on board a sort of Ark they had got.—I went close
to him that afternoon in my Gondola—& he amused himself with
flinging great beams that flew about over the water in all directions—
he was then not *very* angry—but towards midnight he became furious
—& displayed the most extraordinary strength—pulling down every
thing before him.—All Musquetry proved in vain—& when he

[5] This was Byron's first mention in a letter of the Countess Teresa Guiccioli
whom he had met a few days before.
[6] This is Byron's literal translation of the Italian "piantare", to abandon, or
leave in the lurch.

charged the Austrians threw down their musquets & ran.—At last they broke a hole & brought a field-piece the first shot missed the second entered behind—& came out *all but* the Skin at his Shoulder.— I saw him dead the next day—a stupendous fellow.—He went mad for want of a She it being the rutting month.—Fletcher is well.—I have got two monkeys, a fox—& two new mastiffs—Mutz is still in high old age.—The Monkeys are charming.—Last month I had a business about a Venetian Girl[7] who wanted to marry me—a circumstance prevented like Dr. Blifil's Espousals not only by my previous marriage—but by Mr. Allworthy's being acquainted with the existence of Mrs. Dr. Blifil.[8]——I was very honest and gave her no hopes—but there was a scene—I having been found at her window at Midnight and they sent me a Priest and a friend of the family's to talk with me next day both of whom I treated with Coffee.——

[TO DOUGLAS KINNAIRD]   *Venice April 24th. 1819*

Dear Douglas—

"When that the Captain comed for to know it,
He very much applauded what she had done,"

and I only want the command "of the gallant Thunder Bomb" to make you my "first Lieutenant".—I meant "five thousand pounds" and never intend to have so much meaning again—in short—I refer you Gentlemen—to my original letter of instructions which by the blessing of God—seems to bear as many constructions as a Delphic Oracle;—I say I refer you to that when you are at a loss how to avoid paying my money away;—I hate paying—& you are quite right to encourage me.—As to Hanson & *Son*—I make no distinctions—it would be a sort of blasphemy—I should as soon think of untwisting the Trinity—what do they mean by separate bills?—With regard to the Rochdale suit—and the "large discretion" or Indiscretion of a thousand pounds—what could I do? I want to gain my suit—but I will be guided by you—if you think "punds Scottish" will do better—let me know—I am docile.—Pray what could make Farebrother[1] say that

---

[7] The girl's name was Angelina and she was the daughter of a noble. Byron gave more details of the affair in a letter to Murray, May 18, 1819.

[8] Fielding, *Tom Jones,* Book I, Chap. 10.

[1] Farebrother was the auctioneer who twice offered Newstead for sale, once in August, 1812, and again in the summer of 1815. Both times the bids were insufficient and it was withdrawn from sale.

Seventeen thousand pounds had been bidden for the undisputed part of Rochdale manor?—it may be so—but I never heard of it before—not even from Spooney—if anybody bids—take it—& send it me by post—but don't pay away to those low people of tradesmen—they may survive Lady Noel—or me—and get it from the executors and heirs—but I don't approve of any living liquidations—a damned deal too much has been paid already—the fact is that the villains owe me money —& not I to them.—Damn *"the Vampire,"*[2]—what do I know of Vampires? it must be some bookselling imposture—contradict it in a solemn paragraph.—I sent off on April 3rd. the 2nd. Canto of "Don Juan" addressed to Murray—I hope it is arrived—by the Lord! it is a Capo d'Opera—so "full of pastime and prodigality"[3]—but you shan't decimate nor mutilate—no—"rather than that come Critics into the list—and champion me to the uttermost."[4]—Nor you nor that rugged rhinoceros Murray have ever told me in answer to fifty times the question—if he ever received the additions to Canto *first* entitled "Julia's letter" and also some four stanzas for the beginning.—I have fallen in love within the last month with a Romagnuola Countess from Ravenna—the Spouse of a year of Count Guiccioli—who is sixty —the Girl twenty—he has eighty thousand ducats of rent—and has had two wives before—but he is Sixty—he is the first of Ravenna Nobles—but he is sixty—She is fair as Sunrise—and warm as Noon—we had but ten days—to manage all our little matters in beginning middle and end. & we managed them;—and I have done my duty—with the proper consummation.—But She is young—and was not content with what she had done—unless it was to be turned to the advantage of the public—and so She made an eclat which rather astonished even the Venetians—and electrified the Conversazioni of the Benzone—the Albrizzi—& the Michelli—and made her ⟨Lord⟩ husband look embarrassed.—They have been gone back to Ravenna—some time—but they return in the Winter.—She is the queerest woman I ever met with—for in general they cost one something in one way or other—whereas by an odd combination of circumstances—I have proved an expence to HER—which is not my custom,—but an accident—however it don't matter.—She is a sort of an Italian Caroline Lamb, except that She is much prettier, and not so savage.—

[2] *The Vampyre*, written by Dr. Polidori, based on a tale Byron began at Diodati in 1816, was published anonymously in 1819. It was widely supposed to be Byron's work, and was ascribed to him in *Galigani's Messenger*.

[3] Farquhar, *The Recruiting Officer*, Act V, scene 1.

[4] *Macbeth*, Act III, scene 1: "Rather than so, . . . come fate into the list / And champion me to the utterance!"

But She has the same red-hot head—the same noble dis*dain* of public opinion—with the superstructure of all that Italy can add to such natural dispositions.—To be sure they may go much further here with impunity—as her husband's rank ensured their reception at all societies including the Court—and as it was her first outbreak since Marriage—the Sympathizing world was liberal.—She is also of the Ravenna noblesse—educated in a convent—sacrifice to Wealth— filial duty and all that.—I am damnably in love—but they are gone— gone—for many months—and nothing but Hope—keeps me alive seriously.

yrs. [scrawl]

[TO JOHN MURRAY]   *Venice. May 15th. 1819*

Dear Sir—I have received & return by this post under cover—the first proof of "Don Juan."—Before the second can arrive it is probable that I may have left Venice—and the length of my absence is so uncertain—that you had better proceed to the publication without boring me with more proofs—I sent by last post an addition—and a new copy of "Julia's letter," perceiving or supposing the former one in Winter did not arrive.—Mr. Hobhouse is at it again about indelicacy —there is *no indelicacy*—if he wants *that,* let him read Swift—his great Idol—but his Imagination must be a dunghill with a Viper's nest in the middle—to engender such a supposition about this poem.—For my part I think you are all crazed.—What does he mean about "G—d damn"—there is *"damn"* to be sure—but no "G—d" whatever.— And as to what he calls "a p—ss bucket"—it is nothing but simple water—as I am a Sinner—pray tell him so—& request him not "to put me in a phrenzy," as Sir Anthony Absolute says—"though he was not the indulgent father that I am."[1]—I have got yr. extract, & the "Vampire". I need not say it is *not mine*—there is a rule to go by— you are my publisher (till we quarrel) and what is not published by you is not written by me.—The Story of Shelley's agitation is true[2]— I can't tell what seized him—for he don't want courage. He was once with me in a Gale of Wind in a small boat right under the rocks

---

[1] *The Rivals,* Act II, scene 1.

[2] In the Preface to *The Vampyre* is an account of an evening at the Villa Diodati when Shelley was so agitated while ghost stories were being told that he rushed out of the room and later confessed that his imagination had been so stirred that he conceived that one of the ladies (Mary Godwin) had eyes in her breasts.

between Meillerie & St. Gingo—we were five in the boat—a servant —two boatmen—& ourselves. The Sail was mismanaged & the boat was filling fast—he can't swim.—I stripped off my coat—made him strip off his—& take hold of an oar—telling him that I thought (being myself an expert swimmer) I could save him if he would not struggle when I took hold of him—unless we got smashed against the rocks which were high & sharp with an awkward Surf on them at that minute;—we were then about a hundred yards from shore—and the boat in peril.—He answered me with the greatest coolness—"that he had no notion of being saved—& that I would have enough to do to save myself, and begged not to trouble me".—Luckily the boat righted & baling [sic] we got round a point into St. Gingo—where the Inhabitants came down and embraced the boatmen on their escape— the Wind having been high enough to tear up some huge trees from the Alps above us as we saw next day.—And yet the same Shelley who was as cool as it was possible to be in such circumstances—(of which I am no judge myself as the chance of swimming naturally gives self-possession when near shore) certainly had the fit of phantasy which P[olidori] describes—though *not exactly* as he describes it. The story of the agreement to write the Ghost-books is true—but the ladies are *not Sisters*—one is Godwin's daughter by Mary Wolstonecraft—and the other the *present* Mrs. Godwin's daughter by a former husband. So much for Scoundrel Southey's Story of *"incest"*—neither was there *any promiscuous intercourse* whatever—both are an invention of the execrable villain Southey—whom I will term so as publicly as he deserves.— Mary Godwin (now Mrs. Shelley) wrote "Frankenstein"—which you have reviewed thinking it Shelley's—methinks it is a wonderful work for a Girl of nineteen—*not* nineteen indeed—at that time.—I enclose you the beginning of mine[3]—by which you will see how far it resembles Mr. Colburn's publication.—If you choose to publish it in the Edinburgh Magazine (*Wilsons* & *Blackwoods*) you may—*stating why*, & with such explanatory proem as you please.—I never went on with it—as you will perceive by the date.—I began it in an old account-book of Miss Milbanke's which I kept because it contains the word *"Household"* written by her twice on the inside blank page of the Covers— being the only two Scraps I have in the world in her writing, except her name to the deed of Separation.—Her letters I sent back—except those of the quarrelling correspondence—and those being documents

---

[3] This fragment of a story, begun at Diodati, which was the basis for Polidori's *Vampyre*, was published with *Mazeppa* and the *Ode on Venice*.

are placed in possession of a third person (Mr. Hobhouse) with copies of several of my own,—so that I have no kind of memorial whatever of her but these *two* words—and her actions. I have torn the leaves containing the part of the tale out of the book & enclose them with this sheet.—Next week—I set out for Romagna—at least in all probability.—You had better go on with the publications without waiting to hear farther—for I have other things in my head.— "Mazeppa" & "the Ode"—*separate*—what think you?—*Juan anonymous without the dedication*—for I won't be shabby—& attack Southey under Cloud of night.—What do you mean? first you seem hurt by my letter? & then in your next you talk of it's "power" & so forth— "this is a d—d blind Story Beck—but never mind—go on." You may be sure I said nothing *on purpose* to plague you—but if you will put me "in a phrenzy, I will never call you *Jack* again."[4]—I remember nothing of the epistle at present.—What do you mean by Polidori's *diary?*—why—I defy him to say any thing about me—but he is welcome—I have nothing to *reproach* me with on his score—and I am much mistaken if that is not his *own* opinion—but why publish the names of the two girls? & in such a manner?—what a blundering piece of exculpation!—*He* asked Pictet[5] &c. to dinner—and of course was left to entertain them.—I went into *Society solely* to present *him* (as I told him) that he might return into good company if he chose—it was the best thing for his youth & circumstances—for myself I had done with Society—& having presented him—withdrew to my own "way of life."—It is true that I returned without entering Lady Dalrymple Hamilton's—because I saw it full.—It is true—that Mrs. Hervey[6] (She writes novels) fainted at my entrance into Coppet—& then came back again;—on her fainting—the Duchess de Broglie[7] exclaimed: "This is *too much*—at Sixty five years of age!"—I never gave "the English" an opportunity of "avoiding" me—but I trust, that if ever I do, they will seize it.—

I am yrs. very truly

B

[4] *The Rivals*, Act II, scene 1.

[5] Marc-Auguste Pictet, a prominent literary and political figure of Geneva.

[6] There seems to be some doubt as to the identity of this Mrs. Hervey. Prothero (*LJ*, IV, 300–301) identifies three of that name who wrote novels. Elwin (*Lord Byron's Family*) says she was Elizabeth Hervey, half-sister of William Beckford.

[7] Madame de Staël's daughter.

My dearest Love—I have been negligent in not writing, but what can I say[.] Three years absence—& the total change of scene and habit make such a difference—that we have now nothing in common but our affections & our relationship.—

But I have never ceased nor can cease to feel for a moment that perfect & boundless attachment which bound & binds me to you— which renders me utterly incapable of *real* love for any other human being—what could they be to me after *you?* My own XXXX [Short word crossed out] we may have been very wrong—but I repent of nothing except that cursed marriage—& your refusing to continue to love me as you had loved me—I can neither forget nor *quite forgive* you for that precious piece of reformation.—but I can never be other than I have been—and whenever I love anything it is because it reminds me in some way or other of yourself—for instance I not long ago attached myself to a Venetian for no earthly reason (although a pretty woman) but because she was called XXXX [short word crossed out] and she often remarked (without knowing the reason) how fond I was of the name.—It is heart-breaking to think of our long Separation—and I am sure more than punishment enough for all our sins—Dante is more humane in his "Hell" for he places his unfortunate lovers (Francesca of Rimini & Paolo whose case fell a good deal short of, ours—though sufficiently naughty) in company— and though they suffer—it is at least together.—If ever I return to England—it will be to see you—and recollect that in all time—& place—and feelings—I have never ceased to be the same to you in heart—Circumstances may have ruffled my manner—& hardened my spirit—you may have seen me harsh & exasperated with all things around me; grieved & tortured with *your new resolution,*—& the soon after persecution of that infamous fiend who drove me from my Country & conspired against my life—by endeavouring to deprive me of all that could render it precious—but remember that even then *you* were the sole object that cost me a tear? and *what tears!* do you remember *our* parting? I have not spirits now to write to you upon other subjects—I am well in health—and have no cause of grief but the reflection that we are not together—When you write to me speak to me of yourself—& say that you love me—never mind common-place people & topics—which can be in no degree interesting—to me who see nothing in England but the country which holds *you*—or around it but the sea which divides us.—They say absence destroys weak passions—& confirms strong ones—Alas! *mine* for you is the union of all passions & of all affections—Has strengthened itself but will destroy me—I do not speak of *physical* destruction—for I have endured & can endure much—but of the annihilation of all thoughts feelings or hopes—which have not more or less a reference to you & to *our recollections—*

Ever dearest
[Signature erased]

[TO JOHN MURRAY]   *Venice, May 18, 1819*

Dear Sir—Yesterday I wrote to Mr. Hobhouse and returned the proof under cover to you. Tell Mr. Hobhouse that in the Ferrara story I told him, the phrase was *Vi riveresco Signor Cognato* and *not Cognato mio* as I stated yesterday by mistake. I write to you in haste and at past two in the morning—having besides had an accident. In going, about an hour and a half ago, to a rendezvous with a Venetian Girl (unmarried and the daughter of one of their nobles), I tumbled into the Grand Canal—and not choosing to miss my appointment by the delays of changing—I have been perched in a balcony with my wet clothes on ever since—till this minute that on my return I have slipped into my dressing gown. My foot slipped in getting into my Gondola to set out (owing to the cursed slippery steps of their palaces) and in I flounced like a Carp—and went dripping like a Triton to my Sea-nymph—and had to scramble up to a Grated window

"Fenced with iron within and without
Lest the Lover get in, or the Lady get out."

She is a very dear friend of mine—and I have undergone some trouble on her account—for last winter the truculent tyrant her flinty-hearted father—having been informed by an infernal German Countess Vorsperg (their next neighbour) of our meetings—they sent a priest to me—and a Commissary of police—and they locked the Girl up—and gave her prayers and bread and water—and our connection was cut off for some time—but the father hath lately been laid up—and the brother is at Milan—and the mother falls asleep—and the Servants are naturally on the wrong side of the question—and there is no Moon at Midnight just now—so that we have lately been able to recommence;—the fair one is eighteen—her name Angelina—the family name of course I don't tell you. She proposed to me to divorce my mathematical wife—and I told her that in England we can't divorce except for *female* infidelity—"and pray, (said she), how do you know what she may have been doing these last three years?"—I answered *that* I could not tell—but that the status of Cuckoldom was not quite so flourishing in Great Britain as with us here.—But—She said—"can't you get rid of her?"—"not more than is done already" (I answered) —"you would not have me *poison her*?"—would you believe it? She made me *no answer*—is not that a true and odd national trait?—it spoke more than a thousand words—and yet this is a little—pretty— sweet-tempered,—quiet, feminine being as ever you saw—but the Passions of a Sunny Soil are paramount to all other considerations;— an unmarried Girl naturally wishes to be married—if she can marry & love at the same time it is well—but at any rate She must love;—I am not sure that my pretty paramour was herself fully aware of the inference to be drawn from her dead Silence—but even the uncon- sciousness of the latent idea was striking to an Observer of the Passions—and I never strike out a thought of another's or of my own— without trying to trace it to it's Source.—I wrote to Mr. H. pretty fully about our matters—in a few days I leave Venice for Romagna— excuse this scrawl—for I write in a state of shivering from having sat in my dripping drapery—and from some other little accessories which affect this husk of our immortal Kernel.——Tell Augusta that I wrote to her by yesterday's post—addressed to your care—let me know if you come out this Summer—that I may be in the way—and come to me —don't go to an Inn—I do not know that I can promise you any pleasure [;] "our way of life" is so different in these parts, but I insure to myself a great deal in seeing you, and in endeavouring (how- ever vainly) to prove to you that I am

very truly yrs. ever

B

P.S.—I have read Parson Hodgson's "Friends"[1] in which he seems to display his knowledge of the Subject by a covert Attack or two on Some of his own. He probably wants another Living—at least I judge so by the prominence of his Piety—although he was always pious— even when he was kept by a Washerwoman on the New road. I have seen him cry over her picture which he generally wore under his left Armpit.—But he is a good man—and I have no doubt does his duties by

---

[1] *The Friends: a Poem* by the Rev. Francis Hodgson, was published by Murray in 1818. It was dedicated to the Duke of Rutland, a son-in-law of Lord Carlisle, which may have accounted in part for the acerbity of Byron's comments.

his Parish.—As to the poetry of his new-fangled Stanza—I wish they would write the octave or the Spenser—we have no other legitimate measure of that kind.—He is right in defending *Pope*—against the bastard Pelicans of the poetical winter day—who add insult to their Parricide—by sucking the blood of the parent of English *real* poetry— poetry without a fault—and then spurning the bosom which fed them.—

[TO RICHARD BELGRAVE HOPPNER]   *Bologna. June 6th. 1819*

Dear Hoppner—I am at length joined to Bologna—where I am settled like a Sausage—and shall be broiled like one if this weather continues.—Will you thank Mengaldo on my part for the Ferrara acquaintance—which was a very agreeable one—I staid two days at Ferrara—& was much pleased with the Count Mosti and the little the shortness of the time permitted me to see of his family.—I went to his Conversazione which is very far superior to anything of the kind at Venice—the women almost all young—several pretty—and the men courteous & cleanly; the Lady of the mansion who is young—lately married—and with child—appeared very pretty by Candle light (I did not see her by day) pleasing in her manners and very lady-like —or thorough-bred as we call it in England a kind of thing which reminds me of a racer—an Antelope—or an Italian Grey-hound—— She seems very fond of her husband who is amiable and accomplished— he has been in England two or three times—and is young.—The Sister—a Countess Somebody—I forget what—they are both Maffei by birth—and Veronese of course—is a lady of more display—she sings & plays divinely—but I thought She was a d—d long time about it——her likeness to Madame Flahaut—(Miss Mercer that was) is something quite extraordinary—I had but a bird's eye view of these people and shall not probably see them again—but I am very much obliged to Mengaldo for letting me see them at all;—whenever I meet with any-thing agreeable in this world it surprizes me so much —and pleases me so much (when my passions are not interested one way or the other) that I go on wondering for a week to come.—I fell too in great admiration of the Cardinal Legate's red Stockings.—— I found too such a pretty epitaph in the Certosa Cimetery—or rather two—one was

    Martini Luigi
    Implora pace.

201

the other—

> Lucrezia Picini
> "Implora eterna quiete."

that was all—but it appears to me that these two and three words comprize and compress all that can be said on the subject—and then in Italian they are absolute Music.——They contain doubt—hope—and humility—nothing can be more pathetic than the "implora" and the modesty of the request—they have had enough of life—they want nothing but rest—they implore it—and "eterna quieta"—it is like a Greek inscription in some good old Heathen "City of the dead".— Pray— if I am shovelled into the Lido Church-yard—in your time— let me have the "implora pace" and nothing else for my epitaph—I never met with any antient or modern that pleased me a tenth part so much.——In about a day or two after you receive this letter I will thank you to desire Edgecombe to prepare for my return—I shall go back to Venice before I village on the Brenta.——I shall stay but a few days in Bologna, I am just going out to see sights, but shall not present my introductory letters for a day or two till I have run over again the place & pictures——nor perhaps at all if I find that I have books & sights enough to do without the inhabitants.——After that I shall return to Venice where you may expect me about the eleventh— or perhaps sooner—pray make my thanks acceptable to Mengaldo— my respects to the Consuless—and to Mr. Scott;—I hope my daughter is well—ever yrs

> & truly
> BYRON

P.S.—I went over the Ariosto M.S. &c. &c. again at Ferrara—with the Castle—and Cell—and House—&c. &c. &c. One of the Ferrarese asked me if I knew "Lord Byron" an acquaintance of his *now* at Naples—I told him *No*—which was true both ways—for I know not the Impostor—and in the other—no one knows himself.—He stared when told that I was "the real Simon Pure."[1]—Another asked me if I had *not translated* "Tasso".—You see what *fame* is—how *accurate*— how *boundless*;—I don't know how others feel—but I am always the lighter and the better looked on when I have got rid of mine—it *sits* on me like armour on the Lord Mayor's Champion—and I got rid of all the husk of literature—and the attendant babble by answering that I had not translated Tasso.—but a namesake had—and by the blessing

---

[1] Mrs. Susanna Centlivre, *A Bold Stroke for a Wife.*

of Heaven I looked so little like a poet that every body believed me.
——I am just setting off for Ravenna.—June 8th 1819. I changed my
mind this morning & decided to go on———

[TO COUNTESS TERESA GUICCIOLI]   [*no date*] [*June–July 1819?*]

"My thoughts cannot find rest in me"[1]—I was right then: what is
that man doing every evening for so long beside you in your box? "So
we are agreed"—fine words! "*You* are agreed", it appears. I have
noticed that every time I turned my head toward the stage you
turned your eyes to look at that man—and this, after all that had
happened today! But do not fear, tomorrow evening I shall leave the
field clear to him.—I have no strength to bear a fresh torment every
day—you have made me despicable in my own eyes—and perhaps soon
in those of others.—Have you not seen my torments? Have you not
pitied them? I forgive you what you have made me suffer—but I can
never forgive myself the weakness of heart which has prevented me
until now from taking the only honourable step in such circumstances
—that of bidding you good-bye—for ever—

Midnight

My time for sleep before I knew you.

Let me go—it is better to die from the pain of separation, than from
that of betrayal—my life now is a constant agony. I have enjoyed a
unique and final happiness in your arms—but—oh God! how much
more those moments are costing me!—and *they* [cost] *this*!—now that
I am writing to you alone— completely alone. I had no one but you in
the world—and now, not having you any more (without the heart,
what is the rest?) solitude has become as tedious as society—for that
image, which I pictured as so pure, so dear, is now nothing but a
perfidious and menacing shadow,—and yet—always *yours*.[2]

---

[1] Tasso, *Gerusalemme Liberata*, Canto X⁰: "I suoi pensieri in lui dormir non
ponno" ("His thoughts cannot find rest in him"). This was the motto at the
beginning of *The Corsair*.

[2] Teresa wrote a note accompanying this letter in her collection: "Billet de
jalousie *magnifique—passionné—sublime mais* tres injuste. Il ne me connaissait
encore que depuis trop peu!!!" The original letter was written in Italian. Translation by Iris Origo in *The Last Attachment*, page 76.

My dearest Augusta—I am at too great a distance to scold you—
but I *will* ask you—whether *your* letter of the *1st.* July *is an answer* to
the letter I wrote you before I quitted Venice?—What? is it come to
this?—Have you no memory? or no heart?—You *had* both—and I *have*
both—at least for *you.*——I write this presuming that you received
that letter—is it that you fear? do not be afraid of the post—the World
has it's own affairs without thinking of *ours* and you may write safely
—if you do—address as usual to *Venice.*—My house is not in St.
Marc's but on the Grand Canal—within sight of the Rialto Bridge.—
—I do not like at all this pain in your side and always think of your
mother's constitution—you must always be to me the first consideration in the World.—Shall I come to *you?*—or would a warm climate do
you good?—if so say the word—and I will provide you & your whole
family (including that precious baggage your Husband) with the
means of making an agreeable journey—you need not fear about *me*—I
am much altered—and should be little trouble to you—nor would I
give you more of my company than you like.——I confess after three
years and a half—and *such years!* and *such a year* as preceded those three
years! it would be a relief to see you again—and if it would be so to
you—I will come to you.——Pray—answer me—and recollect that I
will do as you like in everything—even to returning to England—
which is *not* the pleasantest of residences were *you* out of it.——I write
from Ravenna—I came here on account of a Countess Guiccioli—a
Girl of Twenty married to a very rich old man of Sixty—about a year
ago;—with her last Winter I had a *liaison* according to the good old
Italian custom—she miscarried in May—and sent for me here—and
here I have been these two months.—She is pretty—a great Coquette—
extremely vain—excessively affected—clever enough—without the
smallest principle—with a good deal of imagination and some
passion;—She had set her heart on carrying me off from Venice out of
vanity—and succeeded—and having made herself the subject of
general conversation has greatly contributed to her recovery.—Her
husband is one of the richest Nobles of Ravenna—threescore years of
age—this is his third wife.——You may suppose what *esteem* I
entertain for *her*—perhaps it is about equal on both sides.—I have my
saddle-horses here and there is good riding in the forest—with these
—and my carriage which is here also—and the Sea—and my books—
and the lady—the time passes—I am very fond of riding and always
was out of England—but I hate your Hyde Park—and your turnpike

roads—& must have forests—downs—or deserts to expatiate in—I detest *knowing* the road—one is to go,—and being interrupted by your damned fingerposts, or a blackguard roaring for twopence at a turn-pike.——I send you a sonnet which this faithful Lady had made for the nuptials of one of her relations in which she swears the most *alarming constancey* to her husband—is not this good? you may suppose my *face* when she showed it to me—I could not help laughing—one of *our* laughs.——All this is very absurd—but you see that I have good morals at bottom.——She is an Equestrian too—but a bore in her rides—for she can't guide her horse—and he runs after mine—and tries to bite him—and then she begins screaming in a high hat and Sky-blue habit—making a most absurd figure—and embarrassing me and both our grooms—who have the devil's own work to keep her from tumbling—or having her clothes torn off by the trees and thickets of the Pine forest.——I fell a little in love with her intimate friend—a certain Geltruda—(that is *Gertrude*) who is very young & seems very well disposed to be perfidious—but alas!—*her* husband is jealous—and the G. also detected me in an illicit squeezing of hands, the consequence of which was that the friend was whisked off to Bologna for a few days—and since her return I have never been able to see her but twice—with a dragon of a mother in law—and a barbarous husband by her side—besides my own dear precious *Amica* —who hates all flirting but her own.—But I have a Priest who be-friends me—and the Gertrude says a good deal with her great black eyes, so that perhaps—but Alas! I mean to give up these things alto-gether.——I have now given you some account of my present state—the Guide-book will tell you about Ravenna—I can't tell how long or short may be my stay—write to me—love me—as ever

yrs. most affectly.

B

P.S.—*This* affair is *not* in the least expensive—being all in the wealthy line—but troublesome—for the lady is imperious—and exigeante—however there are hopes that we may quarrel—when we do you shall hear

[In margin of printed sonnet enclosed]

Ask Hobhouse to translate this to you—and tell him the reason.——

Address yr. answer to Venice however

Dear Sir—Don't be alarmed.—You will see me defend myself gaily—that is—if I happen to be in Spirits—and by *Spirits* I don't mean your meaning of the word—but the spirit of a bull-dog when pinched—or a bull when pinned—it is then that they make best sport— and as my Sensations under an attack are probably a happy compound of the united energies of those amiable animals—you may perhaps see what Marrall calls "rare sport"[1]—and some good tossing and goring in the course of the controversy.—But I must be in the right cue first —and I doubt I am almost too far off to be in a sufficient fury for the purpose—and then I have effeminated and enervated myself with love and the summer in these last two months.—I wrote to Mr. Hobhouse the other day—and foretold that Juan would either fall entirely or succeed completely—there will be no medium—appearances are not favourable—but as you write the day after publication—it can hardly be decided what opinion will predominate.—You seem in a fright— and doubtless with cause.—Come what may—I never will flatter the Million's canting in any shape—circumstances may or may not have placed me at times in a situation to lead the public opinion—but the public opinion—never led nor ever shall lead me.—I will not sit on "a degraded throne" so pray put Messrs. Southey—or Sotheby— or Tom Moore—or Horace Twiss upon it—they will all of them be transported with their coronation.——You have bought Harlow's drawings[2] of Margarita and me rather dear methinks—but since you desire the story of Margarita Cogni—you shall be told it—though it may be lengthy.——Her face is of the fine Venetian cast of the old Time—and her figure though perhaps too tall not less fine—taken altogether in the national dress.——In the summer of 1817, Hobhouse and myself were sauntering on horseback along the Brenta one evening—when amongst a group of peasants we remarked two girls as the prettiest we had seen for some time.—About this period there had been great distress in the country—and I had a little relieved some of the people.—Generosity makes a great figure at very little cost in Venetian livres—and mine had probably been exaggerated—as an

[1] When Sir Giles Overreach curses his daughter in Massinger's *New Way to Pay Old Debts* (Act V, scene 1), Marrall asks: "Is't not brave sport?"

[2] George Henry Harlow, who had painted a portrait of Byron in England in 1815, was in Venice in 1818, and made drawings of the poet and his mistress which Murray bought when the artist returned to England. Margarita Cogni looks very demure in her portrait. Harlow's drawing of Byron shows him with long hair.

Englishman's——Whether they remarked us looking at them or no—
I know not—but one of them called out to me in Venetian—"Why do
not you who relieve others—think of us also?"—I turned round and
answered her—"Cara—tu sei troppo bella e giovane per aver'
bisogno del' soccorso mio"—she answered—["] if you saw my hut and
my food—you would not say so["]—All this passed half jestingly—
and I saw no more of her for some days—A few evenings after—we
met with these two girls again—and they addressed us more seriously
—assuring us of the truth of their statement.—They were cousins—
Margarita married—the other single.—As I doubted still of the
circumstances—I took the business up in a different light—and made an
appointment with them for the next evening.—Hobhouse had taken a
fancy to the single lady—who was much shorter—in stature—but a
very pretty girl also.——They came attended by a third woman—
who was cursedly in the way—and Hobhouse's charmer took fright
(I don't mean at Hobhouse but at not being married—for here no
woman will do anything under adultery), and flew off—and mine made
some bother—at the propositions—and wished to consider of them.—
I told her "if you really are in want I will relieve you without any
conditions whatever—and you may make love with me or no just as
you please—*that* shall make no difference—but if you are not in
absolute necessity—this is naturally a rendezvous—and I presumed
that you understood this—when you made the appointment".——She
said that she had no objection to make love with me—as she was
married—and all married women did it—but that her husband (a
baker) was somewhat ferocious—and would do her a mischief.—In
short—in a few evenings we arranged our affairs—and for two years—
in the course of which I had ⟨almost two⟩ more women than I can
count or recount—she was the only one who preserved over me an
ascendancy—which was often disputed & never impaired.—As she
herself used to say publicly—"It don't matter—he may have five
hundred—but he will always come back to me".——The reasons of
this were firstly—her person—very dark—tall—the Venetian face—
very fine black eyes—and certain other qualities which need not be
mentioned.—She was two & twenty years old—and never having had
children—had not spoilt her figure—nor *anything else*—which is I
assure you—a great desideration in a hot climate where they grow
relaxed and doughy and *flumpity* in a short time after breeding.——
She was besides a thorough Venetian in her dialect—in her thoughts—
in her countenance—in every thing—with all their naïveté and
Pantaloon humour.—Besides she could neither read nor write—and

could not plague me with letters—except twice that she paid sixpence to a public scribe under the piazza—to make a letter for her—upon some occasion when I was ill and could not see her.———In other respects she was somewhat fierce and "prepotente" that is—overbearing—and used to walk in whenever it suited her—with no very great regard to time, place, nor persons—and if she found any women in her way she knocked them down.—When I first knew her I was in "relazione" (liaison) with la Signora Segati—who was silly enough one evening at Dolo—accompanied by some of her female friends—to threaten her—for the Gossips of the Villeggiatura—had already found out by the neighing of my horse one evening—that I used to "ride late in the night" to meet the Fornarina.———Margarita threw back her veil (fazziolo) and replied in very explicit Venetian—"*You* are *not* his *wife*: *I* am *not* his *wife*—*you* are his Donna—and *I* am his *donna*—*your* husband is a cuckold—and mine is another;—for the rest, what *right* have you to reproach me?—if he prefers what is mine—to what is yours—is it my fault? if you wish to secure him—tie him to your petticoat-string—but do not think to speak to me without a reply because you happen to be richer than I am."———Having delivered this pretty piece of eloquence (which I translate as it was related to me by a byestander) she went on her way—leaving a numerous audience with Madame Segati—to ponder at her leisure on the dialogue between them.—When I came to Venice for the Winter she followed:—I never had any regular *liaison* with her—but whenever she came I never allowed any other connection to interfere with her—and as she found herself out to be a favourite she came pretty often.—But She had inordinate Self-love—and was not tolerant of other women—except of the Segati—who was as she said my regular "Amica"—so that I being at that time somewhat promiscuous—there was great confusion—and demolition of head dresses and handkerchiefs—and sometimes my servants in "redding the fray"[3] between her and other feminine persons—received more knocks than acknowledgements for their peaceful endeavours.———At the "Cavalchina" the masqued ball on the last night of the Carnival—where all the World goes—she snatched off the mask of Madame Contarini—a lady noble by birth—and decent in conduct—for no other reason but because she happened to be leaning on my arm.—You may suppose what a cursed noise this made—but this is only one of her pranks.—At last she quarrelled with her husband—and one evening ran away to my house.—I told her this would not do—she said she would lie in the street but not go back to

[3] *Waverley*, Chapter LIV.

208

him—that he beat her (the gentle tigress) spent her money—and scandalously neglected his Oven. As it was Midnight—I let her stay— and next day there was no moving her at all.———Her husband came roaring & crying—& entreating her to come back, *not* She!—He then applied to the Police—and they applied to me—I told them and her husband to *take* her—I did not want her—she had come and I could not fling her out of the window—but they might conduct her through that or the door if they chose it———She went before the Commissary—but was obliged to return with that "becco Ettico" (consumptive cuckold), as she called the *poor* man who had a Ptisick.—In a few days she ran away again.—After a precious piece of work she fixed herself in my house—really & truly without my consent—but owing to my indolence —and not being able to keep my countenance—for if I began in a rage she always finished by making me laugh with some Venetian panta- loonery or other—and the Gipsy knew this well enough—as well as her other powers of persuasion—and exerted them with the usual tact and success of all She-things—high and low—they are all alike for that.—Madame Benzone also took her under her protection—and then her head turned.—She was always in extremes either crying or laughing—and so fierce when angered that she was the terror of men women and children—for she had the strength of an Amazon with the temper of Medea. She was a fine animal—but quite untameable. *I* was the only person that could at all keep her in any order—and when she saw me really angry—(which they tell me is rather a savage sight), she subsided.—But she had a thousand fooleries—in her fazziolo—the dress of the lower orders—she looked beautiful—but alas! she longed for a hat and feathers and all I could say or do (and I said much) could not prevent this travestie.—I put the first into the fire—but I got tired of burning them before she did of buying them—so that she made herself a figure—for they did not at all become her.—Then she would have her gowns with a *tail*—like a lady forsooth—nothing would serve her—but "l'abito colla *coua*", or *cua*, (that is the Venetian for "la *Coda*" the tail or train) and as her cursed pronunciation of the word made me laugh—there was an end of all controversy—and she dragged this diabolical tail after her every where.———In the mean time she beat the women—and stopped my letters.—I found her one day pondering over one—she used to try to find out by their shape whether they were feminine or no—and she used to lament her ignorance—and actually studied her Alphabet—on purpose (as she declared) to open all letters addressed to me and read their contents. ———I must not omit to do justice to her housekeeping qualities—after she came into my house as "donna di governo" the expences were reduced to less than half—and every body did their duty better—the apartments were kept in order—and every thing and every body else except herself.——That she had a sufficient regard for me in her wild way I had many reasons to believe—I will mention one.——In the autumn one day going to the Lido with my Gondoliers—we were overtaken by a heavy Squall and the Gondola put in peril—hats blown away—boat filling—oar lost—tumbling sea—thunder—rain in torrents—night coming—& wind increasing.—On our return—after a tight struggle: I found her on the open steps of the Mocenigo palace on the Grand Canal—with her great black eyes flashing through her tears and the long dark hair which was streaming drenched with rain over her brows & breast;—she was perfectly exposed to the storm—and the wind blowing her hair & dress about her tall thin figure—and the lightning flashing round her—with the waves rolling at her feet—made her look like Medea alighted from her chariot—or the Sibyl of the tempest that was rolling around her—the only living thing within hail at that moment except ourselves.—On seeing me safe—she did not wait to greet me as might be expected—but calling out to me—"Ah! Can' della Madonna xe esto il tempo per andar' al' Lido?" (ah! Dog of the Virgin!—is this a time to go to Lido?) ran into the house—and solaced herself with scolding the boatmen for not foreseeing the "temporale".—I was told by the servants that she had only been prevented from coming in a boat to look after me—by the refusal of all the Gondoliers of the Canal to put out into the harbour in such a moment and that then she sate down on the steps in all the thickest of the Squall—and would neither be removed nor comforted. Her joy at seeing me again—was moderately mixed with ferocity—and gave me the idea of a tigress over her recovered Cubs.——But her reign drew near a close.—She became quite ungovernable some months after—and a concurrence of complaints some true and many false—"a favourite has no friend"—determined me to part with her.—I told her quietly that she must return home—(she had acquired a sufficient provision for herself and mother, &c. in my service,) and She refused to quit the house.—I was firm—and she went—threatening knives and revenge. —I told her—that I had seen knives drawn before her time—and that if she chose to begin—there was a knife—and fork also at her service on the table and that intimidation would not do.—The next day while I was at dinner—she walked in, (having broke open a glass door that led from the hall below to the staircase by way of prologue) and advancing strait up to the table snatched the knife from my hand—cutting me slightly in the thumb in the operation.—Whether she meant to use this against herself or me I know not—probably against neither—but Fletcher seized her by the arms—and disarmed her.—I then called my boatmen—and desired them to get the Gondola ready and conduct her to her own house again—seeing carefully that she did herself no mischief by the way.—She seemed quite quiet and walked down stairs. —I resumed my dinner.—We heard a great noise—I went out—and met them on the staircase—carrying her up stairs.—She had thrown herself into the Canal.—That she intended to destroy herself I do not believe—but when we consider the fear women and men who can't swim have of deep or even of shallow water—(and the Venetians in particular though they live on the waves) and that it was also night— and dark—& very cold—it shows that she had a devilish spirit of some sort within her.—They had got her out without much difficulty or damage except the salt water she had swallowed and the wetting she had undergone.—I foresaw her intention to refix herself, and sent for a Surgeon—enquiring how many hours it would require to restore her from her agitation, and he named the time.—I then said—"I give you that time—and more if you require it—but at the expiration of the prescribed period—if *She* does not leave the house—*I* will".——All my people were consternated—they had always been frightened at her —and were now paralyzed—they wanted me to apply to the police— to guard myself—&c. &c.—like a pack of sniveling servile boobies as they were——I did nothing of the kind—thinking that I might as well end that way as another—besides—I had been used to savage women and knew their ways.—I had her sent home quietly after her recovery —and never saw her since except twice at the opera—at a distance amongst the audience.—She made many attempts to return—but no more violent ones.—And this is the story of Margharita Cogni—as far as it belongs to me.—I forgot to mention that she was very devout —and would cross herself if she heard the prayer-time strike—some- times—when that ceremony did not appear to be much in unison with what she was then about.—She was quick in reply—as for instance;—one day when she had made me very angry with beating somebody or other—I called her a *Cow* (*Cow* in Italian is a sad affront and tantamount to the feminine of dog in English) I called her "Vacca" she turned round—curtsied—and answered "Vacca *tua*— 'Celenza" (i.e. Eccelenza) *your* Cow—please your Excellency.—In short—she was—as I said before—a very fine Animal—of considerable beauty and energy—with many good & several amusing qualities— but wild as a witch—and fierce as a demon.—She used to boast publicly of her ascendancy over me—contrasting it with that of other women—and assigning for it sundry reasons physical and moral which did more credit to her person than her modesty.————True it was that they all tried to get her away—and no one succeeded—till her own absurdity helped them.—Whenever there was a competition, and sometimes—one would be shut in one room and one in another—to prevent battle—she had generally the preference.——

yrs. very truly and affectly

B

P.S.—The Countess G[uiccioli] is much better than she was.—I sent you before leaving Venice—a letter containing the real original sketch—which gave rise to the "Vampire" &c. did you get it?—

[TO JOHN MURRAY]   *Bologna. August 12th. 1819*

Dear Sir—I do not know how far I may be able to reply to your letter—for I am not very well today.—Last night I went to the representation of Alfieri's Mirra[1]—the two last acts of which threw me into convulsions.—I do not mean by that word—a lady's hysterics—but the agony of reluctant tears—and the choaking shudder which I do not often undergo for fiction.—This is but the second time for anything under reality, the first was on seeing Kean's Sir Giles Overreach.[2] —The worst was that the *"dama"* in whose box I was—went off in the same way—I really believe more from fright—than any other sympathy—at least with the players—but she has been ill—and I have been ill and we are all languid & pathetic this morning—with great expenditure of Sal Volatile.—But to return to your letter of the 23d. of July.——You are right—Gifford is right—Crabbe is right—Hobhouse is right—you are all right—and I am all wrong—but do pray let me have that pleasure.—Cut me up root and branch—quarter me in the Quarterly—send round my "disjecti membra poetae" like those of the Levite's Concubine—make—if you will—a spectacle to men and angels—but don't ask me to alter for I can't—I am obstinate and lazy

---

[1] Alfieri's play was suggested by Ovid's *Metamorphoses* (Book 10) where Myrrha became the mother of Adonis by her father. The tragedy of Mirra is linked by Alfieri to the vengeance of Venus. Mirra's mother had said her daughter was more beautiful than the goddess, who then fated the daughter to love her father. On confessing her incestuous love Mirra killed herself.

[2] In *A New Way to Pay Old Debts.*

—and there's the truth.—But nevertheless—I will answer your friend C. V.[3] who objects to the quick succession of fun and gravity—as if in that case the gravity did not (in intention at least) heighten the fun.— His metaphor is that "we are never scorched and drenched at the same time!"—Blessings on his experience!—Ask him these questions about "scorching and drenching".—Did he never play at Cricket or walk a mile in hot weather?—did he never spill a dish of tea over his testicles in handing the cup to his charmer to the great shame of his nankeen breeches?—did he never swim in the sea at Noonday with the Sun in his eyes and on his head—which all the foam of ocean could not cool? did he never draw his foot out of a tub of too hot water damning his eyes & his valet's? did he never inject for a Gonorrhea?—or make water through an ulcerated Urethra?—was he ever in a Turkish bath— that marble paradise of sherbet and sodomy?—was he ever in a cauldron of boiling oil like St. John?—or in the sulphureous waves of hell? (where he ought to be for his "scorching and drenching at the same time") did he never tumble into a river or lake fishing—and sit in his wet cloathes in the boat—or on the bank afterwards "scorched and drenched" like a true sportsman?——"Oh for breath to utter"[4] ——but make him my compliments—he is a clever fellow for all that —a very clever fellow.——You ask me for the plan of Donny Johnny —I *have* no plan—I *had* no plan—but I had or have materials—though if like Tony Lumpkin—I am "to be snubbed so when I am in spirits"[5] the poem will be naught—and the poet turn serious again.—If it don't take I will leave it off where it is with all due respect to the Public—but if continued it must be in my own way—you might as well make Hamlet (or Diggory)[6] "act mad" in a strait waistcoat—as trammel my buffoonery—if I am to be a buffoon—their gestures and my thoughts would only be pitiably absurd—and ludicrously con- strained.—Why Man the Soul of such writing is it's licence?—at least the *liberty* of that *licence* if one likes—*not* that one should abuse it —it is like trial by Jury and Peerage—and the Habeas Corpus—a very fine thing—but chiefly in the *reversion*—because no one wishes to be tried for the mere pleasure of proving his possession of the privilege. ——But a truce with these reflections;—you are too earnest and

[3] Francis Cohen [why Byron used the initials C.V. is not clear], who later took the name of Palgrave, was a scholar specializing in Italian and medieval history.

[4] *Henry IV*, Part I, Act II, scene 4.

[5] *She stoops to Conquer*, Act II. Tony Lumpkin said: "I wish you'd let me and my good alone, then. Snubbing this way when I'm in spirits."

[6] Diggery is a stage-struck servant who proposes to take the part of a madman in Jackman's farce *All the World's a Stage*.

eager about a work never intended to be serious;—do you suppose that I could have any intention but to giggle and make giggle?—a playful satire with as little poetry as could be helped—was what I meant—and as to the indecency—do pray read in Boswell—what *Johnson* the sullen moralist—says of *Prior* and Paulo Purgante[7]—— Will you get a favour done for me?—*you* can by your Government friends—Croker—Canning—or my old Schoolfellow Peel—and I can't. —Here it is—will you ask them to appoint (*without salary or emolument*) a noble Italian (whom I will name afterwards) Consul or Vice Consul for Ravenna.[8]—He is a man of very large property—noble too—but he wishes to have a British protection in case of changes— Ravenna is near the Sea—he wants *no emolument* whatever;—that his office might be useful—I know—as I lately sent off from Ravenna to Trieste—a poor devil of an English Sailor—who had remained there sick sorry and penniless (having been set ashore in 1814) from the want of any accredited agent able or willing to help him homewards. —Will you get this done?—it will be the greatest favour to me?—if you do—I will then send his name and condition—subject of course to rejection if *not* approved—when known.——I know that in the Levant—you make consuls—and Vice Consuls perpetually—of foreigners—this man is a Patrician and has twelve thousand a year.— His motive is a British protection in case of new Invasions.——Don't you think Croker would do it for us? to be sure *my interest* is rare!!— but perhaps a brother-wit in the Tory line might do a good turn at the request of so harmless and long absent a Whig—particularly as there is no *salary* nor *burthen* of any sort to be annexed to the office.——I can assure you I should look upon it as a great obligation—but Alas! that very circumstance may very probably operate to the contrary— indeed it ought.—But I have at least been an honest and an open enemy.——Amongst your many splendid Government Connections— could not you think you? get our Bibulus[9] made a Consul?—Or make me one that I may make him my Vice.—You may be assured that in case of accidents in Italy—he would be no feeble adjunct—as you would think if you knew his property.——What is all this about Tom Moore? but—why do I ask?—since the state of my own affairs would

[7] Johnson defended Prior as "a lady's book," when Boswell questioned whether "Paulo Purgante and his Wife" should have been included in Johnson's edition of the *English Poets*. "There is nothing in Prior that will excite to lewdness", Johnson said. (Boswell, *Life of Johnson*, ed. Hill, III, 192.)

[8] Count Alessandro Guiccioli, husband of Byron's amorosa, sought the appointment.

[9] Bibulus was Consul with Julius Caesar in 59 B.C.

not permit me to be of use to him—although they are greatly improved since 1816,—and may be—with some more luck—and a little prudence become quite Clear.—It seems his Claimants are *American* merchants. —*There* goes *Nemesis*.—Moore abused America.—It is always thus in the long run.—Time the Avenger.—You have seen every trampler down in turn from Buonaparte to the simplest individuals.——You saw how some were avenged even upon my insignificance; and how in turn Romilly paid for his atrocity.—It is an odd World—but the Watch has its mainspring after all.——So the Prince has been repealing Lord Ed. Fitzgerald's forfeiture[10]—"Ecco un' Sonnetto!"—

> To be the father of the fatherless
> To stretch the hand from the throne's height and raise
> *His* offspring, who expired in other days
> To make thy Sire's Sway by a kingdom less,
> *This* is to be a Monarch, and repress
> Envy into unutterable praise,
> Dismiss thy Guard, and trust thee to such traits,
> For who would lift a hand except to bless?—
> Were it not easy, Sir, and is't not sweet
> To make thyself beloved? and to be
> Omnipotent by Mercy's means? for thus
> Thy Sovereignty would grow but more complete,
> A Despot thou, and yet thy people free,
> And by the Heart not Hand enslaving Us

There you dogs—there's a Sonnet for you—you won't have such as that in a hurry from Mr. Fitzgerald.[11]——You may publish it with my name—an' ye wool—He deserves all praise bad & good—it was a very noble piece of principality.—Would you like an Epigram? ⟨upon a female⟩ a translation.——

> If for silver or for gold—
> You could melt ten thousand pimples
> Into half a dozen dimples
> Then your face we might behold
> Looking doubtless much more smugly
> Yet even then 'twould be damned ugly.

---

[10] Lord Edward Fitzgerald (1763–1798), son of the 1st Duke of Leinster, was an adventurous Irish rebel.

[11] William Thomas Fitzgerald, a poetaster whom Byron had ridiculed in *English Bards and Scotch Reviewers*.

This was written on some French-woman, by Rulhières—I believe.—
"And so good morrow t'ye—good Master Lieutenant."———

yrs. [scrawl]

[TO JOHN CAM HOBHOUSE]   *Bologna. August 20th. 1819*

My dear Hobhouse—I have not lately had of your news—and shall
not reproach you because I think that if you had good to send me you
would be the first.—I wrote to you twice or thrice from Ravenna—
and now I am at Bologna—address to me however at Venice.—My
time has been passed viciously and agreeably—at thirty-one so few
years months days hours or minutes remain that "Carpe *diem*" is not
enough—I have been obliged to crop even the seconds—for who can
trust to *tomorrow? tomorrow* quotha? *to-hour—to-minute*——I can *not*
repent me (I try very often) so much of any thing I have done—as of
any thing I have left undone—alas! I have been but idle—and have the
prospect of early decay—without having seized every available
instant of our pleasurable year.—This is a bitter thought—and it will
be difficult for me ever to recover the despondency into which this
idea naturally throws me.—Philosophy would be in vain—let us try
action.——In England I see & read of reform "and there never were
such troublesome times especially for *Constables*" [;] they have wafered
Mr. Birch of Stockport.—There is much of Hunt and Harrison and Sir
Charles (Linsey) Woolsey[1]—but we hear nothing of you & Burdett?
—The "Venerable Cartwright" too—why did you not shorten that
fellow's longevity? I do assure you (though that lust for duelling
of which you used to accuse me in the Stevens's Coffeehouse days has
long subsided into a moderate desire of killing one's more personal
enemies) that I would have Mantoned old Cartwright most readily—
I have no notion of an old fool like that drivelling defiance and
coughing a challenge at his youngers and his betters—*"solder him up"*
as Francis said of his defunct wife.[2]—And now what do you think of
doing? I have two notions—one to visit England in the Spring—the
other to go to South America.——Europe is grown decrepit—besides
it is all the same thing over again—those fellows are fresh as their
world—and fierce as their earthquakes.———Besides I am enamoured

---

[1] Sir Charles Wolseley, 7th Baronet (1769–1846) was one of the founders of the
radical Hampden Club. He was imprisoned in 1820 on a charge of sedition and
conspiracy for his activities as a radical reformer.

[2] Medwin, *Conversations* (ed. Lovell), p. 202.

of General Paez[3]—who has proved that my Grandfather spoke truth about the Patagonians[4]—with his Gigantic Country.—Would that the Dougal of Bishop's Castle, would find a purchaser for Rochdale—I would embark (with Fletcher as a breeding beast of burthen) and possess myself of the pinnacle of the Andes—or a spacious plain of unbounded extent in an eligible earthquake situation.—Will my wife always live? will her mother never die? is her father immortal? what are you about? married and settled in the country I suppose by your silence?—

yrs. [scrawl]

P.S.—I hear nothing of Don Juan but in two letters from Murray— the first very tremulous—the second in better spirits.——Of the fate of the "pome" I am quite uncertain, and [do] not anticipate much brilliancy from your silence.—But I do not care—I am as sure as the Archbishop of Grenada[5]—that I never wrote better—and I wish you all better taste—but will not send you any pistols.——

[TO JOHN CAM HOBHOUSE] *Bologna. August 23d. 1819*

My dear Hobhouse—I have received a letter from Murray containing the "British review's" eleventh article.[1]—Had you any conception of a man's tumbling into such a trap as Roberts has done? why it is precisely what he was wished to do.—I have enclosed an epistle for publication with a queer signature (to Murray who should

[3] José Antonio Paez, Venezuelan revolutionary, who assisted Bolivar in gaining Venezuelan independence, and who later became president and dictator of the country.

[4] Commodore John Byron recorded in his "Journal" (in Hawkesworth's *Voyages*, I, 28) that in passing through the Straits of Magellan they saw natives who were giants, seven to eight feet high. Since no one else (except some of Commodore Byron's companions) ever saw them, this account had been taken for a traveller's tall tale. But in *Blackwood's Edinburgh Magazine* (Vol. V, July, 1819, pp. 431–33), which Byron had undoubtedly seen, there was a note on Patagonia in which it was said that a lieutenant of the navy (unnamed) recently returned from a voyage there reported seeing some natives of enormous size, and particularly two chiefs who measured eight feet in height.

[5] In *Gil Blas*.

[1] The *British Review*, a periodical with Tory and Evangelical views, was edited by William Roberts (1767–1849). In reviewing *Don Juan*, Roberts had taken seriously Byron's playful accusation "I've bribed My Grandmother's Review,— the British!" (*Don Juan*, I, 209).

keep the anonymous still about D Juan) in answer to Roberts[2]—which pray approve if you can—it is written in an evening & morning in haste—with ill health & worse nerves.—I am so bilious—that I nearly lose my head—and so nervous that I cry for nothing—at least today I burst into tears all alone by myself over a cistern of Gold fishes—which are not pathetic animals.[3]—I can assure you it is not Mr. Roberts or any of his crew that can affect me;—but I have been excited—and agitated and exhausted mentally and bodily all this summer—till I really sometimes begin to think not only "that I shall die at top first"[4]—but that the moment is not very remote.—I have had no particular cause of grief—except the usual accompaniments of all unlawful passions;—I have to do with a woman rendered perfectly disinterested by her situation in life—and young and amiable and pretty—in short as good and at least as attractive as anything of the sex can be with all the advantages and disadvantages of being scarcely twenty years old—and only two out of her Romagnuolo Convent at Faenza.——But I feel & I feel it bitterly—that a man should not consume his life at the side and on the bosom—of a woman—and a stranger—that even the recompense and it is much—is not enough—and that this Cisisbean existence is to be condemned.—But I have neither the strength of mind to break my chain, nor the insensibility which would deaden it's weight.—I cannot tell what will become of me—to leave or to be left would at present drive me quite out of my senses—and yet to what have I conducted myself?—I have luckily or unluckily no ambition left—it would be better if I had—it would at least awake me—whereas at present I merely start in my sleep.——I think I wrote to you last week—but really (Like Lord Grizzle)[5] cannot positively tell.—Why don't you write, pray do—never mind "Don Juan"—let him tumble—and let me too—like Jack and Gill.——Write—and believe me—as long as I can keep my sanity

ever yrs. most truly & affectly.

B

[2] Byron's "Letter to the Editor of 'My Grandmother's Review' ", signed "Wortley Clutterbuck", like Swift's Partridge-Bickerstaff papers, set out with mock seriousness to prove that Roberts had actually accepted a bribe and then had not praised Byron's work. The "Letter" was published in the first number of *The Liberal.*

[3] Teresa had gone to the country for a few days with her husband and Byron was disconsolate.

[4] Byron frequently quoted Swift's premonition.

[5] In *Tom Thumb,* a burlesque Opera, altered from Fielding by Kane O'Hara, Act I, scene 3.

My dearest Teresa—I have read this book[1] in your garden;—my Love—you were absent—or I could not have read it.—It is a favourite book of yours—and the writer was a friend of mine.—You will not understand these English words—and *others* will not understand them —which is the reason I have not scribbled them in Italian—but you will recognize the hand-writing of him who passionately loved you— and you will divine that over a book which was yours—he could only think of love. In *that word* beautiful in all languages—but most so in yours—*Amor* mio—is comprized my existence here and hereafter.—— I feel that I exist here—and I fear that I shall exist hereafter—to *what* purpose—you will decide—my destiny rests with you—& you are a woman [nineteen?][2] years of age—and two years out of a Convent.— —I wish that you had staid there with all my heart—or at least that I had never met you in your married state.—but all this is too late—I love you—and you love me—at least you *say* so—and act as if you *did* so—which last is a great consolation in all events.—But *I* more than love you—and cannot cease to love you.—Think of me sometimes when the Alps and the Ocean divide us—but they never will—unless you wish it.

BN

My dear Douglas—My late expenditure has arisen from living at a distance from Venice and being obliged to keep up two establishments, from frequent journeys—and buying some furniture and books as well as a horse or two—and not from any renewal of the EPICUREAN system as you suspect. I have been faithful to my honest liaison with Countess Guiccioli—and I can assure you that *She* has never cost me directly or indirectly a sixpence—indeed the circumstances of herself and family render this no merit.—I never offered her but one present—a broach of brilliants—and she sent it back to me with her *own hair* in it (I shall *not* say of *what part* but *that* is an Italian custom) and a note to say that she was not in the habit of receiving presents of that value—but hoped

---

[1] The book was Madame de Staël's *Corinne* (in Italian), now in the Biblioteca Classense in Ravenna.

[2] Teresa tried to change "[nineteen?] years" to "seventeen".

that I would not consider her sending it back as an affront—nor the value diminished by the enclosure.—I have not had a whore this half-year—confining myself to the strictest adultery.———Why should you prevent Hanson from making a *peer* if he likes it—I think the *"Garret-ting"* would be by far the best parliamentary privilege—I know of. ——Damn your delicacy.—It is a low commercial quality—and very unworthy a man who prefixes "honourable" to his nomenclature. If you say that I must sign the bonds—I suppose that I must—but it is very iniquitous to make me pay my debts—you have no idea of the pain it gives one.—Pray do three things—get my property out of the *funds*—get Rochdale sold—get me some information from Perry about *South America*—and 4thly. ask Lady Noel not to live so very long.——As to Subscribing to Manchester—if I do that—I will write a letter to Burdett—for publication—to accompany the Subscription—which shall be more radical than anything yet rooted—but I feel lazy.—I have thought of this for some time—but alas! the air of this cursed Italy enervates—and disfranchises the thoughts of a man after nearly four years of respiration—to say nothing of emission.—As to "Don Juan" —confess—confess—you dog—and be candid—that it is the sublime of *that there* sort of writing—it may be bawdy—but is it not good English?—it may be profligate—but is it not *life*, is it not *the thing*?— Could any man have written it—who has not lived in the world?—and tooled in a post-chaise? in a hackney coach? in a Gondola? against a wall? in a court carriage? in a vis a vis?—on a table?—and under it?—I have written about a hundred stanzas of a third Canto—but it is damned modest—the outcry has frightened me.—I had such projects for the Don—but the *Cant* is so much stronger than *Cunt*—now a days, —that the benefit of experience in a man who had well weighed the worth of both monosyllables—must be lost to despairing posterity.— After all what stuff this outcry is—Lalla Rookh and Little—are more dangerous than my burlesque poem can be—Moore has been here— we got tipsy together—and were very amicable—he is gone on to Rome—I put my life (in M.S.) into his hands[1]—(*not* for publication) you—or any body else may see it—at his return.—It only comes up to 1816.——He is a noble fellow—and looks quite fresh and poetical— nine years (the age of a poem's education) my Senior—he looks younger—this comes of marriage and being settled in the Country. I want to go to South America—I have written to Hobhouse all about it. —I wrote to my wife—three months ago—under care to Murray—

[1] Byron's famous Memoirs.

has she got the letter—or is the letter got into Blackwood's magazine?
——You ask after my Christmas pye—Remit it any how—*Circulars* is
the best—you are right about *income*—I must have it all—how the
devil do I know that I may live a year or a month?—I wish I knew that
I might regulate my spending in more ways than one.—As it is one
always thinks that there is but a span.—A man may as well break or be
damned for a large sum as a small one—I should be loth to pay the
devil or any other creditor more than sixpence in the pound.—

[scrawl for signature]

P.S.—I recollect nothing of "Davies's landlord"—but what ever
Davies *says*—I will *swear* to—and *that's* more than *he* would.—So pray
pay—has he a landlady too?—perhaps I may owe her something.——
With regard to the bonds I will sign them but—it goes against the
grain.——As to the rest—you *can't* err—so long as you *don't* pay.
——Paying is executor's or executioner's work.——You may write
somewhat oftener—Mr. Galignani's messenger gives the outline of
your public affairs—but I see no results—you have no man yet—
(always excepting Burdett—& you & H[obhouse] and the Gentlemanly
leaven of your two-penny loaf of rebellion) don't forget however my
charge of horse—and commission for the Midland Counties and by the
holies!—You shall have your account in decimals.—Love to Hobby—
but why leave the Whigs?——

[TO JOHN MURRAY]   *Venice. Octr. 29th. 1819*

Dear Murray—Yours of the 15th. came yesterday. I am sorry that
you do not mention a large letter addressed to *your care* for Lady Byron
—from me at Bologna—two months ago. Pray tell me was this letter
received and forwarded?——You say nothing of the Vice Consulate for
the Ravenna patrician—from which it is to be inferred that the thing
will not be done.——I had written about a hundred stanzas of a *third*
Canto to Don Juan—but the reception of the two first is no encouragement to you nor me to proceed.——I had also written about 600 lines
of a poem—the Vision (or Prophecy) of Dante—the subject a view of
Italy in the ages down to the present—supposing Dante to speak in his
own person—previous to his death—and embracing all topics in the
way of prophecy—like Lycophron's Cassandra.[1] But this and the other

---

[1] The *Cassandra* of Lycophron, an Alexandrian poet (c. 284 B.C.) is a long poem
prophesying events in Greek history.

are both at a standstill—for the present.——I gave Moore who is gone to Rome—my Life in M.S. in 78 folio sheets brought down to 1816.[2] ——But this I put into his hands for *his* care—as he has some other M.S.S. of mine—a journal kept in 1814—&c.—Neither are for publication during my life—but when I am cold—you may do what you please. ——In the mean time—if you like to read them—you may—and show them to any body you like—I care not.——The life is *Memoranda*— and not *Confessions*—I have left out all my *loves* (except in a general way) and many other of the most important things—(because I must not compromise other people) so that it is like the play of Hamlet— "the part of Hamlet omitted by particular desire".——But you will find many opinions—and some fun—with a detailed account of my marriage and it's consequences—as true as a party concerned can make such accounts—for I suppose we are all prejudiced.——I have never read over this life since it was written—so that I know not exactly what it may repeat—or contain.——Moore and I passed some merry days together—but so far from "seducing me to England" as you suppose —the account he gave of me and mine—was of any thing but a nature to make me wish to return;—it is not such opinions of the public that would weigh with me one way or the other—but I think they should weigh with others of my friends before they ask me to return to a place for which I have no great inclination.——I probably must return for business—or in my way to America—pray—did you get a letter for Hobhouse—who will have told you the contents.—I understood that the Venezuelan commissioners had orders to treat with emigrants— now I want to go there—I should not make a bad South-American planter, and I should take my natural daughter Allegra with me and settle.——I wrote at length to Hobhouse to get information from Perry who I suppose is the best topographer and trumpeter of the new Republicans. Pray write—

yrs. ever
[Scrawl]

P.S.—Moore and I did nothing but laugh—he will tell you of "my whereabouts" and all my proceedings at this present—they are as usual.——You should not let those fellows publish false "Don

---

[2] Byron added more to his Memoirs later and sent the additions to Moore who sold the whole for posthumous publication to John Murray for 2,000 guineas. The MS. was burned, together with a copy, at 50 Albemarle Street on May 17, 1824, three days after the news of Byron's death reached England. See *The Late Lord Byron* by Doris Langley Moore for the full account.

Juans"[3]—but do not put *my name* because I mean to cut Roberts up like a gourd—in the ⟨anonymous⟩ preface—if I continue the poem.

My dear Hoppner—The Ferrara Story is of a piece with all the rest of the Venetian manufacture—you may judge.—I only changed horses there since I wrote to you after my visit in June last.—*"Convent"*— and *"carry off"* quotha!—and *"girl"*——I should like to know *who* has been carried off—except poor dear *me*—I have been more ravished myself than anybody since the Trojan war—but as to the arrest and it's causes—one is as true as the other—and I can account for the invention of neither.—I suppose it is some confusion of the tale of the For[narina]—and of M[adam]e Guiccioli—and half a dozen more—but it is useless to unravel the web—when one has only to brush it away.— I shall settle with Master Edgecombe who looks very blue at your indecision—and swears that he is the best arithmetician in Europe—and so I think also—for he makes out two and two to be five.——You may see me next week—I have a horse or two more (five in all) and I shall repossess myself of Lido—and I will rise earlier—and we will go and shake our livers over the beach as heretofore—if you like—and we will make the Adriatic roar again with our hatred of that now empty Oyster shell—without it's pearl—the city of Venice.—Murray sent me a letter yesterday—the impostors have published—*two* new *third* Cantos of *Don Juan*—the devil take the impudence of some blackguard bookseller or other there*for*.—Perhaps I did not make myself understood—he told me the sale had not been great—1200 out of 1500 quarto I believe (which is nothing after selling 13000 of the Corsair in one day[1]) but that the "best Judges &c." had said it was very fine and clever and particularly good English & poetry and all those consolatory things which are not however worth a single copy to a bookseller—and as to the author—of course I am in a damned passion at the bad taste of the times—and swear there is nothing like posterity —who of course must know more of the matter than their Grand-

---

[3] The first two cantos of *Don Juan* were published together in a quarto on July 15, 1819. Four days later William Hone's *Don Juan, Canto the Third* appeared. Murray was handicapped in his attempt to prevent piracies and forgeries because Byron's poem had appeared without the name of either the author or the publisher.

[1] Byron's memory must have failed him, or he was thinking of a later report of sales. On Feb. 3, 1814, Murray wrote of the phenomenal sale of *The Corsair*: "I sold on the day of publication, a thing perfectly unprecedented, 10,000 copies."

fathers.—There has been an eleventh commandment to the women not to read it—and what is still more extraordinary they seem not to have broken it.———But that can be of little import to them poor things—for the reading or non-reading a book—will never keep down a single petticoat;—but it is of import to Murray—who will be in scandal for his aiding as publisher.———He is bold howsomedever—wanting two more cantos against the winter—I think that he had better not—for by the larkins!—it will only make a new row for him.—Edgecombe is gone to Venice today—to consign my chattels to t'other fellow.———Count G[uiccioli] comes to Venice next week and I am requested to consign his wife to him, which shall be done—with all her linen.—What you say of the long evenings at the Mira—or Venice—reminds me of what Curran said to Moore—"so—I hear—you have married a pretty woman—and a very good creature too—an excellent creature —pray—*how do you pass your evenings?*["] it is a devil of a question that—and perhaps as easy to answer with a wife as with a mistress—but surely they are longer than the nights. I am all for morality now—and shall confine myself henceforward to the strictest adultery—which you will please to recollect is all that that virtuous wife of mine has left me.———If you go to Milan—pray leave at least a *Vice*-Consul—the only Vice that will ever be wanting in Venice.—Dorville is a good fellow.———But you should go to England in the Spring with me—and plant Mrs. Hoppner at Berne with her relations for a few months. —I wish you had been here (at Venice—I mean not the Mira) when Moore was here—we were very merry and tipsy—he *hated* Venice by the way—and swore it was a sad place.———So—Madame Albrizzi's death is in danger—poor woman.———Saranzo—is of course in the ⟨doleful⟩ crazy recollection of their rancid amours. ———Moore told me that at Geneva they had made a devil of a story of the Fornaretta—"young lady seduced—subsequent abandonment—leap into the Grand Canal—her being in the hospital of *fous* in consequence"—I should like to know who was nearest being made *"fou"* and be damned to them.———Don't you think me in the interesting character of a very ill used gentleman?—I hope your little boy is well —Allegrina is flourishing like a pome-granate blossom.—

yrs. ever
BYRON

My Dearest Friend—Fanny will have told you, with her *usual sublimity,* that Love has won. I have not been able to find enough resolution to leave the country where you are, without seeing you at least once more:—perhaps it will depend on *you* whether I ever again shall leave you. Of the rest we shall speak. You should now know what is more conducive to your welfare, my presence or my absence. I am a citizen of the world—all countries are alike to me. You have always been (since we met) *the only object of my thoughts.* I believed that the best course, both for your peace and for that of your family, was for me to leave, and to go *very far away,* for to remain near and *not* approach you, would have been impossible for me. But you have decided that I am to return to Ravenna. I shall return—and do—and be—what you wish. I cannot say more. Fanny will be much more brilliant—and is probably at this moment in the throes of composition—at great expense to the poor dictionary. I pray you greet respectfully on my behalf—Papa—the Cavaliere—and all who may be glad to have my regards. I hope that your Papa will not be displeased—and that A[lessandro] is *as you say*—in your very dear letter by the last post. In any case inform me of everything—for my guidance. I kiss you 10000+ times from my heart——

P.S.—Since your departure—I have not gone out of the house—and scarcely out of my room—nor shall I go out unless it be—to come to you or to leave Italy. You can learn from others of my conduct—I am sure you will be satisfied.[1]

Dearest Augusta—The health of my daughter Allegra—the cold Season—and the length of the journey—induce me to postpone for some time a purpose (never very willing on my part) to revisit Great Britain.——You can address to me at Venice as usual. Wherever I may be in Italy the letter will be forwarded.——I enclose to you—all that *long hair*—on account [of] which you would not go to see my picture.[1]

---

[1] Translation by Professor Nancy Dersofi. This letter, like most of those written to the Countess Teresa Guiccioli, was written in Italian.

[1] This was the drawing by Harlow, made in Venice in 1818, which shows Byron's hair grown down below his collar.

———You will see that it was not so very long.———I curtailed it yesterday—my head & hair being weakly after my tertian.———I wrote to you not very long ago—and as I do not know that I could [add] anything satisfactory to that letter—I may as well finish this.———In a letter to Murray—I requested him to apprize you that my journey was postponed———but here—there and every where know me

yours ever & very truly
B

[TO JOHN MURRAY]   *Ravenna. February 21st. 1820*

Dear Murray—The Bulldogs will be very agreeable—I have only those of this country who though good—& ready to fly at any thing—yet have not the tenacity of tooth and Stoicism in endurance of my canine fellow citizens, then pray send them—by the readiest conveyance, perhaps best by Sea.———Mr. Kinnaird will disburse for them & deduct from the amount on your application or on that of Captain Fyler.—I see the good old King is gone to his place—one can't help being sorry—though blindness—and age and insanity are supposed to be drawbacks—on human felicity—but I am not at all sure that the latter at least—might not render him happier than any of his subjects.———I have no thoughts of coming to the Coronation—though I should like to see it—and though I have a right to be a puppet in it—but my division with Lady Byron which has drawn an equinoctial line between me and mine in all other things—will operate in this also to prevent my being in the same procession.

———By Saturday's post—I sent you four packets containing Cantos third and fourth of D[on] J[uan]—recollect that these two cantos reckon only as *one* with you and me—being in fact the third Canto cut into two—because I found it too long.—Remember this—and don't imagine that there could be any other motive.—-The whole is about 225 Stanzas more or less—and a lyric of 96 lines—so that they are no longer than the first *single* cantos—but the truth is—that I made the first too long—and should have cut those down also had I thought better.———Instead of saying in future for so many cantos—say so many *Stanzas* or pages—it was Jacob Tonson's way—and certainly the best—it prevents mistakes—I might have sent you a dozen cantos of 40 Stanzas each—those of "the Minstrel" (Beatties's) are no longer—and ruined you at once—if you don't suffer as it is;—but recollect you are not *pinned down* to anything you say in a letter and that calculating even these two cantos as *one* only (which they were and are to be reckoned) you are not bound by your offer,—act as may seem fair to all parties.———I have finished my translation of the first Canto of the "Morgante Maggiore" of Pulci—which I will transcribe and send—it is the parent not only of Whistlecraft—but of all jocose Italian poetry.———You must print it side by side with the original Italian because I wish the reader to judge of the fidelity—it is stanza for stanza—and often line for line if not word for word.——

You ask me for a volume of manners &c.—on Italy; perhaps I am in the case to know more of them than most Englishmen—because I have lived among the natives—and in parts of the country—where Englishmen never resided before—(I speak of Romagna and this place particularly) but there are many reasons why I do not choose to touch in print on such a subject—I have lived in their houses and in the heart of their families—sometimes merely as "amico di casa" and sometimes as "Amico di cuore" of the Dama—and in neither case do I feel myself authorized in making a book of them.———Their moral is not your moral—their life is not your life—you would not understand it—it is not English nor French—nor German—which you would all understand—the Conventual education—the Cavalier Servitude—the habits of thought and living are so entirely different—and the difference becomes so much more striking the more you live intimately with them—that I know not how to make you comprehend a people—who are at once temperate and profligate—serious in their character and buffoons in their amusements—capable of impressions and passions which are at once *sudden* and *durable* (what you find in no other nation) and who *actually* have *no society* (what we would call so) as you may see by their Comedies—they have no real comedy not even in Goldoni—and that is because they have no society to draw it from.——

Their Conversazioni are not Society at *all*.—They go to the theatre to talk—and into company to hold their tongues—The *women* sit in a circle and the men gather into groupes [sic]—or they play at dreary Faro—or "Lotto reale"—for small sums.—Their Academie are Concerts like our own—with better music—and more form.—Their best things are the Carnival balls—and masquerades—when every body runs mad for six weeks.———After their dinners and suppers they make extempore verses—and buffoon one another—but it is in a humour which you would not enter into—ye of the North.——

In their houses it is better—I should know something of the matter—having had a pretty general experience among their women—[from]

227

the fisherman's wife—up to the Nobil' Donna whom I serve.——
Their system has it's rules—and it's fitnesses—and decorums—so as
to be reduced to a kind of discipline—or game at hearts—which
admits few deviations unless you wish to lose it.——They are extremely tenacious—and jealous as furies—not permitting their
Lovers even to marry if they can help it—and keeping them always
close to them in public as in private whenever they can.——In short
they transfer marriage to adultery—and strike the *not* out of that
commandment.—The reason is that they marry for their parents and
love for themselves.—They exact fidelity from a lover as a debt of
honour—while they pay the husband as a tradesman—that is not at
all.——You hear a person's character—male or female—canvassed—
not as depending on their conduct to their husbands or wives—but to
their mistress or lover.——And—and—that's all.—If I wrote a
quarto—I don't know that I could do more than amplify what I
have here noted.——

It is to be observed that while they do all this—the greatest out-
ward respect is to be paid to the husbands—and not only by the ladies
but by their Serventi—particularly if the husband serves no one himself
—(which is not often the case however) so that you would often
suppose them relations—the Servente making the figure of one adopted
into the family.—Sometimes the ladies run a little restive—and
elope—or divide—or make a scene—but this is at starting generally—
when they know no better—or when they fall in love with a foreigner—
or some such anomaly—and is always reckoned unnecessary and
extravagant.——

You enquire after "Dante's prophecy"—I have not done more
than six hundred lines but will vaticinate at leisure.——Of the Bust I
know nothing—no Cameos or Seals are to be cut here or elsewhere
that I know of in any good style.—Hobhouse should write himself
to Thorwalsen—the bust was made and paid for three years ago.——
Pray tell Mrs. Leigh to request Lady Byron—to urge forward the
transfer from the funds—which Hanson is opposing because he has
views of investment for some Client of his own—which I can't consent to—I wrote to Lady B. on business this post addressed to the
care of Mr. D. Kinnaird.—Somebody has sent me some American
abuse of "Mazeppa"—and "the Ode";—in future I will compliment
nothing but Canada—and desert to the English.——

By the king's death[1]—Mr. H[obhouse] I hear will stand for West-

---

[1] On the death of the King a new Parliament had to be elected.

minster—I shall be glad to hear of his standing any where except in the pillory—which from the company he must have lately kept— (I always except Burdett—and Douglas K. and the genteel part of the reformers) was perhaps to be apprehended. I was really glad to hear it was for libel instead of larceny—for though impossible in his own person he might have been taken up by mistake for another at a meeting.——All reflections on his present case and place are so ⟨very⟩ *Nugatory*—that it would be useless to pursue the subject further.——

I am out of all patience to see my friends sacrifice themselves for a pack of blackguards—who disgust one with their Cause—although I have always been a friend to and a Voter for reform.——If Hunt[2] had addressed the language to me—which he did to Mr. H[obhouse] last election—I would not have descended to call out such a miscreant who won't fight—but have passed my sword-stick through his body— like a dog's and then thrown myself on my Peers—who would I hope—have weighed the provocation;—at any rate—it would have been as public a Service as Walworth's chastisement of Wat. Tyler.— If we must have a tyrant—let him at least be a gentleman who has been bred to the business, and let us fall by the axe and not by the butcher's cleaver.——No one can be more sick of—or indifferent to politics than I am—if they let me alone—but if the time comes when a part must be taken one way or the other—I shall pause before I lend myself to the views of such ruffians—although I cannot but approve of a Constitutional amelioration of long abuses.——Lord George Gordon[3]—and Wilkes—and Burdett—and Horne Tooke— were all men of education—and courteous deportment—so is Hobhouse—but as for these others—I am convinced—that Robespierre was a Child—and Marat a quaker in comparison of what they would be could they throttle their way to power.——

[scrawl]

[TO JOHN CAM HOBHOUSE]   *Ravenna. March 3d. 1820*

My dear Hobhouse—I have paused thus long in replying to your letter not knowing well in what terms to write—because though I

---

[2] Henry ("Orator") Hunt, the radical leader.

[3] Lord George Gordon, born 1751, youngest son of the 3rd Duke of Gordon, instigated anti-Roman Catholic riots in 1774. He died in Newgate in 1793.

approve of the object—yet with the exception of Burdett and Doug. K. and one or two others—I dislike the companions of your labours as much as the place to which they have brought you.——I perceive by the papers that "ould Apias Korkus"[1] has not extricated you from the "puddle" into which your wit hath brought you.—However if this be but a prologue to a seat for Westminster—I shall less regret your previous ordeal, but I am glad that I did not come to England—for it would not have pleased me to find on my return from transportation my best friends in Newgate. "Did I ever—no I never"—but I will say no more—all reflections being quite *Nugatory* on the occasion ;— still I admire your Gallantry and think you could not do otherwise *having* written the pamphlet[2]—but *"why bitch* Mr. Wild!"[3]—why write it?—why lend yourself to Hunt and Cobbett—and the bones of Tom Paine? "Death and fiends"—You used to be thought a prudent man—at least by me whom you favoured with so much good counsel— but methinks you are waxed somewhat rash at least in politics.——

However the King is dead—so get out of Mr. Burns's apartments— and get into the House of Commons—and then abuse it as much as you please, and I'll come over and hear you. Seriously—I did not "laugh" as you supposed I would—no more did Fletcher—but we looked both as grave as if we had got to have been your Bail— particularly that learned person who pounced upon the event in the course of spelling the Lugano Gazette.——So—Scrope is gone[4]— down—*diddled*—as Doug. K. writes it—the said Doug. being like the Man who when he lost a friend went to the St. James's Coffee House and took a new one—but to you and me—the loss of Scrope is irreparable—we could have "better spared" not only "a better man"[5]

---

[1] Habeas Corpus.

[2] Soon after the defeat of Hobhouse for the Westminster Parliamentary seat in the autumn of 1819, Lord Erskine, who had been a defender of the people during the treason trials of 1794, was provoked by the Reformers' denunciation of the Whigs, and published a pamphlet in their defence. Hobhouse countered with an anonymous pamphlet, "A Trifling Mistake in Thomas Lord Erskine's Recent Preface", in which he wrote: "What prevents the people from walking down to the House, and pulling out the members by the ears, locking up their doors, and flinging the key into the Thames?" The only reason, he said, was that the members were protected by the Horse Guards. This alone permits "those who have got the tax-power [to] keep it, and hang those who resist." On December 11, 1819, the pamphlet was voted a breach of privilege and Hobhouse, when he admitted the authorship to spare the printer, was committed to Newgate prison where he remained until the dissolution of Parliament in February, 1820.

[3] Fielding's *Life of Mr. Jonathan Wild*, Book III, chapter 8.

[4] Scrope Davies, like Beau Brummell, was ruined by gambling and escaped to the Continent. He spent his last days in Paris.

[5] *Henry IV*, Part 1, Act V, scene 4.

but the "best of Men".—Gone to Bruges—where he will get tipsy with Dutch beer and shoot himself the first foggy morning.——Brummell—at *Calais*—Scrope at Bruges—Buonaparte at St. Helena—you in—your new apartments—and I at Ravenna—only think so many great men!—there has been nothing like it since Themistocles at Magnesia—and Marius at Carthage.——But—Times change—and they are luckiest who get over their worst rounds at the beginning of the battle.—The other day—February 25th. we plucked violets by the way side *here* at Ravenna—and now March 3d. it is snowing for all the world as it may do in Cateaton Street.——

We have nothing new here but the Cardinal from Imola—and the news of the Berricide in France by a Saddler[6] ;—I suppose the Duke had not paid his bill.——I shall let *"dearest Duck"* [Lady Byron] waddle alone at the Coronation—a ceremony which I should like to see and have a right to act Punch in—but the Crown itself would not bribe me to return to England—unless business or actual urgency required it.——I was very near coming—but that was because I had been very much "agitato" with some circumstances of a domestic description—here in Italy—and not from any love of the tight little Island.—Tell Doug. K. that I answered his last letter long ago—and enclosed in the letter an order peremptory to Spooney—to make me an Irish Absentee according to Doug's own directions.——I like the security in Dublin Houses "an empty house on Ormond Quay"—but pray are they insured in case of Conflagration?—Deliver me that—and let us be guaranteed—otherwise what becomes of my fee?—My Clytemnestra stipulated for the security of her jointure—it was delicately done—considering that the poor woman will only have ten thousand a year more or less for life on the death of her mother.——

I sent Murray two more Cantos of Donny Johnny—but they are only to reckon as *one* in arithmetic—because they are but one long one cut into *two*—whilk [which] was expedient on account of tedium.—So don't let him be charged for these two but as one.——I sent him also a translation close and rugged—of the first Canto of the Morgante Maggiore to the published with the original text side by side—"cheek by jowl by Gome!" on account of the superlative merits of both.——All these are to be corrected by you—by way of solace during your probation.——

William Bankes came to see me twice—once at Venice—and he

---

[6] Pierre-Louis Louvel, a saddler, assassinated the Duc de Berri, grandson of Louis XVIII, February 13, 1820.

since came a second time from Bologna to Ravenna on purpose—so I took him to a Ball here and presented him to all the Ostrogothic Nobility—and to the Dama whom I serve;—I have settled into regular Serventismo—and find it the happiest state of all—always excepting Scarmentado's.[7]—I double a shawl with considerable alacrity—but have not yet arrived at the perfection of putting it on the right way—and I hand in and out and know my post in a Conversazione—and theatre—and play at cards as well as [a] man can do who of all the Italian pack can only distinguish "Asso" and "Re" the rest for me are hieroglyphics.—Luckily the play is limited to "Papetti" that is pieces of four Pauls—somewhere in or about two shillings. I am in favour & respect with the Cardinal and the Vice-legato—and in decent inter-course with the Gonfaloniere—and all the Nobiltà of the middle ages.—Nobody has been stabbed this winter—and few new liaisons formed—there is a Sposa Fiorentina—a pretty Girl yet in abeyance—but no one can decide yet who is to be her Servente—most of the men being already adulterated—and she showing no preferences to any who are not.—There is a certain Marchese who I think would run a good chance—if he did not take matters rather too philosophically.—Sgricci is here improvising away with great success—he is also a celebrated Sodomite a character by no means so much respected in Italy as it should be; but they laugh instead of burning—and the Women talk of it as a pity in a man of talent—but with greater tolerance than could be expected—and only express their hopes that he may yet be converted to Adultery.——He is not known to have b———d anybody here as yet but he has paid his addresses "fatto la corte" to two or three.——

[scrawl]

Ravenna, 9bre 19, 1820

Dear Murray,—What you said of the late Charles Skinner Matthews has set me to my recollections; but I have not been able to turn up anything which would do for the purposed Memoir of his brother,—even if he had previously done enough during his life to sanction the introduction of anecdotes so merely personal. He was, however, a very

---

[7] In Voltaire's tale, *Histoire des Voyages de Scarmentado Écrite par lui-même* (1756), the hero like Candide decides after his travels to stay at home, not to cultivate his garden, but "Je me mariai chez moi; je fus cocu, et je vis que c'était l'état le plus doux de la vie."

extraordinary man, and would have been a great one. No one ever succeeded in a more surpassing degree than he did as far as he went. He was indolent, too; but whenever he stripped, he overthrew all antagonists. His conquests will be found registered at Cambridge, particularly his *Downing* one, which was hotly and highly contested, and yet easily *won*. Hobhouse was his most intimate friend, and can tell you more of him than any man. William Bankes also a great deal. I myself recollect more of his oddities than of his academical qualities, for we lived most together at a very idle period of *my* life. When I went up to Trinity, in 1805, at the age of seventeen and a half, I was miserable and untoward to a degree. I was wretched at leaving Harrow, to which I had become attached during the two last years of my stay there; wretched at going to Cambridge instead of Oxford (there were no rooms vacant at Christchurch); wretched from some private domestic circumstances of different kinds, and consequently about as unsocial as a wolf taken from the troop. So that, although I knew Matthews, and met him often *then* at Bankes's (who was my collegiate pastor, and master, and patron,) and at Rhode's, Milnes's, Price's, Dick's, Macnamara's, Farrell's, Gally Knight's, and others of that *set* of contemporaries, yet I was neither intimate with him nor with any one else, except my old schoolfellow Edward Long (with whom I used to pass the day in riding and swimming), and William Bankes, who was good-naturedly tolerant of my ferocities.

It was not till 1807, after I had been upwards of a year away from Cambridge, to which I had returned again to *reside* for my degree, that I became one of Matthews's familiars, by means of Hobhouse, who, after hating me for two years, because I wore a *white hat*, and a *grey* coat, and rode a *grey* horse (as he says himself), took me into his good graces because I had written some poetry. I had always lived a good deal, and got drunk occasionally, in their company—but now we became really friends in a morning. Matthews, however, was not at this period resident in College. I met *him* chiefly in London, and at uncertain periods at Cambridge. Hobhouse, in the mean time, did great things: he founded the Cambridge "Whig Club" (which he seems to have forgotten), and the "Amicable Society," which was dissolved in consequence of the members constantly quarrelling, and made himself very popular with "us youth," and no less formidable to all tutors, professors, and heads of Colleges. William Bankes was gone; while he stayed, he ruled the roast—or rather the *roasting*— and was father of all mischiefs.

Matthews and I, meeting in London, and elsewhere, became great cronies. He was not good tempered—nor am I—but with a little tact his temper was manageable, and I thought him so superior a man, that I was willing to sacrifice something to his humours, which were often, at the same time, amusing and provoking. What became of his *papers* (and he certainly had many), at the time of his death, was never known. I mention this by the way, fearing to skip it over, and *as* he *wrote* remarkably well, both in Latin and English. We went down to Newstead together, where I had got a famous cellar, and *Monks'* dresses from a masquerade warehouse. We were a company of some seven or eight, with an occasional neighbour or so for visiters, and used to sit up late in our friars' dresses, drinking burgundy, claret, champagne, and what not, out of the *skull-cup*, and all sorts of glasses, and buffooning all around the house, in our conventual garments.[1] Matthews always denominated me "the Abbot," and never called me by any other name in his good humours, to the day of his death. The harmony of these our symposia was somewhat interrupted, a few days after our assembling, by Matthews's threatening to throw Hobhouse out of a *window*, in consequence of I know not what commerce of jokes ending in this epigram. Hobhouse came to me and said, that "his respect and regard for me as host would not permit him to call out any of my guests, and that he should go to town next morning." He did. It was in vain that I represented to him that the window was not high, and that the turf under it was particularly soft. Away he went.

Matthews and myself had travelled down from London together, talking all the way incessantly upon one single topic. When we got to Loughborough, I know not what chasm had made us diverge for a moment to some other subject, at which he was indignant. "Come," said he, "don't let us break through—let us go on as we began to our journey's end;" and so he continued, and was as entertaining as ever to the very end. He had previously occupied, during my year's absence from Cambridge, my rooms in Trinity, with the furniture; and Jones, the tutor, in his odd way, had said, on putting him in, "Mr Matthews, I recommend to your attention not to damage any of the moveables, for Lord Byron, Sir, is a young man of *tumultuous passions*." Matthews was delighted with this; and whenever anybody came to visit him, begged them to handle the very door with caution; and used to repeat Jones's admonition in his tone and manner. There was a large mirror

[1] According to Hobhouse, Matthews hid in a stone coffin in the long gallery at Newstead at night, and rose up from it to blow out Hobhouse's candle (Broughton [John Cam Hobhouse], *Recollections of a Long Life*, III, 29).

in the room, on which he remarked, "that he thought his friends were grown uncommonly assiduous in coming to *see him*, but he soon discovered that they only came to *see themselves.*" Jones's phrase of "*tumultuous passions,*" and the whole scene, had put him into such good humour, that I verily believe that I owed to it a portion of his good graces.

When at Newstead, somebody by accident rubbed against one of his white silk stockings, one day before dinner; of course the gentleman apologised. "Sir," answered Matthews, "it may be all very well for you, who have a great many silk stockings, to dirty other people's; but to me, who have only this *one pair*, which I have put on in honour of the Abbot here, no apology can compensate for such carelessness; besides, the expense of washing." He had the same sort of droll sardonic way about every thing. A wild Irishman, named Farrell, one evening began to say something at a large supper at Cambridge, Matthews roared out "Silence!" and then, pointing to Farrell, cried out, in the words of the oracle, "*Orson is endowed with reason.*" You may easily suppose that Orson lost what reason he had acquired, on hearing this compliment. When Hobhouse published his volume of poems, the *Miscellany* (which Matthews *would* call the "*Miss-sell-any*"), all that could be drawn from him was, that the preface was "extremely like *Walsh.*" Hobhouse thought this at first a compliment; but we never could make out what it was, for all we know of *Walsh* is his Ode to King William, and Pope's epithet of "*knowing Walsh,*"[2] When the Newstead party broke up for London, Hobhouse and Matthews, who were the greatest friends possible, agreed, for a whim, to *walk together* to town. They quarrelled by the way, and actually walked the latter half of the journey, occasionally passing and repassing, without speaking. When Matthews had got to Highgate, he had spent all his money but three-pence half-penny, and determined to spend that also in a pint of beer, which I believe he was drinking before a public-house, as Hobhouse passed him (still without speaking) for the last time on their route. They were reconciled in London again.

One of Matthew's passions was "the fancy;"[3] and he sparred uncommonly well. But he always got beaten in rows, or combats with the bare fist. In swimming, too, he swam well; but with *effort* and *labour*, and *too high* out of the water; so that Scrope Davies and myself,

[2] "Granville, the polite, / and *knowing Walsh*, would tell me I could write." (*Epistle to Dr. Arbuthnot*, lines 135–6.)
[3] The common term then used to refer to those intensely interested in the art of pugilism and to the art itself.

of whom he was therein somewhat emulous, always told him that he would be drowned if ever he came to a difficult pass in the water. He was so; but surely Scrope and myself would have been most heartily glad that

> "the Dean had lived,
> And our prediction proved a lie."

His head was uncommonly handsome, very like what *Pope's* was in his youth.

His voice, and laugh, and features, are strongly resembled by his brother Henry's, if Henry be *he* of *King's College*. His passion for boxing was so great, that he actually wanted me to match him with Dogherty (whom I had backed and made the match for against Tom Belcher), and I saw them spar together at my own lodgings with the gloves on. As he was bent upon it, I would have backed Dogherty to please him, but the match went off. It was of course to have been a private fight, in a private room.

On one occasion, being too late to go home and dress, he was equipped by a friend (Mr. Baillie, I believe,) in a magnificently fashionable and somewhat exaggerated shirt and neckcloth. He proceeded to the Opera, and took his station in Fop's Alley. During the interval between the opera and the ballet, an acquaintance took his station by him and saluted him: "Come round," said Matthews, "come round."—"Why should I come round?" said the other; "you have only to turn your head—I am close by you."—"That is exactly what I cannot do," said Matthews; "don't you see the state I am in?" pointing to his buckram shirt collar and inflexible cravat,—and there he stood with his head always in the same perpendicular position during the whole spectacle.

One evening, after dining together, as we were going to the Opera, I happened to have a spare Opera ticket (as subscriber to a box), and presented it to Matthews. "Now, sir," said he to Hobhouse afterwards, "this I call *courteous* in the Abbot—another man would never have thought that I might do better with half a guinea than throw it to a door-keeper;—but here is a man not only asks me to dinner, but gives me a ticket for the theatre." These were only his oddities, for no man was more liberal, or more honourable in all his doings and dealings, than Matthews. He gave Hobhouse and me, before we set out for Constantinople, a most splendid entertainment, to which we did ample justice. One of his fancies was dining at all sorts of out-of-the-way places. Somebody popped upon him in I know not what coffee-house in the Strand—and what do you think was the attraction? Why, that he paid a shilling (I think) to *dine with his hat on*. This he called his *"hat* house," and used to boast of the comfort of being covered at meal times.

When Sir Henry Smith[4] was expelled from Cambridge for a row with a tradesman named "Hiron," Matthews solaced himself with shouting under Hiron's windows every evening

> "Ah me! what perils do environ
> The man who meddles with *hot Hiron*,"[5]

He was also of that band of profane scoffers who, under the auspices of * * * *, used to rouse Lort Mansel (late Bishop of Bristol) from his slumbers in the lodge of Trinity; and when he appeared at the window foaming with wrath, and crying out, "I know you, gentlemen, I know you!" were wont to reply, "We beseeche thee to hear us, good *Lort*!"—"Good *Lort* deliver us!" (Lort was his Christian name.) As he was very free in his speculations upon all kinds of subjects, although by no means either dissolute or intemperate in his conduct, and as I was no less independent, our conversation and correspondence used to alarm our friend Hobhouse to a considerable degree.

You must be almost tired of my packets, which will have cost a mint of postage.

Salute Gifford and all my friends.

Yours,

B

[TO JOHN MURRAY]   *Ravenna. Decr. 9th. 1820*

Dear Murray—I intended to have written to you at some length by this post,—but as the Military Commandant is now lying dead in my house—on Fletcher's bed—I have other things to think of.—— He was shot at 8 o Clock this evening about two hundred paces from our door.—I was putting on my great Coat to pay a visit to the Countess G[uiccioli]—when I heard a shot—and on going into the hall—found all my servants on the balcony—exclaiming that "a Man was murdered".——As it is the custom here to let people fight it through— they wanted to hinder me from going out—but I ran down into the Street—Tita the bravest of them followed me—and we made our way

---

[4] Sir Henry Smyth was expelled in 1805 for "Inciting to disturbance".
[5] Butler, *Hudibras*, Part I, chapter 3 (last two words "cold iron").

to the Commandant who was lying on his back with five wounds—of which three in the body—one in the heart.——There were about him— Diego his Adjutant—crying like a Child—a priest howling—a Surgeon who dared not touch him—two or three confused & frightened Soldiers—one or two of the boldest of the mob—and the Street dark as pitch—with the people flying in all directions.—As Diego could only cry and wring his hands—and the Priest could only pray—and nobody seemed able or willing to do anything except exclaim shake and stare —I made my Servant & one of the mob take up the body—sent off Diego crying to the Cardinal—the Soldiers for the Guard—& had the Commandant carried up Stairs to my own quarters.—But he was quite gone.—I made the Surgeon examine him & examined him myself.— He had bled inwardly, & very little external blood was apparent.— One of the Slugs had gone quite through—all but the Skin, I felt it myself.—Two more shots in the body—one in a finger—and another in the arm.—His face not at all disfigured—he seems asleep—but is growing livid.—The Assassin has not been taken—but the gun was found—a gun filed down to half the barrel.——

He said nothing—but "O Dio!" and "O Gesu" two or three times. The house was filled at last with Soldiers—officers—police—and military—but they are clearing away—all but the Sentinels—and the [body] is to be removed tomorrow.—It seems [that] if I had not had him taken into my house he might have lain in the Street till morning— for here nobody meddles with such things—for fear of the consequences —either of public suspicion, or private revenge on the part of the Slayers.—They may do as they please—I shall never be deterred from a duty of humanity by all the assassins of Italy—and that is a wide word.——He was a brave officer—but an unpopular man.—The whole town is in confusion.—You may judge better of things here by this detail than by anything which I could add on the Subject—communicate this letter to Hobhouse & Douglas K[innair]d—and believe me

yrs. truly
B

P.S.—The poor Man's wife is not yet aware of his death—they are to break it to her in the morning.—The Lieutenant who is watching the body is smoking with the greatest Sangfroid—a strange people.—

RAVENNA JOURNAL

January 4–February 27, 1821

January 5th, 1821

Rose late—dull and drooping—the weather dripping and dense. Snow on the ground, and sirocco above in the sky, like yesterday. Roads up to the horse's belly, so that riding (at least for pleasure) is not very feasible. Added a postscript to my letter to Murray. Read the conclusion, for the fiftieth time (I have read all W. Scott's novels at least fifty times) of the third series of "Tales of my Landlord",— grand work—Scotch Fielding, as well as great English poet—wonderful man! I long to get drunk with him.

Dined versus six o' the clock. Forgot that there was a plum-pudding, (I have added, lately, *eating* to my "family of vices,") and had dined before I knew it. Drank half a bottle of some sort of spirits—probably spirits of wine; for what they call brandy, rum, &c. &c., here is nothing but spirits of wine, coloured accordingly. Did *not* eat two apples, which were placed by way of dessert. Fed the two cats, the hawk, and the tame (but *not* tamed) crow. Read Mitford's History of Greece— Xenophon's Retreat of the Ten Thousand. Up to this present moment writing, 6 minutes before eight o' the clock—French hours, not Italian.

Hear the carriage—order pistols and great coat, as usual— necessary articles. Weather cold—carriage open, and inhabitants somewhat savage—rather treacherous and highly inflamed by politics. Fine fellows, though,—good materials for a nation. Out of chaos God made a world, and out of high passions comes a people.

Clock strikes—going out to make love. Somewhat perilous, but not disagreeable. Memorandum—a new screen put up to-day. It is rather antique, but will do with a little repair.

Thaw continues—hopeful that riding may be practicable to-morrow. Sent the papers to Al[borghett]i[1]—grand events coming.

11 o' the clock and nine minutes. Visited La Contessa G[uiccioli] Nata G[hiselli] G[amba]. Found her beginning my letter of answer to the thanks of Alessio del Pinto of Rome for assisting his brother the

---

[1] Count Giuseppe Alborghetti, Secretary to the Papal Legate in Ravenna, had a taste for poetry and some knowledge of English. He was much impressed with Byron and furnished him with secrets from the Cardinal's mail bag at a time when it might have been considered near treason, for he knew that Byron was connected with the revolutionary Carbonari organization.

late Commandant in his last moments, as I had begged her to pen my reply for the purer Italian, I being an ultramontane, little skilled in the set phrase of Tuscany. Cut short the letter—finish it another day. Talked of Italy, patriotism, Alfieri, Madame Albany,[2] and other branches of learning. Also Sallust's Conspiracy of Catiline, and the War of Jugurtha.[3] At 9 came in her brother, Il Conte Pietro—at 10, her father, Conte Ruggiero.

Talked of various modes of warfare—of the Hungarian and Highland modes of broad-sword exercise, in both whereof I was once a moderate "master of fence". Settled that the R[evolution]. will break out on the 7th or 8th of March, in which appointment I should trust, had it not been settled that it was to have broken out in October, 1820. But those Bolognese shirked the Romagnuoles.

"It is all one to Ranger,"[4] One must not be particular, but take rebellion when it lies in the way. Came home—read the "Ten Thousand" again, and will go to bed.

Mem.—Ordered Fletcher (at four o'clock this afternoon) to copy out 7 or 8 apophthegms of Bacon, in which I have detected such blunders as a school-boy might detect rather than commit. Such are the sages! What must they be, when such as I can stumble on their mistakes or misstatements? I will go to bed, for I find that I grow cynical.

January 6th, 1821

Mist—thaw—slop—rain. No stirring out on horseback. Read Spence's Anecdotes. Pope a fine fellow—always thought him so. Corrected blunders in *nine* apophthegms of Bacon—all historical—and read Mitford's Greece. Wrote an epigram. Turned to a passage in Guinguené[1]—ditto in Lord Holland's Lope de Vega. Wrote a note on Don Juan.

At eight went out to visit. Heard a little music—like music. Talked

---

[2] The Comtesse d'Albany, née Stolberg (1753–1824) married the Young Pretender, Charles Edward Stuart, in 1772. After his death in 1788 she lived with Alfieri in Paris and later in Florence, and was said to have had considerable influence on his literary work.

[3] Jugurtha, King of Numidia, warred against several Roman consuls sent into Africa to defeat him until he was finally captured and brought to Rome in 104 B.C. where he died in prison.

[4] Benjamin Hoadly, *The Suspicious Husband* (1747), Act V, scene 2.

[1] Pierre Louis Ginguené (1748–1816), once French ambassador at Turin, published the beginning of his *Histoire Littéraire de l' Italie* in 1811. After his death the work was completed, in 14 volumes, by Salfi by 1835.

with Count Pietro G. of the Italian comedian Vestris,[2] who is now at Rome—have seen him often act in Venice—a good actor—very. Somewhat of a mannerist; but excellent in broad comedy, as well as in the sentimental pathetic. He has made me frequently laugh and cry, neither of which is now a very easy matter—at least, for a player to produce in me.

Thought of the state of women under the ancient Greeks—convenient enough. Present state, a remnant of the barbarism of the chivalry [chivalric?] and feudal ages—artificial and unnatural. They ought to mind home—and be well fed and clothed—but not mixed in society. Well educated, too, in religion—but to read neither poetry nor politics—nothing but books of piety and cookery. Music—drawing—dancing—also a little gardening and ploughing now and then. I have seen them mending the roads in Epirus with good success. Why not, as well as hay-making and milking?

Came home, and read Mitford again, and played with my mastiff—gave him his supper. Made another reading to the epigram, but the turn the same. To-night at the theatre, there being a prince on his throne in the last scene of the comedy,—the audience laughed, and asked him for a *Constitution*. This shows the state of the public mind here, as well as the assassinations. It won't do. There must be an universal republic,—and there ought to be.

The crow is lame of a leg—wonder how it happened—some fool trod upon his toe, I suppose. The falcon pretty brisk—the cats large and noisy—the monkeys I have not looked to since the cold weather, as they suffer by being brought up. Horses must be gay—get a ride as soon as weather serves. Deuced muggy still—an Italian winter is a sad thing, but all the other seasons are charming.

What is the reason that I have been, all my lifetime, more or less *ennuyé*? and that, if any thing, I am rather less so now than I was at twenty, as far as my recollection serves? I do not know how to answer this, but presume that it is constitutional,—as well as the waking in low spirits, which I have invariably done for many years. Temperance and exercise, which I have practiced at times, and for a long time together vigorously and violently, made little or no difference. Violent passions did;—when under their immediate influence—it is odd, but—I was in agitated, but *not* in depressed spirits.

A dose of salts has the effect of a temporary inebriation, like light

2 Luigi Vestri (1781–1841) was chosen by Alfieri to act the part of Gomez in *Filippo*. He played parts also in Goldoni's comedies in Venice.

champagne, upon me. But wine and spirits make me sullen and savage to ferocity—silent, however, and retiring, and not quarrelsome, if not spoken to. Swimming also raises my spirits,—but in general they are low, and get daily lower. That is *hopeless*: for I do not think I am so much *ennuyé* as I was at nineteen. The proof is, that then I must game, or drink, or be in motion of some kind, or I was miserable. At present, I can mope in quietness; and like being alone better than any company —except the lady's whom I serve. But I feel a something, which makes me think that, if I ever reach near to old age, like Swift, "I shall die at top"[3] first. Only I do not dread idiotism or madness so much as he did. On the contrary, I think some quieter stages of both must be preferable to much of what men think the possession of their senses.

· · · · ·

January 11th, 1821

Read the letters. Corrected the tragedy and the "Hints from Horace". Dined, and got into better spirits.—Went out—returned—finished letters, five in number. Read Poets, and an anecdote in Spence.

Al[borghett]i writes to me that the Pope, and Duke of Tuscany, and King of Sardinia, have also been called to Congress; but the Pope will only deal there by proxy. So the interests of millions are in the hands of about twenty coxcombs, at a place called Leibach![1]

I should almost regret that my own affairs went well, when those of nations are in peril. If the interests of mankind could be essentially bettered (particularly of these oppressed Italians), I should not so much mind my own "sma' peculiar". God grant us all better times, or more philosophy.

In reading, I have just chanced upon an expression of Tom Campbell's;—speaking of Collins, he says that "no reader cares any more about the *characteristic manners* of his Eclogues than about the authenticity of the tale of Troy". 'Tis false—we *do* care about "the authenticity of the tale of Troy". I have stood upon that plain *daily*, for more than a month, in 1810; and, if any thing diminished my pleasure, it was

[3] Edward Young, in his *Conjectures on Original Composition* (1759) recorded that while he was walking with Swift near Dublin, the Dean "earnestly gazing upward at a noble elm, which in its uppermost branches was much withered, and decayed," pointed to it and said: "I shall be like that tree, I shall die at top."

[1] The Congress at Laibach (modern Ljubljana, Yugoslavia) was called by the Czar of Russia, the Emperor of Austria, and the Prince of Prussia in January, 1821. King Ferdinand of Naples was invited to attend. The purpose of it was to suppress the Neapolitan revolt and to declare that the powers would not tolerate a constitution which sprang from a revolution, and that the country would be occupied by the Austrian army.

that the blackguard Bryant[2] had impugned its veracity. It is true I read "Homer Travestied"[3] (the first twelve books), because Hobhouse and others bored me with their learned localities, and I love quizzing. But I still venerated the grand original as the truth of *history* (in the material *facts*) and of *place*. Otherwise, it would have given me no delight. Who will persuade me, when I reclined upon a mighty tomb, that it did not contain a hero?—its very magnitude proved this. Men do not labour over the ignoble and petty dead—and why should not the *dead* be *Homer's* dead? The secret of Tom Campbell's defence of *inaccuracy* in costume and description is, that his Gertrude,[4] &c., has no more locality in common with Pennsylvania than with Penmanmaur. It is notoriously full of grossly false scenery, as all Americans declare, though they praise parts of the Poem. It is thus that self-love for ever creeps out, like a snake, to sting anything which happens, even accidentally, to stumble upon it.

January 12th, 1821

The weather still so humid and impracticable, that London, in its most oppressive fogs, were a summer-bower to this mist and sirocco, which now has lasted (but with one day's interval), chequered with snow or heavy rain only, since the 30th of December, 1820. It is so far lucky that I have a literary turn;—but it is very tiresome not to be able to stir out, in comfort, on any horse but Pegasus, for so many days. The roads are even worse than the weather, by the long splashing, and the heavy soil, and the growth of the waters.

Read the Poets—English, that is to say—out of Campbell's edition. There is a good deal of taffeta in some of Tom's prefatory phrases, but his work is good as a whole. I like him best, though, in his own poetry.

Murray writes that they want to act the Tragedy of Marino Faliero;—more fools they, it was written for the closet. I have protested against this piece of usurpation, (which, it seems, is legal for managers over any printed work, against the author's will) and I

---

[2] Jacob Bryant, *Dissertation concerning the war of Troy, and the expedition of the Grecians, as described by Homer; showing that no such expedition was ever undertaken, and that no such city of Phrigia existed*, 1796. Byron protested against Bryant's view in *Don Juan*, Canto IV, stanza 101.

[3] *Homer Travestie; Being a new translation of that great poet* was published anonymously in 1720. A third edition with the title *A Burlesque Translation of Homer* appeared with the name of the author, T. Bridges, in 1770.

[4] Campbell's *Gertrude of Wyoming* was published in 1809.

hope they will not attempt it. Why don't they bring out some of the numberless aspirants for theatrical celebrity, now encumbering their shelves, instead of lugging me out of the library? I have written a fierce protest against any such attempt; but I still would hope that it will not be necessary, and that they will see, at once, that it is not intended for the stage. It is too regular—the time, twenty-four hours —the change of place not frequent—nothing *melo*dramatic—no surprises, no starts, nor trap-doors, nor opportunities "for tossing their heads and kicking their heels"—and no *love*—the grand ingredient of a modern play.

I have found out the seal cut on Murray's letter. It is meant for Walter Scott—or Sir Walter—he is the first poet knighted since *Sir* Richard Blackmore. But it does not do him justice. Scott's—particularly when he recites—is a very intelligent countenance, and this seal says nothing.

Scott is certainly the most wonderful writer of the day. His novels are a new literature in themselves, and his poetry as good as any—if not better (only on an erroneous system)—and only ceased to be so popular, because the vulgar learned were tired of hearing "Aristides called the Just", and Scott the Best, and ostracised him.

I like him, too, for his manliness of character, for the extreme pleasantness of his conversation, and his good-nature towards myself, personally. May he prosper!—for he deserves it. I know no reading to which I fall with such alacrity as a work of W. Scott's. I shall give the seal, with his bust on it, to Madame la Comtesse G. this evening, who will be curious to have the effigies of a man so celebrated.

How strange are my thoughts!—The reading of the song of Milton, "Sabrina fair"[1] has brought back upon me—I know not how or why— the happiest, perhaps, days of my life (always excepting, here and there, a Harrow holiday in the two latter summers of my stay there) when living at Cambridge with Edward Noel Long,[2] afterwards of the Guards,—who, after having served honourably in the expedition to Copenhagen (of which two or three thousand scoundrels yet survive in plight and pay), was drowned early in 1809, on his passage to Lisbon with his regiment in the St. George transport, which was run foul of, in the night, by another transport. We were rival swimmers— fond of riding—reading—and of conviviality. We had been at Harrow

[1] *Comus*, line 859 ff.
[2] Long was at Harrow and Cambridge with Byron. He is the "Cleon" of "Childish Recollections" and the subject of a separate poem, "To Edward Noel Long, Esq.".

together; but—*there*, at least—his was a less boisterous spirit than mine. I was always cricketing—rebelling—fighting—*rowing* (from *row*, not *boat*-rowing, a different practice), and in all manner of mischiefs; while he was more sedate and polished. At Cambridge— both of Trinity—my spirit rather softened, or his roughened, for we became very great friends. The description of Sabrina's seat reminds me of our rival feats in *diving*. Though Cam's is not a very "trans- lucent wave," it was fourteen feet deep, where we used to dive for, and pick up—having thrown them in on purpose—plates, eggs, and even shillings. I remember, in particular, there was the stump of a tree (at least ten or twelve feet deep) in the bed of the river, in a spot where we bathed most commonly, round which I used to cling, and "wonder how the devil I came there".[3]

Our evenings we passed in music (he was musical, and played on more than one instrument, flute and violoncello), in which I was audience; and I think that our chief beverage was soda-water. In the day we rode, bathed, and lounged, reading occasionally. I remember our buying, with vast alacrity, Moore's new quarto[4] (in 1806), and reading it together in the evenings.

We only passed the summer together;—Long had gone into the Guards during the year I passed in Notts, away from college. *His* friendship, and a violent, though *pure*, love and passion[5]—which held me at the same period—were the then romance of the most romantic period of my life.

.   .   .   .   .

January 13th, 1821, Saturday

Sketched the outline and Drams. Pers. of an intended tragedy of Sardanapalus, which I have for some time meditated. Took the names from Diodorus Siculus, (I know the history of Sardanapalus, and have known it since I was twelve years old), and read over a passage in the ninth vol. octavo of Mitford's Greece, where he rather vindicates the memory of this last of the Assyrians.

Dined—news come—the *Powers* mean to war with the peoples. The intelligence seems positive—let it be so—they will be beaten in the end. The king-times are fast finishing. There will be blood shed like

---

[3] cf. Pope, Epistle to Dr. Arbuthnot (line 172): "But wonder how the devil they got there."

[4] *Epistles, Odes, and other Poems* (1806).

[5] An obvious reference to his attachment to John Edleston, the Cambridge chorister.

water, and tears like mist; but the peoples will conquer in the end. I shall not live to see it, but I foresee it.

I carried Teresa the Italian translation of Grillparzer's Sappho, which she promises to read. She quarrelled with me, because I said that love was *not the loftiest* theme for true tragedy; and, having the advantage of her native language, and natural female eloquence, she overcame my fewer arguments. I believe she was right. I must put more love into "Sardanapalus" than I intended. I speak, of course, *if* the times will allow me leisure. That *if* will hardly be a peace-maker.

January 14th, 1821

Turned over Seneca's tragedies. Wrote the opening lines of the intended tragedy of Sardanapalus. Rode out some miles into the forest. Misty and rainy. Returned—dined—wrote some more of my tragedy.

Read Diodorus Siculus—turned over Seneca, and some other books. Wrote some more of the tragedy. Took a glass of grog. After having ridden hard in rainy weather, and scribbled, and scribbled again, the spirits (at least mine) need a little exhilaration, and I don't like laudanum now as I used to do. So I have mixed a glass of strong waters and single waters, which I shall now proceed to empty. Therefore and thereunto I conclude this day's diary.

The effect of all wines and spirits upon me is, however, strange. It *settles*, but it makes me gloomy—gloomy at the very moment of their effect, and not gay hardly ever. But it composes for a time, though sullenly.

January 15th, 1821

Weather fine. Received visit. Rode out into the forest—fired pistols. Returned home—dined—dipped into a volume of Mitford's Greece—wrote part of a scene of "Sardanapalus". Went out—heard some music—heard some politics. More ministers from the other Italian powers gone to Congress. War seems certain—in that case, it will be a savage one. Talked over various important matters with one of the initiated. At ten and half returned home.

I have just thought of something odd. In the year 1814, Moore ("the poet", *par excellence*, and he deserves it) and I were going together, in the same carriage, to dine with Earl Grey, the Capo Politico of the remaining whigs. Murray, the magnificent (the illustrious publisher of that name), had just sent me a Java gazette—I know not why, or wherefore. Pulling it out, by way of curiosity, we found it to contain a dispute (the said Java gazette) on Moore's merits and mine. I think, if I had been there, that I could have saved them the trouble of disputing on the subject. But, there is *fame* for you at six and twenty! Alexander had conquered India at the same age; but I doubt if he was disputed about, or his conquests compared with those of Indian Bacchus, at Java.

It was a great fame to be named with Moore; greater to be compared with him; greatest—*pleasure*, at least—to be *with* him; and, surely, an odd coincidence, that we should be dining together while they were quarrelling about us beyond the equinoctial line.

Well, the same evening, I met Lawrence the painter, and heard one of Lord Grey's daughters (a fine, tall, spirit-looking girl, with much of the *patrician, thorough-bred look* of her father, which I dote upon) play on the harp, so modestly and ingenuously, that she *looked music*. Well, I would rather have had my talk with Lawrence (who talked delightfully) and heard the girl, than have had all the fame of Moore and me put together.

The only pleasure of fame is that it paves the way to pleasure; and the more intellectual our pleasure, the better for the pleasure and for us too. It was, however, agreeable to have heard our fame before dinner, and a girl's harp after.

.   .   .   .   .

January 25th, 1821

Received a letter from Lord S. O.,[1] state secretary of the Seven Islands—a fine fellow—clever—dished in England five years ago, and came abroad to retrench and to renew. He wrote from Ancona, in his way back to Corfu, on some matters of our own. He is son of the late Duke of L[eeds] by a second marriage. He wants me to go to Corfu. Why not?—perhaps I may, next spring.

Answered Murray's letter—read—lounged. Scrawled this additional page of life's log-book. One day more is over of it, and of me;—

[1] Lord Sidney Godolphin Osborne (1789–1861) was the son of the second wife of the Duke of Leeds whom the Duke married after divorcing Augusta Leigh's mother, the Marchioness of Carmarthen, who eloped with and later married Byron's father.

but "which is best, life or death, the gods only know," as Socrates said to his judges, on the breaking up of the tribunal.[2] Two thousand years since that sage's declaration of ignorance have not enlightened us more upon this important point; for, according to the Christian dispensation, no one can know whether he is *sure* of salvation—even the most righteous—since a single slip of faith may throw him on his back, like a skaiter, while gliding smoothly to his paradise. Now, therefore, whatever the certainty of faith in the facts may be, the certainty of the individual as to his happiness or misery is no greater than it was under Jupiter.

It has been said that the immortality of the soul is a "grand peut-être"—[3] but still it is a *grand* one. Every body clings to it—the stupidest, and dullest, and wickedest of human bipeds is still persuaded that he is immortal.

January 28th, 1821

Memoranda.

What is Poetry?—The feeling of a Former world and Future.

Thought Second.

Why, at the very height of desire and human pleasure,—worldly, social, amorous, ambitious, or even avaricious,—does there mingle a certain sense of doubt and sorrow—a fear of what is to come—a doubt of what *is*—a retrospect to the past, leading to a prognostication of the future? (The best of Prophets of the future is the Past.) Why is this? or these?—I know not, except that on a pinnacle we are most susceptible of giddiness, and that we never fear falling except from a precipice—the higher, the more awful, and the more sublime; and, therefore, I am not sure that Fear is not a pleasurable sensation; at least, *Hope* is; and *what Hope* is there without a deep leaven of Fear? and what sensation is so delightful as Hope? and, if it were not for Hope, where would the Future be?—in hell. It is useless to say *where* the Present is, for most of us know; and as for the Past, *what* predominates in memory?—*Hope baffled*. Ergo, in all human affairs, it is Hope—Hope—Hope. I allow sixteen minutes, though I never counted them, to any given or supposed possession. From whatever place we

---

[2] In Plato's *Phaedo* (62) Socrates is quoted as saying that "at some times and to some persons it is better to die than to live".

[3] This was one of the apocryphal legends about the death-bed utterances of Rabelais: "La farce est jouée", "Je vais chercher un grand peut-être."

commence, we know where it all must end. And yet, what good is there in knowing it? It does not make men better or wiser. During the greatest horrors of the greatest plagues, (Athens and Florence, for example—see Thucydides and Machiavelli) men were more cruel and profligate than ever. It is all a mystery. I feel most things, but I know nothing, except——

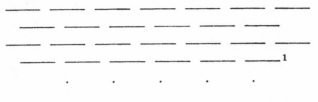

February 2d, 1821

I have been considering what can be the reason why I always wake, at a certain hour in the morning, and always in very bad spirits—I may say, in actual despair and despondency, in all respects—even of that which pleased me over night. In about an hour or two, this goes off, and I compose either to sleep again, or, at least, to quiet. In England, five years ago, I had the same kind of hypochondria, but accompanied with so violent a thirst that I have drank as many as fifteen bottles of soda-water in one night, after going to bed, and been still thirsty—calculating, however, some lost from the bursting out and effervescence and overflowing of the soda-water, in drawing the corks, or striking off the necks of the bottles from mere thirsty impatience. At present, I have *not* the thirst; but the depression of spirits is no less violent.

I read in Edgeworth's Memoirs of something similar (except that his thirst expended itself on *small beer*) in the case of Sir F. B. Delaval; —but then he was, at least, twenty years older. What is it?—liver? In England, Le Man (the apothecary) cured me of the thirst in three days, and it had lasted as many years. I suppose that it is all hypochondria.

What I feel most growing upon me are laziness, and a disrelish more powerful than indifference. If I rouse, it is into fury. I presume that I shall end (if not earlier by accident, or some such termination) like Swift—"dying at top." I confess I do not contemplate this with so much horror as he apparently did for some years before it happened.

---

[1] "Thus marked, with impatient strokes of the pen in the original." (Moore, II, 420). The indented lines seem to indicate that the omission was in verse form.

But Swift had hardly *begun life* at the very period (thirty-three) when I feel quite an *old sort* of feel.

Oh! there is an organ playing in the street—a waltz, too! I must leave off to listen. They are playing a waltz which I have heard ten thousand times at the balls in London, between 1812 and 1815. Music is a strange thing.

·　　·　　·　　·　　·

February 16th, 1821

Last night Il Conte P. G. sent a man with a bag full of bayonets, some muskets, and some hundreds of cartridges to my house, without apprizing me, though I had seen him not half an hour before. About ten days ago, when there was to be a rising here, the Liberals and my brethren C[arbonar]i asked me to purchase some arms for a certain few of our ragamuffins. I did so immediately, and ordered ammunition, etc., and they were armed accordingly. Well—the rising is prevented by the Barbarians marching a week sooner than appointed; and an *order* is issued, and in force, by the Government, "that all persons having arms concealed, &c. &c., shall be liable to," &c. &c.—and what do my friends, the patriots, do two days afterwards? Why, they throw back upon my hands, and into my house, these very arms (without a word of warning previously) with which I had furnished them at their own request, and at my own peril and expense.

It was lucky that Lega was at home to receive them. If any of the servants had (except Tita and F[letcher] and Lega) they would have betrayed it immediately. In the mean time, if they are denounced, or discovered, I shall be in a scrape.

At nine went out—at eleven returned. Beat the crow for stealing the falcon's victuals. Read "Tales of my Landlord"—wrote a letter—and mixed a moderate beaker of water with other ingredients.

·　　·　　·　　·　　·

February 18th, 1821

To-day I have had no communication with my Carbonari cronies; but, in the mean time, my lower apartments are full of their bayonets, fusils, cartridges, and what not. I suppose that they consider me as a depôt, to be sacrificed, in case of accidents. It is no great matter, supposing that Italy could be liberated, who or what is sacrificed. It is a grand object—the very *poetry* of politics. Only think—a free Italy!!! Why, there has been nothing like it since the days of Augustus. I reckon the times of Caesar (Julius) free; because the commotions left every body a side to take, and the parties were pretty equal at the set out. But, afterwards, it was all praetorian and legionary business—and since!—we shall see, or, at least, some will see, what card will turn up. It is best to hope, even of the hopeless. The Dutch did more than these fellows have to do, in the Seventy Years' War.

· · · · ·

[TO JOHN MURRAY]   *Ravenna—Feb[brai]o 16o 1821*

Dear Moray—In the month of March will arrive from Barcelona—*Signor Curioni*[1] engaged for the Opera.—He is an acquaintance of mine—and a gentlemanly young man—high in his profession.—I must request your personal kindness and patronage in his favour.——Pray introduce him to such of the theatrical people—Editors of Papers—and others, as may be useful to him in his profession publicly and privately.—He is accompanied by the Signora Arpalice Taruscelli[2]—a Venetian lady of great beauty and celebrity and a particular friend of mine—your natural gallantry will I am sure induce you to pay her proper attention.—Tell Israeli—that as he is fond of *literary* anecdotes—she can tell him some of your acquaintance abroad.—I presume that he speaks Italian.—Do not neglect this request, but do them and me this favour in their behalf.——I shall write to some others to aid you in assisting them with your countenance.

I agree to your request of leaving in abeyance the terms for the three D. J.s till you can ascertain the effect of publication.—If I refuse to alter—you have a claim to so much courtesy in return.—I had let you off your proposal about the price of the Cantos, last year (the 3d. & 4th. always to reckon as *one* only—which they originally were) and I do not call upon you to renew it.—You have therefore no occasion to fight so shy of such subjects as I am not conscious of having given you occasion.——The 5th. is so far from being the last of D. J. that it is hardly the beginning.—I meant to take him the tour of Europe—with a proper mixture of siege—battle—and adventure—and to make him finish as *Anacharsis Cloots*[3]—in the French revolution.—To how many

---

[1] Alberico Curioni, an Italian tenor, sang operatic parts in London from 1821 to 1832.

[2] A Ballerina with whom Byron had a brief affair in Venice in 1818.

[3] Jean Baptiste (Anacharsis) Clootz was a Prussian baron who became involved in the French Revolution. He described himself before the National Convention as "l'orateur du genre humain". He later came under the suspicion of Robespierre and was executed in 1794.

cantos this may extend—I know not—nor whether (even if I live) I shall complete it—but this was my notion.—I meant to have made him a Cavalier Servente in Italy and a cause for a divorce in England—and a Sentimental "Werther-faced man"[4] in Germany—so as to show the different ridicules of the society in each of those countries—— and to have displayed him gradually gaté and blasé as he grew older—as is natural.—But I had not quite fixed whether to make him end in Hell—or in an unhappy marriage,—not knowing which would be the severest.—The Spanish tradition says Hell—but it is probably only an Allegory of the other state.——You are now in possession of my notions on the subject.—

You say "the Doge" will not be popular—did I ever write for *popularity?*——I defy you to show a work of mine (except a tale or two) of a popular style or complexion.—It appears to me that there is room for a different style of the drama—neither a servile following of the old drama—which is a grossly erronious one—nor yet *too French*—like those who succeeded the older writers.—It appears to me that good English—and a severer approach to the rules—might combine something not dishonourable to our literature.——I have also attempted to make a play without love.——And there are neither rings—nor mistakes—nor starts—nor outrageous ranting villains—nor melodrame—in it.—All this will prevent it's popularity, but does not persuade me that it is *therefore* faulty.—Whatever faults it has will arise from deficiency in the conduct—rather than in the conception—which is simple and severe.—So—*you epigrammatize* upon *my epigram.*——I will *pay you* for *that*—mind if I don't—some day.—I never let anyone off in the long run—(*who first begins*)—remember *Sam*—and see if I don't do you as good a turn.—You unnatural publisher!—what—quiz your own authors!—You are a paper Cannibal.—

In the letter on Bowles—(which I sent by Tuesday's post) after the words *"attempts had been made"* (alluding to the republication of "English Bards")—add the words *"in Ireland"* for I believe that Cawthorn did not begin his attempts till after I had left England the second time.—Pray attend to this.—Let me know what you & your Synod think of the letter on Bowles.——I did not think the second *Seal* so bad—surely it is far better than the Saracen's head with which you have sealed your *last letter*—the larger in *profile* was surely much better than that.—[So] Foscolo says he will get you a [*seal*] *cut* better

---

[4] Byron borrowed the phrase from Letter 5 of Moore's *Fudge Family in Paris* (1818): "A fine, sallow, sublime, sort of Werther-faced man".

in Italy—he means a *throat*—that is the only thing they do dexterously. —The Arts—all but Canova's and Morghen's[5]—and Ovid's[6];—(I don't *mean poetry*) are as low as need be—look at the Seal which I gave to Wm. Bankes—and own it.—How came George Bankes[7] to quote English Bards in the House of Commons? all the World keep flinging that poem in my face.——Belzoni[8] *is* a grand traveller and his English is very prettily broken.——As for News—the Barbarians are marching on Naples——and if they lose a single battle, all Italy will be up.—It will be like the Spanish war if they have any bottom.—— "*Letters opened!*" to be sure they are—and that's the reason why I always put in my opinion of the German Austrian Scoundrels;—there is not an Italian who loathes them more than I do—and whatever I could do to scour Italy and the earth of their infamous oppression— would be done "con amore".—

yrs. ever & truly
BYRON

Recollect that the *Hints* must be printed with the *Latin* otherwise there is no sense.—

[TO PERCY BYSSHE SHELLEY]   *Ravenna, April 26th, 1821*

The child continues doing well, and the accounts are regular and favourable. It is gratifying to me that you and Mrs. Shelley do not disapprove of the step which I have taken, which is merely temporary.

---

[5] Raphael Morghen (1758–1835) was a famous Italian engraver who settled in Florence.

[6] Ovid's *Ars Amatoria*.

[7] George Bankes, M.P. for Corfe Castle, in an address at the opening of Parliament on January 23, 1821, said that "the new springs of knowledge were endeavoured to be poisoned at their source "which reminded him of "the lines of the poet, when he expressed the keen pangs of the bird, wounded by the arrow feathered from his own wing". He then quoted two lines from *English Bards and Scotch Reviewers:*

> "Keen were his pangs, but keener far to feel
> He nursed the pinion which impelled the steel."

[8] Giovanni Battista Belzoni (1778–1823), an Italian explorer, insisted on writing in English the account of his travels, though his knowledge of the language was imperfect. Murray published in 1820 his *Narrative of the Operations and Recent Discoveries within the Pyramids, Temples, Tombs, and Excavations in Egypt and Nubia.*

I am very sorry to hear what you say of Keats—is it *actually* true? I did not think criticism had been so killing. Though I differ from you essentially in your estimate of his performances, I so much abhor all unnecessary pain, that I would rather he had been seated on the highest peak of Parnassus than have perished in such a manner. Poor fellow! though with such inordinate self-love he would probably have not been very happy. I read the review of "Endymion" in the Quarterly. It was severe,—but surely not so severe as many reviews in that and other journals upon others.

I recollect the effect on me of the Edinburgh on my first poem; it was rage, and resistance, and redress—but not despondency nor despair. I grant that those are not amiable feelings; but, in this world of bustle and broil, and especially in the career of writing, a man should calculate upon his powers of *resistance* before he goes into the arena.

> "Expect not life from pain nor danger free,
> Nor deem the doom of man reversed for thee."[1]

You know my opinion of *that second-hand* school of poetry. You also know my high opinion of your own poetry,—because it is of *no* school. I read Cenci—but, besides that I think the *subject* essentially *un-*dramatic, I am not an admirer of our old dramatists *as models*. I deny that the English have hitherto had a drama at all. Your Cenci, however, was a work of power, and poetry. As to *my* drama, pray revenge yourself upon it, by being as free as I have been with yours.

I have not yet got your Prometheus,[2] which I long to see. I have heard nothing of mine, and do not know that it is yet published. I have published a pamphlet on the Pope controversy, which you will not like. Had I known that Keats was dead—or that he was alive and so sensitive—I should have omitted some remarks upon his poetry, to which I was provoked by his *attack* upon *Pope*, and my disapprobation of *his own* style of writing.

You want me to undertake a great Poem—I have not the inclination nor the power. As I grow older, the indifference—*not* to life, for we love it by instinct—but to the stimuli of life, increases. Besides, this late failure of the Italians has latterly disappointed me for many reasons,—some public, some personal. My respects to Mrs. S.

Yours ever,

B

---

[1] Johnson's *Vanity of Human Wishes*, lines 155–156.
[2] Shelley's *Cenci* was published at Leghorn in 1818; his *Prometheus Unbound* in London in 1820.

P.S.—Could not you and I contrive to meet this summer? Could not you take a run *alone?*

Ravenna, July 5th, 1821

How could you suppose that I ever would allow any thing that *could* be said on your account to weigh with *me?* I only regret that Bowles had not *said* that you were the writer of that note, until afterwards, when out he comes with it, in a private letter to Murray, which Murray sends to me.[1] D—n the controversy!

> "D—n Twizzle,
> D—n the bell.
> And d—n the fool who rung it—Well!
> From all such plagues I'll quickly be delivered."[2]

I have had a friend of your Mr. Irving's—a very pretty lad—a Mr. Coolidge, of Boston—only somewhat too full of poesy and "entusymusy." I was very civil to him during his few hours' stay, and talked with him much of Irving, whose writings are my delight. But I suspect that he did not take quite so much to me, from his having expected to meet a misanthropical gentleman, in wolf-skin breeches, and answering in fierce monosyllables, instead of a man of this world. I can never get people to understand that poetry is the expression of *excited passion,* and that there is no such thing as a life of passion any more than a continuous earthquake, or an eternal fever. Besides, who would ever *shave* themselves in such a state?

I have had a curious letter to-day from a girl in England (I never saw her), who says she is given over of a decline, but could not go out of the world without thanking me for the delight which my poesy for several years, &c. &c. &c. It is signed simply N. N. A. and has not a word of "cant" or preachment in it upon *any* opinions. She merely says that she is dying, and that as I had contributed so highly to her existing pleasure, she thought that she might say so, begging me to *burn* her *letter*—which, by the way, I can *not* do, as I look upon such a letter, in such circumstances, as better than a diploma from Gottingen. I once had a letter from Drontheim in *Norway* (but not from a dying

---

[1] Bowles had quoted a gentleman "of the highest literary, etc." as saying that in his pamphlet he (Bowles) had "hit the right nail on the head, and * * * * too." Byron had taken this to refer to Pope, but he was amused to learn from Bowles that he meant Moore.

[2] George Colman the Younger, *Broad Grins* (1811). Byron has quoted, slightly inaccurately, from "The Elder Brother".

woman), in verse, on the same score of gratulation. These are the things which make one at times believe one's self a poet. But if I must believe that * * * * *, and such fellows, are poets also, it is better to be out of the corps.

I am now in the fifth act of "Foscari" being the third tragedy in twelve months, besides *proses*; so you perceive that I am not at all idle. And are you, too, busy? I doubt that your life at Paris draws too much upon your time, which is a pity. Can't you divide your day, so as to combine both? I have had plenty of all sorts of worldly business on my hands last year, and yet it is not so difficult to give a few hours to the *Muses*. This sentence is so like * * * * that—

Ever, &c.

If we were together, I should publish both my plays (periodically) in our *joint* journal. It should be our plan to publish all our best things in that way.

[TO JOHN MURRAY]   R[avenn]a *August 23d. 1821*

Dear Sir/—Enclosed are the two notes corrected.—With regard to the charges about the "Shipwreck"[1]—I think that I told both you and Mr. Hobhouse years ago—that [there] was not a *single circumstance* of it—*not* taken from *fact*—not indeed from any *single* shipwreck —but all from *actual* facts of different wrecks.—Almost all Don Juan is *real* life—either my own—or from people I knew.——By the way much of the description of the *furniture* in Canto 3d. is taken from *Tully's Tripoli*[2]—(pray *note this*)—and the rest from my own observation.——Remember I never meant to conceal this at all—& have only not stated it because D[on] Juan had no preface nor name to it.— If you think it worth while to make this statement—do so—in your own way.—*I* laugh at such charges—convinced that no writer ever borrowed less—or made his materials more his own.——Much is Coincidence[;] for instance—Lady Morgan (in a really *excellent* book I assure you on Italy) calls Venice an *Ocean Rome*—I have the very

[1] Byron's indebtedness for his shipwreck scenes in the second canto of *Don Juan* to Sir J. G. Dalyell's *Shipwrecks and Disasters at Sea* (1812) was pointed out by the *Monthly Review*. (Vol. III, Aug. 1821, pp. 19–22).
[2] Richard Tully's *Narrative of a Ten Years' Residence at the Court of Tripoli* was the source of some of Byron's description of the furnishings of the Pirate Lambro's palace in *Don Juan*, Canto III, stanzas 67–69.

same expression in *Foscari*—& yet *you* know that the play was written months ago & was sent to England.—The "Italy" I received only on the 16th. Inst.——Your friend—like the public is not aware that my dramatic Simplicity is *studiously* Greek—& must continue so—*no* reform ever succeeded at first.——I admire the old English dramatists —but this is quite another field—& has nothing to do with theirs.—I want to make a *regular* English drama—no matter whether for the Stage or not—which is not my object—but a *mental theatre*——

yrs. [Scrawl]

P.S.—*Can't* accept your courteous offer,[3]——
> For Orford and for Waldegrave
> You give much more than me you *gave*
> Which is not fairly to behave
>> My Murray!
>
> Because if a live dog, 'tis said,
> Be worth a Lion fairly sped,
> A *live lord* must be worth *two* dead,
>> My Murray!
>
> And if, as the opinion goes,
> Verse hath a better sale than prose—
> Certes, I should have more than those
>> My Murray!
>
> But now—this sheet is nearly crammed,
> So—if *you will*—*I* shan't be shammed,
> And if you *wont*—*you* may be damned,
>> My Murray!

These matters must be arranged with Mr. Douglas K[innaird].—He is my trustee—and a man of honour.—To him you can state all your mercantile reasons which you might not like to state to me personally —such as "heavy season" ["]flat public" "don't go off"—["]Lordship writes too much—Won't take advice—declining popularity—deductions for the trade—make very little—generally lose by him— pirated edition—foreign edition—severe criticisms. &c.["] with other hints and howls for an oration—which I leave Douglas who is an orator to answer.——You can also state them more freely—to a third person—as between you and me they could only produce some smart postscripts which would not adorn our mutual archives.——I am

---

[3] Murray had offered 2000 guineas for three cantos of *Don Juan*, *Sardanapalus*, and *The Two Foscari*.

sorry for the Queen[4]—and that's more than you are.———Is the bust[5] arrived?

[TO JOHN MURRAY] *Ravenna Septr. 24th. 1821*

Dear Murray/—I have been thinking over our late correspondence and wish to propose the following articles for our future.—1stly—That you shall write to me of yourself—of the health wealth and welfare of all friends—but of *me* (*quoad me*) little or nothing.—
2dly—That you shall send me Soda powders—tooth-paste—tooth-brushes—or any such anti-odontalgic or chemical articles as heretofore "ad libitum" upon being re-imbursed for the same.—
3dly—That you shall *not* send me any modern or (as they are called) *new* publications in *English—whatsoever*—save and excepting any writing prose or verse of (or reasonably presumed to be of) Walter Scott — Crabbe — Moore — Campbell — Rogers — Gifford — Joanna Baillie—*Irving* (the American) Hogg—Wilson (Isle of Palms Man) or any especial *single* work of fancy which is thought to be of considerable merit.—*Voyages* and *travels*—provided that they are *neither in Greece Spain Asia Minor Albania nor Italy* will be welcome—having travelled the countries mentioned—I know that what is said of them can convey nothing further which I desire to know about them.—No other *English* works whatsoever.——
4thly—That you send me *no periodical works* whatsoever—*no* Edinburgh—Quarterly—Monthly—nor any Review—Magazine—Newspaper English or foreign of any description——
5thly—That you send me *no* opinions whatsoever either *good—bad—* or *indifferent*—of yourself or your friends or others—concerning any work or works of mine—past—present—or to come.—
6thly—That all Negotiations in matters of business between you and me pass through the medium of the Hon[oura]ble Douglas Kinnaird— my friend and trustee, or Mr. Hobhouse—as "Alter Ego" and tantamount to myself during my absence.—or presence.——

Some of these propositions may at first seem strange—but they are founded.—The quantity of trash I have received as books is incalculable, and neither amused nor instructed.—Reviews & Magazines— are at the best but ephemeral & superficial reading—*who thinks* of the

---

[4] Queen Caroline, wife of George IV, died August 7, 1821.
[5] The Thorwaldsen bust of Byron which was being sent to England for Hobhouse.

grand article of *last year* in any *given review*? in the next place—if they regard *myself*—they tend to increase *Egotism*,—if favourable—I do not deny that the praise *elates*—and if unfavourable that the abuse *irritates*—the latter may conduct me to inflict a species of Satire—which would neither do good to you nor to your friends—*they* may smile *now*, and so may *you* but if I took you all in hand—it would not be difficult to cut you up like gourds. I did as much by as powerful people at nineteen years old—& I know little as yet in three & thirty—which should prevent me from making all your ribs—Gridirons for your hearts—if such were my propensity.—But it is *not*.—Therefore let me hear none of your provocations—if anything occurs so very *gross* as to require my notice—I shall hear of it from my personal friends.—For the rest—I merely request to be left in ignorance.—

The same applies to opinions *good—bad* or *indifferent* of persons in conversation or correspondence; these do not *interrupt* but they *soil* the *current* of my *Mind*;—I am sensitive enough—but *not* till I am *touched* & *here* I am beyond the touch of the short arms of literary England—except the few feelers of the Polypus that crawl over the Channel in the way of Extract.——All these precautions *in* England would be useless —the libeller or the flatterer would there reach me in spite of all—but in Italy we know little of literary England & think less except what reaches us through some garbled & brief extract in some miserable Gazette.——For *two years* (except two or three articles cut out & sent by *you*—by the post) I never read a newspaper—which was not forced upon me by some accident—& know upon the whole as little of England—as you all do of Italy—& God knows—*that* is little enough with all your travels &c. &c. &c.—The English travellers *know Italy* as *you* know Guernsey—how much is *that*?—If any thing occurs so violently gross or personal as to require notice, Mr. D[ougla]s Kinnaird will let me *know*—but of *praise* I desire to hear *nothing*.—— You will say—"to what tends all this?—" I will answer THAT——to keep my mind *free and* unbiased—by all paltry and personal irritabilities of praise or censure;—To let my Genius take it's natural direction,—while my feelings are like the dead—who know nothing and feel nothing of all or aught that is said or done in their regard.—— If you can observe these conditions you will spare yourself & others some pain—let me not be worked upon to rise up—for if I do—it will not be for a little;—if you can *not* observe these conditions we shall cease to be correspondents,—but *not friends*—for I shall always be yrs. ever & truly

BYRON

P.S.—I have taken these resolutions not from any irritation against *you* or *yours* but simply upon reflection that all reading either praise or censure of myself has done me harm.—When I was in Switzerland and Greece I was out of the way of hearing either—& *how I wrote there!*—In Italy I am out of the way of it too—but latterly partly through my fault—& partly through your kindness in wishing to send me the *newest* & most periodical publications—I have had a crowd of reviews &c. thrust upon me—which have bored me with their jargon of one kind or another—& taken off my attention from greater objects. ——You have also sent me a parcel of trash of poetry for no reason that I can conceive—unless to provoke me to write a new "English Bards"—Now *this* I wish to avoid—for if ever I *do*—it will be a strong production—and I desire peace as long as the fools will keep their nonsense out of my way.——

*

My dearest Augusta/—Has there been nothing to make it grey? to be sure the *years* have not.——Your parcel will not find me here—I am going to *Pisa*—for the winter.—The late political troubles here have occasioned the exile of all my friends & connections—& I am going there to join them.—You know or you do *not* know that Madame La Comtesse G[uiccioli] was separated from her husband last year (on account of P. P. Clerk of this parish) that the Pope decided in her favour & gave her a separate maintenance & that we lived very quietly & decently—she at her father's (as the Pope decided) and I at home— till this Summer.—When her father was exiled—she was obliged either to accompany him or retire into a Convent—such being the terms of his Holiness's deed of divorcement.——They went to Pisa— by my recommendation & there I go to join them.——So there's a *romance* for you—I assure you it was not my wish nor fault altogether —her husband was old—rich—& must have left her a large jointure in a few years—but he was jealous—& insisted &c. & *she* like all the rest—*would* have her own way.—You know that all my loves go crazy—and make scenes—and so—"She is the sixteenth Mrs. Shuffleton".[1]——Being very young—very romantic—and odd—and being contradicted by her husband besides—& being of a country

---

[1] In George Colman the Younger's *John Bull*, Act III, Shuffleton says: ". . . she is to be the fifteenth Mrs. Shuffleton".

where morals are no better than in England—(though elopements and divorces are rare—and this made an uncommon noise—the first that had occurred at Ravenna for two hundred years—that is in a *public* way with appeals to the Pope &c.) you are not to wonder much at it;—she being too a beauty & the great Belle of the four Legations—and married not quite a year (at our first acquaintance) to a man *forty years older* than herself—who had had two wives already—& a little suspected of having poisoned his first.——

We have been living hitherto decently & quietly—these things here do not exclude a woman from all society as in yr. hypocritical country. ——It is very odd that all my *fairs* are such romantic people—and always daggering or divorcing—or making scenes.——But this is "positively the last time of performance" (as the play-bills say) or of my getting into such scrapes for the future.—Indeed—I have had my share.—But this is a finisher—for you know when a woman is separated from her husband for her Amant—he is bound both by honour (and inclination at least I am) to live with her all his days, as long as there is no misconduct.—So you see that I have closed as papa *begun*——and you will probably never see me again as long as you live.—Indeed you don't deserve it—for having behaved so *coldly*—⟨when I was ready to have sacrificed every thing for you—and after *you* had taken the farther . . . always⟩—It is nearly three years that this "liaison" has lasted——I was dreadfully in love—and she blindly so—for she has sacrificed every thing to this headlong passion.—That comes of being romantic—I can say that without being so *furiously* in love as at first—I am more attached to her—than I thought it possible to be to any woman after three years—⟨except one & who was she *you* can guess⟩ and have not the least wish—nor prospect of separation from her.—She herself—(and it is now a year since her separation a year too of all kinds of vicissitudes &c.) is still more decided—of course the *step* was a decisive one.—If Lady B[yron] would but please to die—and the Countess G[uiccioli]'s husband—(for Catholics can't marry though divorced) we should probably have to marry—though I would rather *not*—thinking it the way to hate each other—for all people whatsoever.——However—you must not calculate upon seeing me again in a hurry, if ever.——How have you sent the *parcel*—& how am I to receive it at Pisa?—I am anxious about the Seal—not about Hodgson's nonsense—what is the fool afraid of the *post* for? it is the *safest*—the only *safe* conveyance—they never meddle but with political packets.

yrs. [Scrawl]

P.S.—*You* ought to be a great admirer of the *future* Lady B. for *three* reasons. 1stly. She is a grand patroness of the *present* Lady B.— and always says "that she had no doubt that she was exceedingly ill-used by me["]—2dly. She is an admirer of yours—and I have had great difficulty in keeping her from writing to you eleven pages—(for she is a grand Scribe) and 3dly. she having read "Don Juan" in a *French* translation—made me promise to write *no more* of it—declaring that it was abominable &c. &c.—that *Donna Inez* WAS meant for Ly. B.—& in short made me vow *not* to continue it—(*this* occurred lately & since the last cantos were sent to England last year) is not this altogether odd enough?—She has a good deal of *us* too—I mean that turn for ridicule like Aunt Sophy and you and I & all the B's. Desire Georgiana to write me a letter I suppose she can by this time.—Opened by me— and the Seal taken off—so—don't accuse the post-office without cause

B—that's a sign—a written one where the wax was.

DETACHED THOUGHTS
October 15, 1821–May 18, 1822

5

I have never heard any one who fulfilled my Ideal of an Orator.—
Grattan would have been near it but for his Harlequin delivery.——
Pitt I never heard.—Fox but once—and then he struck me as a debater
—which to me seems as different from an Orator as an Improvisatore
or a versifier from a poet.——Grey is great—but it is not oratory.—
Canning is sometimes very like one.—Windham I did not admire
though all the world did—it seemed sad sophistry.——Whitbread
was the Demosthenes of bad taste and vulgar vehemence—but strong
and English.——Holland is impressive from sense and sincerity—Ld.
Lansdowne good—but still a debater only—Grenville I like vastly—if
he would prune his speeches down to an hour's delivery——Burdett
is sweet and silvery as Belial himself—and *I* think the greatest favourite
in Pandemonium—at least I always heard the Country Gentleman &
the ministerial devilry praise his speeches *up*stairs—and run down from
Bellamy's[2] when he was upon his legs.——I heard Bob Milnes make
his second speech—it made an impression.——I like Ward,—studied
—but keen and sometimes eloquent.—Peel—my School and form-
fellow—(we sate within two of each other) strange to say I have never
heard—though I often wished to do so—but from what I remember of
him at Harrow—he *is* or *should* be—among the best of them. Now I do
not admire Mr. Wilberforce's speaking—it is nothing but a flow of
words—"words—words alone".[3]——

I doubt greatly if the English *have* any eloquence—properly so
called—and am inclined to think that the Irish *had* a great deal, and
that the French *will* have—and have had in Mirabeau.—Lord Chatham
& Burke are the nearest approach to Oratory in England.——I don't
know what Erskine may have been at the *bar*, but in the house I wish
him at the Bar once more. Lauderdale is shrill—& Scotch, and acute.
——Of Brougham—I shall say nothing as I have a personal feeling of
dislike to the man.—But amongst all these good—bad—and indifferent

---

[1] Continued in the same notebook in which the Journal dated May 15, 1821, was
begun.

[2] A famous pastry cook.

[3] *Troilus and Cressida*, Act V, scene 3.

—I never heard the speech which was not too long for the auditors—& not very intelligible except here and there.——The whole thing is a grand deception—and as tedious and tiresome as may be to those who must be often present. I heard Sheridan only once—and that briefly— but I liked his voice—his manner—and his wit—he is the only one of them I ever wished to hear at greater length.——In society I have met him frequently—he was superb!—he had a sort of liking for me—and never attacked me—at least to my face, and he did every body else— high names & wits and orators some of them poets also——I have seen [him] cut up Whitbread—quiz Me. de Stael—annihilate Colman—and do little less by some others—(whose names as friends I set not down) of good fame and abilities.—Poor fellow! he got drunk very thoroughly and very soon.—It occasionally fell to my lot to convey him home—no sinecure—for he was so tipsy that I was obliged to put on his cock'd hat for him—to be sure it tumbled off again and I was not myself so sober as to be able to pick it up again.——

6

There was something odd about Sheridan. One day at a dinner he was slightly praising that pert pretender and impostor Lyttelton[1]— (The Parliament puppy, still alive, I believe)——I took the liberty of differing from him—he turned round upon me—and said "is that your real opinion?" I confirmed it.—Then said he—"fortified by this con- currence I beg leave to say that it in fact is also *my* opinion—and that he is a person—whom I do absolutely and utterly—despise,—abhor—and detest"—he then launched out into a description of his despicable qualities—at some length—& with his usual wit—and evidently in earnest (for he hated Lyttelton) his former compliment had been drawn out by some preceding one—just as it's reverse was by my hinting that it was unmerited.—

7

One day I saw him take up his own "Monody ⟨to⟩ on Garrick".—He lighted upon the dedication to the Dowager Lady Spencer—on seeing it he flew into a rage—exclaimed "that it must be a forgery—that he had never dedicated anything of his to such a d——d canting b——h &c. &c. &c." and so went on for half an hour abusing his own dedication, or at least—the object of it—if all writers were equally sincere—it would be ludicrous.——

[1] William Henry Lyttelton, third Baron Lyttelton of the second creation (1782–1837), was M.P. for Worcestershire, 1807–1820. He was a Whig and had the reputation of an eloquent orator.

He told me that on the night of the grand success of his S[chool] for S[candal]—he was knocked down and put into the watch house for making a row in the Street & being found intoxicated by the watch-men.—— —

10

Sheridan's liking for me (whether he was not mystifying me I do not know—but Lady C[arolin]e L[amb] & others told me he said the same both before and after he knew me) was founded upon "English Bards & S[cotch] Reviewers"—he told me that he did not care about poetry (or about mine—at least any but *that* poem of mine) but that he was sure from *that* and other symptoms—I should make an Orator if I would but take to speaking and grow a parliament man—he never ceased harping upon this to me—to the last—and I remember my old tutor Dr. Drury had the same notion when I was a *boy*—but it never was my turn of inclination to try—I spoke once or twice as all young *peers* do—as a kind of introduction into public life—but dissipation—shyness —haughty and reserved opinions—together with the short time I lived in England—after my majority (only about five years in all) prevented me from resuming the experiment—as far as it went it was not dis-couraging—particularly my *first* speech (I spoke three or four times in all) but just after it my poem of C[hild]e H[arol]d was published— & nobody ever thought about my *prose* afterwards, nor indeed did I—it became to me a secondary and neglected object, though I sometimes wonder to myself *if* I should have succeeded?—

11

The Impression of Parliament upon me—was that it's members are not formidable as *Speakers*—but very much so as an *audience*—because in so numerous a body there may be little Eloquence (after all there were but *two* thorough Orators in all Antiquity—and I suspect still *fewer* in modern times) but must be a leaven of thought and good sense sufficient to make them *know* what is right—though they can't express it nobly.—— —

13

Whenever an American requests to see me—(which is *not* un-frequently) I comply—1stly. because I respect a people who acquired their freedom by firmness without excess—and 2dly. because these transatlantic visits "few and far between"[1] make me feel as if talking with Posterity from the other side of the Styx;—in a century or two the

---

[1] Campbell, *The Pleasures of Hope*, Part II, line 378, p. 265.

new English & Spanish Atlantides will be masters of the old Countries in all probability—as Greece and Europe overcame their Mother Asia in the older or earlier ages as they are called.

14

Sheridan was one day offered a bet by M. G. Lewis[1]——"I will bet you, Mr. Sheridan, a very large sum—I will bet you what you *owe me* as Manager for my 'Castle Spectre'"——"I never make *large bets*— said Sheridan—but I will lay you a *very small* one—I will bet you *what it is worth!*["]

16

Lewis at Oatlands[2] was observed one morning to have his eyes red— & his air sentimental—being asked why?—replied—"that when people said any thing *kind* to him—it affected him deeply—and just now the Duchess has said something *so* kind to me that"——here "tears began to flow" again——"Never mind, Lewis—said Col. Armstrong to him —never mind—don't cry— *She could not mean it.*"

17

Lewis was a good man—a clever man—but a bore—a damned bore—one may say.—My only revenge or consolation used to be setting him by the ears with some vivacious person who hated Bores especially—Me. de Stael or Hobhouse for example.—But I liked Lewis—he was a Jewel of a Man had he been better set—I don't mean *personally,* but less *tiresome*—for he was tedious—as well as contra-dictory to every thing and every body.——Being short-sighted—when we used to ride out together near the Brenta in the twilight in Summer he made me go *before* to pilot him—I am absent at times—especially towards evening—and the consequence of this pilotage was some narrow escapes to the Monk on horseback.——Once I led him *into* a ditch—over which I had passed as usual forgetting to warn my Convoy —once I led him nearly into the river instead of *on* the *moveable* bridge which *in*commodes passengers—and twice did we both run against the diligence which being heavy and slow did communicate less damage than it received in its leaders who were *terrassé'd* by the charge.— Thrice did I lose him in the gray of the Gloaming and was obliged to bring to to his distant signals of distance and distress.—All the time he went on talking without interruption for he was a man of many words.

---

[1] Matthew Gregory Lewis had gained the nickname of "Monk" from his popular Gothic tale, *Ambrosio, or the Monk,* which on its publication in 1795 made him famous.

[2] The estate near Weybridge, Surrey, bought by the Duke of York in 1794.

—Poor fellow—he died a martyr to his new riches—of a second visit to Jamaica—

> "I'd give the lands of Deloraine—
> Dark Musgrave were alive again!"[1]

---

that is

I would give many a Sugar Cane
Monk Lewis were alive again!

25

A young American named Coolidge called on me not many months ago—he was intelligent—very handsome and not more than twenty years old according to appearances.—A little romantic but that sits well upon youth—and mighty fond of poesy as may be suspected from his approaching me in my cavern.——He brought me a message from an old Servant of my family (Joe Murray) and told me that *he* (Mr. Coolidge) had obtained a copy of my bust from Thorwal[d]sen at Rome to send to America—I confess I was more flattered by this young enthusiasm of a solitary trans-atlantic traveller than if they had decreed me a Statue in the Paris Pantheon—(I have seen Emperors and demagogues cast down from their pedestals even in my own time—& Grattan's name razed from the Street called after him in Dublin) I say that I was more flattered by it—because it was *single—un-political* & was without motive or ostentation—the pure and warm feeling of a boy for the poet he admired.——It must have been expensive though——*I* would not pay the price of a Thorwaldsen bust for any human head & shoulders—except Napoleon's—or my children's—or some *"absurd Womankind's"* as Monkbarns[1] calls them—or my Sister's.—If asked —*why* then I sate for my own—answer—that it was at the request particular of J. C. Hobhouse Esqre.—and for no one else.—A *picture* is a different matter—every body sits for their picture—but a bust looks like putting up pretensions to permanency—and smacks something of a hankering for *public* fame rather than private remembrance.——

26

One of the cleverest men I ever knew in Conversation was Scrope Beardmore [sic] Davies—Hobhouse is also very good in that line, though it is of less consequence to a man who has other ways of showing his talents than in company—Scrope was always ready—and often

---

[1] Scott's *Lay of the Last Minstrel*, Canto 5.
[1] Jonathan Oldbuck, the Laird of Monckbarns, in Scott's *The Antiquary*.

witty—H[obhouse] as witty—but not always so ready—being more diffident.—

28

When Brummell was obliged (by that affair of poor Meyler[1]—who thence acquired the name of "Dick the Dandy-killer"—it was about money and debt & all that) to retire to France—he knew no French & having obtained a Grammar for the purpose of Study—our friend Scrope Davies was asked what progress Brummell had made in French —to which he responded—"that B[rummell] had been stopped like Buonaparte in Russia by the *Elements*"—I have put this pun into "Beppo"[2] which is "a fair exchange and no robbery"—for Scrope made his fortune at several dinners (as he owned himself) by repeating occasionally as his own some of the buffooneries with which I had encountered him in the Morning.—

29

I liked the Dandies—they were always very civil to *me*—though in general they disliked literary people—and persecuted and mystified Me. de Stael,—Lewis,—Horace Twiss—and the like—damnably.— They persuaded Me. de Stael that Alvanley[1] had a hundred thousand a year &c. &c. till she praised him to his *face* for his *beauty!*—and made a set at him for Albertine—(*Libertine* as Brummell baptized her—though the poor Girl was—& is as correct as maid or wife can be—& very amiable withal—) and a hundred fooleries besides—The truth is— that though I gave up the business early—I had a tinge of Dandyism in my minority—& probably retained enough of it—to conciliate the great ones—at four & twenty.——I had gamed—& drank—& taken my degrees in most dissipations—and having no pedantry & not being overbearing—we ran quietly together.——I knew them all more or less—and they made me a Member of Watier's (a superb Club at that time) being I take it—the only literary man (except *two others* both men of the world M.—& S.[2]) in it.—Our Masquerade was a grand one

---

[1] Richard Meyler, a wealthy sugar-baker, a frequenter of Harriette Wilson's drawing room (and bedroom), entered into a deal with others to raise £30,000 for Brummell. Meyler's contribution was £7,000. When he learned that there was not the remotest prospect of ever getting any of his money back he was furious, and he exposed Brummell at White's Club. By this he earned the nickname of "Dick the Dandy-killer". (See *Harriette Wilson's Memoirs*, 1929, pp. 602–604.)

[2] Stanza 61.

[1] Lord Alvanley, one of the Dandies, was a close friend of Beau Brummell.

[2] Moore and William Robert Spencer (1769–1843), poet and wit, writer of society verse.

—as was the Dandy Ball—too at the Argyle—but *that* (the latter) was given by the four Chiefs—B. M. A. and P.[3]—if I err not.—

33

I have a notion that Gamblers are as happy as most people—being always *excited*;—women—wine—fame—the table—even Ambition—*sate* now & then—but every turn of the card—& cast of the dice—keeps the Gambler alive—besides one can Game ten times longer than one can do any thing else.—I was very fond of it when young—that is to say of "Hazard" for I hate all *Card* Games even Faro—When Macco (or whatever they spell it) was introduced I gave up the whole thing —for I loved and missed the *rattle* and *dash* of the box & dice—and the glorious uncertainty not only of good luck or bad luck—but of *any luck at all*—as one had sometimes to throw *often* to decide at all.——I have thrown as many as fourteen mains running—and carried off all the cash upon the table occasionally—but I had no coolness or judgement or calculation.—It was the *delight* of the thing that pleased me.—Upon the whole I left off in time without being much a winner or loser.— Since One and twenty years of age—I played but little & then never above a hundred or two—or three.——

36

I have been called in as Mediator or Second at least twenty times in violent quarrels—and have always contrived to settle the business without compromising the honour of the parties or leading them to mortal consequences, & often too sometimes in very difficult and delicate circumstances—and having to deal with very hot and haughty Spirits—Irishmen—Gamesters—Guardsmen—Captains & Cornets of horse—and the like.—This was of course in my youth—when I lived in hot-headed company.—I have had to carry challenges—from Gentlemen to Noblemen—from Captains to Captains—from lawyers to Counsellors—and once from a Clergyman to an officer in the Lifeguards —it may seem strange—but I have found the latter by far the most difficult

> ". . . to compose
> The bloody duel without blows."[1]

The business being about a woman.—I must add that I never saw a *woman* behave so ill—like a cold-blooded heartless whore as she was— but very handsome for all that.—A certain Susan C. was she called—I never saw her but once—and that was to induce her but to say two

---

[3] Brummel, Mildmay, Alvanley, and Pierrepoint?
[1] Samuel Butler, *Hudibras*, First Part, Canto I, lines 721–726.

words (which in no degree compromised herself) & which would have had the effect of saving a priest or a Lieutenant of Cavalry.—She would *not* say them—and neither N. or myself (the son of Sir E. N. and a friend of one of the parties)—could prevail upon her to say them—though both of us used to deal in some sort with Womankind.—At last I managed to quiet the combatants without her talisman—and I believe to her great disappointment.—She was the d——st bitch—that I ever saw—& I have seen a great many.———Though my Clergyman was sure to lose either his life or his living—he was as war-like as the Bishop of Beauvais—& would hardly be pacified—but then he was in love—and that is a martial passion.[2]———

39

At Venice in the year 1817—an order came from Vienna for the Archbishop to go in State to Saint Mark's in his Carriage and four horses—which is much the same as commanding the Lord Mayor of London to proceed through Temple Bar in his Barge.———

40

When I met Hudson Lowe the Jailor at Lord Holland's before he sailed for Saint Helena, the discourse turned on the battle of Waterloo. —I asked him whether the dispositions of Napoleon were those of a great General?—he answered disparageingly—"that they were very *simple*"———I had always thought that a degree of Simplicity was an ingredient of Greatness.—

51

It is singular how soon we lose the impression of what ceases to be *constantly* before us.—A year impairs, a lustre obliterates.—There is little distinct left without an *effort* of memory,—*then* indeed the lights are rekindled for a moment—but who can be sure that the Imagination is not the torch-bearer?—Let any man try at the end of *ten* years to bring before him the features—or the mind—or the sayings—or the habits of his best friend—or his *greatest* man—(I mean his favourite—his Buonaparte—his this—that, or tother)[.] And he will be surprized at the extreme confusion of his ideas.———I speak confidently on this point having always past for one who had a good eye—an excellent memory.—I except indeed—our recollections of Womankind—— there is no forgetting *them*—(and be d——d to them) any more than any other remarkable Era—such as "the revolution" or "the

---

[2] The clergyman was the Rev. Robert Bland, a close friend of Byron's friend Francis Hodgson.

plague"—or "the Invasion" or "the Comet"—or "the War" of such—
and such an Epoch—being the favourite dates of Mankind who have so
many *blessings* in their lot that they never make their Calendars from
them—being too common.—For instance you see "the great drought"
—"the Thames frozen over"—"the Seven years war broke out"—the
E[nglish] or F[rench] or S[panish] "Revolution commenced"—"The
Lisbon Earthquake"—"the Lima Earthquake"—"the Earthquake of
Calabria"—"the Plague of London"—"Ditto of Constantinople"—
"the Sweating Sickness"—"The Yellow fever of Philadelphia" &c. &c.
&c.—but you don't see "the abundant harvest"—"the fine Summer"—
"the long peace"—"the wealthy speculation"—"the wreckless voyage" recorded so emphatically?—By the way there has been a *thirty
years war* and a *Seventy years war*—was there ever a *Seventy or a thirty
years peace?*—or was there even a day's *Universal* peace—except perhaps in China—where they have found out the miserable happiness of a
stationary & unwarlike mediocrity?—And is all this—because Nature
is niggard or savage? or Mankind ungrateful?—let philosophers
decide.——I am none.—

53

In general I do not draw well with Literary men—not that I dislike
them but—I never know what to say to them after I have praised their
last publication.—There are several exceptions to be sure—but they
have either been men of the world—such as Scott—& Moore &c. or
visionaries out of it—such as Shelley &c. but your literary every day
man—and I never went well in company——especially your foreigner
—whom I never could abide—except Giordani[1] & and—and (I really
can't name any other)—I do not remember a man amongst them—
—whom I ever wished to see twice—except perhaps Mezzophanti[2]—
who is a Monster of Languages—the Briareus[3] of parts of Speech—a
walking Polyglott and more—who ought to have existed at the time
of the tower of Babel as universal Interpreter.—He is indeed a Marvel
—unassuming also—I tried him in all the tongues of which I knew a
single oath (or adjuration to the Gods against Postboys—Lawyers—
Tartars — boatmen, — Sailors, pilots, — Gondoliers — Muleteers —
Camel-drivers—Vetturini—Postmasters—post-horses—post-houses
—post-everything) and Egad! he astonished me even to my English.—

[1] Byron met Pietro Giordani in Venice.

[2] Giuseppe Mezzofanti was the librarian of the Bologna Library. He later
became a Cardinal.

[3] In Greek mythology one of three hundred-handed monsters, children of
Heaven and Earth.

54

Three Swedes came to Bologna knowing no tongue but Swedish——
the inhabitants in despair presented them to Mezzophanti.—Mezzophanti (though a great Linguist) knew no more Swedish than the
Inhabitants.—But in two days by dint of dictionary he talked with them
fluently and freely, so that they were astonished—and every body else,
at his acquisition of another tongue in forty eight hours—I had this
anecdote first from Me. Albrizzi—& afterwards confirmed by *himself*
—& he is not a boaster.—

55

I sometimes wish that—I had studied languages with more attention
—those which I know, even the classical (Greek and Latin in the usual
proportion of a sixth form boy) and a smattering of modern Greek—
the Armenian & Arabic Alphabets—a few Turkish & Albanian phrases,
oaths, or requests—Italian tolerably—Spanish less than tolerably—
French to read with ease—but speak with difficulty—or rather not at
all——all have been acquired by ear or eye—& never by anything like
Study:—like "Edie Ochiltree"——"I never dowed to bide a hard turn
o'wark in my life"[1]——To be sure—I set in zealously for the Armenian
and Arabic—but I fell in love with some absurd womankind both times
before I had overcome the Characters and at Malta & Venice left the
profitable Orientalists for—for—(no matter what—) notwithstanding
that my master the Padre Pasquale Aucher (for whom by the way I
compiled the major part of two Armenian & English Grammars) assured me "that the terrestrial Paradise had been certainly in *Armenia*"
—I went seeking it—God knows where—did I find it?—Umph!—Now
& then—for a minute or two.

58

I have more than once heard Sheridan say that he never "had a
shilling of his own"—to be sure he contrived to extract a good many of
other people's.——In 1815—I had occasion to visit my Lawyer—in
Chancery Lane—he was with Sheridan.—After mutual greetings &c.
Sheridan retired first.—Before recurring to my own business—I could
not help enquiring *that* of S.——"Oh (replied the Attorneo) the usual
thing—to stave off an action from his Wine-Merchant—my Client.
—["] "Well (said I) & what do you mean to do?" "Nothing at all for
the present—said he—would you have us proceed against old Sherry?
—what would be the use of it?["]—And here he began laughing &
going over Sheridan's good gifts of Conversation.——Now from per-

---

[1] In Scott's *The Antiquary*.

sonal experience I can vouch that my Attorneo is by no means the tenderest of men, or particularly accessible to any kind of impression out of the Statute or record.—And yet Sheridan in half an hour had found a way to soften and seduce him in such a manner that I almost think he would have thrown his Client (an honest man with all the laws and some justice on his side) out of the window had he come in at the moment.—Such was Sheridan!—he could soften an Attorney!—there has been nothing like it since the days of Orpheus.———

65

When I was fifteen years of age—it happened that in a Cavern in Derbyshire—I had to cross in a boat—(in which two people only could lie down—) a stream which flows under a rock—with the rock so close upon the water—as to admit the boat only to be pushed on by a ferry-man (a sort of Charon) who wades at the stern stooping all the time.— —The Companion of my transit was M[ary] A. C[haworth] with whom I had been long in love and never told it—though *she* had discovered it without.—I recollect my sensations—but cannot describe them—and it is as well.———We were a party—a Mr. W.—two Miss W's—Mr. & Mrs. Cl[ar]ke—Miss R. and *my* M. A. C.—Alas! why do I say *My?* —our Union would have healed feuds in which blood had been shed by our fathers—it would have joined lands—broad and rich—it would have joined at least *one* heart and two persons not ill-matched in years (she is two years my elder) and—and—and—what has been the result?—*She* has married a man older than herself—been wretched— and separated.—I have married—& am separated.—and yet *we* are *not* united.———

67

When I belonged to the D[rury] L[ane] Committee and was one of the S[ub] C[ommittee] of Management—the number of *plays* upon the shelves were about *five* hundred;—conceiving that amongst these there must be *some* of merit—in person & by proxy I caused an investigation. —I do not think that of those which I saw—there was one which could be conscientiously tolerated.———There never were such things as most of them.—Mathurin was very kindly recommended to me by Walter Scott—to whom I had recourse—firstly—in the hope that he would do something for us himself—& secondly—in my despair—that he would point out to us any young (or old) writer of promise.—Mathurin sent his Bertram—and a letter *without* his address—so that at first—I could give him no answer.—When I at last hit upon his residence I sent him a favourable answer and something more substantial.—His play succeeded—but I was at that time absent from England.——I tried Coleridge too—but he had nothing feasible in hand at the time.—Mr. Sotheby obligingly offered *all* his tragedies—and I pledged myself—and notwithstanding many squabbles with my Committe[e]d Brethren—did get "Ivan" accepted—read—& the parts distributed.—But lo! in the very heart of the matter—upon some *tepid*-ness on the part of Kean—or warmth upon that of the Authour—Sotheby withdrew his play.——Sir J. B. Burgess[1] did also present four tragedies and a farce—and I moved Green-room & S[ub] Committee—but they would not.—Then the Scenes I had to go through!—the authours—and the authoresses——the Milliners—the wild Irishmen—the people from Brighton—from Blackwell—from Chatham—from Cheltenham—from Dublin—from Dundee—who came in upon me!—to all of whom it was proper to give a civil answer—and a hearing—and a reading——Mrs. Glover's father an Irish dancing Master of Sixty years—called upon me to request to play *"Archer"*—drest in silk stockings on a frosty morning to show his legs—(which were certainly good & Irish for his age—& had been still better)—Miss Emma Somebody with a play entitled the "Bandit of Bohemia"—or some such title or production—Mr. O' Higgins—then resident at Richmond—with an Irish tragedy in which the unities could not fail to be observed for the protagonist was chained by the leg to a pillar during the chief part of the performance.—He was a wild man of a salvage appearance—and the difficulty of *not* laughing at him was only to be got over—by reflecting upon the probable consequences of such cachinnation.——As I am really a civil & polite person—and *do* hate giving pain—when it can be avoided—I sent them up to Douglas Kinnaird—who is a man of business—and sufficiently ready with a negative—and left them to settle with him—and as at the beginning of next year—I went abroad—I have since been little aware of the progress of the theatres.

72

When I first went up to College—it was a new and a heavy hearted scene for me.—Firstly—I so much disliked leaving Harrow that though it was time—(I being seventeen) it broke my very rest for the last quarter—with counting the days that remained.—I always *hated* Harrow till the last year and a half—but then I liked it.—2dly. I wished to go to Oxford and not to Cambridge.—3dly. I was so completely alone in this new world that it half broke my Spirits.—My companions were not unsocial but the contrary—lively—hospitable—of rank—&

[1] Sir James Bland Burges, an uncle by marriage of Lady Byron.

274

fortune—& gay far beyond my gaiety—I mingled with—and dined—& supped &c. with them—but I know not how—it was one of the deadliest and heaviest feelings of my life to feel that I was no longer a boy.—From that moment I began to grow old in my own esteem—and in my esteem age is not estimable.—I took my gradations in the vices—with great promptitude—but they were not to my taste—for my early passions though violent in the extreme—were concentrated—and hated division or spreading abroad.—I could have left or lost the world with or for that which I loved—but though my temperament was naturally burning—I could not share in the common place libertinism of the place and time—without disgust.——And yet this very disgust and my heart thrown back upon itself—threw me into excesses perhaps more fatal than those from which I shrunk—as fixing upon one (at a time) the passions which spread amongst many would have hurt only myself.—

73

People have wondered at the Melancholy which runs through my writings.—Others have wondered at my personal gaiety——but I recollect once after an hour in which I had been sincerely and particularly gay—and rather brilliant in company—my wife replying to me when I said (upon her remarking my high spirits) "and yet Bell—I have been called and mis-called Melancholy—you must have seen how falsely frequently." "No—B—(she answered) it is not so—at *heart* you are the most melancholy of mankind, and often when apparently gayest. ["]——

74

If I could explain at length the *real* causes which have contributed to increase this perhaps *natural* temperament of mine—this Melancholy which hath made me a bye-word—nobody would wonder——but this is impossible without doing much mischief.——I do not know what other men's lives have been—but I cannot conceive anything more strange than some of the earlier parts of mine——I have written my memoirs—but omitted *all* the really *consequential* & *important* parts—from deference to the dead—to the living—and to those who must be both.—

75

I sometimes think that I should have written the *whole*—as a *lesson*——but it might have proved a lesson to be *learnt*—rather than *avoided*—for passion is a whirlpool, which is not to be viewed nearly without attraction from it's Vortex.——

One night Scrope Davies at a Gaming house—(before I was of age) being tipsy as he mostly was at the Midnight hour—& having lost monies—was in vain intreated by his friends one degree less intoxicated than himself to come or go home.—In despair—he was left to himself and to the demons of the dice-box.——Next day—being visited about two of the Clock by some friends just risen with a severe headache and empty pockets—(who had left him losing at four or five in the morning) he was found in a sound sleep—without a nightcap—& not particularly encumbered with bed-cloathes——a Chamber-pot stood by the bed-side—*brim-full* of—*Bank Notes!*—all won—God knows how—and crammed—Scrope knew not where—but *there* they were—all good legitimate notes—and to the amount of some thousand pounds.—

My first dash into poetry, was as early as 1800.——It was the ebullition of a passion for my first Cousin Margaret Parker (daughter and grand-daughter of the two Admirals Parker) one of the most beautiful of Evanescent beings.—I have long forgotten the verses—but it would be difficult for me to forget her——Her dark eyes!—her long eyelashes! her completely Greek cast of face and figure!—I was then about twelve—She rather older—perhaps a year.——She died about a year or two afterwards—in consequence of a fall which injured her spine and induced consumption.—Her Sister Augusta—(by some thought still more beautiful) died of the same malady—and it was indeed in attending her that Margaret met with the accident which occasioned her own death.—My Sister told me that when she went to see her shortly before her death—upon accidentally mentioning my name—Margaret coloured through the paleness of mortality to the eyes—to the great astonishment of my Sister—who (residing with her Grand-mother Lady Holderness—saw at that time but little of me for family reasons) knew nothing of our attachment—nor could conceive why my name should affect her at such a time.——I knew nothing of her illness—(being at Harrow and in the country) till she was gone.——Some years after I made an attempt at an Elegy.—A very dull one.—I do not recollect scarcely anything equal to the *transparent* beauty of my cousin—or to the sweetness of her temper—during the short period of our intimacy——she looked as if she had been made out of a rainbow—all beauty and peace.—My passion had it's effects upon me—I could not sleep—I could not eat—I could not rest—and although I had reason to know that she loved me—it was the torture of my life—to think of the time which must elapse before we could meet again—being usually about *twelve hours*—of separation!——But I was a fool then—and am not much wiser now.

80

My passions were developed very early—so early—that few would believe me—if I were to state the period—and the facts which accompanied it.—Perhaps this was one of the reasons which caused the anticipated melancholy of my thoughts—having anticipated life.—My earlier poems are the thoughts of one at least ten years older than the age at which they were written,—I don't mean for their solidity—but their Experience—the two first Cantos of C[hild]e H[arold]e were completed at twenty two—and they were written as if by a man—older than I shall probably ever be.—

83

Like Sylla—I have always believed that all things depend upon Fortune & nothing upon ourselves.—I am not aware of any one thought or action worthy of being called good to myself or others—which is not to be attributed to the Good Goddess—*Fortune!*—

91

My School friendships were with *me passions* (for I was always violent) but I do not know that there is one which has endured (to be sure some have been cut short by death) till now—that with Lord Clare began one of the earliest and lasted longest—being only interrupted by distance—that I know of.—I never hear the word *"Clare"* without a beating of the heart—even *now*, & I write it—with the feelings of 1803–4–5—ad infinitum.—

95

If I had to live over again—I do not know what I would change in my life—unless it were *for*—*not to have lived at all*[.] All history and experience—and the rest—teaches us that the good and evil are pretty equally balanced in this existence—and that what is most to be desired is an easy passage out of it.——What can it give us but *years*? & those have little of good but their ending.—

96

Of the Immortality of the Soul—it appears to me that there can be little doubt—if we attend for a moment to the action of Mind.—It is in perpetual activity;—I used to doubt of it—but reflection has taught me better.—It acts also so very independent of body—in dreams for instance incoherently and madly—I grant you;—but still it is *Mind* & much more *Mind*—than when we are awake.——Now—that *this* should not act *separately*—as well as jointly—who can pronounce?—The Stoics Epictetus & Marcus Aurelius call the present state "a Soul which drags a Carcase"——a heavy chain to be sure, but all chains being material may be shaken off.—How far our future life will be *individual*—or rather—how far it will at all resemble our *present* existence is another question—but that the *Mind* is *eternal*—seems as possible as that the body is not so.—Of course—I have venture[d] upon the question without recurring to Revelation—which however is at least as rational a solution of it—as any other.—A *material* resurrection seems strange and even absurd except for purposes of punishment—and all punishment which is to *revenge* rather than *correct*—must be *morally wrong*—and *when* the *World is at an end*—what moral or warning purpose *can* eternal tortures answer?—human passions have probably disfigured the divine doctrines here—but the whole thing is inscrutable. —It is useless to tell one *not* to *reason* but to *believe*——you might as well tell a man not to wake but *sleep*—and then to *bully* with torments! —and all that!—I cannot help thinking that the *menace* of Hell makes as many devils as the severe penal codes of inhuman humanity make villains.——Man is born *passionate* of body—but with an innate though secret tendency to the love of Good in his Main-spring of Mind.—— But God help us all!—It is at present a sad jar of atoms.——

97

Matter is eternal—always changing—but reproduced and as far as we can comprehend Eternity—Eternal—and why not Mind?—Why should not the Mind act with and upon the Universe?—as portions of it act upon and with the congregated dust—called Mankind?—See—how one man acts upon himself and others—or upon multitudes?—The same Agency in a higher and purer degree may act upon the Stars &c. ad infinitum.

98

I have often been inclined to Materialism in philosophy—but could never bear it's introduction into *Christianity*—which appears to me essentially founded upon the *Soul*.—For this reason, Priestley's Christian Materialism—always struck me as deadly.—Believe the resurrection of the *body*—if you will—but *not without* a *Soul*—the devil's in it—if after having had a Soul—(as surely the *Mind* or whatever you call it—*is*)—in this world we must part with it in the next— even for an Immortal Materiality;—I own my partiality for *Spirit*.—

I am always most religious upon a sunshiny day—as if there was some association between an internal approach to greater light and purity—and the kindler of this dark lanthorn of our external exist-ence.——

The Night is also a religious concern—and even more so—when I viewed the Moon and Stars through Herschell's telescope—and saw that they were worlds.—

What a strange thing is the propagation of life!—A bubble of Seed which may be spilt in a whore's lap—or in the Orgasm of a voluptuous dream—might (for aught we know) have formed a Caesar or a Buonaparte—there is nothing remarkable recorded of their Sires—that I know of.——

I have met George Colman occasionally and thought him extremely pleasant and convivial—Sheridan's humour or rather wit—was always saturnine—and sometimes savage—but he never laughed (at least that *I* saw—and I watched him) but Colman did—I have got very drunk with them both—but if I had to *choose*—and could not have both at a time—I should say—"let me begin the evening with Sheridan and finish it with Colman."—Sheridan for dinner—Colman for Supper—Sheridan for Claret or port—but Colman for every thing—from the Madeira & Champaigne—at dinner—the Claret with a *layer* of *port* between the Glasses—up to the Punch of the Night—and down to the Grog—or Gin and water of day-break—all these I have threaded with both the same——Sheridan was a Grenadier Company of Life-Guards —but Colman a whole regiment of *light Infantry* to be sure—but still a regiment.

There is nothing left for Mankind but a Republic—and I think that there are hopes of Such—the two Americas (South and North) have it —Spain and Portugal approach it—all thirst for it—Oh Washington!—

116

I have lately been reading Fielding over again. —They talk of Radicalism—Jacobinism &c. in England (I am told) but they should turn over the pages of "Jonathan Wild the Great".—The inequality of conditions and the littleness of the great—were never set forth in stronger terms—and his contempt for Conquerors and the like is such that had he lived *now* he would have been denounced in the "Courier" as the grand Mouth-piece and Factionary of the revolutionists.—And yet I never recollect to have heard this turn of Fielding's mind noticed though it is obvious in every page.——

117

The following dialogue passed between me and a very pretty peasant Girl (Rosa Benini married to Domenico Ovioli or Oviuoli the Vetturino) at Ravenna.—

Rosa. "*What* is the Pope?"

I. "Don't *you* know?"

Rosa. "No, I don't know, what or who is he—is he a Saint?"

I. "He is an old man."

Rosa. "What nonsense to make such a fuss about an old man.—have *you ever* seen him?"

I. "Yes—at Rome."—

Rosa. "You English don't believe in the Pope?"

I. "No—we don't—but you do—"

Rosa. "I don't know what I believe—but the priests talk about him——I am sure I did not know what he was."

This dialogue I have translated nearly verbatim—& I don't think that I have either added to or taken away from it.——The speaker was under eighteen & an old acquaintance of mine.——It struck me as odd that I should have to instruct her *who* the Pope was—I think they might have found it out without me—by this time.——The fact is indisputable & occurred but a few weeks ago, before I left Ravenna.—

Pisa Novr. 6th. 1821

[TO JOHN MURRAY]   *Pisa Novr. 3d. 1821*

Dear Moray/—The two passages cannot be altered without making Lucifer talk like the Bishop of Lincoln—which would not be in the character of the former.——The notion is from Cuvier[1] (that of the *old Worlds*) as I have explained in an additional note to the preface.— The other passage is also in Character—if *nonsense*—so much the better—because then it can do no harm—& the sillier Satan is made the safer for every body.——As to "alarms" &c. do you really think such things ever led anybody astray? are these people more impious than Milton's Satan?—or the Prometheus of Æschylus?—or

[1] The reference is to Cuvier's "Essay on the Theory of the Earth", translated in 1813 by Robert Kerr.

even than the Sadducees of your envious parson the "Fall of Jerusalem" fabricator?[2]—Are not Adam—Eve—Adah—and Abel as pious as the Catechism?—Gifford is too wise a man to think that such things can have any *serious* effect—*who* was ever altered by a poem? I beg leave to observe that there is no creed nor personal hypothesis of mine in all this—but I was obliged to make Cain and Lucifer talk consistently—and surely this has always been permitted to poesy.———Cain is a proud man—if Lucifer promised him kingdoms &c.—it would *elate* him—the object of the demon is to *depress* him still further in his own estimation than he was before—by showing him infinite things—& his own abasement—till he falls into the frame of mind—that leads to the Catastrophe—from mere *internal* irritation—*not* premeditation or envy—ot *Abel*—(which would have made him contemptible) but from rage and fury against the inadequacy of his state to his Conceptions—& which discharges itself rather against Life—and the author of Life—than the mere living.——His subsequent remorse is the natural effect of looking on his sudden deed—had the *deed* been premeditated—his repentence would have been tardier.—

The three last M.S. lines of Eve's curse are replaced from *memory* on the proofs—but incorrectly (for I keep no copies)—Either keep *these three*—or *replace* them with the *other three*—whichever are thought least bad by Mr. Gifford——There is no occasion for a *revise*—it is only losing time.—Either dedicate it to Walter Scott[3]—or if you think—he would like the dedication to "the Foscaris" better—put the dedication to "the Foscaris"—Ask him which.——Your first note was queer enough—but your two other letters with Moore's & Gifford's opinions set all right again—I told you before that I can never *recast* anything.—I am like the Tiger—if I miss the first spring—I go growling back to my Jungle again—but if I *do hit*—it is crushing. ——Now for Mr. Mawman.——I received him civilly as *your* friend—and he spoke of you in a friendly manner.—As one of the Squadron of Scribblers—I could not but pay due reverence to a commissioned officer.—I gave him that book with the inscription to show to *you*—that you might correct the errors.—With the rest I can have nothing to do—but he served you very *right*.—You have played the Stepmother to D[on] J[uan]—throughout.—Either ashamed—or afraid—or negligent—to your own loss and nobody's credit. ——Who ever heard before of a *publisher's not* putting *his* name?—The reasons for *my anonyme*—I stated—they were family ones entirely.——Some

[2] The Rev. H. H. Milman.
[3] *Cain* was dedicated to Scott.

travelling Englishmen whom I met the other day at Bologna told me—that you affect to wish to be considered as *not* having anything to do with that work—which by the way—is sad half and half dealing— for you will be a long time before you publish a better poem.——

You seem hurt at the words *"the publisher" what*! *you*—who won't put your name on the title page—would have had me stick J. M. Esqre. on the blank leaf—no—Murray—you are an excellent fellow— a little variable—& somewhat of the opinion of every body you talk with—(particularly the last person you see) but a good fellow for all that—yet nevertheless—I can't tell you that I think you have acted very gallantly by that persecuted book—which has made it's way entirely by *itself*—without the light of your countenance—or any kind of encouragement—critical—or bibliopolar.—You disparaged the last three cantos to me—& kept them back above a year—but I have heard from England—that (notwithstanding the errors of the press) they are well thought of—for instance—by American Irving—which last is a feather in my (fool's) Cap.——You have received my letter (open) through Mr. Kinnaird—& so pray—send me no more reviews of any kind.——I will read no more of evil or good in that line.—— Walter Scott has not read a review of *himself* for *thirteen years*.—The bust is not *my* property—but *Hobhouse's*—I addressed it to you as an Admiralty man great at the custom house—pray—deduct the expences of the same—& all others.—

yrs. ever & [most?]
BYRON

[TO THOMAS MOORE]   *Pisa, March 4th, 1822*

Since I wrote the enclosed,[1] I have waited another post, and now have your answer acknowledging the arrival of the packet—a troublesome one, I fear, to you in more ways than one, both from weight external and internal.

The unpublished things in your hands, in Douglas K.'s, and Mr. John Murray's, are "Heaven and Earth, a lyrical kind of Drama upon the Deluge, etc."; "Werner," *now with you*;—a translation of the First Canto of the Morgante Maggiore;—*ditto* of an Episode in Dante; —some stanzas to the Po, June 1st, 1819;—Hints from Horace, written in 1811, but a good deal, *since*, to be omitted; several prose things, which may, perhaps, as well remain unpublished;—"The Vision, &c., of Quevedo Redivivus," in verse.

---

[1] The previous letter (March 1) to Moore.

Here you see is "more matter for a May morning;"[2] but how much of this can be published is for consideration. The Quevedo (one of my best in that line) has appalled the Row already, and must take its chance at Paris, if at all. The new Mystery is less speculative than "Cain," and very pious; besides, it is chiefly lyrical. The Morgante is the *best* translation that ever was or will be made; and the rest are—whatever you please to think them.

I am sorry you think Werner even *approaching* to any fitness for the stage, which, with my notions upon it, is very far from my present object. With regard to the publication, I have already explained that I have no exorbitant expectations of either fame or profit in the present instances; but wish them published because they are written, which is the common feeling of all scribblers.

With respect to "Religion," can I never convince you that *I* have no such opinions as the characters in that drama, which seems to have frightened every body? Yet *they* are nothing to the expressions in Goethe's Faust (which are ten times hardier), and not a whit more bold than those of Milton's Satan. My ideas of a character may run away with me: like all imaginative men, I, of course, embody myself with the character while I *draw* it, but not a moment after the pen is from off the paper.

I am no enemy to religion, but the contrary. As a proof, I am educating my natural daughter a strict Catholic in a convent of Romagna; for I think people can never have *enough* of religion, if they are to have any. I incline, myself, very much to the Catholic doctrines; but if I am to write a drama, I must make my characters speak as I conceive them likely to argue.

As to poor Shelley,[3] who is another bugbear to you and the world, he is, to my knowledge, the *least* selfish and the mildest of men—a man who has made more sacrifices of his fortune and feelings for others than any I ever heard of. With his speculative opinions I have nothing in common, nor desire to have.

The truth is, my dear Moore, you live near the *stove* of society, where you are unavoidably influenced by its heat and its vapours. I did so once—and too much—and enough to give a colour to my whole

---

[2] *Twelfth Night*, Act. III, scene 4.

[3] Byron apparently read to Shelley some of Moore's letters, including one in which he deprecated Shelley's influence on Byron's views, especially in *Cain*. Shelley wrote to Horace Smith on April 11, 1822: "Pray assure him [Moore] that I have not the smallest influence over Lord Byron, in this particular, and if I had, I certainly should employ it to eradicate from his great mind the delusions of Christianity, which, in spite of his reason, seem perpetually to recur . . . ."

future existence. As my success in society was *not* inconsiderable, I am surely not a prejudiced judge upon the subject, unless in its favour; but I think it, as now constituted, *fatal* to all great original undertakings of every kind. I never courted it *then*, when I was young and high in blood, and one of its "curled darlings;"[4] and do you think I would do so *now*, when I am living in a clearer atmosphere? One thing *only* might lead me back to it, and that is, to try once more if I could do any good in *politics*; but *not* in the petty politics I see now preying upon our miserable country.

Do not let me be misunderstood, however. If you speak your *own* opinions, they ever had, and will have, the greatest weight with *me*. But if you merely *echo* the "monde", (and it is difficult not to do so, being in its favour and its ferment,) I can only regret that you should ever repeat any thing to which I cannot pay attention.

But I am prosing. The gods go with you, and as much immortality of all kinds as may suit your present and all other existence.

Yours, &c.

[TO THOMAS MOORE] *Pisa, March 6th, 1822*

The enclosed letter from Murray hath melted me; though I think it is against his own interest to wish that I should continue his connexion. You may, therefore, send him the packet of "Werner," which will save you all further trouble. And pray, *can you* forgive me for the bore and expense I have already put upon you? At least, *say* so—for I feel ashamed of having given you so much for such nonsense.

The fact is, I cannot *keep* my *resentments*, though violent enough in their onset. Besides, now that all the world are *at* Murray on my account, I neither can nor ought to leave him; unless, as I really thought, it were better for *him* that I should.

I have had no other news from England, except a letter from Barry Cornwall,[1] the bard, and my old school-fellow. Though I have sickened you with letters lately, believe me.

Yours, &c.

P.S.—In your last letter you say, speaking of Shelley, that you would almost prefer the "damning bigot" to the "annihilating infidel." Shelley believes in immortality, however—but this by the way. Do you remember Frederick the Great's answer to the remonstrance of the villagers whose curate preached against the eternity of hell's

---

[4] *Othello*, Act I, scene 2.
[1] The pseudonym of Bryan Waller Proctor.

torments? It was thus:—"If my faithful subjects of Schrausenhaussen prefer being eternally damned, let them."

Of the two, I should think the long sleep better than the agonised vigil. But men, miserable as they are, cling so to any thing *like* life, that they probably would prefer damnation to quiet. Besides, they think themselves so *important* in the creation, that nothing less can satisfy their pride—the insects!

[TO THOMAS MOORE]   *Pisa, March 8th, 1822*

You will have had enough of my letters by this time—yet one word in answer to your present missive. You are quite wrong in thinking that your "advice" had offended me;[1] but I have already replied (if not answered) on that point.

With regard to Murray as I really am the meekest and mildest of men since Moses (though the public and mine "excellent wife" cannot find it out), I had already pacified myself and subsided back to Albemarle-street, as my yesterday's *ye*pistle will have informed you. But I thought that I had explained my causes of bile—at least to you. Some instances of vacillation, occasional neglect, and troublesome sincerity, real or imagined, are sufficient to put your truly great author and man into a passion. But reflection, with some aid from hellebore, hath already cured me "pro tempore", and, if it had not, a request from you and Hobhouse would have come upon me like two out of the "tribus Anticyris,"[2]—with which, however, Horace despairs of purging a poet. I really feel ashamed of having bored you so frequently and fully of late. But what could I do? You are a friend—an absent one, alas!—and as I trust no one more, I trouble you in proportion.

This war of "Church and State" has astonished me more than it disturbs; for I really thought "Cain" a speculative and hardy, but still a harmless production. As I said before, I am really a great admirer of tangible religion; and am breeding one of my daughters a Catholic, that she may have her hands full. It is by far the most elegant worship, hardly excepting the Greek mythology. What with incense, pictures, statues, altars, shrines, relics, and the real presence, confession, absolution,—there is something sensible to grasp at. Besides, it leaves no possibility of doubt; for those who swallow their Deity, really and truly, in transubstantiation, can hardly find any thing else otherwise than easy of digestion.

[1] Moore's advice to avoid religious scepticism and the influence of Shelley.
[2] Horace, *Ars Poetica*, line 300: "For oh! he shines a bard confessed, be sure,/ Whose poll (which three Anticyras could not cure)/To barber Licinus was ne'er consigned!"

I am afraid that this sounds flippant, but I don't mean it to be so; only my turn of mind is so given to taking things in the absurd point of view, that it breaks out in spite of me every now and then. Still, I do assure you that I am a very good Christian. Whether you will believe me in this, I do not know; but I trust you will take my word for being

Very truly and affectionately yours, &c.

P.S.—Do tell Murray that one of the conditions of peace is, that he publisheth (or obtaineth a publisher for * * * [Taaffe]'s Commentary on Dante, against which there appears in the trade an unaccountable repugnance. It will make the man so exuberantly happy. He dines with me and half-a-dozen English to-day; and I have not the heart to tell him how the bibliopolar world shrink from his Commentary;—and yet it is full of the most orthodox religion and morality. In short, I made it a point that he shall be in print. He is such a good-natured, heavy * * Christian, that we must give him a shove through the press. He naturally thirsts to be an author, and has been the happiest of men for these two months, printing, correcting, collating, dating, anticipating, and adding to his treasures of learning. Besides, he has had another fall from his horse into a ditch the other day, while riding out with me into the country.

[TO JOHN MURRAY]   *Montenero. May 26th. 1822*
                                    near Leghorn.——

Dear Sir,—The body is embarked—in what ship—I know not—neither could I enter into the details; but the Countess G[amba] G[uiccioli] has had the goodness to give the necessary orders to Mr. Dunn—who superintends the embarkation[1]—& will write to you. ——I wish it to be buried in Harrow Church—there is a spot in the Churchyard near the footpath on the brow of the hill looking toward Windsor—and a tomb under a large tree (bearing the name of Peachee —or Peachey) where I used to sit for hours & hours when a boy—this was my favourite spot—but as I wish to erect a tablet to her memory —the body had better be deposited in the Church.—Near the door— on the left as you enter—there is a monument with a tablet containing these words—

"When Sorrow weeps o'er Virtue's sacred dust,
Our tears become us, and our Grief is just,

---

[1] Byron's illegitimate daughter Allegra died at the age of five in the convent school at Bagnacavallo near Ravenna. Henry Dunn, a merchant at Leghorn, superintended the embarkation of her body when it was sent to England.

Such were the tears she shed, who grateful pays
This last sad tribute to her love, and praise."

I recollect them (after seventeen years) not from any thing remarkable in them—but because—from my seat in the Gallery—I had generally my eyes turned towards that monument——as near it as convenient I would wish Allegra to be buried—and on the wall—a marble tablet placed with these words.—

In memory of
Allegra—
daughter of G. G. Lord Byron—
who died at Bagnacavallo
in Italy April 20th. 1822.
aged five years and three months.—
"I shall go to her, but she shall not return to me.—"[2]
2d. Samuel 12.—23.—

The funeral I wish to be as private as is consistent with decency—and I could hope that Henry Drury will perhaps read the service over her. —If he should decline it—it can be done by the usual Minister for the time being.—I do not know that I need add more just now.——I will now turn to other subjects.—

Since I came here I have been invited by the Americans on board of their Squadron where I was received with all the kindness which I could wish, and with *more ceremony* than I am fond of.—I found them finer ships than your own of the same class—well manned & officered. —A number of American gentlemen also were on board at the time & some ladies.—As I was taking leave—an American lady asked for a *rose* which I wore—for the purpose she said of sending to America something which I had about me as a memorial.—I need not add that I felt the compliment properly.—Captain Chauncey showed me an American and very pretty edition of my poems, and offered me a passage to the United States—if I would go there.——Commodore Jones was also not less kind and attentive.—I have since received the enclosed letter desiring me to sit for my picture for some Americans.[3]—It is singular that in the same year that Lady Noel leaves by will an inter-

---

[2] Because of the objection of J. W. Cunningham, Vicar of Harrow, and some of his influential parishioners, no memorial inscription to Allegra was placed in the church, though the body was buried near the entrance. (See *LJ*, VI, 70–72.)

[3] The request came from George H. Bruen of New York, then in Leghorn, for Byron to sit for his portrait to William Edward West (1788–1857) of Philadelphia, who had come to Italy to study painting in 1819. He later painted in London from 1825 to 1839.

diction for my daughter to see her father's portrait for many years—
the individuals of a nation not remarkable for their liking to the English
in particular—nor for flattering men in general, request me to sit for my
"portraicture"—as Baron Bradwardine[4] calls it.———I am also told of
considerable literary honours in Germany.———Goëthe I am told is my
professed patron and protector.—At Leipsic this year—the highest
prize was proposed for a translation of two Cantos of Childe Harold.—
—I am not sure that this was at *Leipsic*—but Mr. Bancroft[5] was my
authority—a good German Scholar (a young American) and an acquaintance of Goëthe's.———Goëthe and the Germans are particularly
fond of Don Juan—which they judge of as a work of Art.—I had heard
something like this before through Baron Lutzerode.[6]—The translations have been very frequent of several of the works—and Goëthe
made a comparison between Faust and Manfred.———All this is some
compensation for your English native brutality so fully displayed this
year—(I mean *not your* individually) to it's brightest extent.—I forgot
to mention a little anecdote of a different kind—I went over the Constitution (the Commodore's flag ship) and saw among other things
worthy of remark a little boy *born* on board of her by a sailor's wife.—
They had christened him "Constitution Jones"—I of course approved
the name—and the woman added—"Ah Sir—if he turns out but half as
good as his name!"

yrs. ever & truly
N B

[TO JOHN MURRAY] *Pisa. ⟨July⟩ August 3d. 1822*

Dear Sir/—I have received your scrap—with H[enry] D[rury]'s
letter enclosed.—It is just like him—always kind and ready to oblige
his old friends.—Will you have the goodness to *send immediately* to
Mr. Douglas Kinnaird—and inform him that I have *not* received the
remittances due to me from the funds a month & more ago—& *promised
by him to be sent by every post*—which omission is of great inconvenience
to me——and indeed inexcusable—as well as unintelligible.—As I
have written to *him* repeatedly I suppose that *his* or *my* letters have
miscarried.—I presume you have heard that Mr. Shelley & Capt.
Williams were lost on the 7th Ulto. [actually the 8th.] in their passage

4 *Waverley*, Chap. 13.
5 George Bancroft, the American historian, then a young man on his travels,
who had just returned from studying in Germany, visited Byron at Montenero
on May 22, 1822.
6 Baron Lutzerode had translated *Cain* and was a Byron enthusiast.

from Leghorn to Spezia in their own open boat. You may imagine the state of their families—I never saw such a scene—nor wish to see such another.—You are all brutally mistaken about Shelley who was without exception—the *best* and least selfish man I ever knew.—I never knew one who was not a beast in comparison.—

yrs. ever
N B

[TO MARY SHELLEY]   *Octr. 4th. 1822*

    The Sopha which I request is *not* of your furniture—it was purchased by me at Pisa since you left it.——It is convenient for my room though of little value (about 12 pauls) and I offered to send another (now sent) in it's stead.—I preferred retaining the purchased furniture—but always intended that you should have as good or better in it's place.—I have a particular dislike to any thing of S[helley]'s being within the same walls with Mr. Hunt's children.—They are dirtier and more mischievous than Yahoos[;] what they can['t] destroy with their filth they will with their fingers.—I presume that you received ninety and odd crowns from the wreck of the D[on] J[uan] and also the price of the boat purchased by Capt. R[oberts].—if not you will have *both*—Hunt has these in hand.——With regard to any difficulties about money I can only repeat that I will be your banker till this state of things is cleared up—and you can see what is to be done—so—there is little to trouble you on that score.——I was confined four days to my bed at Lerici.——Poor Hunt with his six little blackguards—are coming slowly up—as usual—he turned back⟨twice⟩ once—was there ever such a *kraal* out of the Hottentot Country before?——

[scrawl]

[TO MARY SHELLEY]   *9bre. 14th. 1822*

    Dear M.—The letter is all very well—but I wish that he would press upon his brother (what is of more importance at least to the *quantity* of the publication) the expediency of seeing Mr. K[innair]d the moment he is well enough to receive visitors—else he may never get the M.S.S. at all from Murray—who seems to stick at nothing in all that relates to Hunt's family. As to any expressions in private letters about Hunt or others—I am not a cautious letter-writer and generally say what comes uppermost at the moment, but I remember in my more deliberate Memoirs (which Murray bought of Moore) having done his character justice—why didn't M. allude to them?—it were less a breach of confidence than the other?——The whole thing has been a piece of officious Malice on the part of M. & not very discreet zeal on the part of Hunt's friends.—

yrs. ever
N B

P.S.—I send you the completion of the *first* part—of the drama[1]— as I think it may be as well to divide it—although *intended* to be *irregular* in all it's branches.

[TO MARY SHELLEY]   [*Nov. 16?*] *1822*

✻ ✻ ✻ ✻ ✻ ✻ ✻ ✻ ✻ ✻ ✻ ✻ ✻ ✻ ✻ ✻

I presume that you, at least, know enough of me to be sure that I could have no intention to insult Hunt's poverty. On the contrary, I honour him for it; for, I know what it is, having been as much embarrassed as ever he was, without perceiving aught in it to diminish an honourable man's self-respect. If you mean to say that, had he been a wealthy man, I would have joined in this Journal, I answer in the negative. ✻ ✻ ✻ I engaged in the Journal from good-will towards him, added to respect for his character, literary and personal; and no less for his political courage, as well as regret for his present circumstances: I did this in the hope that he might, with the same aid from literary friends of literary contributions (which is requisite for all journals of a mixed nature), render himself independent.

✻ ✻ ✻ ✻ ✻ ✻ ✻ ✻ ✻ ✻ ✻ ✻ ✻ ✻ ✻ ✻

I have always treated him, in our personal intercourse, with such scrupulous delicacy, that I have forborne intruding advice, which I thought might be disagreeable, lest he should impute it to what is called "taking advantage of a man's situation".

As to friendship, it is a propensity in which my genius is very limited. I do not know the *male* human being, except Lord Clare, the

---

[1] Byron had since Shelley's death been sending Mary his first drafts of poems for her to make fair copies. This was a service to both, for Byron hated to copy a poem after he had written it and it gave Mary occupation and increased her income when she needed it. The drama mentioned here was *The Deformed Transformed*.

friend of my infancy, for whom I feel any thing that deserves the name. All my others are men-of-the-world friendships. I did not even feel it for Shelley, however much I admired and esteemed him; so that you see not even vanity could bribe me into it, for, of all men, Shelley thought highest of my talents,—and, perhaps of my disposition.

I will do my duty by my intimates, upon the principle of doing as you would be done by. I have done so, I trust, in most instances. I may be pleased with their conversation—rejoice in their success—be glad to do them service, or to receive their counsel and assistance in return. But as for friends and friendship, I have (as I already said) named the only remaining male for whom I feel any thing of the kind, excepting, perhaps, Thomas Moore. I have had, and may have still, a thousand friends, as they are called, in *life,* who are like one's partners in the waltz of this world—not much remembered when the ball is over, though very pleasant for the time. Habit, business, and companionship in pleasure or in pain, are links of a similar kind, and the same faith in politics is another. * * *

[TO LADY HARDY]   *Albaro. 10bre. 1 0 1822*

My dear "Cousin (*not*) of *Buckingham* and sage grave Woman"[1] it was my intention to have answered yr. letter sooner—but in the interim yr. Chevalier arrived[2]—and calling upon me had not been two minutes in the room (though I had not seen him for these nine years) before he began a long story about you—which I cut short as well as I could by telling him that I *knew* you—and was a *relative* and was not desirous of his confidence on the subject.—He—however—persisted in declaring himself an illused Gentleman—and describing you—as a kind of cold Calypso—who lead astray people of an amatory disposition —without giving them any sort of compensation—contenting yourself it seems—with only making *one* fool—instead of *two*—which is the more approved method of proceeding on such occasions.—For my part —I think you quite right—and be assured from me that a woman who —(as Society is constituted in England—) gives any advantage to a man—may expect a lover—but will sooner or later find a tyrant.— And this may not perhaps be the Man's fault neither—but is the necessary and natural result of the Circumstances of Society which in fact tyrannize over the Man equally with the woman—that is to say—

---

[1] *Richard III,* Act III, scene 7: "Cousin of Buckingham, and sage, grave men."
[2] James Wedderburn Webster.

291

if either of *them* have any feeling or honour.—He (the Chevalier) bored me so upon the subject that I greatly fear (Heaven forgive me for you won't) that I said something about the "transmutation of hair" but I was surprized into it—by his wanting to [swear?] me out that his black wig—was the shock (or shocking) flaxen poodle furniture with which Nature had decorated his head ten years ago.———

He is gone post to Leghorn in pursuit of you—having (I presume in consequence of your disappearance) actually—(*no* jest I assure you) advertised "for an agreeable companion in a post-chaise["] in the Genoa Gazette.—I enclose you the paragraph.—Have you found any benefit for your girl from the L[eghorn] Baths? or are you gone to Florence.—You can write to me at yr. own leisure and inclination.—I have always laid it down as a maxim—and found it justified by experience—that a man and a woman—make far better friendships than can exist between two of the same sex—but *then* with the condition—that they never have made—or are to make love with each other.[3]— Lovers may [be]—and indeed generally are—enemies—but they never can be friends—because there must always be a spice of jealousy—and a something of Self in all their speculations.—Indeed I rather look upon Love altogether as a sort of hostile transaction—very necessary to make—or to break—matches and keep the world a-going—but by no means a sinecure to the parties concerned.——Now—as *my* Love perils are—I believe pretty well over—and yours by all accounts are never to begin;—we shall be the best friends imaginable—as far as both are concerned—and with this advantage—that we may both fall to loving right and left through all our acquaintance—without either sullenness or sorrow from that amiable passion—which are it's [unnoble?] attributes.———I address this at hazard to Leghorn—believe me my dear Coz

ever & affectly yrs.
N B

[TO DOUGLAS KINNAIRD]   *Genoa. Jy. 18th. 1823*

My dear Douglas—By ye. post of yesterday—or rather of ye. 16 o —I forwarded a packet to you containing a letter—the revise of [Don] J[uan] and certain poeshies for any ensuing number of "the Liberal"— to be transmitted by you to Mr. J[ohn] H[unt] in time.—This is merely a line of Advice to your Honour.—I have already written more

---

[3] Byron carried this thought into *Don Juan*:

> "No friend like to a woman Earth discovers,
> So that you have not been nor will be lovers."
> (Canto XIV, stanza 93).

than once to express my willingness to accept the—or almost any mortgage—anything to get out of the tremulous funds of these oscillatory times.—There will be a war somewhere—no doubt—and wherever it may be the funds will be affected more or less—so pray— get us out of them with all proper expedition.—It has been the burthen of my song to you these three years and better and about as useful as better Counsels.——With regard to Chancery—Appeals—Arbitrations— Surveyings— Bills— fees— receipts— disbursements— copy-*rights*—manorial ditto—funds—land—&c. &c. &c.—I shall always be disposed to follow your more practical—and practicable experience.— I will economize—and *do* as I have partly proved to you by my surplus revenue of 1822—(which almost equals the ditto of the United States of America—vide—President's report to Congress—in proportion) & do *you* second my parsimony by judicious disbursements of what is requisite—and a moderate liquidation,—also such an investment of any spare monies—as may render some usance to the owner because however little—"every little makes a mickle" as we of the North say with more reason than rhyme.—I hope that you have *all receipts* &c. &c. &c. and acknowledgements of monies paid towards liquidation of debts,— to prevent confusion and ⟨prevent⟩ hinder the fellows from coming *twice*—of which they would be capable—particularly—as my absence would lend a pretext to the pretension.——

You will perhaps wonder at this recent & furious fit of accumulation and retrenchment—but—it is not so unnatural—I am not naturally ostentatious—although once careless and expensive *because careless*— —and my most extravagant passions have pretty well subsided--as it is time that they should on the very verge of thirty five.——I always looked to about thirty as the barrier of any real or fierce delight in the passions—and determined to work them out in the younger ore and better veins of the Mine—and I flatter myself (perhaps) that I have pretty well done so—and now the *dross* is coming—and I loves lucre— for one must love something. At least if I have not quite worked out the others—it is not for want of labouring hard to do so—but perhaps I deceive myself.—At any rate then I have a passion the more—and thus a feeling. However it is not for myself—but I should like (God willing) to leave something to my relatives more than a mere name; and besides that to be able to do good to others to a greater extent. If nothing else—will do—I must try bread & water—which by the way —are very nourishing—and sufficient—if good of their kind.—

yrs. ever

N B

Illustrious Sir—I cannot thank you as you ought to be thanked for the lines which my young friend Mr. Sterling[1] sent me of yours,—and it would but ill become me to pretend to exchange verses with him who for fifty years has been the undisputed Sovereign of European literature.—You must therefore accept my most sincere acknowledgements in prose—and in hasty prose too—for I am at present on my voyage to Greece once more—and surrounded by hurry and bustle which hardly allow a moment even to Gratitude and Admiration to express themselves.——I sailed from Genoa some days ago—was driven back by a Gale of Wind—and have since sailed again—and arrived here (Leghorn) this morning to receive on board some Greek passengers for their struggling Country.——*Here* also I found your lines and Mr. Sterling's letter—and I could not have had a more favourable Omen or more agreeable surprise than a word from Goethe written by his own hand.——I am returning to Greece to see if I can be of any little use there;—if ever I come back I will pay a visit to Weimar to offer the sincere homage of one of the many Millions of your admirers.—I have the honour to be ever & most respectfully

yr. obliged adm[irer] & Se[rvant]

NOEL BYRON

Aux Soins de Monsieur Sterling.

---

[1] Charles Sterling, son of the British Consul at Genoa, when he left for Germany carried a note from Byron expressing homage to the great German writer. Goethe's German verses in reply sent by young Sterling are printed in Moore, II, 676.

JOURNAL IN CEPHALONIA

June 19th. 1823

The Dead have been awakened—shall I sleep?
The World's at war with tyrants—shall I crouch?
The harvest's ripe—and shall I pause to reap?
I slumber not—the thorn is in my Couch—
Each day a trumpet soundeth in mine ear—
It's Echo in my heart————[1]

Metaxata—Cephalonia—Septr. 28th.

1823

On the sixteenth (I think) of July I sailed from Genoa on the English Brig Hercules—Jno. Scott Master—on the 17th.[2] a Gale of wind occasioning confusion and threatening damage to the horses in the hold—we bore up again for the same port—where we remained four and twenty hours longer and then put to sea—touched at Leghorn—and pursued our voyage by the straits of Messina for Greece—passing within sight of Elba—Corsica—the Lipari islands including Stromboli Sicily Italy &c.—about the 4th of August[3] we anchored off Argostoli, the chief harbour of the Island of Cephalonia.——

Here I had some expectation of hearing from Capt. B[laquiere] who was on a mission from the G[ree]k Committee in London to the Gr[eek] Provisional Gov[ernmen]t of the Morea—but rather to my surprise learned that he was on his way home—though his latest letters to me from the peninsula—after expressing an anxious wish that I should come up without delay—stated further that he intended to remain in the Country for the present.——I have since received various letters from him addrest to Genoa—and forwarded to the Islands—partly explaining the cause of his unexpected return—and also (contrary to his former opinion) requesting me not to proceed to

---

[1] These lines, with the above date, are written at the head of the first page of the manuscript of the Journal. Byron told Dr. Henry Muir, the health officer at Argostoli, that he began to keep a journal when he first arrived in Cephalonia, but that he left off because he could not help abusing the Greeks in it.

[2] With so many false starts, Byron did not remember the date. They left Genoa finally on the 16th of July.

[3] On August 3 Byron wrote to Blaquiere from Argostoli.

Greece *yet*—for sundry reasons, some of importance.—I sent a boat to Corfu in the hope of finding him still there—but he had already sailed for Ancona.—

In the island of Cephalonia Colonel Napier commanded in chief as Resident—and Col. Duffie the 8th. a King's regiment then forming the Garrison. We were received by both those Gentlemen—and indeed by all the Officers as well as the Civilians with the greatest kindness and hospitality—which if we did not deserve—I still hope that we have done nothing to forfeit—and it has continued unabated—even since the Gloss of new acquaintance has been worn away by frequent inter-course.——We have learned what has since been fully confirmed— that the Greeks are in a state of political dissention amongst them-selves—that Mavrocordato was dismissed or had resigned (L'Un vaut bien l'autre) and that Colocotroni with I know not what or whose party was paramount in the Morea.—The Turks were in force in Acarnania &c. and the Turkish fleet blockaded the coast from Mis-solonghi to Chiarenza—and subsequently to Navarino——the Greek Fleet from the want of means or other causes remained in port in Hydra—Ipsara and Spezas[?]—and for aught that is yet certainly known may be there still. As rather contrary to my expectations I had no advices from Peloponnesus—and had also letters to receive from England from the Committee I determined to remain for the interim in the Ionian Islands—especially as it was difficult to land on the opposite coast without risking the confiscation of the Vessel and her Contents— which Capt. Scott naturally enough declined to do—unless I would insure to him the full amount of his possible damage.——

To pass the time we made a little excursion over the mountains to Saint Eufemia—by worse roads than I ever met in the course of some years of travel in rough places of many countries.—At Saint Euphemia we embarked for Ithaca—and made the tour of that beautiful Island— as a proper pendant to the Troad which I had visited several years before.—The hospitality of Capt. Knox (the resident) and his lady was in no respect inferior to that of our military friends of Cephalonia. —That Gentleman with Mrs. K. and some of their friends conducted us to the fountain of Arethusa—which alone would be worth the voyage—but the rest of the Island is not inferior in attraction to the admirers of Nature;—the arts and tradition I leave to the Antiquaries, —and so well have those Gentlemen contrived to settle such questions —that as the existence of Troy is disputed—so that of Ithaca (as *Homer's Ithaca* i.e.) is not yet admitted.—Though the month was August and we had been cautioned against travelling in the Sun—yet as I had during my former experience never suffered from the heat as long as I continued in *motion*—I was unwilling to lose so many hours of the day on account of a sunbeam more or less—and though our party was rather numerous no one suffered either illness or inconvenience as far as could be observed, though one of the Servants (a Negro)[4]— declared that it was as hot as in the West Indies.—I had left our thermometer on board—so could not ascertain the precise degree.— We returned to Saint Eufemia and passed over to the monastery of Samos on the opposite part of the bay and proceeded next day to Argostoli by a better road than the path to Saint Eufemia.—The land Journey was made on Mules.——

Some days after our return, I heard that there were letters for me at Zante—but a considerable delay took place before the Greek to whom they were consigned had them properly forwarded—and I was at length indebted to Col. Napier for obtaining them for me;—*what* occasioned the demur or delay—was never explained.—I learned by my advices from England—the request of the Committee that I would act as their representative near the G[ree]k Gov[ernmen]t and take charge of the proper disposition and delivery of certain Stores &c. &c. expected by a vessel which has not yet arrived up to the present date (Septr. 28th)[5]—Soon after my arrival I took into my own pay a body of forty Suliotes under the Chiefs Photomara—Giavella—and Drako— and would probably have increased the number—but I found them not quite united among themselves in any thing except raising their de- mands on me—although I had given a dollar per man more each month —than they could receive from the G[ree]k Gov[ernmen]t and they were destitute[,] at the time I took them[,] of every thing.———I had acceded too to their own demand—and paid them a month in advance. ——But set on probably by some of the trafficking shopkeepers with whom they were in the habit of dealing on credit—they made various attempts at what I thought extortion—so that I called them together stating my view of the case—and declining to take them on with me— but I offered them another month's pay—and the price of their passage to Acarnania—where they could now easily go as the Turkish fleet was gone—and the blockade removed.—This part of them accepted—

[4] Benjamin Lewis, an American Negro, was employed briefly by Trelawny, but Byron took him into his service. He had a smattering of French and Italian and understood cooking and horses. See Doris Langley Moore, *Lord Byron: Accounts Rendered*, p. 374.

[5] The *Ann*, with the London Greek Committee's stores and the fire-master Parry and a number of mechanics, left England on November 10, 1823, and did not arrive at Missolonghi until Feb. 5, 1824.

and they went accordingly.—Some difficulty arose about restoring their arms by the Septinsular Gov[ernmen]t but these were at length obtained—and they are now with their compatriots in Etolia or Acarnania.——

I also transferred to the resident in Ithaca—the sum of two hundred and fifty dollars for the refugees there—and I had conveyed to Cephalonia—a Moriote family who were in the greatest helplessness —and provided them with a house and decent maintenance under the protection of Messrs. Corgialegno—wealthy merchants of Argostoli— to whom I had been recommended by my Correspondents.——I had caused a letter to be written to Marco Bozzari the acting Commander of a body of troops in Acarnania—for whom I had letters of recommended [sic];—his answer was probably the last he ever signed or dictated—for he was killed in action the very day after it's date—with the character of a good Soldier—and an honourable man—which are not always found together nor indeed separately.——I was also invited by Count Metaxa the Governor of Missolonghi to go over there—but it was necessary in the present state of parties that I should have some communication with the existing Gov[ernmen]t on the subject of their opinion *where* I might be—if not *most* useful—at any rate *least* obnoxious.——

As I did not come here to join a faction but a nation—and to deal with honest men and not with speculators or peculators—(charges bandied about daily by the Greeks of each other) it will require much circumspection ⟨for me⟩ to avoid the character of a partizan—and I perceive it to be the more difficult—as I have already received invitations from more than one of the contending parties—always under the pretext that *they* are the "real Simon Pure"[6].——After all—one should not despair—though all the foreigners that I have hitherto met with from amongst the Greeks—are going or gone back disgusted.—

Whoever goes into Greece at present should do it as Mrs. Fry went into Newgate—not in the expectation of meeting with any especial indication of existing probity—but in the hope that time and better treatment will reclaim the present burglarious and larcenous tendencies which have followed this General Gaol delivery.—When the limbs of the Greeks are a little less stiff from the shackles of four centuries— they will not march so much "as if they had gyves on their legs".[7]—— At present the Chains are broken indeed—but the links are still clank-

---

[6] Mrs Centlivre, *A Bold Stroke for a Wife*. In the play, Col. Feignwell pretends to be Simon Pure.

[7] *Henry IV*, Part I, Act IV, scene 2.

ing—and the Saturnalia is still too recent to have converted the Slave into a sober Citizen.—The worst of them is—that (to use a coarse but the only expression that will not fall short of the truth) they are such d————d liars;—there never was such an incapacity for veracity shown since Eve lived in Paradise.—One of them found fault the other day with the English language—because it had so few shades of a Negative —whereas a Greek can so modify a No—to a yes—and vice versa—by the slippery qualities of his language—that prevarication may be carried to any extent and still leave a loop-hole through which perjury may slip without being perceived.——This was the Gentleman's own talk—and is only to be doubted because in the words of the Syllogism —"Now Epimenides was a Cretan".[8] But they may be mended by and bye.—

Sept. 30th.

After remaining here some time in expectation of hearing from the G[ree]k G[overnmen]t I availed myself of the opportunity of Messrs B[rowne] and T[relawny] proceeding to Tripolitza—subsequently to the departure of the Turkish fleet to write to the acting part of the Legislature. My object was not only to obtain some accurate information so as to enable me to proceed to the Spot where I might be if not most safe at least more serviceable but to have an opportunity of forming a judgement on the real state of their affairs. In the mean time I hear from Mavrocordato—and the Primate of Hydra—the latter inviting me to that island—and the former hinting that he should like to meet me there or elsewhere.

1823
10bre. 17th.

My Journal was discontinued abruptly and has not been resumed sooner—because on the day of it's former date I received a letter from my Sister Augusta—that intimated the illness of my daughter—and I had not then the heart to continue it.——Subsequently I had heard through the same channel that she was better—and since that she is well—if so—for me all is well. But although I learned this early in 9bre.—I know not why—I have not continued my journal, though many things which would have formed a curious record have since occurred.—I know not why I resume it even now except that standing at the window of my apartment in this beautiful village—the calm though cool serenity of a beautiful and transparent Moonlight—

[8] The line, attributed to Epimenides, is in the New Testament (*Titus*, 1: 12): "The Cretans are always liars, evil beasts, slow bellies."

showing the Islands—the Mountains—the Sea—with a distant outline of the Morea traced between the double Azure of the waves and skies —have quieted me enough to be able to write—from [sic] which (however difficult it may seem for one who has written so much publicly— to refrain) is and always has been to me—a task and a painful one—— I could summon testimonies were it necessary—but my handwriting is sufficient—it is that of one who thinks much, rapidly—perhaps deeply —but rarely with pleasure.——

But—"En Avant!"—The Greeks are advancing in their public progress—but quarrelling amongst themselves.——I shall probably bon grè mal grè be obliged to join one of the factions—which I have hitherto strenuously avoided in the hope to unite them in one common interest.—Mavrocordato—has appeared at length with the Idriote Squadron in these seas—which apparition would hardly have taken place had I not engaged to pay two hundred thousand piastres (10 piastres per dollar being the present value—on the Greek Continent) in aid of Messolonghi—and has commenced operations somewhat successfully but not very prudently.—Fourteen (some say Seventeen) Greek Ships attacked a Turkish vessel of 12 guns—and took her—— This is not quite an Ocean-Thermopylæ—but n'importe—they (on dit) had found on board 50000 dollars—a sum of great service in their present exigencies—if properly applied.—This prize however has been made within the bounds of Neutrality on the Coast of Ithaca—and the Turks were (it is said) pursued on shore—and some slain.—All this may involve a question of right and wrong with the not very Tolerant Thomas Maitland[9]—who is not very capable of distinguishing either. I have advanced the sum above noted to pay the said Squadron—it is not very large—but it is double that with which Napoleon the Emperor of Emperors—began his campaign in Italy, withal—vide—Las Cases —passim vol 1 (tome premier).[10]

The Turks have retired from before Messolonghi—nobody knows why—since they left provisions and ammunition behind them in quantities—and the Garrison made no sallies or none to any purpose—they never invested Messolonghi this year—but bombarded Anatoliko—(a sort of village which I recollect well having passed through the whole of that country with 50 Albanians in 1809 Messolonghi included) near the Achelous—some say that S[irota?] Pacha heard of an insurrection

[9] Sir Thomas Maitland, High Commissioner of the Ionian Islands, maintained a strict neutrality.

[10] According to Las Cases (Mémorial . . . , tome I, p. 173) Napoleon could raise no more than two thousand louis for his Italian campaign.

near Scutari—some one thing some another—for my part I have been in correspondence with the Chiefs—and their accounts are not unanimous.—The Suliotes both there—here—and elsewhere—having taken a kind of liking *to*, or at least formed or renewed a sort of acquaintance *with* me—(as I have aided them and their families in all that I could according to circumstances) are apparently anxious that I should put myself forward as their Chief—(If I may so say) I would rather not for the present—because there are too many divisions and Chiefs already—but if it should appear necessary—why—as they are admitted to be the best and bravest of the present combatants—it might—or may—so happen—that I could would—should—or shall take to me the support of such a body of men—with whose aid—I think something might be done both *in* Greece and *out* of it—(for there is a good deal to put to rights in both)[.] I could maintain them out of my own present means (always supposing my present income and means to be permanent) they are not above a thousand—and of those not six hundred *real* Suliotes—but they are allowed to be equal (that seems a bravado though but it is in print recently) *one* to 5 European Moslems—and *ten* Asiatics—be it as it may—they are in high esteem—and my very good friends.——

A soldier may be maintained on the Mainland—for 25 piastres (rather better than two dollars a month) monthly—and find his rations out of the Country—or for *five dollars*—including his paying for his rations—therefore for between two and three thousand dollars a month—(and the dollar here is to be had for 4 and 2 pence instead of 4 and 6 pence—the price in England) I could maintain between five hundred and a thousand of these warriors for as long as necessary—and I have more means than are—(supposing them to last) [sufficient] to do so—for my own personal wants are very simple (except in horses for I am no great pedestrian) and my income considerable for any country but England—(being equal to the President's of the United States—the English Secretaries' of State's or the French Ambassador's at Vienna and the greater courts—150000 Francs—I believe) and I have hope to have sold a Manor besides for nearly 3000000 francs more—thus I could (with what We should extract according to the usages of war—also) keep on foot a respectable clan or Sept or tribe or horde—for some time—and as I have not any motive for so doing but the well-wishing to Greece I should hope with advantage.—

My dear Hobhouse—I write a few lines by a private conveyance to inform you that I have sent you two packets—whence you will extract information for the Committee—one by Capt. Scott of the Brig Hercules—and the other by Mr. Peacock agent for a Society on his return from his mission to the G[reek] G[overnmen]t——The documents are in considerable number—and will tell you all that is requisite up to their respective dates.——The Greek disputes amongst themselves are in statu quo——the fleet is at length said to be at sea—but has done nothing—indeed there has been (except in the case of Bozzari [Botzaris] who was killed in Rumelia—) a kind of contest of *inaction* on both sides Greek and Mussulman during the present year. —But the Turks have at length come down in force (sixteen thousand they say) on Messolonghi—which however is stronger than it was last year—when they were repulsed in a similar attempt.—There is a squadron of some sort in sight from our windows in the village here at this present writing—but whether Greek or Turk—is not easily made out—two sail one three masted vessel—and apparently ships of war. We are very anxious for your Committee Argo with it's continents— and Congreve rockets—which I will direct to the place where they seem needful.—I have not had any answer yet from the G[ree]k G[overnmen]t but I have heard of a packet directed to me by their order some time ago—which is said to have been searched or destroyed by some of the factions or their adherents at Zante. When Mrs. Fry has done with Newgate it would not be amiss if the Committee would send her into Greece—she would find plenty of exercise for her *re*-moralizing talents by all accounts.—It is my duty and business to conceal nothing either of my own impressions or of the general belief upon the score of the Greeks from the Committee—but when I add that I do not despair—but think still every exertion should be used in their behalf—in the hope that time and freedom will revive for them what tyranny has kept under but perhaps not extinguished—I conceive that you will not despond nor believe me desponding because I state things as they really are.—They want a regular force to support a regular System quite as much as to repel their enemies—in the interim every man that can pay or command from one hundred to a thousand Gillies is independent—and seems to act for himself.—When I state to you that I have had half a dozen offers of different kinds and from different parties to put myself at the head of some hundred boys of the belt and of the blade——all of whom might be maintained for any purpose—with less means than those which I can at present command —you may judge for yourself—how far there is any actual order or regularity.—I have hitherto steered clear of such matters—and avoided committing myself with any of the parties—being a peaceable man—but really if they go on in this way—and I get up in a bad humour some morning there is no saying what one may be provoked into.——

I have got over most of the Suliotes (their best παλι καρια [soldiers]) who were here, to recruit the ranks in Acarnania—one of their bravest Chiefs (Drako) went a few days ago—and is to let me know (he as well as Kosta Bozzari Marco's surviving brother) the exact state of *their* affairs.—They have lately lost another Chief in action—Giavella —whose widow is here—she sent her little boy a child of four years old to pay me a visit the other day—who is a sturdy little Lion's whelp with an immense head—and neither cries nor laughs like other children—but sits still and blows out his lips and snorts as the High-landers do when they are angry.—He already talks of revenging his father's death on the followers of Mahomet—according to the good old custom which of course his mother carefully patronizes.—His organ of Combativeness seems considerably developed—and he will doubtless if he lives be a Credit to the Courage line of business.—Of my present position here I have little further to say—I hear that the Canteen has got as far as Zante—but I neither know the name—nor the probable time of Arrival of that same Caraval [sic] or Argosie which is to waft Mr. Parry and his fire-enginry to the seat of warfare. —Blaquiere has probably got back amongst you; he had evaporated before I arrived here.—My own motions will partly depend upon the arrival of your Brigade—or it may be on the answer I may have from the actual G[ree]k G[overnmen]t now in Congress at Salamis (Colouri hodie) or Egina——I have two correspondents there awaiting a reply. —Another English Gentleman volunteer is gone over to Mesolonghi this day—or going.—It is not yet sure that it *is* besieged—and to say the *truth*—no *truth* or very little is to be extracted from the Greek accounts of any kind till *long* after any given occurrence.—

I have had a letter from Bowring (to whom make me remembered) dated August 18th.—in which he mentions (among other matter) the possible or even probable prospect of a loan for the Hellenes but at the same time imposes on me to impress on them the necessity of the most *santa-sacred* (an Italianism of mine—pardon it) observance of engage-ments—and of a speciality their regular payment of *interest*.—As Henry Morton says to Cuthbert Headrigg—I doubt "that the *penny fee* will be a hard chapter"[1] for the actual members of the G[overnmen]t do not pass for being great dilettanti in the matter of pecuniary punctuality.—But this by the way.—But I doubt that the news of Mavrocordato's being out—and their other slight discrepancies—will enhance the scruples of our monied people.—Besides the deputies to treat for the said loan—are *not yet* embarked! I have written and railed to urge their *immediate* departure—but no!—they are not gone —nor for aught I know—going.—Mr. Peacock (an important personage for he was authorized to offer large sums) came away much disgusted with them—as almost all foreigners have hitherto done.—I laboured to put him in better humour with them—and perhaps partly succeeded.—I mean (unless something out of the way occurs to recal[l] me) to stay up in the country itself or the neighbourhood of Greece—till things are either better or hopeless—and in every case will take advantage of circumstances to serve the *Cause* if the patriots will permit me—but it must be *the Cause*—and not individuals or *parties* that I endeavour to benefit.—

yrs. ever
N B

P.S.—Remember me to D[ouglas] K[innaird]—from whom I have not heard—tell him as usual—to muster all my possible monies—as well for the present—as for the ensuing year—that I may take the field in force in case it should be proper or prospective of Good that I should do so.—I send you a minute of my answer to Mavrocordato's epistle.——Tell Douglas K[innair]d that I cannot make out from his statement whether the 950—deducted in the first year (1822) from the Kirkby Mallory rental on account of Ly N[oe]ll *is* to return to Lady B[yron] and to me or no—but whether it is or not—there was still better than 5000 £ to divide between Ly B. and myself the rental being 6336 £ of which in all I have as yet received but *nine* hundred in two separate payments.—There is therefore or ought to be in any case still due to me from the *1822* rental fully sixteen hundred pounds being my balance of two thousand five hundred—without adverting to the present year—so that I have the better part of two years to receive.—My *own* income is I take it paid more regularly;—as to anything from publications I do not calculate on much but Murray ought to have settled for Werner before this time. Tell Lord E[rskine] that I have at length received his brochure on the G[ree]ks for which many thanks—I shall try and get it translated into Romaic.—

---

[1] In Scott's *Old Mortality*.

Dear Barry—A barrel containing three thousand dollars to my address has been consigned to S.S. Corgialegno—and as I choose to keep my Genoese Credit intact for the present I shall remit to yr. house by some early opportunity bills on Messrs Ransom for six hundred and twenty or thirty pounds which I conjecture to be about the equivalent more or less—but in case there be any balance for or against me you can rectify it from my own accompt with your house.—I have still between 7 and 8000 dollars of those which I brought up with me—so that the reinforcement though not unacceptable was for the present unnecessary.——

Messrs Corgialegno—at first—either had not or pretended not to have funds to supply above a certain sum per month—and for this they required two and a half per cent—as I believe—because they were not aware of the monies I had in hand—and wished to profit by the letters of *Credit*—not much to their *own*. I told them that I had several thousand dollars in hand—and that even were it otherwise I would see them d——d before I agreed to such terms of exchange for the bills of and on respectable houses in Italy and England.—I further added that I had enough for my own occasions for a year to come and that as my *extra*-expenditure was to have been for the Greeks—he might settle it with his compatriots—for whom if I spent my monies—it must naturally be on equitable terms.—They have since changed *their note*— and offer to change *my notes* and to advance whatever I require on fair terms of exchange—but I made their proposition (the original one) pretty public—and the Greeks (as might be expected when their own interest was concerned—) clamoured pretty loudly against this Hebrew proceeding of the Sieurs Corgialegno—so that they grew ashamed of it themselves—and explained it away—something about the scarcity of dollars &c.—and I have allowed them the benefit of their explanation.——They have however been very *civil*—and have opened a correspondence with Napoli di Romania—so that I may draw there too for what I want.—I am invited over by the Greek Gov[ern-men]t who have received Messrs Browne and Trelawney [sic] with great hospitality.—— They have sent an Agent to conduct me to that city—for which I expect to set out early in November.—Continue to address to Cephalonia however, till I direct otherwise.——The various letters of Credit from Messrs Webb—the Corgialegnos declare to be superfluous—as they wish to be the intermediate agents in our business.—So that all seems very well so far.——

The states of parties in Greece are still the same—I have transmitted by private hands several packets of documents and Correspondence to Mr. Hobhouse M.P. to be laid by him before Mr. *Bowring* for his inspection and the Committee's.—If you write to that Gentleman say —that I do not address directly to him especially by the *post*—as *his* letters are liable to be looked into by the curious in correspondence on the Continent—ever since his adventure in France[1]—but the letters to Mr. H[obhouse] are in fact meant for his perusal with their enclosed papers.—It is very expedient that the Committee should support me with their authority—and if they were to frame a memorial to the Greek Gov[ernmen]t on the subject of their existing differences and the expulsion or secession of Mavrocordato—it would probably have more effect than any *individual* attempt of mine to reconcile the parties—and until they *are* reconciled—it seems to be allowed very generally—that their internal affairs will be in an unpleasant state of weakness—I would of course present such a memorial and enforce it by all lawful means in my power.——

All the stories of the Greek victories by sea and land are exaggerated or untrue—they *have* had the advantage in some skirmishes—but the Turks have also had the same in others—and are now before Mesalonghi in force—and as for the fleet—it has never been to sea at all until very lately—and as far as can be ascertained has done little or nothing to the purpose.—The deputies for the loan are not yet set out —though I have written (to urge their departure) to the G[ree]k G[overnmen]t.—I neither despond nor despair of the Cause—but it is *my* business to state things as they are to the Committee—were it only to show the expediency of further exertion.—I offered to advance a thousand dollars per month for the succour of Mesalonghi—and the Suliotes under Bozzari (who was since killed) but the Gov[ernmen]t have answered me (through Count Delladecima[2] of this island) that they wish to confer with me previously—which is in fact saying that they wish me to spend my money in some other direction.———Now—I will

---

[1] John Bowring was Secretary of the London Greek Committee. On Oct. 5, 1822, he had been arrested by order of the French Government at Calais and he was imprisoned for a time in Boulogne. His papers, which were seized, included a letter to a Peruvian agent in London and to the Portuguese Ambassador. This link to revolutionary governments made him anathema to the Bourbon regime in France.

[2] Millingen (*Memoirs*, p. 18) called Count Demetrius Delladecima "a Cephaloniot nobleman of considerable shrewdness, sound judgment, and deep acquaintance with Greek character." He was in close contact with many mainland Greeks and gave Byron his appraisal of their recommendations and of their reliability. (Byron generally spelled his name Della Decima.)

take especial care that it *is* for the public cause—otherwise—I will not advance a parà.—The Opposition say they want to cajole me—and the party in power say the others want to seduce me—so between the two I have a difficult part to play—however I will have nothing to do with their factions—unless to reconcile them if possible.—I know not whether it be true that "Honesty is the best policy"—but it is the only kind that I am disposed to practice or to sanction.—

The Committee should hasten their brigade as it's announcement has been gratefully received by the G[ree]k Gov[ernmen]t who are also profuse in their civilities and acknowledgements to the Committee &c. and are preparing to receive me with all regard.——It is not of their ill-usage (which I should know how to repel or at least endure perhaps) but of *their good* treatment that I am apprehensive—for it is difficult not to allow our private impressions to predominate—and if these Gentlemen *have* any undue interest and discover my weak side— viz—a propensity to be governed—and were to set a pretty woman or a clever woman about me—with a turn for political or any other sort of intrigue—why—they would make a fool of me—no very difficult matter probably even without such an intervention.——But if I can keep passion—at least that passion—out of the question—(which may be the more easy as I left my heart in Italy) they will not weather me with quite so much facility.——

If the Committee expect to do much good—they must increase their funds—to which I will add all that I can spare of my own——and they should appoint at least *three* persons in whom they have confidence to direct their expenditure—I would rather *not* myself have anything to do with *that* department—not being a good accomptant—but in superintending all or any thing—*not* relative to the pecuniary detail—I am at their commandment.—Mr. Blaquiere's report in the papers is not quite the same with that in his private letters to Col. Napier—but he may be in the right to conceal partly the extent of the Greek divisions —especially as Mavrocordato was still in power when Mr. B. left the Morea.—I hope that his statement will be of some utility.—

8bre. 27th.

I was interrupted by a visitor on the 25th. and yesterday was Sunday.—With reference to what you say of the purchase of the Schooner—I can only answer that he is not likely to buy it—and *if* he buys—perhaps as little likely to pay the price—but you are—or *were* of a contrary opinion.—I shall be happy to confess your superior discernment. I hope you will give a careful look at my travelling carriage which I wish to have kept in good order.—The Prints also and some of my books (a life of Marceau the French General sent me by his Sister—) and some volumes inscribed tracts &c. which I believe I mentioned in a recent letter I wish to have reserved in case of disposal of the furniture &c.——It is not very probable that I should return before Spring—if even then—but it were idle to anticipate what must so much depend upon circumstances.—Here is a long epistle for you—will you tell the Hon[oura]ble Douglas Kinnaird that I have written to him to approve and sanction his proposal on a matter of business with reference to a Manor of mine—he will understand what is meant—I add this—in case he should not have received my reply to his letter—of the 14th. August—which I only got not very long ago.——My respects to Messrs Webb and B[arker?] I have received all their letters to which I presume the previous part of this will serve for answer without troubling them with a postage—Remember me to Mr. Sterling and all acquaintances—

Ever yrs. and truly
N B

8bre. 29th. 1823

P.S.—You surely care little (on my account) or should do for newspaper tattle or gossip of any kind—if any fact is falsely stated which appears to be of consequence—you have it in your power to contradict it—for you know as much nearly of my affairs public or private as I do myself.—I have recently seen something of a zealous Dr. Kennedy—a very good Calvinist—who has a taste for controversy and conversion—and thinks me so nearly a tolerable Christian that he is trying to make me a whole one.—I have found indeed one indisputable text in St. Paul's epistle to the Romans (Chapter 10th. I believe) which disposes me much to credit all the rest of the dicta of that powerful Apostle—— It is this (see the Chapter) *"For there is no difference between a* JEW *and a* GREEK"*[3]*—tell Messrs Webb and B[arker?] that I intend to preach from this text to Carridi and Corgialegno.—What think you? I hope that it is not a sin to say so.

[TO JOHN BOWRING] 10bre. 26th. 1823

Dear Sir—Little need be added to the enclosed Which have arrived this day except that I embark tomorrow for Messolonghi.—The intended operations are detailed in the annexed documents.——I have

---

[3] *Romans,* 10: 12.

308

only to request that the Committee will use every exertion to forward our views—by all it's influence and credit.—I have also to request you *personally* from myself to urge my friend and trustee Douglas Kinnaird (from whom I have not heard these four months nearly) to forward to me all the resources of my *own* we can muster for the ensuing year since it is no time to menager *purse*—or perhaps—*person*—I *have* advanced—and am advancing all that I have in hand—but I shall require all that can be got together—and (if Douglas has completed the sale of Rochdale—*that* and my years income for next year ought to form a good round sum) as you may perceive that there will be little cash of their own amongst the Greeks—(unless they get the loan) it is the more necessary that those of their friends who have any should risk it.——

The Supplies of the Committee are some useful—and all excellent in their kind—but occasionally hardly *practical* enough—in the present state of Greece—for instance the Mathematical instruments are thrown away—none of the Greeks know a problem from a poker—we must conquer first—and plan afterwards.—The use of the trumpets too may be doubted—unless Constantinople were Jericho—for the Hellenists have no ear for Bugles—and you must send us somebody to listen to them.—We will do our best—and I pray you to stir your English hearts at home to more *general* exertion—for my part—I will stick by the cause while a plank remains which can be honourably clung to—if I quit it—it will be by the Greek's conduct—and not the holy Allies or the holier Mussulmans—but let us hope better things.

ever yrs.
N B

P.S.—As much of this letter as you please is for the Committee— the rest may be "entre nous".——

P.S.[1]—I am happy to say that Colonel Leicester Stanhope and myself are acting in perfect harmony together—he is likely to be of great service both to the cause and to the Committee, and is publicly as well as personally a very valuable acquisition to our party on every account. He came up (as they all do who have not been in the country before) with some high-flown notions of the sixth form at Harrow or Eton, &c.; but Col. Napier and I set him to rights on those points, which is absolutely necessary to prevent disgust, or perhaps return; but now we can set our shoulders *soberly* to the *wheel*, without quarrelling with the mud which may clog it occasionally.

[1] This postscript is not with the manuscript, but is given in Moore, II, 699–700.

I can assure you that Col. Napier and myself are as decided for the cause as any German student of them all; but like men who have seen the country and human life, there and elsewhere, we must be permitted to view it in its truth, with its defects as well as beauties,— more especially as success will remove the former *gradually*.

N B

[TO JOHN CAM HOBHOUSE]   *27th. 10bre. 1823*

Dear Hobhouse—I embark for Messolonghi. Douglas K[innair]d and Bowring can tell you the rest—I particularly require and entreat you to desire Douglas K[innair]d to send me soon Credits to the uttermost—that I may get the Greeks to keep the field—never mind *me*— so that the Cause goes on—if that is well—all is well.——Douglas must send me *my money* (Rochdale Manor included—if the sale is completed and the purchase money paid) the Committee must furnish *their* money—and the monied people *theirs*—with these we will soon have men enough—and all that.——

yrs. ever

N B

P.S.—Mavrocordato's letter says that my presence will *"electrify* the troops" so I am going over to "electrify" the Suliotes—as George Primrose went to Holland "to teach the Dutch English—who were fond of it to distraction."[1]

[TO HENRY MUIR][1]   *Dragomestri. J[anua]ry 2d. 1823 [1824]*

My dear Muir—I wish you many returns of the season—and happiness therewithal.—Gamba and the Bombarda (there is strong reason to believe) are carried into Patras by a Turkish frigate—which we saw chase them at dawn on the 31st.[2]—We had been down under the stern

---

[1] *Vicar of Wakefield*, Chap. 20.

[1] Dr. Henry Muir was Health Officer at Argostoli. It was at his house that Dr. Kennedy, a Methodist, expounded his doctrines of Christianity and tried to convert Byron and the officers of the garrison. Muir shared Byron's skeptical views and was one of his most intimate friends during his stay in Argostoli. His recollections of Byron were published in *Notes and Queries*, 6th series, Vol. IX, p. 81, 1884.

[2] Byron and his party left Argostoli the evening of Dec. 29, 1823, and arrived at Zante the next morning. They were travelling in two boats. Byron was in one called a "mistico", a long fast-sailing boat drawing little water. He had with him Dr. Bruno, his servant Fletcher, his Newfoundland dog Lyon, and the Moreote boy Lukas Chalandritsanos. Count Gamba was in the "bombard", a larger vessel, with most of the supplies and the servants. They left Zante in the evening and toward morning were intercepted by some Turkish warships. The mistico was able to escape and landed near the Scrofe rocks in a sheltered cove. The bombard was captured by the Turks.

in the night believing her a Greek till within pistol shot—and only escaped by a miracle of all the Saints (our Captain says) and truly I am of his opinion—for we should never have got away of ourselves.— They were signalizing their Consort with lights—and had illuminated the ship between decks—and were shouting like a Mob—but then why did they not fire? perhaps they took us for a Greek brulotte—and were afraid of *kindling* us—they had no colours flying even at dawn nor after.—At daybreak my boat was on the coast—but the wind unfavourable for *the port*—a large vessel with the wind in her favour standing between us and the Gulph—and another in chace of the Bombard— about 12 miles off or so.—Soon after they stood (i.e. the Bombard and frigate—) apparently towards Patras and a Zantiote boat making signals to us from the shore to get away—away we went before the wind—and ran into a Creek called Scrofes (I believe) where I landed Luke and another (as Luke's life was in most danger) with some money for themselves and a letter for Stanhope and sent them up the country to Messolonghi, where they would be in safety,—as the place where we were could be assailed by armed boats in a moment—and Gamba had all our arms except two carbines—a fowling piece—and some pistols.—In less than an hour—the vessel in chace neared us— and we dashed out again—and showing our stern (our boat sails very well) got in before night to Dragomestre[3]—where we now are.—But where is the Greek fleet? I don't know—do *you?* I told our Master of the boat that I was inclined to think the two large vessels (there were none else in sight) Greeks—but he answered "they are too large— why don't they show their colours?["] and his account was confirmed be it true or false—by several boats which we met or passed. As we could not at any rate have got in with that wind—without beating about for a long time—and as there was much property and some lives to risk (the boy's especially) without any means of defence—it was necessary to let our boatmen have their own way.——I dispatched yesterday another messenger to Messolonghi—for an escort—but we have yet no answer. We are here (those of my boat) for the fifth day— without taking our cloathes off—and sleeping on deck in all weathers —but are all very well and in good spirits.—It is to be supposed that the Govt. will send for their own sakes an escort as I have 16000 dollars on board—the greater part for their service.——I had (besides personal property to the amount of about 5000 more) 8000 dollars in specie of my own—without reckoning the Committee's stores—so

[3] Modern Astakos on the coast above Missolonghi.

that the Turks will have a good thing of it—if the prize be good.—I regret the detention of Gamba &c.—but the rest we can make up again—so tell Hancock to set my bills into cash—as soon as possible—and Corgialegno to prepare the remainder of my credit with Messrs Webb to be turned into monies.—I shall remain here (unless something extraordinary occurs) till Mavrocordato sends—and then go on —and act according to circumstances.—My respects to the two Colonels—and remembrances to all friends—tell *"Ultima Analise"*[4] that his friend Raidi[5] [sic] did not make his appearance with the brig—though I think that he might as well have spoken with us *in* or *off* Zante—to give us a gentle hint of what we had to expect.

yrs. ever affectly.
N B

P.S.—Excuse my scrawl on account of the pen and the frosty morning at daybreak—I write in haste a boat starting for Kalamo.[6]—I do not know whether the detention of the Bombard (*if* she be detained for I cannot swear to it and can only judge from appearances—and what all these fellows say) be an affair of the Govt. and Neutrality and &c.—but she *was stopped* at least 12 distant miles from any port—and had all her papers regular from *Zante* for *Kalamo* and *we also.*—I did not land at Zante being anxious to lose as little time as possible—but Sir F[rederick] S[toven][7] came off to invite me &c. and every body was as kind as could be—even in Cephalonia.—

[On cover] Lord Byron presents his respects to the Commandant of Kalamo and will feel particularly obliged if that Gentleman will forward this letter to Argostoli. [Request]ing his pardon for the trouble.

[TO CHARLES HANCOCK[1]] *Messolonghi. Jy. 13th. 1824*

Dear Sr. H.—Many thanks for yrs. of ye 5th. ditto to Muir for his. —You will have heard that Gamba and my vessel got out of the hands of the Turks safe and intact—nobody knows well how or why—for there is a mystery in the story somewhat melodramatic—Captain

---

[4] "Count Delladecima, to whom he gave this name, in consequence of a habit which that gentleman had of using the phrase 'in ultima analise', frequently in conversation." (Moore, II, 708.) See Oct. 25, 1823, to Barry, note 2.

[5] It should be Praidi, who was secretary to Prince Mavrocordatos.

[6] Kalamos was one of the smaller Ionian Islands near the mainland.

[7] British Resident at Zante.

[1] A British merchant at Argostoli, who with his partner Samuel Barff on Zante handled Byron's bills of exchange. See Biographical Sketch in Appendix II.

Valsamachi[2]—has I take it spun a long yarn by this time in Argostoli;
—I attribute their release entirely to Saint Dionysius of Zante—and
the Madonna ot the Rock near Cephalonia.—The adventures of my
separate bark were also not finished at Dragomestre.—We were conveyed out by some Greek Gunboats—and found the Leonidas brig of
war at Sea to look after us.—But blowing weather coming on we were
driven on the rocks—*twice*—in the passage of the Scrophes—and the
dollars had another narrow escape.—Two thirds of the Crew got
ashore over the bowsprit—the rocks were rugged enough—but water
very deep close in shore—so that she was after much swearing and
some exertion got off again—and away we went with a third of our
crew leaving the rest on a desolate island—where they might have been
now—had not one of the Gunboats taken them off—for we were in no
condition to take them off again.—Tell Muir that Dr. Bruno did not
show much fight on the occasion—for besides stripping to the flannel
waistcoat—and running about like a rat in an emergency—when I was
talking to a Greek boy[3] (the brother of the G[ree]k Girls in Argostoli)
and telling him the fact that there was no danger for the passengers
whatever there might be for the vessel—and assuring him that I could
save both him and myself—without difficulty (though he can't swim)
as the water though deep was not very rough—the wind *not* blowing
right on shore—(it was a blunder of the Greeks who missed stays)
the Doctor exclaimed—"Save *him* indeed—by G–d—save *me* rather—
I'll be first if I can" a piece of Egotism which he pronounced with such
emphatic simplicity—as to set all who had leisure to hear him laughing
—and in a minute after—the vessel drove off again after striking twice
—she sprung a small leak—but nothing further happened except that
the Captain was very nervous afterwards.—To be brief—we had bad
weather almost always—though not contrary—slept on deck in the wet
generally—for seven or eight nights—but never was in better health
(I speak personally) so much so that I actually bathed for a quarter of
an hour on the evening of the fourth inst. in the sea—(to kill the fleas
and others) and was all the better for it.———We were received at
Messolonghi with all kinds of kindness and honours—and the sight of
the fleet saluting &c. and the crowds and different costumes was

[2] Captain of the Greek "bombard" when it was captured by the Turkish vessel
and taken into harbour at Patras. The fact that he had once saved the life of the
Captain of the Turkish ship accounted for the good treatment of Gamba and his
eventual release with all his cargo.

[3] Lukas Chalandritsanos, who had been sent to Missolonghi by land but
apparently returned with a Greek boat which came to escort Byron into port.

really picturesque.—We think of undertaking an expedition soon[4]— and I expect to be ordered with the Suliotes to join the army—all well at present—we found Gamba already arrived—and every thing in good condition.—Remembrance to all friends—

yrs. ever

N B

P.S.—You will I hope use every exertion to realize the Assetts— for besides what I have already advanced—I have undertaken to maintain the Suliotes for a year—([and] accompany them either as a Chief or [word torn out with seal] whichever is most agreeable to the Government) besides sundries.—I do not quite understand Browne's *"letter of Credit"*—I neither gave nor ordered a letter of Credit that I know of—(and though of course if you have done it—I will be responsible) I was not aware of any thing—except that I would have backed his bills—which you said was unnecessary.—As to *orders*—I ordered nothing but some *red* cloth—and oil cloth—both of which I am ready to receive—but if Gamba has exceeded my commission the other things must be sent back *for I cannot permit anything of the kind nor will.* —The Servants' journey will of course be paid for—though *that* is exorbitant.—As for Browne's letter—I do not know anything more than I have said—and I really cannot defray the charges of half Greece and the Frank adventurers besides.——Mr. Barff must send us some dollars soon—for the expences fall on me for the present.——

P.S. 2d.—Jy. 14th. 1824 Will you tell Saint (Jew) Geronimo Corgialegno—that I mean to draw for the balance of my credit with Messrs Webb & Co;—I shall draw for two thousand dollars—(that being about the amount more or less—)but to facilitate the business I shall make the draft payable also at Messrs Ransom and Co's Pall Mall East London.—I believe I already showed you my letters (but if not I have them to show) by which besides the Credits now realizing—you will have perceived that I am not limited to any particular amount of credit with my bankers—The Honourable Douglas my friend and trustee is a principal partner in that house—and having the direction of my affairs—is aware to what extent my present resources may go— and the letters in question were from him.—I can merely say that

---

[4] This was the proposed attack on the fortress of Lepanto (Navpactos), on the north side of the Gulf of Corinth. Byron counted much on leading his Suliote soldiers to the siege, but the assault was postponed and never took place, for the Suliotes were unruly and thought of nothing but extorting money from their foreign leader and refused to "fight against stone walls".

within *the current* year, 1824, besides the money already advanced to the Greek Govt. and the credits now in your hands and yr. partner— (Mr. Barff) which are all from the income of 1823 (I have anticipated nothing from that of the present year hitherto) I shall—or ought to have at my disposition upwards of an hundred thousand dollars— (including my income—and the purchase money of a manor recently sold) and perhaps more—without impinging on my income for 1825— and not including the remaining balance of 1823.—

yrs. ever
N B

P.S.—Many thanks to Colonel Wright and Muir for their exertions about the vessell.—

[TO YUSUFF PASHA]   *J[anuary] 23d. 1824*

Highness—A ship with some of my friends and servants on board was brought under the turrets of a Turkish frigate. It was then released on the order of Your Highness. I thank you, not for having released the ship—since it had a neutral flag and was under English protection, so that no one had the right to detain it—but for having treated my friends with the utmost courtesy—while they were at your disposition. ——In the hope of performing an action not displeasing to Your Highness I have asked the Greek Government here to place four Mussulman prisoners in my hands.—I now release them to Your Highness in recompense, as far as is possible, for your Courtesy.—They are sent without conditions—but if the circumstances could win a place in your memory I would only beg Your Highness to treat with humanity any Greek who may be [captured?] or fall into the hands of the Mussulmans—Since the horrors of war are sufficient in themselves without adding cold-blooded ruthlessness on either side.—

I have the honour to be etc. etc. etc.[1]

[TO THOMAS MOORE]   *Messolonghi. Western Greece. March 4th. 1824*

My dear Moore/—Your reproach is unfounded. I have received two letters from you and answered both previous to leaving Cephalonia.— I have not been "quiet" in an Ionian Island but much occupied with

---

[1] The original draft of this letter was written by Byron in Italian and copied by Count Gamba. Translated by Antony Peattie.

business—as the G[ree]k Deputies (if arrived) can tell you.—Neither have I continued "Don Juan"—nor any other poem—you go as usual—I presume by some newspaper report or other.[1]——When the proper moment to be of some use—arrived—I came here—and am told that my arrival (with some other circumstances—) *has* been of at least temporary advantage to the Cause.—I had a narrow escape from the Turks—and another from Shipwreck on my passage.—On the 15th. (or 16th.) Fy.—I had an attack of Apoplexy or Epilepsy—the physicians have not exactly decided *which*—but the Alternative is agreeable.——My Constitution therefore remains between the two opinions—like Mahomet's sarcophagus between the Magnets.[2]——All that I can say is—that they nearly bled me to death—by placing the leeches too near the temporal Artery—so that the blood could with difficulty be stopped even with Caustic. I am supposed to be getting better, slowly however—but my homilies will, I presume, for the future—be like the Archbishop of Granada's.—In this case "I order you a hundred ducats from my treasurer and wish you a little more taste."[3]—

For Public matters I refer you to Col. Stanhope's and Capt. Parry's reports—and to all other reports whatsoever.——There is plenty to do—war without—and tumult within—they "kill a man a week" like Bob Acres in the country.[4]—Parry's Artificers have gone away in alarm—on account of a dispute—in which some of the natives and foreigners were engaged—and a Swede was killed—and a Suliote wounded.—In the middle of their fright—there was a strong shock of an Earthquake—so between that and the sword—they boomed off in a hurry—in despite of all dissuasions to the contrary.——A Turkish brig ran ashore the other day—and was burnt to prevent her from being taken.—I have obtained the release of about thirty Turkish prisoners—and have adopted one little girl of about nine years old—her name is Hato or Hatagée—her family were nearly all destroyed in the troubles.—If I live—she will be provided for respectably—as I mean to send her to my daughter.—I hope that she will turn out well.

---

[1] Moore had written that he had heard that "instead of pursuing heroic and war-like adventures, he was residing in a delightful villa, continuing 'Don Juan'" (Gamba, *Narrative*, p. 48). Byron was irritated by this conception of his activities and was cooler than usual in his reply to Moore.

[2] It was common legend that Mahomet's tomb was suspended in air between two loadstones. It was referred to by Prior (*Alma*, II, 199, 200), and by Scott in *Quentin Durward* (Chapter 4).

[3] *Gil Blas*, Book IV, Chap. 4.

[4] *The Rivals*, Act IV, scene 1.

—You—I presume—are either publishing or meditating that same.—
Let me hear from and of you—and believe me in all events

ever and truly[5] yrs.
N B

P.S.—Tell Mr. Murray that I wrote to him the other day—and hope
that he has received or will receive the letter.

[TO COUNTESS TERESA GUICCIOLI]   *March 17th, 1824*

[At end of letter from Pietro Gamba to Teresa]

My dearest T.—The Spring is come—I have seen a Swallow to-day
—and it was time—for we have had but a wet winter hitherto—even in
Greece.—We are all very well, which will I hope—keep up your
hopes and Spirits. I do not write to you letters about politics—which
would only be tiresome, and yet we have little else to write about—
except some private anecdotes which I reserve for "viva voce" when
we meet—to divert you at the expense of Pietro and some others.—
The Carnival here is curious—though not quite so elegant as those of
Italy.——

We are a good many foreigners here of all Nations—and a curious
mixture they compose.——I write to you in English without apologies
—as you say you have become a great proficient in that language of
birds.——To the English and Greeks—I generally write in Italian—
from a Spirit of contradiction, I suppose—and to show that I am
Italianized by my long stay in your Climate.——Salute Costa and his
lady—and Papa and Olimpia and Giulia and Laurina—and believe
me—dearest T. t.A.A.—in E.[1]

N Bn

[TO JOHN BOWRING]   *Messolonghi. March 30th. 1824*

Dear Sir—Signor Zaimi the third Greek Deputy will deliver this
letter of introduction—which he has requested—although I told him
that it was superfluous as his name and nation were ample recommendation in themselves.—I have received yrs of the 4th. February in which

---

[5] When he printed this letter, Moore, who could not bear to have the public
think that Byron was less cordial than usual in his last letter to him, changed this to
"Ever and affectionately yours".

[1] Tua Amico ed Amante in Eterno (Your friend and lover forever).

you mention having received mine of the 10th and 12th 9bre. 1823.—
—As you merely allude to them—and do not state the receipt of
several other communications—addrest either to yourself or to Mr.
Hobhouse for your perusal—some of them containing documents of
considerable importance relative to the Cause or information connected
with it—I am to conclude that these have not arrived.——

Col. Stanhope's and Capt. Parry's reports will have informed the
Committee of what is doing or has been done here—and Signor Zaimi
will be able to communicate still further—what will render any detail
of mine unnecessary.———I shall observe the Committee's directions
with regard to the Officers and Medical men. Mr. Tyndale [sic][1] had
stated to me—that he *had* a claim on the Committee for 35 £ Sterling
—as passage money—and some others of the Officers foreign or native
—have preferred in a slighter degree—similar pretensions.—To Mr.
Tyndale I advanced 100 dollars—and to the Germans a smaller sum.
——I am not stating this—as calling upon the Committee to *repay me*
—sensible that such advances are at my own risk—but I do wish
seriously to impress upon the Committee—either *not* to send out
officers of any description—or to provide for their maintenance.———I
am at this moment paying nearly *thirty Officers**, of whom five and
twenty would not have bread to eat (in Greece that is) if I did not.
——Even their rations are obtained with difficulty—and their actual
pay comes from myself.———I am called to a meeting at Salona—with
Ulysses and other Chiefs—on business in a few days—the weather and
the flooding of the rivers has delayed P[rince] Mavrocordato and myself for some time—but appear to be now settling.——

The News of the Loan have [has] excited much expectation and
pleasure amongst the Greeks[2]—the dissensions in the Morea still

* [Byron's marginal note] It is to be observed however that most of
these are either German or other foreigners, but very few of the
English are better provided—it is true that they do not claim actual
pay from the Committee—but they state that hopes were held out to
them which the Greek Govt have not realized.——

[1] Tindall helped Dr. Millingen establish a dispensary in Missolonghi in
January and then left for Athens.

[2] The first loan to the Greeks was signed by the Deputies, Jean Orlando and
Andreas Luriottis on February 21, 1824. It was in the name of the London Greek
Committee, but it was actually negotiated by the bankers Loughnan, Son, and
O'Brien, who acted as agents and took a large commission. The loan was ostensibly
for £800,000, but it was discounted at 41 per cent, so that the purchasers paid only
£59 for £100 of stock. It was guaranteed by the whole national wealth of Greece.
Since two years' interest at 5 per cent was withheld, the Greek Government was to
receive only about £300,000 after all deductions. Byron, Stanhope, and Col.

continue—and hamper them a good deal—but the Opening of the Campaign will probably re-unite the parties—at least—if that do not —nothing will.——P[rince] Mavrocordato will write to you by this opportunity—I cashed some bills for him (for 550 £ Sterling) lately-drawn by him on you—for which—he says that S.S. Orlando and Luriotti have assetts to answer the amount.—This you will know better than I can do.—I have the honour to be

yr. very obedt. and faithful Servt.

Noel Byron

P.S.—I shall continue to pursue my former plan of stating to the Committee things as they *really* are—I am an enemy to Cant of all kinds—but it will be seen in time—who are or are not the firmest friends of the Greek Cause—or who will stick by them longest—the Lempriere dictionary quotation Gentlemen—or those who neither dissemble their faults nor their virtues.—"I could mouthe"[3] as well as any of them if I liked it—but I reserved (when I was in the habit of writing) such things for verse—in business—plain prose is best—and simplest—and was so—I take it even amongst the antient Greeks themselves—if we may judge from their history. You surprize me by what you say of Baring[4]—I thought that he had been a wiser man.—It would have been a very good reason for not lending money to the offender—but I do not see what the Greeks had to do with the offence. ——They may say what they will of the work in question[5]—but it will stand—and as high as most others in time.——This latter observation is addrest to you—as an *author*—I have only recently received your translation[6]—from which I promise myself much pleasure—the Russians are greatly obliged to you—but I did not know that you so greatly admired their Czar—their poetry—at least in your version—will be [words torn off with seal] than [words torn off] princes. Remember me to any acquaintances or friends of the C[ommitt]ee and to the two Deputies.

Napier were named as commissioners. But when the first instalment arrived in Zante in May in the *Florida*, Byron was dead and it was held by Samuel Barff for some time before a new commissioner was appointed. In the meantime the *Florida* carried Byron's body back to England. For an account of the complicated speculations and peculations connected with the Loan both in England and in Greece, see St. Clair, *That Greece Might Still Be Free*, p. 209 ff.

[3] *Hamlet*, Act V, scene 1.

[4] Baring Brothers were international bankers. The particular reference here is not clear, but it must have had something to do with the Greek loan.

[5] *Don Juan?*

[6] Bowring had published *Specimens of the Russian Poets*, his own English translations of selected Russian authors.

On This Day I Complete My
Thirty-Sixth Year

'Tis time this heart should be unmoved,
   Since others it hath ceased to move:
Yet though I cannot be beloved,
     Still let me love!

My days are in the yellow leaf;
   The flowers and fruits of Love are gone;
The worm—the canker, and the grief
     Are mine alone!

The fire that on my bosom preys
   Is lone as some Volcanic Isle;
No torch is kindled at its blaze
     A funeral pile!

The hope, the fear, the jealous care,
   The exalted portion of the pain
And power of Love I cannot share,
     But wear the chain.

But 'tis not *thus*—and 'tis not *here*
   Such thoughts should shake my Soul, nor *now*
Where Glory decks the hero's bier
     Or binds his brow.

The Sword, the Banner, and the Field,
   Glory and Greece around us see!
The Spartan borne upon his shield
     Was not more free!

Awake (not Greece—she *is* awake!)
   Awake, my Spirit! think through *whom*
Thy life-blood tracks its parent lake
     And then strike home!

Tread those reviving passions down
    Unworthy Manhood—unto thee
Indifferent should the smile or frown
    Of Beauty be.

If thou regret'st thy Youth, *why live?*
    The land of honourable Death
Is here:—up to the Field, and give
    Away thy Breath'.

Seek out—less often sought than found—
    A Soldier's Grave, for thee the best;
Then look around, and choose thy Ground,
    And take thy Rest!

Missolonghi,
January 22, 1824

    Byron's final entry in his last journal

ANTHOLOGY OF MEMORABLE PASSAGES IN BYRON'S LETTERS AND JOURNALS

AGE

. . . it was one of the deadliest and heaviest feelings of my life to feel that I was no longer a boy.—From that moment I began to grow old in my own esteem—and in my esteem age is not estimable.

"Detached Thoughts", No.72 (Vol.9, p. 37)

1821. Here lies interred in the Eternity of the Past, from whence there is no Resurrection for the Days—whatever there may be for the Dust —the Thirty-Third Year of an ill-spent Life, which, after a lingering disease of many months sunk into a lethargy, and expired, January 22d, 1821, A.D. leaving a successor Inconsolable for the very loss which occasioned its Existence.

Ravenna Journal, Jan.22, 1822 (Vol.8, p.32)

[Bartolini bust] . . . it exactly resembles a superannuated Jesuit. . . . though my mind misgives me that it is hideously like. If it is—I can not be long for this world—for it overlooks seventy.

Sept.23, 1822, to Murray (Vol.9, p.213)

AMERICA

America is a Model of force and freedom & moderation—with all the coarseness and rudeness of its people.

Oct.12, 1821, to Hobhouse (Vol.8, p.240)

I would rather . . . have a nod from an American, than a snuff-box from an emperor.   *June 8, 1822, to Moore (Vol.9, p.171)*

ATHENS

I am living in the Capuchin Convent, Hymettus before me, the Acropolis behind, the temple of Jove to my right, the Stadium in front, the town to the left, eh, Sir, there's a situation, there's your picturesque! nothing like that, Sir, in Lunnun, no not even the Mansion House. And I feed upon Woodcocks & red Mullet every day, & I have three horses (one a present from the Pacha of the Morea) and I ride to Piraeus, & Phalerum & Munichia . . . I wish to be sure I had a few books, one's own works for instance, any damned nonsense on a long Evening.

Jan.20, 1811, to Hodgson (Vol.2, p.37)

CAVALIER SERVENTE

But I feel & feel it bitterly—that a man should not consume his life at the side and on the bosom—of a woman—and a stranger—that even the recompense and it is much—is not enough—and that this Cicisbean existence is to be condemned.—But I have neither the strength of mind to break my chain, nor the insensibility which would deaden it's weight.   *Aug.23, 1819, to Hobhouse (Vol.6, p.214)*

I am not tired of Italy—but a man must be a Cicisbeo and a singer in duets and a Connoisseur of operas—or nothing here—I have made some progress in all these accomplishments—but I can't say that I don't feel the degradation.—Better be a[n] unskilful planter—an awkward settler—better be a hunter—or anything than a flatterer of fiddlers—and a fan-carrier of a woman.—I like women—God he knows —but the more their system here developes upon me—the worse it seems—after Turkey too—here the *polygamy* is all on the female side. —I have been an intriguer, a husband, and now I am a Cavalier Servente.—by the holy!—it is a strange sensation.
                    Oct.3, 1819, to Hobhouse (Vol.6, p.226)

I have settled into regular Serventismo—and find it the happiest state of all—always excepting Scarmentado's.
                    Mar.3, 1820, to Hobhouse (Vol.7, p.51)

CHILDREN

I hear you have been increasing his Majesty's Subjects, which in these times of War & tribulation is really patriotic, notwithstanding Malthus tells us that were it not for Battle, Murder, & Sudden death, we should be overstocked, I think we have latterly had a redundance of these national benefits, & therefore I give you all credit for your matronly behaviour.   *Aug.21, 1811, to Augusta Leigh (Vol.2, p.74)*

I don't know what Scrope Davies meant by telling you I liked Children, I abominate the sight of them so much that I have always had the greatest respect for the character of *Herod*.
                    Aug.30, 1811, to Augusta Leigh (Vol.2, p.84)

If we meet in Octbr. we will travel in my *Vis*—& can have a cage for the children & a Cart for the Nurse.
                    Sept.2, 1811, to Augusta Leigh (Vol.2, p.88)

The place is very well & quiet & the children only scream in a low voice. *Sept.21, 1813, to Lady Melbourne (Vol.3, p.116)*

I have a particular dislike to anything of S[helley]'s being within the same walls with Mr. Hunt's children.—They are dirtier and more mischievous than Yahoos[;] what they can['t] destroy with their filth they will with their fingers. . . . Poor Hunt with his six little blackguards are coming slowly up . . . was there ever such a *kraal* out of the Hottentot Country before?
Oct.4, 1822, to Mary Shelley (Vol.10, p.11)

CONSISTENCY

You accuse yourself of "apparent inconsistencies"—to me they have not appeared—on the contrary—your consistency has been the most *formidable* Apparition I have encountered.
Sept.7, 1814, to Annabella Milbanke (Vol.4, p.168)

COURAGE

. . . the French Courage proceeds from vanity—the German from phlegm—the Turkish from fanaticism & opium—the Spanish from pride—the English from coolness—the Dutch from obstinacy—the Russian from insensibility—but the *Italian* from *anger*—so you will see that they will spare nothing.
Aug.31, 1820, to Murray (Vol.7, p.169)

CUCKOLDOM

I am still remote from *marriage*, & presume whenever that takes place, "even-handed Justice" will return me cuckoldom in abundance.
Nov.27, 1812, to Hobhouse (Vol.2, p.251)

DEATH

I have seen a thousand graves opened—and always perceived that whatever was gone—the *teeth and hair* remained of those who had died with them.——Is not this odd?—they go the very first things in youth —& yet last the longest in the dust . . .
Nov.18, 1820, to Murray (Vol.7, p.228)

DON JUAN

It is called "Don Juan", and is meant to be a little quietly facetious upon every thing. *Sept.19, 1818, to Moore (Vol.6, p.67)*

. . . but I *protest*. If the poem has poetry—it would stand—if not—fall
—the rest is "leather and prunella" . . . Dullness is the only annihil-
ator in such cases.—As to the Cant of the day—I despise it—as I have
ever done all its other finical fashions,—which become you as paint
became the Antient Britons.—If you admit this prudery—you must
omit half Ariosto—La Fontaine—Shakespeare—Beaumont—Fletcher
—Massinger—Ford—all the Charles second writers—in short, *Something* of most who have written before Pope—and are worth reading—
and much of Pope himself. . . *Jan.25, 1819, to Murray (Vol.6, p.95)*

You sha'n't make *Canticles* of my Cantos. The poem will please if it is
lively—if it is stupid it will fail—but I will have none of your damned
cutting & slashing. . . . So you and Mr. Foscolo &c. want me to undertake what you call a "great work" an Epic poem I suppose or some
such pyramid.—I'll try no such thing—I hate tasks—and then "seven
or eight years!" God send us all well this day three months—let alone
years—if one's years can't be better employed than in sweating poesy
—a man had better be a ditcher.—And works too!—is Childe Harold
nothing? you have so many *"divine"* poems, is it nothing to have
written a *Human* one? without any of your worn out machinery.
                    April 6, 1819, to Murray (Vol.6, p.105)

Don Juan shall be an entire horse or none. . . . I will not give way to
all the Cant of Christendom.
                    Jan.19, 1819, to Hobhouse and Kinnaird (Vol.6, p.91)

You talk of "approximations to indelicacy"—this reminds me of
George Lamb's quarrel at Cambridge with Scrope Davies—"Sir—
said George—he *hinted at my illegitimacy*," "Yes," said Scrope—"I
called him a damned adulterous bastard"—the approximation and the
hint are not unlike.   *May 21, 1819, to Murray (Vol.6, p.138)*

. . . you are too earnest and eager about a work never intended to be
serious;—do you suppose that I could have any intention but to giggle
and make giggle?—a playful satire with as little poetry as could be
helped—was what I meant. . . *Aug.12, 1819, to Murray (Vol.6, p.208)*

As to "Don Juan"—confess—confess—you dog—and be candid—
that it is the sublime of *that there* sort of writing—it may be bawdy—
but is it not good English?—it may be profligate—but is it not *life*, is
it not *the thing*?—Could any man have written it—who has not lived
in the world?—and tooled in a post-chaise? in a hackney coach? in a

Gondola? Against a wall? in a court carriage? in a vis a vis?—on a table?—and under it?   *Oct.26, [1819], to Kinnaird (Vol.6, p.232)*

There has been an eleventh commandment to the women not to read it—and what is still more extraordinary they seem not to have broken it.——But that can be of little import to them poor things—for the reading or non-reading a book—will never keep down a single petti-coat. . . .   *Oct.29, 1819, to Hoppner (Vol.6, p.237)*

The truth is that *it is too true*—and the women hate every thing which strips off the tinsel of *Sentiment*—& they are right—or it would rob them of their weapons.   *Oct.12, 1820, to Murray (Vol.7, p.202)*

The 5th. is so far from being the last of D. J. that it is hardly the beginning.—I meant to take him the tour of Europe—with a proper mixture of siege—battle—and adventure—and to make him finish as *Anacharsis Cloots*—in the French revolution.—To how many cantos this may extend—I know not—nor whether (even if I live) I shall complete it—but this was my notion.—I meant to have him made a Cavalier Servente in Italy and a cause for divorce in England—and a Sentimental "Werther-faced man" in Germany—so as to show the different ridicules of the society in each of those countries——and to have displayed him gradually gaté and blasé as he grew older—as is natural.—But I had not quite fixed whether to make him end in Hell—or in an unhappy marriage,—not knowing which would be the severest. —The Spanish tradition says Hell—but it is probably only an Allegory of the other state.   *Feb.16, 1821, to Murray (Vol.8, p.78)*

D[on] Juan will be known by and bye for what it is intended a *satire* on *abuses* of the present *states* of Society—and not an eulogy of vice;—it may be now and then voluptuous—I can't help that—Ariosto is worse —Smollett (see Lord Strutwell in vol 2d. of R[oderick] R[andom]) ten times worse—and Fielding no better.——No Girl will ever be seduced by reading D[on] J[uan]—no—no—she will go to Little's poems—& Rousseau's romans—for that—or even to the immaculate De Stael—— they will encourage her—and not the Don—who laughs at that—and —and—most other things.   *Dec.25, 1822, to Murray (Vol.10, p.68)*

DRINKING
Like other parties of the kind, it was first silent, then talky, then argu-mentative, then disputatious, then unintelligible, then altogethery,

then inarticulate, and then drunk. When we had reached the last step of this glorious ladder, it was difficult to get down again without stumbling;—and, to crown all, Kinnaird and I had to conduct Sheridan down a d——d corkscrew staircase, which had certainly been constructed before the discovery of fermented liquors, and to which no legs, however crooked, could possibly accomodate themselves. . . . Both he and Colman were, as usual, very good; but I carried away much wine, and the wine had previously carried away my memory; so that all was hiccup and happiness for the last hour or so, and I am not impregnated with any of the conversation.

Oct.31, 1815, to Moore (Vol. 4, pp.326–327)

ENNUI
J[ohn] Claridge is here, improved in person a good deal, & amiable, but not amusing, now here is a good man, a handsome man, an honourable man, a most inoffensive man, a well informed man, and a *dull* man, & this last damned epithet undoes all the rest; there is S[crope] B[erdmore] D[avies] with perhaps not better intellects, & certes not half his sterling qualities, is the life & soul of me, & every body else; but my old friend with the soul of honour & the zeal of friendship & a vast variety of insipid virtues, can't keep me or himself awake.

Sept.20, 1811, to Hobhouse (Vol.2, pp.102–103)

I shall not entertain you with a long list of *attributes* [of Lady Oxford], but merely state that I have not been guilty of once *yawning* in the eternity of two months under the same roof—a phenomenon in my history. . . .   *Dec.31, 1812, to Lady Melbourne (Vol.2, p.265)*

FREEDOM
There is no freedom in Europe—that's certain—it is besides a worn out portion of the globe.

Oct.3, 1819, to Hobhouse (Vol.6, pp.226–227)

FRIENDSHIP
I have always laid it down as a maxim—and found it justified by experience—that a man and a woman—make far better friendships than can exist between two of the same sex—but *then* with the condition— that they never have made—or are to make love to each other.— Lovers may [be]—and indeed generally are—enemies—but they never can be friends—because there must always be a spice of jealousy—and a something of Self in all their speculations.—Indeed I rather look

upon Love altogether as a sort of hostile transaction—very necessary to make—or to break—matches and keep the world a-going—but by no means a sinecure to the parties concerned.

Dec.1, 1822, to Lady Hardy (Vol.10, p.50)

GAMBLING

I have a notion that Gamblers are as happy as most people—being always *excited*;—women—wine—fame—the table—even Ambition—*sate* now & then—but every turn of the card—& cast of the dice—keeps the Gambler alive—besides one can Game ten times longer than one can do any thing else.

"Detached Thoughts", No.33 (Vol.9, p.23)

GREEKS

The supplies of the Committee are some useful—and all excellent in their kind—but occasionally hardly *practical* enough—in the present state of Greece—for instance the Mathematical instruments are thrown away—none of the Greeks know a problem from a poker—we must conquer first—and plan afterwards. The use of the trumpets too may be doubted—unless Constantinople were Jericho.

Dec.26, 1823, to Bowring (Vol.11, p.83)

The opposition say they want to cajole me—and the party in power say the others want to seduce me. . . . It is not of their ill-usage (which I should know how to repel or at least endure perhaps) but of *their good* treatment that I am apprehensive—for it is difficult not to allow our private impressions to predominate—and if these Gentlemen *have* any undue interest and discover my weak side—viz—a propensity to be governed—and were to set a pretty woman or a clever woman about me—with a turn for political or any other sort of intrigue—why—they would make a fool of me—no very difficult matter probably even without such an intervention.———But if I can keep passion—at least that passion—out of the question—(which may be the more easy as I left my heart in Italy) they will not weather me with quite so much facility.

Oct.25, 1823, to Barry (Vol.11, pp.54–55)

As I did not come here to join a faction but a nation—and to deal with honest men and not with speculators or peculators—(charges bandied about daily by the Greeks of each other) it will require much circumspection to avoid the character of a partizan. . . . Whoever goes into Greece at present should do it as Mrs. Fry went into Newgate—not in the expectation of meeting with any especial indication of existing probity—but in the hope that time and better treatment will reclaim the present burglarious and larcenous tendencies which have followed this General Gaol delivery.

Journal in Cephalonia, Sept.28, 1823 (Vol.11, p.32)

HOMOSEXUALS

[Veli Pasha] He said he wished all the old men . . . to go to his father, but the young ones to come to him, to use his own expression "vecchio con vecchio, Giovane con Giovane". . . . All this is very well, but he has an awkward manner of throwing his arm round one's waist, and squeezing one's hand in *public*, which is a high compliment, but very much embarrasses *"ingenuous youth"*. . . . He asked if I did not think it very proper that as *young* men (he has a beard down to his middle) we should live together, with a variety of other sayings, which made Stranè stare and puzzled me in my replies.

Aug.16, 1810, to Hobhouse (Vol.2, p.10)

At Vostitza I found my dearly-beloved Eustathius—ready to follow me not only to England, but to Terra Incognita. . . . The next morning I found the dear soul upon horseback clothed very sprucely in Greek Garments, with those ambrosial curls hanging down his amiable back, and to my utter astonishment and the great abomination of Fletcher, a *parasol* in his hand to save his complexion from the heat.

July 29, 1810, to Hobhouse (Vol.2, p.6)

But my friend as you may easily imagine is Nicolo, who by the bye, is my Italian master, and we are already very philosophical.—I am his "Padrone" and his "amico" and the Lord knows what besides, it is about two hours since that after informing me he is most desirous to follow *him* (that is me) over the world, he concluded by telling me it was proper for us not only to live but "morire insieme".

Aug.23, 1810, to Hobhouse (Vol.2, p.12)

ILLNESS

Here be also two physicians, one of whom trusts to his Genius (never having studied) the other to a campaign of eighteen months against the sick of Otranto, which he made in his youth with great effect.— When I was seized with my disorder, I protested against both these assassins, but what can a helpless, feverish, toasted and watered poor wretch do? in spite of my teeth & tongue, the English Consul, my

Tartar, Albanians, Dragoman forced a physician upon me, and in three days vomited and glystered me to the last gasp.—In this state I made my epitaph, take it,

> Youth, Nature, and relenting Jove
> To keep my *lamp in* strongly strove,
> But Romanelli was so stout
> He beat all three—and *blew* it *out.*—

But Nature and Jove being piqued at my doubts, did in fact at last beat Romanelli, and here I am well but weakly, at your service.

Oct.3, 1810, to Hodgson (Vol.2, pp.18–19)

I am in bad health & worse spirits, being afflicted in body with what Hostess Quickly in Henry 5th. calls a villainous "*Quotidian Tertian.*" It killed Falstaff & may me. I had it first in the Morea last year, and it returned in Quarantine [at Malta] in this infernal oven, and the fit comes on every other day, reducing me first to the chattering penance of Harry Gill, and then mounting me up to a Vesuvian pitch of fever, lastly quitting me with sweats that render it necessary for me to have a man and horse all night to change my linen.

May 15, 1811, to Hobhouse (Vol.2, p.44)

ITALIANS

As a very pretty woman said to me a few nights ago, with the tears in her eyes, as she sat at the harpsichord, "Alas! the Italians must now return to making operas." I fear *that* and macaroni are their forte...
[On the failure of the Carbonari uprising]

April 28, 1821, to Moore (Vol.8, p.105)

LANGUAGES

By way of divertisement, I am studying daily, at an Armenian monastery, the Armenian language. I found that my mind wanted something craggy to break upon; and this—as the most difficult thing I could discover here for an amusement—I have chosen to torture me into attention.

Dec.5, 1816, to Moore (Vol.5, p. 130)

... I fell in love ... I shall think that—and the Armenian Alphabet—will last the winter—the lady has luckily for me been less obdurate than the language—or between the two I should have lost my remains of sanity.

Dec.4, 1816, to Murray (Vol.5, p. 138)

LIFE AND CHARACTER

... I am so convinced of the advantages of looking at mankind instead of reading about them, and of the bitter effects of staying at home with all the narrow prejudices of an Islander, that I think there should be a law amongst us to set our young men abroad for a term among the few allies our wars have left us.

Jan.14, 1811, to Mrs. Byron (*Vol.2, p. 34*)

. . . anything that confirms or extends one's observations on life & character delights me even when I don't know people. . . .

Oct.1, 1813, to Lady Melbourne (*Vol.3, p. 129*)

All are inclined to believe what they covet, from a lottery-ticket up to a passport to Paradise,—in which, from description, I see nothing very tempting.

Journal, Nov.27, 1813 (*Vol. 3, p.225*)

When one subtracts from life infancy (which is vegetation),—sleep, eating, and swilling—buttoning and unbuttoning—how much remains of downright existence? The summer of a dormouse.

Journal, Dec.7, 1813 (*Vol.3, p.235*)

. . . but what is Hope? nothing but the paint on the face of Existence; the least touch of truth rubs it off, and then we see what a hollow-cheeked harlot we have got hold of.

Oct.28, 1815, to Moore (*Vol.4, p.323*)

. . . whenever I meet with any-thing agreeable in this world it surprizes me so much—and pleases me so much (when my passions are not interested in one way or the other) that I go on wondering for a week to come. *June 6, 1819, to Hoppner* (*Vol.6, p.147*)

The lapse of ages *changes* all things—time—language—the earth—the bounds of the sea—the stars of the sky, and every thing "about, around, and underneath" man, *except man himself*, who has always been, and always will be, an unlucky rascal. The infinite variety of lives conduct but to death, and the infinity of wishes lead but to disappointment. All the discoveries which have yet been made have multiplied little but existence. *Jan.9, 1821, Journal* (*Vol.8, pp.19–20*)

What a strange thing is the propagation of life!—A bubble of Seed which may be spilt in a whore's lap—or in the Orgasm of a voluptuous dream—might (for aught we know) have formed a Caesar or a Buona-

parte—there is nothing remarkable recorded of their Sires—that I
know of—   *"Detached Thoughts"*, No.102 (*Vol.9, p.47*)

LITERATI
[No affectations in Scott, Gifford, and Moore] . . . as for the rest
whom I have known—there was always more or less of the author
about them—the pen peeping from behind the ear—& the thumbs a
little inky or so.   *Mar.25, 1817, to Murray (Vol.5, p.192)*

In general I do not draw well with Literary men—not that I dislike
them but—I never know what to say to them after I have praised their
last publication.   *"Detached Thoughts"*, No.53 (*Vol.9, p.30*)

LITERATURE
But I hate things *all fiction* . . . there should always be some foundation
of fact for the most airy fabric—and pure invention is but the talent of
a liar.   *April 2, 1817, to Murray (Vol.5, p.203)*

If I live ten years longer, you will see, however, that it is not over with
me—I don't mean in literature, for that is nothing; and it may seem
odd enough to say, I do not think it my vocation.
                            Feb.28, 1817, to Moore (Vol.5, p.177)

LONDON
And so—you want to come to London—it is a damned place—to be
sure—but the only one in the world—(at least in the English world)
for fun—though I have seen parts of the Globe that I like better—still
upon the whole it is the completest either to help one in feeling oneself
alive—or forgetting that one is so.
                            Mar.1, 1816, to James Hogg (Vol.5, p.38)

LOVE
. . . to give you some idea of my late life, I have this moment received
a prescription from Pearson, not for any *complaint* but from *debility*,
and literally *too much Love*.—You know my devotion to woman, but
indeed Southwell was much mistaken in conceiving my adorations were
paid to any Shrine there, no, my Paphian Goddesses are elsewhere, and
I have sacrificed at their altar rather too liberally.—In fact, my blue
eyed Caroline, who is only sixteen, has been lately so *charming*, that
though we are both in perfect health, we are at present commanded to
repose, being nearly worn out. *Feb.26, 1808, to Becher (Vol.1, p.157)*

Bland (the *Revd*) has been challenging an officer of Dragoons, about a *whore*, & my assistance being required, I interfered in time to prevent him from losing his *life* or his *Living*.—The man is mad, Sir, mad, frightful as a Mandrake, & lean as a rutting Stag, & all about a bitch not worth a Bank token.—She is a common Strumpet as his Antagonist assured me, and he means to marry her, Hodgson meant to marry her, the officer meant to marry her, her first Seducer (seventeen years ago) meant to marry her, and all this is owing to the *Comet*!

Nov.16, 1811, to Hobhouse (Vol.2, pp.129–130)

It is true from early habit, one must make love mechanically as one swims, I was once very fond of both, but now as I never swim unless I tumble into the water, I don't make love till almost obliged. . . .

Sept.10, 1812, to Lady Melbourne (Vol.2, p.193)

I . . . determined—not to *pursue*, for pursuit it was not—but to *sit* still, and in a week after I was convinced—not that [Caroline] loved me— for I do not believe in the existence of what is called Love—but that any other man in my situation would have believed that he *was* loved.

Sept.13, 1812, to Lady Melbourne (Vol.2, p.194)

As to *Love*, that is done in a week (provided the Lady has a reasonable share) besides marriage goes on better with esteem & confidence than romance, & she is quite pretty enough to be loved by her husband, without being so glaringly beautiful as to attract too many rivals.

Sept.18, 1812, to Lady Melbourne (Vol.2, p.199)

I cannot exist without some object of Love.

Nov.9, 1812, to Lady Melbourne (Vol.2, p.243)

. . . but hatred is a much more delightful passion—& never cloys—it will make us all happy for the rest of our lives.

April 19, 1813, to Lady Melbourne (Vol.3, p.41)

[Lady Charlotte Harley, Lady Oxford's daughter] . . . whom I should love forever if she could always be only eleven years old—& whom I shall probably marry when she is old enough & bad enough to be made into a modern wife. *April 5, 1813, to Lady Melbourne (Vol.3, p.36)*

. . . one generally *ends & begins* with Platonism—& as my proselyte is only twenty—there is time enough to materialize—I hope neverthe- less this spiritual system won't last long—and at any rate must make

the experiment.—I remember my last case was the reverse—as Major O'Flaherty recommends "we fought first and explained afterwards."
Oct.8, 1813, to Lady Melbourne (Vol.3, p.135)

This business is growing serious—& I think *Platonism* in some peril.
Oct.8, 1813, to Lady Melbourne (Vol.3, p.136)

We have progressively improved into a less spiritual species of tenderness—but the seal is not yet fixed though the wax is preparing for the impression.   *Oct.14, 1813, to Lady Melbourne (Vol.3, p.145)*

I do detest everything which is not perfectly mutual.
Oct.21, 1813, to Lady Melbourne (Vol.3, p.151)

. . . if people will stop at the first tense of the verb "aimer" they must not be surprised if one finishes the conjugation with somebody else.
Jan.13, 1814, to Lady Melbourne (Vol.4, p.28)

. . . the fact is that my wife if she had common sense would have more power over me—than any other whatsoever—for my heart always alights upon the nearest *perch.* . . .
April 30, 1814, to Lady Melbourne (Vol.4, p.111)

[To a Swiss girl] Excepting your compliments (which are only excusable because you don't know me) you write like a clever woman for which reason I hope you *look* as *un*like one as possible—I never knew but one of your country—Me. de Stael—and she is frightful as a precipice. . . . . If you will become acquainted with me—I will promise not to make love to you unless you like it. . . .
June 8, 1814, to Henrietta D'Ussières (Vol.4, p.122)

[Francis Hodgson] . . . an excellent-hearted fellow, as well as one of the cleverest; a little, perhaps, too much japanned by preferment in the church and the tuition of youth, as well as inoculated with the disease of domestic felicity, besides being over-run with fine feelings about women and *constancy* (that small change of Love, which people exact so rigidly, receive in such counterfeit coin, and repay in baser metal).
Nov.17, 1816, to Moore (Vol.5, p.131)

. . . my Goddess is only the wife of a "Merchant of Venice"—but she is pretty as an Antelope,—is but two & twenty years old—has the large black Oriental eyes—with the Italian countenance—and dark glossy hair of the curl & colour of Lady Jersey's—then she has the voice of a lute—and the song of a Seraph (though not quite so sacred) besides a long postscript of graces—virtues and accomplishments—enough to furnish out a new Chapter for Solomon's song.—But her great merit is finding out mine—there is nothing so amiable as discernment.   *Nov.25, 1816, to Murray (Vol.5, pp.133–134)*

I meant to have given up gallivanting altogether—on leaving your country—where I had been totally sickened of that & every thing else but I know not how it is—my health growing better—& my spirits not worse—the "besoin d'aimer" came back upon my heart again—after all there is nothing like it. *Nov.27, 1816, to Kinnaird (Vol.5, p.135)*

. . . I have fallen in love with a very pretty Venetian of two and twenty with great black eyes—she is married—and so am I—which is very much to the purpose—we have found & sworn an eternal attachment—which has already lasted a lunar month—& I am more in love than ever—& so is the lady—at least she says so,—& seems so,—she does not plague me (which is a wonder—) and I verily believe we are one of the happiest—unlawful couples on this side of the Alps.
                     Dec.18, 1816, to Augusta Leigh (Vol.5, p.141)

[Claire Clairmont] You know—& I believe saw once that odd-headed girl—who introduced herself to me shortly before I left England—but you do not know—that I found her with Shelley and her sister at Geneva—I never loved nor pretended to love her—but a man is a man —& if a girl of eighteen comes prancing to you at all hours—there is but one way—the suite of all this is that she was with *child*—& returned to England to assist in peopling that desolate island . . . This comes of "putting it about" (as Jackson calls it) & be damned to it—and thus people come into the world. *Jan.20, 1817, to Kinnaird (Vol.5, p.162)*

I have fallen in love within the last month with a Romagnuola Countess from Ravenna—the Spouse of a year of Count Guiccioli—who is sixty the Girl twenty—he has eighty thousand ducats of rent—and has had two wives before—but he is Sixty—he is the first of Ravenna Nobles but he is sixty—She is fair as Sunrise—and warm as Noon—we had but ten days—to manage all our little matters in beginning middle and end, & we managed them;—and I have done my duty—with the proper consummation.
                     April 24, 1819, to Kinnaird (Vol.6, p.114)

Farewell, my dearest *Evil*—farewell, my torment—farewell, my *all* (but *not all mine!*) I kiss you more often than I have ever kissed you— and this (if Memory does not deceive me) should be a fine number, counting from the beginning.

Aug.7, 1819, to Countess Guiccioli (*Vol.6, p.203*)

I am all for morality now—and shall confine myself henceforward to the strictest adultery—which you will please to recollect is all that that virtuous wife of mine has left me.

Oct.29, 1819, to Hoppner (*Vol.6, p.238*)

. . . my attachment has neither the blindness of the beginning—nor the microscopic accuracy of the close of such liaisons. . . .

Jan.10, 1820, to Hoppner (*Vol.7, p.24*)

I verily believe that nor you, nor any man of poetical temperament, can avoid a strong passion of some kind. It is the poetry of life. What should I have known or written, had I been a quiet, mercantile politician or a lord in waiting? A man must travel, and turmoil, or there is no existence. Besides, I only meant to be a Cavalier Servente, and had no idea it would turn out a romance, in the Anglo fashion.

Aug.31, 1820, to Moore (*Vol.7, p.170*)

It is awful work, this love, and prevents all a man's projects of good or glory. I wanted to go to Greece lately (as every thing seems up here) with her brother, who is a fine, brave fellow (I have seen him put to the proof), and wild about liberty. But the tears of a woman [Countess Teresa Guiccioli] who has left her husband for a man, and the weakness of one's own heart, are paramount to these projects, and I can hardly indulge them.   *Sept.19, 1821, to Moore* (*Vol.8, p.214*)

I can say that without being so *furiously* in love as at first—I am more attached to her [Countess Guiccioli]—than I thought it possible to be to any woman after three years.

Oct.5, 1821, to Augusta Leigh (*Vol.8, p.234*)

MARRIAGE

[Newstead Abbey] . . . the premises are so delightfully extensive, that two people might live together without ever seeing hearing or meeting,—but I can't feel the comfort of this till I marry.—In short it would be the most amiable matrimonial mansion, & *that* is another great in-

ducement to my plan,—my wife & I shall be so happy,—one in each
Wing. *Aug.30[31?], 1811, to Augusta Leigh (Vol.2, p.86)*

Besides I do not know a single gentlewoman who would venture upon
me, but that seems the only rational outlet from this adventure [his
love affair with Lady Caroline Lamb].——I admired your niece, but
she is engaged to Eden——Besides she deserves a better heart than
mine. What shall I do—shall I *advertise?*
[Sept.30 ?], 1812, to Lady Melbourne (Vol.2, p.222)

. . . as Moore says "a pretty wife is something for the fastidious vanity
of a roué to *retire* upon."
Jan.16, 1814, to Lady Melbourne (Vol.4, p.34)

I have great hopes that we shall love each other all our lives as much
as if we had never married at all.
Dec.5, 1814, to Annabella Milbanke (Vol.4, p.239)

MATHEMATICS
I thank you again for your efforts with my Princess of Parallelograms
[Annabella Milbanke], who has puzzled you more than the Hypothen-
use; . . . her proceedings are quite rectangular, or rather we are two
parallel lines prolonged to infinity side by side but never to meet.
Oct.18, 1812, to Lady Melbourne (Vol.2, p.231)

I agree with you quite upon Mathematics too—and must be content to
admire them at an incomprehensible distance—always adding them to
the catalogue of my regrets—I know that two and two make four—&
should be glad to prove it too if I could—though I must say if by any
sort of process I could convert 2 & 2 into *five* it would give me much
greater pleasure.—The only part I remember which gave me much
delight were those theorems (is that the word?) in which after ringing
the changes upon—A–B & C–D &c. I at last came to "which is
absurd—which is impossible" and at this point I have always arrived
& I fear always shall through life . . .
No.10, 1813, to Annabella Milbanke (Vol.3, p.159)

MEMORY
It is singular how soon we lose the impression of what ceases to be
constantly before us.—A year impairs, a lustre obliterates.—There is
little distinct left without an *effort* of memory,—*then* indeed the lights

are rekindled for a moment—but who can be sure that the Imagination is not the torch-bearer? *"Detached Thoughts", No.51 (Vol.9, p.29)*

MISCELLANY

As for expectations, don't talk to me of "expects" . . . the Baronet is eternal—the Viscount immortal—and my Lady (*senior*) without end.— They grow more healthy every day and I verily believe Sir R[alph] Ly. M[ilbanke] and Lord W[entworth] are at this moment cutting a fresh set of teeth and unless they go off by the usual fever attendant on such children as don't use the "American soothing syrup" that they will live to have them all drawn again.

Jan.26, 1815, to Hobhouse (Vol.4, p. 260)

. . . if I could but manage to arrange my pecuniary concerns in England —so as to pay my debts—& leave me what would be here a very fair income—(though nothing remarkable at home) you might consider me as posthumous—for I would never willingly dwell in the "tight little island".   *Nov.27, 1816, to Kinnaird (Vol.5, p.136)*

Lord G[uilford] died of an inflamation of the bowels: so they took them out, and sent them (on account of their discrepancies), separately from the carcass, to England. Conceive a man going one way, and his intestines another, and his immortal soul a third!—was there ever such a distribution? One certainly has a soul; but how it came to allow itself to be enclosed in a body is more than I can imagine. I only know if once mine gets out, I'll have a bit of a tussle before I let it get in again to that of any other.   *April 11, 1817, to Moore (Vol.5, p.210)*

An old Woman at Rome reading Boccaccio exclaimed "I wish to God that this was saying one's prayers."

July 30, 1819, to Hobhouse (Vol. 6, p.190)

The Cardinal [at Ravenna] is at his wit's end—it is true—that he had not far to go.   *July 22, 1820, to Murray (Vol. 7, p.137)*

Your letter of excuses has arrived.—I receive the letter but do not admit the excuses except in courtesy—as when a man treads on your toes and begs your pardon—the pardon is granted—but the joint aches —especially if there is a corn upon it.

Feb.2, 1821, to Murray (Vol.8, p.73)

As to Lady Noel—what you say of her declining health—would be very well to any one else—but the way to be immortal (I mean *not* to die at all) is to have me for your heir.—I recommend you to put me in your will—& you will see that (as long as *I* live at least) you will never even catch cold.   *Mar.23, 1821, to Kinnaird (Vol.8, p.96)*

MONEY

Whatever Brain-money—you get on my account from Murray—pray remit to me—I will never consent to pay away what I *earn*—that is *mine*—& what I get by my brains—I will spend on my b——ks— as long as I have a tester or a testicle remaining.

Jan.19, 1819, to Kinnaird (Vol.6, p.92)

I have imbibed such a love for money that I keep some Sequins in a drawer to count, & cry over them once a week. . . .

Jan.27, 1819, to Kinnaird (Vol.6, p.98)

If you say that I must sign the bonds—I suppose that I must—but it is very iniquitous to make me pay my debts—you have no idea of the pain it gives one.   *Oct.26, 1819, to Kinnaird (Vol.6, p.232)*

I believe M[urray] to be a good man with a personal regard for me.— But a bargain is in its very essence a *hostile* transaction. . . . do not all men try to abate the price of all they buy?—I contend that a bargain even between brethren—is a declaration of war.—

July 14, 1821, to Kinnaird (Vol.8, p.153)

I will trust no man's honour in affairs of barter.—I will tell you why.— A state of bargain is Hobbes's "state of nature—a state of war."—It is so with all men.—If I come to a friend—and say "friend, lend me five hundred pounds!" he either does it or says he can't or won't.— But if I come to Ditto—and say "Ditto,—I have an excellent house— or horse—or carriage—or M.S.S. or books—or pictures—&c. &c. &c. &c. &c. honestly worth a thousand pounds, you shall have them for five hundred["]——what does Ditto say?—Why he looks at them —he *hums*—he *ha's*—he *humbugs*—if he can—because *it is* a bargain— this is the blood and bone of mankind—and the same man who would lend another a thousand pounds without interest—would not buy a horse of him for half it's value if he could help it.—It is so—there's no denying it—& therefore I will have as much as I can—& you will give

342

as little.—And there's an end.—All men are intrinsical rascals,—and I am only sorry that not being a dog I can't bite them.—
Oct.20, 1821, to Murray (Vol.8, pp.244–245)

As my notions upon the score of monies coincide with yours and all men's who have lived to see that every guinea is a philosopher's stone —or at least his *touch*-stone—you will doubt me the less when I pronounce my firm belief that Cash is Virtue.
Feb.23, 1822, to Kinnaird (Vol.9, p.113)

I always looked to about thirty as the barrier of any real or fierce delight in the passions—and determined to work them out in the younger ore and better veins of the Mine—and I flatter myself (perhaps) that I have pretty well done so—and now the dross is coming— and I loves lucre. . . . *Jan.18, 1823, to Kinnaird (Vol.10, p.87)*

OPINIONS
Opinions are made to be changed—or how is truth to be got at? we don't arrive at it by standing on one leg? or on the first day of our setting out—but though we may jostle one another on the way that is no reason why we should strike or trample—*elbowing's* enough.—I am all for moderation which profession of faith I beg leave to conclude by wishing Mr. Southey damned—not as a poet—but as a politician.
May 9, 1817, to Murray (Vol.5, p.221)

PAINTING
. . . as for Rubens . . . he seems to me (who by the way know nothing of the matter) the most glaring—flaring—staring—harlotry imposter that ever passed a trick upon the senses of mankind—it is not nature— it is not art—with the exception of some linen (which hangs over the cross in one of his pictures) which to do it justice looked like a very handsome table cloth—I never saw such an assemblage of florid nightmares as his canvas contains—his portraits seem clothed in pulpit cushions. *May 1, 1816, to Hobhouse (Vol.5, p.73)*

You must recollect however—that I know nothing of painting—& that I detest it—unless it reminds me of something I have seen or think it possible to see—for which [reason] I spit upon & abhor all the saints & subjects of one half the impostures I see in the churches & palaces. . . . Depend upon it of all the arts it is the most artificial & unnatural—& that by which the nonsense of mankind is the most imposed upon.
April 14, 1817, to Murray (Vol.5, p.213)

COGNI, MARGARITA

. . . with great black eyes and fine [figure]—fit to breed gladiators
from.   *Mar.11, 1818, to Murray (Vol.6, p.23)*

In the autumn one day going to the Lido with my Gondoliers—we
were overtaken by a heavy Squall and the Gondola put in peril—hats
blown away—boat filling—oar lost—tumbling sea—thunder—rain in
torrents—night coming—& wind increasing.—On our return—after a
tight struggle: I found her on the steps of the Mocenigo palace on the
Grand Canal—with her great black eyes flashing through her tears and
the long dark hair which was streaming drenched with rain over her
brows & breast;—she was perfectly exposed to the storm—and the
wind blowing her hair & dress about her tall thin figure—and the
lightning flashing round her—with the waves rolling at her feet—
made her look like Medea alighted from her chariot. . . . Her joy at
seeing me again—was moderately mixed with ferocity—and gave me
the idea of a tigress over her recovered Cubs.
                         Aug.1, 1819, to Murray (Vol.6, p.196)

LAMB, LADY CAROLINE

Then your heart—my poor Caro, what a little volcano! that pours *lava*
through your veins, & yet I cannot wish it a bit colder . . . I have
always thought you the cleverest most agreeable, absurd, amiable,
perplexing, dangerous fascinating little being that lives now or ought
to have lived 2000 years ago.
             [April, 1812?], to Lady Caroline Lamb (Vol.2, pp.170–171)

[*Glenarvon*] It seems to me that, if the authoress had written the *truth*
and nothing but the truth—the whole truth,—the romance would not
only have been more *romantic*, but more entertaining. As for the likeness, the picture can't be good—I did not sit long enough.
                            Dec.5, 1816, to Moore (Vol.5, p.131)

LEIGH, HON. AUGUSTA

I have received all your letters—I believe—which are full of woes—as
usual—megrims & mysteries—but my sympathies remain in suspense
—for—for the life of me I can't make out whether your disorder is a
broken heart or the ear-ache. . . .
                   June 3, 1817, to Hon. Augusta Leigh (Vol.5, p.231)

MELBOURNE, LADY

To Lady Melbourne I write with most pleasure—and her answers, so sensible, so *tactique*—I never met with half her talent. If she had been a few years younger, what a fool she would have made of me, had she thought it worth her while,—and I should have lost a valuable and most agreeable *friend*.   *Journal, Nov.24, 1813 (Vol.3, p.219)*

MILBANKE, ANNABELLA

I have no desire to be better acquainted with Miss Milbank[e], she is too good for a fallen spirit to know or wish to know, & I should like her more if she were less perfect.

May 1, 1812, to Lady Caroline Lamb (Vol.2, p.176)

As to Annabella she requires time & all the cardinal virtues, & in the interim I am a little verging towards one who demands neither, & saves me besides the trouble of marrying by being married already.

Sept.25, 1812, to Lady Melbourne (Vol.2, p.208)

I congratulate A[nnabella] & myself on our mutual escape.—That would have been but a *cold collation*, & I prefer hot suppers.

Nov.14, 1812, to Lady Melbourne (Vol.2, p.246)

. . . here is the strictest of St. Ursula's what do you call 'ems [St. Ursula and her 11,000 virgins]—a wit—a moralist—& religionist— enters into a clandestine correspondence with a personage generally presumed a great Roué—& drags her aged parents into this secret treaty . . . but this comes of *infallibility*.

Sept.28, 1813, to Lady Melbourne (Vol.3, pp.124–125)

I am not now in love with her—but I can't at all foresee that I should not be so if it came "a warm June" (as Falstaff observes) and seriously —I do admire her as a very superior woman a little encumbered with Virtue. . . .   *April 29, 1814, to Lady Melbourne (Vol.4, p.109)*

WEBSTER, JAMES WEDDERBURN

His wife is very pretty, & I am much mistaken if five years from hence she don't give him reason to think so.—Knowing the man, one is apt to fancy these things, but I really thought, she treated him even already with a due portion of conjugal contempt, but I dare say this was only the megrim of a Misogynist.——At present he is the happiest of men, & has asked me to go with them to a tragedy to see his *wife cry*.

Nov.3, 1811, to Hobhouse (Vol.2, p.126)

POETS

BURNS

What an antithetical mind!—tenderness, roughness—delicacy, coarseness—sentiment, sensuality—soaring and grovelling, dirt and deity—all mixed up in that one compound of inspired clay! It is strange; a true voluptuary will never abandon his mind to the grossness of reality. It is by exalting the earthly, the material, the *physique* of our pleasures, by veiling these ideas, by forgetting them altogether, or, at least, never naming them hardly to one's self, that we alone can prevent them from disgusting.   *Journal, Dec.13, 1813 (Vol.3, p.239)*

COLERIDGE

"Christabel"—I won't have you sneer at Christabel—it is a fine wild poem.   *Sept.30, 1816, to Murray (Vol.5, p.108)*

HUNT, LEIGH

He is a good man, with some poetical elements in his chaos; but spoilt by the Christ-Church Hospital and a Sunday newspaper,—to say nothing of the Surry Jail, which conceited him into a martyr. But he is a good man. When I saw "Rimini" in MSS., I told him that I deemed it good poetry at bottom, disfigured only by a strange style. His answer was, that his style was a system, or *upon system*, or some such cant; and, when a man talks of system, his case is hopeless.
                              June 1, 1818, to Moore (Vol.6, p.46)

... I cannot describe to you the despairing sensation of trying to do something for a man who seems incapable or unwilling to do any thing further for himself,—at least, to the purpose. It is like pulling a man out of a river who directly throws himself in again.
                              April 2, 1823, to Murray (Vol.10, p.138)

KEATS

Johnny Keats's *p–ss a bed* poetry. . . .
                              Oct.12, 1820, to Murray (Vol.7, p.200)

The Edinburgh praises Jack Keats or Ketch or whatever his names are;—why his is the *Onanism* of Poetry. . . .
                              Nov.4, 1820, to Murray (Vol.7, p.217)

... such writing is a sort of mental masturbation—he is always f—g-g—g his *Imagination*.—I don't mean that he is *indecent* but viciously soliciting his own ideas into a state which is neither poetry nor any thing else but a Bedlam vision produced by raw pork and opium.

Nov. 9, 1820, to Murray (Vol.7, p.225)

Had I known that Keats was dead—or that he was alive and so sensitive—I should have omitted some remarks upon his poetry, to which I was provoked by his *attack* upon Pope, and my disapprobation of *his own* style of writing. *April 26, 1821, to Shelley (Vol.8, p.104)*

You know very well that I did not approve of Keats's poetry or principles of poetry—or of his abuse of Pope—but as he is dead—omit *all* that is said *about him* in any *M.S.S.* of mine—or publication.—His Hyperion is a fine monument & will keep his name. . . .

July 30, 1821, to Murray (Vol.8, p.163)

POPE

I took Moore's poems & my own & some others—& went over them side by side with Pope's—and I was really astonished (I ought not to have been so) and mortified—at the ineffable distance in point of sense —harmony—effect—and even *Imagination* Passion—& *Invention*— between the little Queen Anne's Man—& us of the lower Empire. . . .

Sept.15, 1817, to Murray (Vol.5, p.265)

ROGERS

Rogers is silent,—and, it is said, severe. When he does talk, he talks well; and, on all subjects of taste, his delicacy of expression is pure as his poetry. If you enter his house—his drawing-room—his library— you of yourself say, this is not the dwelling of a common mind. There is not a gem, a coin, a book thrown aside on his chimney-piece, his sofa, his table, that does not bespeak an almost fastidious elegance in the possessor. But this very delicacy must be the misery of his existence. Oh the jarrings his disposition must have encountered through life. *Journal, Nov.22, 1813 (Vol.3, p.214)*

. . . and a likeness to the *death* of Mr. Rogers . . . by Denon also—I never saw so good a portrait—"And the trumpet shall sound and the dead shall be raised." *Dec.3, 1817, to Murray (Vol.5, p.277)*

. . . if he values his quiet—let him look to it—in three months I could restore him to the Catacombs. *Feb.20, 1818, to Murray (Vol.6, p.13)*

. . . There is a mean minuteness in his mind & tittle-tattle that I dislike
—ever since I *found him out* (which was but slowly) besides he is not
a good man——why don't he go to bed?—what does he do travelling?

Sept.20, 1821, to Murray (Vol.8, p.218)

SHAKESPEARE
You will find all this [*The Two Foscari*] very *un*like Shakespeare—and
so much the better in one sense—for I look upon him to be the *worst*
of models—though the most extraordinary of writers.

July 14, 1821, to Murray (Vol.8, p.152)

SHELLEY
. . . *Shelley* is *truth* itself—and *honour* itself—notwithstanding his out-
of-the-way notions about religion.

June 2, 1821, to Kinnaird (Vol.8, p.132)

As to poor Shelley, who is another bugbear to you and the world, he
is, to my knowledge, the *least* selfish and the mildest of men—a man
who has made more sacrifices of his fortune and feelings for others
than any I ever heard of. With his speculative opinions I have nothing
in common, nor desire to have.

Mar.4, 1822, to Moore (Vol.9, p.119)

You are all brutally mistaken about Shelley who was without exception—the *best* and least selfish man I ever knew.—I never knew one
who was not a beast in comparison.

Aug.3, 1822, to Murray (Vol.9, pp.189–190)

You do not know—how mild—how tolerant—how good he was in
Society—and as perfect a Gentleman as ever crossed a drawing room;
—when he liked—& where he liked.

Dec.25, 1822, to Murray (Vol.10, p.69)

SOUTHEY
. . . once at Holland House I met Southey—he is a person of very *epic*
appearance—& has a fine head as far as the outside goes—and wants
nothing but taste to make the inside equally attractive.

Sept.30, 1813, to Webster (Vol.3, p.127)

. . . the best looking bard I have seen for some time. To have that
poet's head and shoulders, I would almost have written his Sapphics.

He is certainly a prepossessing person to look on, and a man of talent and all that, and—*there* is his eulogy.

Sept.27, 1813, to Moore (Vol.3, p.122)

His appearance is *Epic*; and he is the only existing entire man of letters. All the others have some pursuits annexed to their authorship. His manners are mild, but not those of a man of the world, and his talents of the first order. His prose is perfect. Of his poetry there are various opinions: there is, perhaps, too much of it for the present generation; posterity will probably select. He has *passages* equal to any thing. At present, he has a *party*, but no *public*—except for his prose writings. The life of Nelson is beautiful. *Journal, Nov.22, 1813, (Vol.3, p.214)*

With regard to Southey please to recollect that in his preface to his "Vision"—he actually called upon the legislature to fall upon Moore[,] me—& others—now such a cowardly cry deserves a dressing.—He is also the vainest & most intolerant of men—and a rogue besides.

Nov.16, 1821, to Kinnaird (Vol.9, p.62)

WORDSWORTH

... his performances since "Lyrical Ballads"—are miserably inadequate to the ability which lurks within him—there is undoubtedly much natural talent spilt over "the Excursion" but it is rain upon rocks where it stands & stagnates—or rain upon sands where it falls without fertilizing—who can understand him?—let those who do make him intelligible. *Oct.30, 1815, to Leigh Hunt (Vol.4, p.324)*

POETRY

I by no means rank poetry high in the scale of intelligence——this may look like Affectation—but it is my real opinion—it is the lava of the imagination whose eruption prevents an earth-quake. . . .

Nov.29, 1813, to Annabella Milbanke (Vol.3, p.179)

I am glad you like it [third canto of *Childe Harold*]; it is a fine indistinct piece of poetical desolation, and my favourite. I was half mad during the time of its composition, between metaphysics, mountains, lakes, love unextinguishable, thoughts unutterable, and the nightmare of my own delinquencies. I should, many a good day, have blown my brains out, but for the recollection that it would have given pleasure to my mother-in-law; and, even *then*, if I could have been certain to haunt her. . . . *Jan.28, 1817, to Moore (Vol.5, p.165)*

I can never get people to understand that poetry is the expression of *excited passion*, and that there is no such thing as a life of passion any more than a continuous earthquake, or an eternal fever. Besides, who would ever *shave* themselves in such a state?

July 5, 1821, to Moore (Vol.8, p.146)

POLITICS

. . . my parliamentary schemes are not much to my taste—I spoke twice last Session—& was told it was well enough—but I hate the thing altogether—& have no intention to "strut another hour" on that stage.   *Mar.26, 1813, to Augusta Leigh (Vol.3, p.32)*

I have declined presenting the Debtor's Petition, being sick of parliamentary mummeries.   *Journal, Nov.14, 1813 (Vol.3, p.206)*

But Men never advance beyond a certain point;—and here we are, retrograding to the dull, stupid old system,—balance of Europe—poising straws upon kings' noses instead of wringing them off! Give me a republic, or a despotism of one, rather than the mixed government of one, two, three. A Republic!—look in the history of the Earth. . . . To be the first man—not the Dictator—not the Sylla, but the Washington or the Aristides—the leader in talent and truth—is next to the Divinity!   *Journal, Nov.23, 1813 (Vol.3, p.218)*

. . . I have simplified my politics into an utter detestation of all existing governments; and, as it is the shortest and most agreeable and summary feeling imaginable, the first moment of an universal republic would convert me into an advocate for single and uncontradicted despotism. The fact is, riches are power, and poverty is slavery all over the earth, and one sort of establishment is no better, nor worse, for a *people* than another.   *Journal, Jan.16, 1814 (Vol.3, p.242)*

. . . we have had lately such stupid mists—fogs—rains—and perpetual density—that one would think Castlereagh had the foreign affairs of the kingdom of Heaven also—upon his hands.

July 29, 1816, to Rogers (Vol.5, p.86)

Weather cold—carriage open, and inhabitants somewhat savage—rather treacherous and highly inflamed by politics. Fine fellows, though,—good materials for a nation. Out of chaos God made a world, and out of high passions comes a people.

Ravenna Journal, Jan.5, 1821 (Vol.8, p.13)

The king-times are fast finishing. There will be blood shed like water, and tears like mist; but the peoples will conquer in the end. I shall not live to see it, but I foresee it.

Ravenna Journal, Jan.13, 1821 (Vol.8, p.26)

It is no great matter, supposing that Italy could be liberated, who or what is sacrificed. It is a grand object—the very *poetry* of politics. Only think—a free Italy!!!

Ravenna Journal, Feb.18, 1821 (Vol.8, p.47)

There is, in fact, no law or government at all [in Italy]; and it is wonderful how well things go on without them.

Jan.2, 1821, to Moore (Vol.8, p.55)

God will not be always a Tory. . . .

Feb.2, 1821, to Murray (Vol.8, p.74)

. . . after all it is better playing at Nations than gaming at Almacks or Newmarket or in piecing or dinnering. . . .

Dec.23, 1823, to Kinnaird (Vol.11, p.80)

RELIGION

As to miracles, I agree with Hume that it is more probable men should *lie* or be *deceived*, than that things out of the course of nature should so happen.   *Sept.13, 1811, to Hodgson (Vol.2, p.97)*

And our carcases, which are to rise again, are they worth raising? I hope, if mine is, that I shall have a better *pair of legs* than I have moved on these two-and-twenty years, or I shall be sadly behind in the squeeze into Paradise.   *Sept.13, 1811, to Hodgson (Vol.2, p.98)*

. . . there is something Pagan in me that I cannot shake off. In short, I deny nothing, but doubt everything.

Dec.4, 1811, to Hodgson (Vol.2, p.136)

I am no Bigot to Infidelity—& did not expect that because I doubted the immortality of Man—I should be charged with denying ye existence of a God.—It was the comparative insignificance of ourselves & *our world* when placed in competition with the mighty whole of which it is an atom that first led me to imagine that our pretensions to eternity might be overrated.

June 18, 1813, to William Gifford (Vol.3, p.64)

My restlessness tells me I have something within that "passeth show". It is for Him, who made it, to prolong that spark of celestial fire which illumines, yet burns, this frail tenement; but I see no such horror in a "dreamless sleep", and I have no conception of any existence which duration would not render tiresome.

Journal, Nov.27, 1813 (Vol.3, p.225)

Is there any thing beyond?—*who* knows? *He* that can't tell. Who tells that there *is*? He who don't know. And when shall he know? perhaps, when he don't expect it, and, generally when he don't wish it. In this last respect, however, all are not alike; it depends a good deal upon education,—something upon nerves and habits—but most upon digestion.

Journal, Feb.18, 1814 (Vol.3, p.244)

. . . if ever I feel what is called devout—it is when I have met with some good of which I did not conceive myself deserving—and then I am apt to thank anything but mankind . . . why I came here—I know not—where I shall go it is useless to enquire—in the midst of myriads of the living & the dead worlds—stars—systems—infinity—why should I be anxious about an atom?

Mar.3, 1814, to Annabella Milbanke (Vol.4, p.78)

I remember a methodist preacher who on perceiving a profane grin on the faces of part of his congregation—exclaimed "no *hopes* for *them* as *laughs*" . . .

Dec.19, 1816, to Augusta Leigh (Vol.5, p.144)

. . . when I turn thirty—I will turn devout—I feel a great vocation that way in Catholic Churches—& when I hear the Organ.

April 9, 1817, to Murray (Vol.5, p.208)

. . . I do not know what to believe—which is the devil—to have no religion at all—all sense & senses are against it—but all belief & much evidence is for it—it is walking in the dark over a rabbit warren—or a garden with steel traps and spring guns.—for my part I have such a detestation of *some* of the articles of faith—that I would not subscribe to them—if I were as sure as St. Peter *after* the Cock crew.

April 14, 1817, to Hobhouse (Vol.5, p.216)

Some of the epitaphs at Ferrara pleased me more than the more splendid monuments of Bologna—for instance

"Martini Luigi
Implora pace."
"Lucrezia Picini
Implora eterna quiete."

Can any thing be more full of pathos! those few words say all that can be said or sought—the dead had had enough of life—all they wanted was rest—and this they *"implore"*. there is all the helplessness—and humble hope and deathlike prayer that can arise from the Grave— *"implore pace"*. I hope, whoever may survive me and shall see me put in the foreigners' burying-Ground at the Lido—within the fortress by the Adriatic—will see those two words and no more put over me. I trust they won't think of "pickling and bringing me home to Clod or Blunderbuss Hall". I am sure my Bones would not rest in an English grave—or my Clay mix with the earth of that Country.

June 7, 1819, to Murray (Vol.6, p.149)

It has been said that the immortality of the soul is a "grand peut-être"—but still it is a *grand* one. Everybody clings to it—the stupidest, and dullest, and wickedest of human bipeds is still persuaded that he is immortal. *Ravenna Journal, Jan.25, 1821 (Vol.8, p.35)*

. . . the Padre Pasquale Aucher . . . assured me "that the terrestrial Paradise had been certainly in *Armenia*"—I went seeking it—God knows where—did I find it?—Umph!—Now & then—for a minute or two. *"Detached Thoughts", No.55 (Vol.9, p.31)*

A *material* resurrection seems strange and even absurd except for purposes of punishment—and all punishment which is to *revenge* rather than *correct*—must be *morally* wrong—and *when* the *World* is at an end— what moral or warning purpose *can* eternal tortures answer?

"Detached Thoughts", No.96 (Vol.9, p.45)

I cannot help thinking that the *menace* of Hell makes as many devils as the severe penal codes of inhuman humanity make villains. Man is born passionate of body—but with an innate though secret tendency to the love of Good in his Main-spring of Mind.—— But God help us all!— It is at present a sad jar of atoms.

"Detached Thoughts", No.96 (Vol.9, p.46)

I am always most religious upon a sunshiny day. . . .

"Detached Thoughts", No.99 (Vol.9, p.46)

. . . I am really a great admirer of tangible religion; and am breeding one of my daughters a Catholic, that she may have her hands full. It is by far the most elegant worship, hardly excepting the Greek mythology. What with incense, pictures, statues, altars, shrines, relics, and the real presence, confession, absolution,—there is something to grasp at. Besides, it leaves no possibility of doubt; for those who swallow their Deity, really and truly, in transubstantiation, can hardly find any thing else otherwise than easy of digestion.

Mar.8, 1822, to Moore (Vol.9, p.123)

REVIEWS

Reviews & Magazines—are at the best but ephemeral & superficial reading—*who thinks* of the *grand article* of *last year*—in any *given review?* in the next place—if they regard *myself*—they tend to increase *Egotism*, if favourable—I do not deny that the praise *elates*—and if unfavourable that the abuse *irritates*—the latter may conduct me to inflict a species of Satire—which would neither do good to you nor to your friends. . . . The same applies to opinions *good*—*bad* or *indifferent* of persons in conversation or correspondence; these do not *interrupt* but they *soil* the *current* of my *Mind*. . . . You will say—"to what tends all this?—" I will answer *that*——to keep my mind *free and* unbiased—by all paltry and personal irritabilities of praise or censure;— to let my Genius take it's natural direction,—while my feelings are like the dead—who know nothing and feel nothing of all or aught that is said or done in their regard. . . . all reading either praise or censure of myself has done me harm.—When I was in Switzerland and Greece I was out of the way of hearing either—& *how I wrote there!*

Sept.24, 1821, to Murray (Vol.8, pp.220–221)

SELF-ANALYSIS

. . . we are all selfish & I no more trust myself than others with a good motive. . . .   *Sept.28, 1813, to Lady Melbourne (Vol.3, p.124)*

I hate sentiment—& in consequence my epistolary levity—makes you believe me as hollow & heartless as my letters are light—Indeed it is not so.   *[Oct.25, 1813?] to Lady Melbourne (Vol.3, p.155)*

It is odd I never set myself seriously to wishing without attaining it— and repenting.   *Journal, Nov.14, 1813 (Vol.3, p.205)*

. . . I will *not* be the slave of *any* appetite.

Journal, Nov.17, 1813 (Vol.3, p.212)

I only go out to get me a fresh appetite for being alone.

Journal, Dec.12, 1813 (Vol.3, p.238)

My great comfort is, that the temporary celebrity I have wrung from the world has been in the very teeth of all opinions and prejudices. I have flattered no ruling powers; I have never concealed a single thought that tempted me. *April 9, 1814, to Moore (Vol.4, pp.92–93)*

. . . it is her fault if she don't govern me properly—for never was anybody more easily managed.

Oct.7, 1814, to Lady Melbourne (Vol.4, p.199)

. . . I am about to be married—and am of course in all the misery of a man in pursuit of happiness.

Oct.15, 1814, to Leigh Hunt (Vol.4, p.209)

. . . it is odd but agitation or contest of any kind gives a rebound to my spirits and sets me up for a time. . . .

Mar.8, 1816, to Moore (Vol.5, p.45)

. . . I was not, and, indeed, am not even *now*, the misanthropical and gloomy gentleman he takes me for, but a facetious companion, well to do with those with whom I am intimate, and as loquacious and laughing as if I were a much cleverer fellow.

Mar.10, 1817, to Moore (Vol.5, p.186)

[Carnival adventures] I will work the mine of my youth to the last vein of the ore, and then—good night. I have lived, and am content.

Feb.2, 1818, to Moore (Vol.6, pp.10–11)

My time has been passed viciously and agreeably—at thirty-one so few years months days hours or minutes remain that *"Carpe diem"* is not enough—I have been obliged to crop even the seconds—for who can trust to *tomorrow? tomorrow* quotha? *to-hour—to-minute*—I can *not* repent me (I try very often) so much of any thing I have done—as of any thing I have left undone—alas! I have been but idle—and have the prospect of early decay—without having seized every available instant of our pleasurable year. *Aug.20, 1819, to Hobhouse (Vol.6, p.211)*

I am afraid that this sounds flippant, but I don't mean it to be so; only my turn of mind is so given to taking things in the absurd point of view, that it breaks out in spite of me every now and then.

Mar.8, 1822, to Moore (Vol.9, p.123)

SENSATION

The great object of life is Sensation—to feel that we exist—even though in pain—it is this "craving void" which drives us to Gaming—to Battle—to Travel—to intemperate but keenly felt pursuits of every description whose principal attraction is the agitation inseparable from their accomplishment.

Sept.6, 1813, to Annabella Milbanke (Vol.3, p.109)

And yet a little *tumult*, now and then, is an agreeable quickener of sensation; such as a revolution, a battle, or an *aventure* of any lively description. *Journal, Nov.22, 1813 (Vol.3, p.213)*

SERVANTS

Besides the perpetual lamentations after beef & beer, the stupid bigoted contempt for every thing foreign, and insurmountable incapacity of acquiring even a few words of any language, rendered him [Fletcher] like all other English servants, an incumbrance.

Jan.14, 1811, to Mrs. Byron (Vol.2, p.34)

SEVILLE

Seville is a fine town, and the Sierra Morena, part of which we crossed a very sufficient mountain,—but damn description, it is always disgusting. *Aug.6, 1809, to Hodgson (Vol.1, p.216)*

SOCIETY

The truth is, my dear Moore, you live near the *stove* of society, where you are unavoidably influenced by its heat and its vapours. I did so once—and too much—and enough to give a colour to my whole future existence. As my success in society was *not* inconsiderable, I am surely not a prejudiced judge upon the subject unless in its favour; but I think it, as now constituted, *fatal* to all original undertakings of every kind. I never courted it *then*, when I was young and in high blood, and one of its "curled darlings"; and do you think I would do so *now*, when I am living in a clearer atmosphere?

Mar.4, 1822, to Moore (Vol.9, p.119)

SPONTANEITY

. . . I can't *furbish*—I am like the tyger (in poesy) if I miss my first Spring—I go growling back to my jungle.

Nov.18, 1820, to Murray (Vol.7, p.229)

... it will be difficult for me not to make sport for the Philistines by pulling down a house or two—since when I take pen in hand—I *must* say what comes uppermost—or fling it away. "Lara" ... I wrote while undressing after coming home from balls and masquerades in the year of revelry *1814*.　　　*June 6, 1822, to Murray (Vol.9, p.168)*

STIMULANTS

How do you manage? I think you told me, at Venice, that your spirits did not keep up without a little claret. I *can* drink, and bear a good deal of wine (as you may recollect in England); but it don't exhilarate —it makes me savage and suspicious, and even quarrelsome. Laudanum has a similar effect; but I can take much of *it* without any effect at all. The thing that gives me the highest spirits (it seems absurd. but true) is a dose of *salts*—I mean in the afternoon, after their effect. But one can't take *them* like champagne.

　　　　　Oct.6, 1821, to Moore (Vol.8, p.236)

THEATRE

I am acquainted with no *im*material sensuality so delightful as good acting. . . .　　　*[May 8?, 1814], to Moore (Vol.4, p.115)*

. . . I could not resist the *first* night of any thing. . . .
　　　　　April 23, 1815, to Moore (Vol.4, p.290)

TRAVEL

I remember my friend Hobhouse used to say in Turkey that I had no notion of comfort because I could sleep where none but a *brute* could— & certainly where *brutes did* for often have the *Cows* turned out of their apartment *butted* at the door all night extremely discomposed with the unaccountable ejectment.—Thus we lived—one day in the palace of the Pacha & the next perhaps in the most miserable hut of the Mountains—I confess I preferred the former but never quarrelled with the latter. . . .　　　*Aug.23, 1813, to Lady Melbourne (Vol.3, p.97)*

Now my friend Hobhouse—when we were wayfaring men used to complain grievously of hard beds and sharp insects—while I slept like a top—and to awaken me with his swearing at them—he used to damn his dinners daily both quality & cookery and quantity—& reproach me for a sort of "brutal" indifference as he called it to these particulars . . . *he* knows that I was always *out* of bed before him—though it is true that my ablutions detained me longer in dressing—than his noble contempt for that "oriental scrupulosity" permitted.

Nov.9, 1820, to Murray (Vol.7, pp.223–224)

VENICE

[Venice] has always been (next to the East) the greenest island of my imagination.   *Nov.17, 1816, to Moore (Vol.5, p.129)*

Venice pleases me as much as I expected—and I expected much—it is one of those places which I know before I see them—and has always haunted me the most—after the East——I like the gloomy gaiety of their gondolas—and the silence of their canals . . .

Nov.25, 1816, to Murray (Vol.5, p.132)

VICE AND VIRTUE

I should wish to gaze away another [year] at least in these evergreen climates, but I fear Business, Law business, the worst of employments, will recall me. . . . If so, you shall have due notice, I hope you will find me an altered personage, I do not mean in body, but in manner, for I begin to find out that nothing but virtue will do in this damned world.

May 5, 1810, to Hodgson (Vol.1, p.241)

Every day confirms my opinion on the superiority of a vicious life— and if Virtue is not it's own reward I don't know any other stipend annexed to it.   *Dec.18, 1813, to Henry Drury (Vol.3, p.202)*

I am as comfortless as a pilgrim with peas in his shoes—and as cold as Charity—Chastity or any other Virtue.

Nov.16, 1814, to Annabella Milbanke (Vol.4, p.232)

The general race of women appear to be handsome—but in Italy as on almost all the Continent—the highest orders are by no means a well looking generation . . . Some are exceptions but most of them as ugly as Virtue herself.   *Nov.25, 1816, to Murray (Vol.5, p.134)*

In England the only homage which they pay to Virtue—is hypocrisy.

May 11, 1821, to Hoppner (Vol.8, p.113)

WOMEN

I only wish she [an Italian woman] did not swallow so much supper, chicken wings—sweetbreads,—custards—peaches & *Port* wine—a woman should never be seen eating or drinking, unless it be *lobster sallad* & *Champagne*, the only true feminine & becoming viands.

Sept.25, 1812, to Lady Melbourne (*Vol.2, p.208*)

There is something to me very softening in the presence of a woman,—some strange influence, even if one is not in love with them,—which I cannot at all account for, having no very high opinion of the sex. But yet,—I always feel in better humour with myself and every thing else, if there is a woman within ken. *Journal, Feb.27, 1814* (*Vol.3, p.246*)

... the women [in Venice] *kiss* better than those of any other nation—which is notorious—and is attributed to the worship of images and the early habit of osculation induced thereby.

Mar.25, 1817, to Murray (*Vol.5, p.193*)

I should like to know *who* has been carried off—except poor dear *me*—I have been more ravished myself than anybody since the Trojan war. . . . *Oct.29, 1819, to Hoppner* (*Vol.6, p.237*)

Your Blackwood accuses me of treating women harshly—it may be so —but I have been their martyr.—My whole life has been sacrificed *to* them & *by* them. *Dec.10, 1819, to Murray* (*Vol.6, p.257*)

WRITING

I have but with some difficulty *not* added any more to this snake of a poem [*The Giaour*]—which has been lengthening its rattles every month. . . . *Aug.26, 1813, to Murray* (*Vol.3, p.100*)

All convulsions end with me in rhyme; and, to solace my midnights, I have scribbled another Turkish story. . . .

Nov.30, 1813, to Moore (*Vol.3, p.184*)

... I do think ... the mighty stir made about scribbling and scribes, by themselves and others—a sign of effeminacy, degeneracy, and weakness. Who would write, who had any thing better to do?

Journal, Nov.24, 1813 (*Vol.3, p.220*)

To withdraw *myself* from *myself* (oh that cursed selfishness!) has ever been my sole, my entire, my sincere motive in scribbling at all . . . . If I valued fame, I should flatter received opinions, which have gathered strength by time, and will yet wear longer than any living works to the contrary. But for the soul of me, I cannot and will not give the lie to my own thoughts and doubts, come what may.

Journal, Nov.27, 1813 (Vol.3, p.225)

I can forgive whatever can be said of or against me—but not what they make me say or sing for myself—it is enough to answer for what I have written—but it were too much for Job himself to bear what one has not—I suspect that when the Arab Patriarch wished that "his Enemy had written a book" he did not anticipate his own name on the title page. *July 22, 1816, to Murray (Vol.5, pp.84–85)*

. . . but poetry is—I fear—incurable—God help me—if I proceed in this scribbling—I shall have frittered away my mind before I am thirty,—but it is at times a real relief to me.

Oct.5, 1816, to Murray (Vol.5, p.112)

I feel exactly as you do about our "art", but it comes over me in a kind of rage every now and then, like * * * *, and then, if I don't write to empty my mind, I go mad. As to that regular, uninterrupted love of writing, which you describe in your friend, I do not understand it. I feel it as a torture, which I must get rid of, but never as a pleasure. On the contrary, I think composition a great pain.

Jan.2, 1821, to Moore (Vol.8, p.55)

I sent two more Poeshies to A[lbemarle] Street—"Cain", a tragedy in three acts—[and] "a Vision of Judgment" by way of reversing Rogue Southey's—in my finest ferocious Caravaggio style. . . .

Oct.12, 1821, to Hobhouse (Vol.8, p.240)

GEORGE GORDON BYRON, 6th BARON
(1788–1824)

BIOGRAPHICAL SUMMARY

George Gordon Byron was born in London on January 22, 1788, of a long line of aristocratic ancestors, but with a club foot. His mother, Catherine Gordon, a Scottish heiress proud of her descent from James I of Scotland, had married the handsome but profligate Captain John Byron in 1785 after the death of his first wife, with whom he had eloped while she was the wife of the Marquis who later became the 5th Duke of Leeds. One child came from that marriage, Augusta, the poet's half-sister, of whom he saw very little until they were both grown. Mrs. Byron's fortune (she was the only daughter of George Gordon, laird of Gight in Aberdeenshire) had been wasted by the extravagance of Captain Byron before her son was born, and she took the boy to Aberdeen where she could live more cheaply in her straitened circumstances. In the meantime the Captain had retreated to Paris to escape his creditors and lived a wastrel and philandering life there until he died in 1791, three years after the birth of his son.

The Captain's father, Admiral John Byron, a noted explorer, was a younger brother of the 5th Baron Byron, who had squandered his inherited estate of Newstead Abbey, granted to the Byrons by Henry VIII, before he died in 1798, predeceased by his son and grandson, so that the title came to the "little lame boy" in Aberdeen. His mother proudly took him to Newstead, and then sent him to a school in London, and with the assistance of her solicitor John Hanson, procured him a government allowance for his education at Harrow and later at Trinity College, Cambridge. He quarrelled with his mother, who was alternately affectionate and given to fits of temper, when she reviled him for his disobedience and extravagance. After a term at Cambridge he retired to London, indulged in some mild dissipations, and piled up debts with money-lenders. The boasting in his letters about his exploits with women should be read with an understanding of his habitual mode of expression, a facetiousness that often concealed the depth of his true feelings. The fact is that he was never as callous in his treatment of women as his flippant remarks suggest. Part of it was compensation for his lameness just as was his boasting of his swimming exploits. Although he had early been initiated into sex play by a pious Scottish maid under circumstances which might have caused a permanent trauma in a less resilient character, he had a naturally affectionate nature. A nineteenth-century biographer, J. Cordy Jeaffreson, observed astutely of his later philandering in Venice: "However dissolute she might be, the woman he regarded with passion became for the moment the object of an affection that was no less tender than transient."

Byron's homosexual tendencies, which began with his attachment to younger boys at Harrow, seemed fully developed with his "violent, though *pure* love and passion" for John Edleston, a Cambridge choir-boy. Since so much has been made of it in recent books on Byron (notably those of G. Wilson Knight and Bernard Grebanier) I hope I may set the record straight by repeating what I said in my own biography of Byron: "How early Byron was aware of the sexual implications of these passionate friendships it is difficult to know: possibly before he left Harrow, probably while he was at Cambridge, and certainly while he was in Greece on his first pilgrimage. There seems little doubt, if one considers dispassionately the total evidence now available, that a strong attraction to boys persisted in Byron from his Harrow days throughout his life. But there is no evidence that he felt guilt or shame about any of the friendships he formed at Harrow. . . . Byron's attraction to women, however, did, on the whole, fulfill his emotional needs much more extensively and through longer periods of his life, though it was not necessarily stronger in individual instances".* Certainly his strongest feelings for boys were on an idealized plane, as attested by his Thyrza poems to Edleston's memory and the last three poems he wrote in Greece to Lukas Chalandritsanos. But G. Wilson Knight's suggestion that Byron's relations with Caroline Lamb and even the Countess Guiccioli were merely Platonic is patently absurd.

Byron's debts had mounted to £13,000 before he embarked for a grand tour in July, 1809. In order to have the company of his friend John Cam Hobhouse, he made him a loan from his own borrowings from usurers. The pilgrims landed in Portugal, traversed war-torn Spain on horseback, and sailed from Gibraltar for Malta, where Byron fell in love with a married woman and nearly fought a duel over her. Then they sailed for Greece and Albania. They penetrated the mountain passes to Tepelene, to visit Ali Pasha, the mild-mannered but

* *Byron: A Biography I,* 90.

362

cruel ruler of Albania and much of Northern Greece. They arrived in Athens on Christmas Day and took lodgings with the widow Macri, whose three young daughters, all under fifteen, enchanted Byron. He immortalized the youngest, Teresa, as "The Maid of Athens". On their way to Constantinople Byron swam the Hellespont and never allowed his friends or the public to forget it. Hobhouse left for home and Byron spent another year in those sunlit climes, chiefly in Athens.

Before leaving England he had published a volume of juvenile poems, imitative but showing some originality. When it was ridiculed in the *Edinburgh Review*, he struck back in a satire called *English Bards and Scotch Reviewers*, modelled on the Popean style of William Gifford. On his return in July, 1811, he carried with him the manuscript of a long autobiographical poem in Spenserian stanzas. It was a rambling travelogue of his journey, interspersed with melancholy reflections and disillusioned observations which fitted the moods of many people following the Napoleonic war. When it was published the following March by the enterprising publisher John Murray, Byron awoke one morning to find himself famous. He had just delivered his maiden speech in the House of Lords, but the poem drove thoughts of a parliamentary career out of his mind.

He became a lion of society and was invited everywhere. He found himself thrown into the highest circles of a society of which he had known little in his youth, and he became intimate with some of its leading figures. His handsome features added to the fame of his melancholy poetry to arouse the liveliest interest in the feminine part of that society. Lady Caroline Lamb, an eccentric and spoiled child of the aristocracy, became infatuated with him and he temporarily succumbed to her until her total lack of discretion and the violence of her emotions cooled his ardour and finally disgusted him. After Caroline's scenes, he found Lady Oxford's calm "autumnal charms" a relief. In the meantime he toyed with the idea of marrying Annabella Milbanke, Caroline's seemingly sensible and learned cousin. He enlisted Caroline's mother-in-law, Lady Melbourne, who had become his confidante, to sound out Annabella's feelings (he had met her only briefly). She politely turned him down but wanted to remain his friend. After Lady Oxford went abroad with her husband in 1813, Byron fell deeply in love with his half-sister Augusta Leigh, then married to her cousin Colonel George Leigh and mother of a growing family. Lady Melbourne, in an attempt to save him from this dangerous liaison, encouraged his flirtation with Lady Frances Webster.

When his infatuation subsided Byron returned to Augusta, admitting to Lady Melbourne that that attachment was the strongest after all. But Augusta agreed with Lady Melbourne that marriage was his only salvation and he turned again to Annabella Milbanke, who had started a correspondence with him. In September, 1814, he sent a tentative proposal which she took for a real one and accepted, for she had come to believe that it was her destiny to rescue and reform this wayward spirit. The fatal marriage took place on January 2, 1815, and lasted only a year. A month after her daughter Ada was born she took her to her mother's home in the country, parting from her husband with apparent mutual affection and writing him a playful and loving letter after her arrival. Two weeks later her father wrote proposing a separation. Augusta with whom she was on the best of terms, remained with Byron, but Lady Byron would communicate with her husband only through her lawyers. Rumours of incest and worse persisted. The real causes of the separation were never revealed by either side. Byron finally signed the separation papers and on April 25, 1816, sailed from Dover and never saw England again.

— During the four years since the publication of *Childe Harold*, he had become a figure of world renown, with a popularity far exceeding that of any other English literary figure of his time. His Oriental tales had an even wider circulation. *The Corsair* sold 10,000 copies on the day of publication. He had come to know and mingle intimately with the most famous of his contemporaries. Murray introduced him to Walter Scott who became his lifelong friend though they met only a few times in London. He associated and drank with Sheridan, was on the Drury Lane Theatre committee and urged Coleridge to write a tragedy for it, wrote the prologue for the opening of the new theatre, and lived an active social life. His poetry was the safety valve of his emotions and was written after returning from parties late at night or in the early hours of the morning. His letters rarely reflect the melancholy and disillusionment of his poems.

— In Geneva Byron first met Shelley on May 27, 1816, and was closely associated with him and with Mary Godwin (later Shelley) and her step-sister Claire Clairmont throughout the summer. That summer produced not only the 3rd canto of *Childe Harold*, *The Prisoner of Chillon*, and *Manfred*, but also an illegitimate daughter Allegra by Claire, born in England the following year and sent to him in Italy to rear. Allegra pleased Byron but he would have nothing to do with her importunate mother. The child was placed in a convent school near Ravenna where she died at the age of five.

Hobhouse joined Byron in Geneva in September, 1816, and after a tour of the Bernese Alps, they journeyed to Italy. Settled in Venice, "the greenest island" of his imagination, Byron lodged with a tolerant "Merchant of Venice" and promptly fell in love with his wife, Marianna Segati. This liaison lasted more than a year during which Byron, more content than he had been for some time, studied Armenian at the monastery of San Lazzaro, attended the theatre, where he heard Rossini operas, rode his horses on the Lido, went to the *conversazioni* of the Countess Albrizzi and the Countess Benzoni, and wrote a fourth canto of *Childe Harold*. This was a tribute to Italy and a pageant of Roman history, and followed his journey to Rome in the spring of 1817.

The next year, after Hobhouse took the manuscript of that poem to England, Byron indulged in the frivolities and buffooneries of the Carnival and wore himself out physically and emotionally with brief encounters with dozens (he once estimated 200) of Venetian women from every level of society. Margarita Cogni, the "Fornarina" or baker's wife, was a favourite.

He had broken with Marianna Segati, who sold his gifts for profit, and he rented the Palazzo Mocenigo on the Grand Canal. Two things changed the course of his life. One was the discovery of his facility in the ottava rima verse in a lively and uninhibited story of Venetian life called *Beppo*, which led to the use of that same style and verse in *Don Juan*, a poem that gave full scope to his unconventional expression of every thought and mood.

The second event which changed his life was the meeting in the spring of 1819 with the Countess Teresa Guiccioli, daughter of a Ravenna aristocrat, aged 20 and married a year to a man of 57, rich but eccentric, who had had two wives already. Byron who was tired of light philandering, fell more deeply in love than he had thought possible, and the Countess was swept off her feet by the handsome poet. They discussed Dante together, and in ten days before she was forced to return to Ravenna with her husband they had cemented their pact and consummated their union. Byron followed her to Ravenna and after some stormy scenes of jealousy and frustration, he leased the upper floor of the Palazzo Guiccioli, and not only was he outwardly accepted as her Cavalier Servente, but he cuckolded the Count in his own house. This liaison lasted the rest of Byron's life until he left for Greece in 1823, and he confined himself, as he said, to "the strictest adultery". After the Countess was separated from her husband by Papal decree, Byron followed her to Pisa, where her father and brother had taken political exile. She continued to live under her father's roof to preserve her alimony, but for all practical purposes Byron had settled into a contented marriage.

In Ravenna Byron spent some of his most productive years. He had been drawn into the Carbonari, the secret revolutionary society aimed at overthrowing the Austrian yoke, by Teresa's father and brother, the Counts Ruggero and Pietro Gamba. After the failure of that movement because of the lack of Italian unity, Byron stayed on for several months before he joined the exiles. Even during the tense days when the insurrection was expected to break out at any moment, he wrote one poetic drama and planned another. His questioning of orthodox religious views in *Cain* together with his freedom in dealing with sexual matters in *Don Juan* had caused his publisher grave concern and his popularity waned. But he would not alter his writing for "all the Cant in Christendom", and before he left Ravenna he had composed the highly amusing but explosively unorthodox "Vision of Judgment", ridiculing George III and Southey, the poet laureate who had written a fawning tribute to the king on his death in 1820.

In Pisa Byron was associated again with Shelley and his circle, including Thomas Medwin, who later Boswellized his conversation, and the imitator of Byron's Corsair, Edward John Trelawny, who later accompanied him to Greece. Shelley's death by drowning left Byron with the maintenance of Leigh Hunt and his numerous family who had come to Italy at Shelley's invitation to edit with them a new periodical, *The Liberal*, in which Byron's "Vision of Judgment" finally appeared and stirred up a violent reaction in England.

The second exile of the Gambas from Tuscany after Shelley's death caused Byron to move the whole Pisan enclave to Genoa, including the Hunts and Mary Shelley. After he quarrelled with Murray, Byron turned all his work over to John Hunt, Leigh's brother, publisher of *The Examiner*, who published all of *Don Juan* after Canto 5, and all the rest of Byron's poems. After swimming in the hot sun at Viareggio while Trelawny was cremating the body of Shelley on the beach, Byron's health deteriorated. He had grown thin and was subject to various ailments. In the spring of 1823 two events lifted his spirits. In April the Earl and Countess of Blessington, with their travelling companion Count Alfred D'Orsay, arrived in Genoa for a stay of several weeks. Byron rode and dined with them. It was the first time he had been associated for any length of time with English people of his own social level since he came abroad and it aroused a certain nostalgia and encouraged him to converse freely about his years of fame in England. This conversation Lady Blessington recorded and published after his death. The other event was the opportunity to return to Greece, which came with the invitation to join the London Greek Committee and to act as their agent at the seat of war. He gladly accepted the commission to gather information and to offer what assistance he could to the Greeks in their struggle for independence from the Turks. He was elated at the prospect of a more active life. He was beginning to chafe at the quiet domesticity into which he had settled in Genoa.

On July 16, 1823, he left on the brig *Hercules* with Pietro Gamba, Teresa's brother, whose head was ''hot for revolution'', and Trelawny, ready for any adventure. They landed at Argostoli on the Ionian island of Cephalonia on August 3, where Byron remained until the end of the year, waiting for more and better news from the mainland of Greece. After the first successes of the revolution, the various factions, each with their own leaders, some little more than bandit chiefs such as Kolokotrones, were engaged in bitter rivalry, and there was no effective central government. The legislative and executive were on the verge of civil war. Alexander Mavrocordatos, the best educated and least venal of the leaders, had given up his post as head of the legislative branch, under threats from Kolokotrones, and had fled to the island of Hydra. Byron wisely did not ally himself with any faction and made every effort to unite the Greeks for their fight against the Turks. In the meantime Trelawny went off to the mainland and joined forces with the wily Odysseus Androutsos, who had made himself master of the region around Athens.

With a personal loan of £4,000 Byron activated the Greek fleet which sailed for Missolonghi with Mavrocordatos, who became governor-general of Western Greece. Byron joined him there at the beginning of 1824. He never gave up hope for the success of the Greek cause and continued his efforts to unite the self-seeking and irreconcilable factions, though he was depressed and disillusioned by the realization that even the Suliote soldiers, whom he had idealized as the bravest of the Greeks, and whom he had undertaken to finance and lead, were interested only in their pay. In the end they refused to march against the Turkish fort of Lepanto on the Gulf of Corinth. He found some satisfaction in trying to encourage both the Turks and the Greeks to practice a more humane treatment of captives by getting the Greeks to let him return some Turkish prisoners. His last days were made more melancholy by an unrequited attachment to a Greek boy Lukas Chalandritsanos whom he had brought as a page from Cephalonia. His last three poems including the famous one on his 36th birthday were addressed to him. Byron died of a fever and the treatment of three doctors, who knew no remedy but bleeding, on April 19, 1824. His body was brought back to England, and, refused burial in Westminster Abbey, was interred with his ancestors at Hucknall Torkard church, near Newstead Abbey. Subsequently, in 1968, the Dean of Westminster Abbey approved the reception of a plaque into the Abbey.

BIOGRAPHICAL SKETCHES
OF CORRESPONDENTS

ADAIR, SIR ROBERT (1763–1855). Son of Robert Adair, who had been sergeant-surgeon to George III, and friend of Charles James Fox. He was sent to Constantinople in 1806 to open negotiation for peace with the Porte.

BARRY, CHARLES F. (17 ?–18 ?) Genoa partner of Webb & Co., bankers of Leghorn. He became Byron's banker, business agent, and friend during the poet's residence in Genoa, and continued to handle his affairs after Byron left for Greece. Byron consigned his papers, books, and furniture to him, and wrote some of his most confidential letters to him from Cephalonia and Missolonghi.

BECHER, REV. JOHN THOMAS (17 ?–18 ?). Vicar of Rumpton and of Midsomer Norton, and later prebendary and then Vicar-general of Southwell Minster. He was related to Byron's friends the Pigots in Southwell. Byron trusted him as a literary adviser while he was preparing his early poems for publication. When Becher objected that the erotic images in his poem "To Mary" in his privately printed *Fugitive Pieces* were "too warmly drawn", Byron suppressed the volume and destroyed most of the copies. Only four survived, including Becher's copy.

BOWRING, JOHN (1792–1872). A Benthamite and Philhellenist, he was secretary of the London Greek Committee, of which Byron had become a member before he left Genoa. Bowring was a man of many talents, master of many languages, and a voluminous writer. He was later an editor and biographer of Jeremy Bentham. Byron at times found him a little too doctrinaire and lacking in knowledge of the Greeks and their problems.

BYRON, CATHERINE GORDON (1765–1811). Byron's mother was proud of her descent from the second Earl of Huntly and his wife Princess Annabella Stewart, daughter of James I of Scotland. She was the only daughter of George Gordon, the twelfth laird of Gight. She married

Capt. John Byron in 1785 after the death of his first wife. After wasting most of her fortune he died in 1791 in Paris three years after the birth of their son. She lived in Aberdeen until the ten-year-old son inherited the title in 1798, when they moved to England. Byron avoided her a good deal after he went to Harrow because of her flighty temper, and she was alarmed by his debts and dissipation, but she was truly devoted to him.

COLERIDGE, SAMUEL TAYLOR (1772–1834). Byron had been an admirer of "The Rime of the Ancient Mariner" and other poems, but he had ridiculed Coleridge's "To a Young Ass" in *English Bards and Scotch Reviewers*. It was at Byron's urging that Murray published *Christabel, Kubla Khan,* and other poems. As a member of the sub-committee of management of Drury Lane Theatre, Byron tried to get Coleridge to write a tragedy for that theatre, but nothing came of it.

DAVIES, SCROPE BERDMORE (1782–1852). Son of a country vicar of Horsley in Gloucestershire, Scrope was educated at Eton and King's College, Cambridge, where he was awarded a Fellowship in 1805. Byron met him through Hobhouse and other friends at Cambridge and was attracted by his wit and man-of-the-world attitudes. He was at home in the fashionable society of London, and at the gaming tables where he won and lost huge sums. He borrowed several thousand pounds from usurers to enable Byron to go abroad in 1809, which Byron could not repay until 1814. He was finally ruined by gambling losses and fled to Bruges and later to Paris. He left in London a trunk, recently opened, full of papers including 14 of Byron's best letters to him.

DRURY, HENRY JOSEPH (1778–1841). As assistant master at Harrow School, he was Byron's tutor until they quarrelled. But after Byron left Harrow, he became very friendly with Drury and wrote some of his most facetious letters to him.

D'USSIÈRES, HENRIETTA, a Swiss girl who, like many others after Byron became famous, wrote asking to meet him. Several of her letters to him were published by Peter Quennell in *"To Lord Byron"*. She could not have impressed him much when he met her, for the correspondence soon lapsed.

FOX, HENRY RICHARD VASSALL, 3rd Baron Holland (1773–1840),

Leader of the Moderate Whigs in the House of Lords. He encouraged Byron as a new member of the Opposition and helped him in his preparation of a maiden speech. He was a champion of liberal and humane causes, and he and Lady Holland took a personal interest in Byron and he was always welcome at their famous salon in Holland House.

GUICCIOLI, COUNTESS TERESA (1799?–1873). Born Teresa Gamba Ghiselli, eldest daughter of Count Ruggero Gamba, of an old aristocratic family of Ravenna, she was married three months after she left the convent school of Santa Chiara at Faenza to the wealthy but eccentric Count Alessandro Guiccioli. The next year (April, 1819) she met Byron at the Countess Benzoni's in Venice and fell desperately in love, enticing him to Ravenna where he became her Cavalier Servente. After she was granted a separation from her husband by the Pope, Byron continued, as he said in "the strictest adultery" with her, though she in accordance with the Pope's decree lived under the roof of her father, with whom Byron was on the best of terms.

HANCOCK, CHARLES (1793–1858). A merchant-banker on the island of Cephalonia in partnership with Samuel Barff on Zante. He negotiated most of Byron's bills of exchange, and with Barff performed many other services for him on the islands after Byron left for Missolonghi.

HANSON, JOHN (17 ?–1841). Byron's solicitor, business agent, and friend from the time he inherited his title in 1798. Mrs. Byron had employed him earlier to look out for her son's interests when he became heir-apparent to his great-uncle, the 5th Lord Byron. Throughout Byron's life Hanson continued to serve and sometimes to exasperate him by his delays and procrastination.

HARDY, ANNE LOUISA EMILY (1790?–18 ?). Daughter of Admiral Sir George Berkeley. She married in 1807 Sir Thomas Masterman Hardy who was with Nelson when he died on the *Victory*. Hardy, later a vice-admiral, was sent on an expedition to South America in 1819 and did not return until 1824. Lady Hardy, who had met Byron in London in 1814, was travelling for the health of her children. She could claim a distant cousinship with Byron because the 4th Lord Byron had married a Berkeley.

HOBHOUSE, JOHN CAM (1786–1869). Oldest son of Benjamin Hobhouse, a Whig M.P. Byron first became friendly with him at Cambridge in 1807. They shared an interest in Juvenalian satire and Byron contributed some poems to his *Imitations and Translations* (1809). He accompanied Byron on his first pilgrimage to Albania, Greece, and Turkey in 1809, continued to be his closest friend during his years of fame, and was with him again in Switzerland and Italy. Hobhouse was elected to Parliament from Westminster in 1820, representing a radical constituency. He was largely responsible for the burning of Byron's Memoirs after his death, fearing they would ruin the poet's reputation. In 1851 he was created Baron Broughton de Gyfford.

HODGSON, FRANCIS (1781–1852). Educated at Eton and King's College, Cambridge, in the classics, he had literary ambitions and was a facile rhymer and a good Latinist. When Byron met him in 1807 he was a resident tutor at King's. They soon became close friends and shared literary interests. Byron, in financial trouble himself, cleared Hodgson's debts so that he could marry. Later before Hodgson took orders in the Church of England in 1812, he tried to win Byron from his sceptical views, and their correspondence is full of arguments on religion. The friendship lapsed after Byron went abroad in 1816.

HOGG, JAMES (1770–1835). While working as a shepherd he began to write verses, and was commonly known as ''The Ettrick Shepherd''. He made the acquaintance of Sir Walter Scott and helped him to gather material for his *Minstrelsy of the Scottish Border*, and later published his own ballads and gained poetical recognition. Byron helped him to make contact with his publisher John Murray. In ''The Poetic Mirror'' (1816) Hogg wrote clever parodies of various poets including Byron.

HOLLAND, LORD. See Fox, Henry Richard Vassall.

HOPPNER, RICHARD BELGRAVE (1786–1872). Second son of John Hoppner, R.A., the portrait painter. He was appointed British Consul in Venice in 1814. He had studied painting and had some literary interests and ability. After Hobhouse left for England in 1818, Byron became intimate with him and they rode together on the Lido sands. After Byron followed the Countess Guiccioli to Ravenna, Hoppner attended to his affairs in Venice and the Hoppners at various times looked after his daughter Allegra.

KINNAIRD, HON. DOUGLAS (1788–1830). He was educated at Eton and at Trinity College, Cambridge, where Byron met him. Like his friend Hobhouse, he entered politics, gaining a seat in Parliament for Bishop's Castle in 1819. In the same year he became a manager of the banking firm of Ransom and Company, of which he was a principal partner. After Byron went abroad in 1816 Kinnaird became his literary and business agent as well as banker, and the recipient of some of Byron's frankest and most facetious letters.

LAMB, LADY CAROLINE (1785–1828). Daughter of Frederick Ponsonby, 3rd Earl of Bessborough, and his wife Lady Henrietta Frances Spencer, sister of Georgiana, Duchess of Devonshire. Caroline was clever and pretty but eccentric. Byron called her "a little volcano". She married in 1805 Lord Melbourne's second son, William Lamb, (later, Lord Melbourne, Prime Minister under Queen Victoria). She fell madly in love with Byron when she met him in 1812. Her indiscretions in the end repelled him, though he was for a time enchanted with her. The affair for him lasted only about three months, but she never forgot him and his image haunted her for the rest of her life. He was the hero-villain of her novel *Glenarvon* which she published after he went abroad. She later had periods of mental derangement and died four years after Byron.

LEIGH, HON. AUGUSTA (1783–1851). Byron's half-sister was the daughter of Capt. John Byron and the woman with whom he eloped and later married in scandalous circumstances, Amelia D'Arcy, Baroness Conyers, the divorced wife of Francis, Marquis of Carmarthen (later 5th Duke of Leeds). She was born in Paris and her mother died soon after, following which her father married the poet's mother. She was raised by her maternal grandmother, Lady Holderness, and saw little of her half-brother until they were grown. She married in 1807 her first cousin, Col. George Leigh, and bore him a numerous family. Byron and his sister were almost strangers when they met in London in 1813 and formed a dangerous liaison. After his marriage to Miss Milbanke she resisted Byron's advances and was loyal to her sister-in-law, but when rumours of the incest were spread after the separation of the Byrons, Lady Byron tried to make Augusta confess and persecuted her unknown to Byron who had gone abroad.

MELBOURNE, LADY (1752?–1818). Elizabeth, only daughter of Sir Ralph Milbanke of Halnaby, Yorkshire, married in 1769 Sir Peniston

Lamb, who later became an Irish baron as Lord Melbourne and an English peer in 1815. She was past 60 when Byron met her in 1812. After his whirlwind affair with her daughter-in-law Lady Caroline Lamb ended, she became his friend and confidante. He was fascinated by her, respecting her wisdom and tolerance. He called her "the best, the kindest, and ablest female I have ever known, old or young".

MILBANKE, ANNE ISABELLA (ANNABELLA) (1792–1860). Only daughter of Sir Ralph and Lady (Judith) Milbanke (later Noel) of Seaham, near Durham. She met Byron first at the home of her aunt, Lady Melbourne, just after he became famous with the publication of *Childe Harold*. She was precocious, widely read and had a penchant for mathematics. But she was a spoiled child, smug in her moral judgments, and confident of her ability to read character. Byron was intrigued by her at the same time that he had misgivings about her priggishness. He called her "a very superior woman a little encumbered with Virtue". But when he sought marriage to escape from his dangerous liaisons, he unfortunately chose a woman who thought she could reform him. The fatal marriage lasted only a year, and she spent the rest of her life in self-justification.

MOORE, THOMAS (1779–1852). The Irish poet had come to London in 1799 and soon made a name for himself and became a favourite in aristocratic circles. Byron had admired his pseudonymous sentimental-erotic *Poetical Works of the Late Thomas Little* (1801). But Moore's reputation, when Byron met him in 1811, was based on his *Irish Melodies* (1807). They met after avoiding a threatened duel because of some lines in Byron's *English Bards and Scotch Reviewers*, and soon became fast friends, going to theatres and parties together. The friendship continued throughout Byron's life and some of his most amusing letters were written to Moore from Italy. When Moore visited him in Venice, Byron gave him the manuscript of his Memoirs, later sold to Murray but burned against Moore's protest after Byron's death. Moore wrote the first official "life and letters" of Byron in 1830.

MUIR, DR. HENRY (17 ?–18 ?). Health Officer at Argostoli. He was one of Byron's closest friends during his stay on the island of Cephalonia. Muir's sceptical views coincided with Byron's own.

MURRAY, JOHN (1778–1843). The first John Murray founded a bookselling and publishing business at 32 Fleet Street in 1768. His son,

John Murray II, became one of the most prestigious publishers in London. He was one of the founders of the Tory *Quarterly Review*, begun in 1809 with William Gifford as editor, and later edited by John G. Lockhart, Scott's son-in-law and biographer. In 1812 Murray moved to 50 Albemarle Street, which has been the home of the firm ever since. His reputation was enhanced by the publication of Byron's *Childe Harold* in 1812 and the poet's succeeding works for the next ten years. Ten thousand copies of *The Corsair* were sold the first day of publication. In the fireplace of Murray's parlour (now the Byron Room) the poet's Memoirs were burned in 1824. Murray continued to publish some of the most notable writers of his day, and later initiated the popular guidebooks which bore his name. Byron quarrelled with him in 1822 and turned over his subsequent works to John Hunt, but he continued his friendship to the end of his life.

NOEL, SIR RALPH (1747–1825). Sir Ralph Milbanke, 6th Baronet, who took the name of Noel when he inherited the property of his wife's brother (her maiden name was Judith Noel) in 1815. He was the brother of Lady Melbourne and the father of Anne Isabella Milbanke who married Byron in 1815.

SHELLEY, MARY (GODWIN) (1797–1851). Daughter of William Godwin and Mary Wollstonecraft. She eloped with Shelley in 1814 and married him after the death of his first wife Harriet. She saw much of Byron during the summer of 1816, when she, Shelley, and Claire Clairmont went boating with him on the lake or gathered for long evenings of conversation at Byron's Villa Diodati. One of these discussions of ghost stories led Mary to the idea for her novel *Frankenstein*. They were less closely associated at Pisa, where it was a man's world. After Shelley's death Byron did all he could for her, writing to Sir Timothy Shelley for support for her child, and employing her to copy the manuscripts of his poems. Though she quarrelled with him before he went to Greece, partly because of Hunt, she continued to cherish his memory after his death, and modelled the heroes of several of her novels on him.

SHELLEY. PERCY BYSSHE (1792–1822). Byron met Shelley in Geneva in the summer of 1816 through Claire Clairmont. They were closely associated during the summer, and his interest in Byron's illegitimate daughter by Claire brought them into contact again in Italy. They saw each other daily in Pisa in 1822. Shelley was a genuine admirer of

Byron's poetry, but Byron liked and respected him more as a man than as a poet. Shelley's drowning affected him profoundly, and he was present at the cremation of his body at Viareggio.

WEBSTER, JAMES WEDDERBURN (1789–1840). Byron met Webster at Cambridge and continued to associate with him on a friendly basis though he always considered him something of a butt and a buffoon. He was amused rather than offended by Webster's absurdities and vanities. In 1810 Webster married Lady Frances Annesley, daughter of Arthur, 1st Earl of Mountnorris and 8th Viscount Valentia. Some of Byron's most amusing letters to Lady Melbourne recount the progress of his flirtation with Lady Frances, who passed love notes to him under the nose of her conceited, philandering, and jealous husband. In later years Webster was separated from his wife and Byron tried unsuccessfully to reconcile them.

YUSUFF PASHA, Turkish commander at Patras.

LETTERS AND JOURNALS
IN THIS VOLUME

Nov. 23, 1805, to John Hanson (Vol. 1, p. 81)

Nov. 30, 1805, to John Hanson (Vol. 1, p. 82)

Feb. 26, 1808, to Rev. John Becher (Vol. 1, p. 157)

June 25, 1809, to Henry Drury (Vol. 1, p. 208)

July 16, 1809, to Francis Hodgson (Vol. 1, p. 215)

Aug. 11, 1809, to Mrs. Catherine Gordon Byron (Vol. 1, p. 218)

Nov. 12, 1809, to Mrs. Catherine Gordon Byron (Vol. 1, p. 226)

May 3, 1810, to Henry Drury (Vol. 1, p. 237)

July 4, 1810, to Robert Adair (Vol. 1, p. 256)

July 31, 1810, to Scrope Berdmore Davies (Vol. 11, p. 157)

Aug. 16, 1810, to John Cam Hobhouse (Vol. 2, p. 9)

Oct. 3, 1810, to Frances Hodgson (Vol. 2, p. 18)

Jan. 20, 1811, to Francis Hodgson (Vol. 2, p. 36)

May 22, 1811, Reasons for a change (Vol. 2, p. 47)

July 7, 1811, to Henry Drury (Vol. 2, p. 58)

Aug. 21, 1811, to Augusta Leigh (Vol. 2, p. 74)

Aug. 30, 1811, to Augusta Leigh (Vol. 2, p. 84)

Sept. 2, 1811, to Augusta Leigh (Vol. 2, p. 88)

Sept. 3, 1811, to Francis Hodgson (Vol. 2, p. 88)

Sept. 13, 1811, to Francis Hodgson (Vol. 2, p. 97)

Nov. 16, 1811, to John Cam Hobhouse (Vol. 2, p. 129)

Feb. 25, 1812, to Lord Holland (Vol. 2, p. 165)

[April, 1812?], to Lady Caroline Lamb (Vol. 2, p. 170)

May 1, 1812, to Lady Caroline Lamb (Vol. 2, p. 175)

Sept. 15, 1812, to Lady Melbourne (Vol. 2, p. 198)

Sept. 25, 1812, to Lady Melbourne (Vol. 2, p. 208)

Oct. 18, 1812, to Lady Melbourne (Vol. 2, p. 229)

Sept. 5, 1813, to Lady Melbourne (Vol. 3, p. 108)

Sept. 6, 1813, to Annabella Milbanke (Vol. 3, p. 108)

Sept. 21, 1813, to Lady Melbourne (Vol. 3, p. 115)

Sept. 28, 1813, to Lady Melbourne (Vol. 3, p. 123)

Oct. 8, 1813, to Lady Melbourne (Vol. 3, p. 133)

Oct. 10, 1813, to Lady Melbourne (Vol. 3, p. 136)

Oct. 17, 1813, to Lady Melbourne (Vol. 3, p. 145)

Nov. 10, 1813, to Annabella Milbanke (Vol. 3, p. 158)

Nov. 29, 1813, to Annabella Milbanke (Vol. 3, p. 178)

Journal, Nov. 14, 1813–April 19, 1814 (extracts) (Vol. 3, pp. 204–258)

Jan. 13, 1814, to Lady Melbourne (Vol. 4, p. 26)

March 24, 1814, to James Hogg (Vol. 4, p. 84)

April 29, 1814, to Lady Melbourne (Vol. 4, p. 108)

April 30, 1814, to Lady Melbourne (Vol. 4, p. 110)

June 8, 1814, to Henrietta D'Ussières (Vol. 4, p. 122)

Sept. 7, 1814, to Annabella Milbanke (Vol. 4, p. 168)

Sept. 9, 1814, to Annabella Milbanke (Vol. 4, p. 169)

Sept. 19, 1814, to Annabella Milbanke (Vol. 4, p. 176)

Nov. 13, 1814, to Lady Melbourne (Vol. 4, p. 231)

Nov. 16, 1814, to Annabella Milbanke (Vol. 4, p. 232)

Jan. 26, 1815, to John Cam Hobhouse (Vol. 4, p. 259)

Sept. 4, 1815, to J. W. Webster (Vol. 4, p. 310)

Sept. 18, 1815, to J. W. Webster (Vol. 4, p. 312)

Oct. 18, 1815, to S. T. Coleridge (Vol. 4, p. 318)

Oct. 30, 1815, to Leigh Hunt (Vol. 4, p. 324)

Oct. 31, 1815, to Thomas Moore (Vol. 4, p. 326)

Feb. 2, 1816, to Sir Ralph Noel (Vol. 5, p. 20)

Feb. 3, 1816, to Lady Byron (Vol. 5, p. 21)

Feb. 5, 1816, to Lady Byron (Vol. 5, p. 22)

Feb. 8, 1816, to Lady Byron (Vol. 5, p. 24)

May 1, 1816, to John Cam Hobhouse (Vol. 5, p. 72)

Sept. 8, 1816, to Augusta Leigh (Vol. 5, p. 91)

Alpine Journal, Sept. 17–28, 1816 (Vol. 5, pp. 96–105)

Oct. 15, 1816, to Augusta Leigh (Vol. 5, p. 114)

Oct. 28, 1816, to Augusta Leigh (Vol. 5, p. 119)

Nov. 17, 1816, to Thomas Moore (Vol. 5, p. 129)

Nov. 25, 1816, to John Murray (Vol. 5, p. 132)

Nov. 27, 1816, to Douglas Kinnaird (Vol. 5, p. 134)

Dec. 18, 1816, to Augusta Leigh (Vol. 5, p. 140)

Dec. 19, 1816, to Augusta Leigh (Vol. 5, p. 144)

Dec. 24, 1816, to Thomas Moore (Vol. 5, p. 146)

Jan. 2, 1817, to John Murray (Vol. 5, p. 154)

Jan. 20, 1817, to Douglas Kinnaird (Vol. 5, p. 160)

Feb. 28, 1817, to Thomas Moore (Vol. 5, p. 176)

April 11, 1817, to Thomas Moore (Vol. 5, p. 210)

May 30, 1817, to John Murray (Vol. 5, p. 229)
June 3–4, 1817, to Augusta Leigh (Vol. 5, p. 231)
Aug. 21, 1817, to John Murray (Vol. 5, p. 257)
Sept. 15, 1817, to John Murray (Vol. 5, p. 264)
Jan. 8, 1818, to John Murray (Vol. 6, p. 3)
Feb. 20, 1818, to John Murray (Vol. 6, p. 11)
June 1, 1818, to Thomas Moore (Vol. 6, p. 45)
June 25, 1818, to John Cam Hobhouse (Vol. 6, p. 54)
Sept. 8, 1818, to J. W. Webster (Vol. 6, p. 65)
Sept. 19, 1818, to Thomas Moore (Vol. 6, p. 66)
Nov. 11, 1818, to John Cam Hobhouse (Vol. 6, p. 76)
Jan. 19, 1819, to John Cam Hobhouse and Douglas Kinnaird (Vol. 6, p. 91)
Jan. 26, 1819, to Scrope Berdmore Davies (Vol. 11, p. 170)
Jan. 27, 1819, to Douglas Kinnaird (Vol. 6, p. 97)
April 6, 1819, to John Murray (Vol. 6, p. 105)
April 6, 1819, to John Cam Hobhouse (Vol. 6, p. 106)
April 24, 1819, to Douglas Kinnaird (Vol. 6, p. 113)
May 15, 1819, to John Murray (Vol. 6, p. 125)
May 17, 1819, to Augusta Leigh (Vol. 6, p. 129)
May 18, 1819, to John Murray (Vol. 6, p. 133)
June 6, 1819, to R. B. Hoppner (Vol. 6, p. 146)
[June–July?], 1819, to Countess Guiccioli (Vol. 6, p. 170)
July 26, 1819, to Augusta Leigh (Vol. 6, p. 185)
Aug. 1, 1819, to John Murray (Vol. 6, p. 192)
Aug. 12, 1819, to John Murray (Vol. 6, p. 206)
Aug. 20, 1819, to John Cam Hobhouse (Vol. 6, p. 211)
Aug. 23, 1819, to John Cam Hobhouse (Vol. 6, p. 213)
Aug. 23, 1819, to Countess Guiccioli (Vol. 6, p. 215)
Oct. 26, 1818 [1819], to Douglas Kinnaird (Vol. 6, p. 231)
Oct. 29, 1819, to John Murray (Vol. 6, p. 235)
Oct. 29, 1819, to R. B. Hoppner (Vol. 6, p. 236)
Dec. 10, 1819, to Countess Guiccioli (Vol. 6, p. 258)
Dec. 23, 1819, to Augusta Leigh (Vol. 6, p. 259)
Feb. 21, 1820, to John Murray (Vol. 7, p. 41)
March 3, 1820, to John Cam Hobhouse (Vol. 7, p. 49)
Nov. 19, 1820, to John Murray (Vol. 7, p. 230)
Dec. 9, 1820, to John Murray (Vol. 7, p. 247)
Ravenna Journal, Jan. 5, 1821–Feb. 27, 1821 (Vol. 8, pp. 11–51)
Feb. 16, 1821, to John Murray (Vol. 8, p. 77)
April 26, 1821, to P. B. Shelley (Vol. 8, p. 103)

July 5, 1821, to Thomas Moore (Vol. 8, p. 146)

Aug. 23, 1821, to John Murray (Vol. 8, p. 186)

Sept. 24, 1821, to John Murray (Vol. 8, p. 219)

Oct. 5, 1821, to Augusta Leigh (Vol. 8, p. 233)

Detached Thoughts, Oct. 15, 1821–May 8, 1822 (Vol. 9, pp. 11–52)

Nov. 3, 1821, to John Murray (Vol. 9, p. 53)

March 4, 1822, to Thomas Moore (Vol. 9, p. 118)

March 6, 1822, to Thomas Moore (Vol. 9, p. 120)

March 8, 1822, to Thomas Moore (Vol. 9, p. 122)

May 26, 1822, to John Murray (Vol. 9, p. 163)

Aug. 3, 1822, to John Murray (Vol. 9, p. 189)

Oct. 4, 1822, to Mary Shelley (Vol. 10, p. 11)

Nov. 14, 1822, to Mary Shelley (Vol. 10, p. 33)

[Nov. 16?], 1822, to Mary Shelley (Vol. 10, p. 34)

Dec. 1, 1822, to Lady Hardy (Vol. 10, p. 49)

Jan. 18, 1823, to Douglas Kinnaird (Vol. 10, p. 87)

July 22, 1823, to Goethe (Vol. 10, p. 213)

Journal in Cephalonia, Sept. 28, 1823–Dec. 17, 1823 (Vol. 11, pp. 29–35)

Oct. 6, 1823, to John Cam Hobhouse (Vol. 11, p. 39)

Oct. 25, 1823, to Charles F. Barry (Vol. 11, p. 52)

Dec. 26, 1823, to John Bowring (Vol. 11, p. 82)

Dec. 27, 1823, to John Cam Hobhouse (Vol. 11, p. 85)

Jan. 2, 1824, to Henry Muir (Vol. 11, p. 87)

Jan. 13, 1824, to Charles Hancock (Vol. 11, p. 91)

Jan. 23, 1824, to Yusuff Pasha (Vol. 11, p. 98)

March 4, 1824, to Thomas Moore (Vol. 11, p. 125)

March, 17, 1824, to Countess Guiccioli (Vol. 11, p. 137)

March 30, 1824, to John Bowring (Vol. 11, p. 145)

INDEX

British Museum, 171
British Review, 218 and n
Brocket Hall, 69
Broglie, Duchesse de, 197
Brompton, 126
Brønsted, Peter Oluf, 46 and n
Brothers, Messrs, 38n
Brothers, Richard, 54 and n
Brougham, Henry, 263; reviewed *Hours of Idleness*, 21n
Broughton, 126
Browne, James Hamilton, 299, 305, 314
Bruen, George H., 287 and n
Bruges, 122, 231
Brummell, George Bryan ("Beau"), 230n, 268 and n
Bruno, Dr. Francesco, 310n, 313
Brutus, 85, 88, 92
Bryant, Jacob, *Dissertation Concerning the War of Troy*, 243 and n
Buckingham, Duke of, 67
Bugden, 68
Buonaparte, Napoleon, 154, 177n, 215, 267, 268; Ali Pasha compared to, 31; and Moreau, 71 and n; his digestion, 87; pared away, 88; B.'s Ode to, 96; relics of at Antwerp, 123; at St. Helena, 231; as a general, 270; his sire not remarkable, 279; campaign in Italy, 300 and n
Burdett, Sir Francis, 191, 220, 221, 229, 230; as orator, 263
Burges, Sir James Bland, 274 and n
Burke, Edmund, 90, 116, 117n, 176, 263
Burney, Fanny (Madame D'Arblay), *Cecilia*, 127
Burns, Robert, 85, 93, 101
Bury, Lord, 67 and n
Busby, Dr. Thomas, 86
Buyukderé, 83 and n
Butler, Dr. George, 22, 24 and n, 37
Butler, Samuel, *Hudibras*, 237 and n, 269 and n
Byron, Allegra, 180, 224, 225, 253, 286 and n, 286–7
Byron, Anne Isabella (Annabella), Lady (Noel) (née Anne Isabella Milbanke, q.v.), 117, 178, 304; expects child in December, 111, 118; truth itself, 118; B.'s appeals to her, 120, 121; has been kind to Augusta, 124; menaced and frightened Augusta, 135n; B.'s "moral Clytemnestra",

145, 182; destroyed B.'s moral existence, 156; her magnanimity, 162; satire on in *Don Juan*, 187 and n; her account book, 196–7; "that infamous fiend", 198; B. wrote to, 221; and coronation, 226, 231; and the funds, 228; would she please die, 261; on B.'s melancholy, 275
Byron, Augusta Ada (B.'s daughter), 124, 146, 152, 299, 316
Byron, Mrs. Catherine Gordon (B.'s mother), 19, 20, 22, 51n, 88, 89
Byron, Eliza, 81
Byron, George, 162
Byron, Hon. Mrs. George, 110
Byron (works)
American edition of his poems, 287
Beppo, 141n, 168 and n, 169n, 174, 180, 182, 268 and n
Blues, The, 174n
Bride of Abydos, The, 29n, 86, 91n
Cain, 281, 283, 285, 288 and n, 360
"Childish Recollections", 22, 244n
Childe Harold, 190; note on Lisbon, 24n; Zitsa, 29n; Canto II, Mt. Tomerit, 35n; praised by Mackintosh, 90n; diverted B. from politics, 265; written as if by an older man, 277; Canto III, 151–2, 166 and n; Canto III, original MS., 152; 4th Canto completed, 166; Canto IV, Hobhouse carried MS., 168 and n; B. questions its success, 174
Corsair, The, 151–2, 167, 203n, 223 and n
Deformed Transformed, The, 290n
Don Juan, 141n, 191, 292, 319 and n; father of Haidée, 29n; Canto X, St. Ursula, 71n; "words are things", 85n; Canto I finished, 180 and n; 1st Canto sent to England, 182; dedicated to Southey, 185n; B.'s friends objected to publication, 187n; Canto II finished, 187, 189, 194; "you sha'n't make canticles of my cantos", 189; will make 50 cantos, 190; first proof, 195; anonymous and without dedication, 197; will never flatter the million's canting, 206; B. has no plan, 213; to giggle and make giggle, 214; B. never wrote better, 217; "My Grandmother's Review", 218 and n; bawdy but good English, 220;

Byron (works)—*continued*
3rd Canto started, 221; Cantos I and II and forgeries, 222–3 and n; women forbidden to read, 224; Cantos III and IV sent, 226, 231; notes, 240; Bryant's view of Troy, 243n; plans for, 251–2; shipwreck scenes, 256 and n; B. promised not to continue, 262; Murray played stepmother to, 281; Goethe fond of, 288; no friend like a woman, 292n; B.'s not continuing, 316 and n; B.'s defense of, 327–9

English Bards and Scotch Reviewers, on Gell, 36n; 2nd edition, 37; 3rd edition, 40; Lord Carlisle, 51n; made Augusta laugh, 52; lines on Moore and Jeffrey, 56n; Fitzgerald, 175n, 215n; piracies, 252; B. threatens a new one, 260; admired by Sheridan, 265

Francesca of Rimini, 282
Giaour, The, 80, 70 and n, 86, 359
Heaven and Earth, 282, 283
Hebrew Melodies, 111
Hints from Horace, 242, 253, 282
Hours of Idleness, 21n
Lament of Tasso, 160
Letter on Bowles, 252
Lara, 357
Manfred, 160, 164 and n, 288
Marino Faliero, 243–4, 252
Mazeppa, 183, 186, 196n, 197, 228
Memoirs, 220 and n, 222
Monody on the Death of Sheridan, 143n, 183
Morgante Maggiore (translation), 227, 231, 282
"Ode to Napoleon Buonaparte", 96
Prophecy of Dante, 221, 228
Sardanapalus, 245, 246, 257n
Siege of Corinth, 151n, 154
"Song", 21n
"Stanzas to the Po", 282
Two Foscari, The, 256, 257, 281, 348
Vampyre, B.'s original, 212
Vision of Judgment, The, 282, 360
Werner, 283, 284, 304
Byron, Hon. Isabella, 51n
Byron, Commodore John, 217 and n
Byron, Juliana, 162n
Byron, Sophia Maria, 145, 262
Byron, William, 5th Baron, 50n
Byzantium, 24

Caesar, Julius, 88, 214n, 251, 279
Cadiz, 22, 37, 47; B's account of his visit, 26–7
Cagliari, 27
Calabria earthquake, 271
Calais, 306n
Caligari, 186
Calvinism, 308
Cam (river), 245
Cambridge, 52, 53, 55, 67, 153, 233, 235, 237; B's opinion of, 19; B's life at, 20; B. with Long at, 233, 244; B. at first unhappy at, 274–5
Cambridge Whig Club, 22n, 233
Campbell, Thomas, 101, 165, 167, 175, 242, 258; his edition of English poets, 243; *Gertrude of Wyoming*, 243 and n; *Pleasures of Hope*, 265 and n
Canada, 228
Canning, George, 141n, 170, 171n, 214
Canning, Stratford (later Lord Stratford de Redcliffe), 80 and n
Canova, Antonio, 140 and n, 149, 253
Cannstatt, 46n
Cape Colonna, 35, 45
Capuchin Convent, 46
Caravaggio, Michelangelo Amerighi, 360
Carbonari, 239n, 250, 333
Cardinal Legate, 201
Carlisle, 4th Earl of, 51n
Carlisle, Frederick Howard, 5th Earl of, 51 and n, 200n
Carlotta, 186
Carlton House, 94
Carmarthen, Marchioness of, 247n
Caroline (B's 16-year-old lover), 21 and n
Caroline, Queen, death, 258 and n
Carr, Sir John, 27
Carridi (Carrithi), banker, 308
Carrington, Baron, 67n
Carthage, 231
Cartwright, Major John, 216
Cary, Capt., 36n
Cassius, 88
Castaños, General Francisco Janier de, Duke of Baylen, 28 and n
Castle Eden, 109
Castiglione, Marchesa, 148, 149
Castlereagh, Robert Stewart, Viscount, 2nd Marquess of Londonderry, 185 and n, 187 and n, 350
Castri (Delphos), 95

Catalani, Mme. Angelica, 156
Cateaton, 231
Catholic churches, 352
Catholicism, 285
Cawthorn, James, 252
Centlivre, Mrs. Susanna, *A Bold Stroke for a Wife*, 202 and n, 298 and n
Cephalonia, 295, 296, 298, 305, 312, 313, 315
Certosa Cemetery, 201
Ceylon, 53n
Chalandritsanos, Lukas, 310n, 311, 313 and n
Chalmers, George, *Life of Mary Queen of Scots*, 169n
Chamouni, 126, 131
Chancery Lane, 183, 272
Chantery, Sir Francis, 165n
Chaonia, 35
Charles I, 126
Charles II, 328
Chatham, 274
Chatham, William Pitt, 1st Earl of, 263
Chaucer, Geoffrey, 185
Chauncey, Capt. Isaac, 287
Chaworth, Mary A., 82 and n, 273
Chaworth-Musters, Mrs. 98 and n
Cheltenham, 274
Chesterfield, 2nd Earl of, 77 and n
Chiarenza, 296
Chillon, Castle of, 126, 127
China, 271
Chrisso, 95
Chrisso, Bishop of, 49
Christ, 54, 55
Christchurch, Oxford, 233
Christ-Church Hospital, 175
Christianity, 53, 278, 283 and n, 310n
Christians, 53, 54
Cibber, Colley, 100
Cicero, 85
Cintra (Sintra), 23, 25 and n, 29
Clairmont, Claire, 125 and n, 145 and n, 155–6, 182, 196
Clare, John Fitzgibbon, 2nd Earl of, 64 and n, 277, 290
Clarens, 126, 127, 166
Claridge, John, 37, 330
Clarke, Mr. and Mrs., 273
Clarke, physician, 78
Claudianus, Claudius, 167
Claughton, Thomas, 39n, 99, 105, 111, 154
Cleopatra, 85

Clermont, Mrs. Mary Anne, 162
Clootz, Jean Baptiste (Anacharsis), 251 and n
Clutterbuck, Wortley, 218n
Clytemnestra, 182, 231
Cobbett, William, 230
Cockburn, Robert, 89n
Cockerell, Charles Robert, 46 and n
Cogni, Margarita (Fornarina, Fornaretta), 186, 223, 224; described by B., 181; her story, 206–12; fit to breed gladiators from, 344
Cohen, Francis (Palgrave), 213 and n
Colburn, Henry, 196
Coldham, Mr 57
Coleridge, S. T., 33n; in the *Poetic Mirror*, 99n; best of the Lakers, 101; *Christabel*, 114 and n, 150–1 and n, 346; *Edinburgh Review* on, 158; asked to write drama for Drury Lane, 274
Collins, William, 82, 242
Colman, George the Younger, B. drinking with, 117, 279; *Bluebeard*, 44–5 and n; *Broad Grins*, 255; *John Bull*, 260 and n; and Sheridan, 264
Colocotroni, *see* Kolokotrones, Theodore
Cologne, 71n
Commons, House of, 230 and n, 253 and n
Congreve rockets, 302
Constantinople, 22, 30n, 35, 37, 39, 43, 45, 46n, 47, 60, 83n, 158, 236, 309
Constantinople, Plague of, 271
Constitution, flagship, 288
Contarini, Madame, 208
Coolidge, Joseph, of Boston, 255, 267
Copenhagen, 46 and n, 244
Coppet, 125, 138, 166
Cordova, Admiral, 26–7
Cordova, Signorita, 27
Corfe Castle, 253n
Corfu, 32, 149, 296
Corgialegno, Geronimo, 298, 305, 308, 312, 314
Corinth, 39; Gulf of, 32, 43, 314n
Cornwall, Barry, see Procter, Bryan Waller
Corsica, 295
Courier, The, 280
Court of Chancery, 20n
Covent Garden Theatre, 94, 117, 122n
Cowper, William, 82, 175 and n

Crabbe, George, 165 and n, 167, 175, 212, 258
Craven Street, 78
Croker, John Wilson, 165, 214
Cruger, Henry, 116 and n
Cunningham, J. W., 287n
Curioni, Alberico, 251 and n
Curran, John Philpot, 224
Cuvier, Léopold, Chrétien, 280 and n
Cyanean Rocks, 49

Da Bezzi, Eleanora, 186
d'Albany, Comtesse (née Stolberg), 240 and n
Dallas, Robert Charles, 59 and n; his farce, 44 and n
Dalmatia, 124
Dalrymple, Sir Hew, 25 and n
Dalyell, Sir J. G., *Shipwrecks and Disasters at Sea*, 256n
Da Mosta, Elena, 186 and n
Dante, 198, 221, 286
Danube, 41
Dardanelles (Hellespont), 35 and n
Davies, Scrope Berdmore, 45, 163, 221; B's debt to, 39n; said B. liked children, 50; B. to visit at Cambridge, 51, 53; B. sought his advice, 56; B. paid off debt, 96 and n, 110; B. wants him to come to Geneva, 123; carrying packets to England, 124; objected to publication of *Don Juan*, 187; escaped to Continent, 230 and n; and Matthews, 235–6; clever in conversation, 267–8; quip on Brummell, 268; his gambling winnings, 276; life and soul of everybody, 330
Dawes, 42
Defoe, Daniel, *Robinson Crusoe*, 22
Delaval, Sir F. B., 249
Delladecima, Count Demetrius, 306 and n, 312 and n
Delphi, 35, 49; Oracle, 193
Demosthenes, 109, 263
Denon, Dominique Vivant, Baron de, 347
Dent, John, 165 and n
Dent d'Argent, 131
Dent Jamant, 128
Derbyshire, 138, 273
Dermody, Thomas, 59 and n
Dersofi, Professor Nancy, 225n
Dibdin, Thomas, 114, 142 and n; *The British Raft*, 143n

Dick, 233
Diego, 238
Diodati, 125, 126, 133, 139, 194n
D'Israeli, Isaac, 251
Dogherty, Dan, 236
Doncaster, 69
Don Juan (Shelley's boat), 289
Dorville (D'Orville), Henry, 224
Downing Fellowship, Cambridge, 233
Dragomestre, 311 and n, 313
Drako, George, 297, 303
Drontheim, Norway, 255
Drummond, Sir William, 171
Drury, Rev. Henry, 24, 45, 47, 287, 288
Drury, Dr. Joseph, 265
Drury Lane Theatre, 44 and n, 115 and n, 122n, 142n, 143n, 150, 166n; Committee, 115 and n, 273
Dryden, John, 40; *All for Love*, 85 and n
Dublin, 242n, 267, 274
Duck puddle, 48
Duff, Helen, 89
Duff, Mary, 86, 88–90
Duffie, Lt. Col. John, 296
Dundee, 274
Dunn, Henry, 286n
Dupont, General, 28n
Durham, 59n, 133
D'Ussières, Henrietta, 104n
Dutens, Louis, *Memoirs of a Traveller*, 171 and n
Dwyer, 24, 37

Edgecombe, clerk, 202, 223
Edgeworth, Richard, 249
Edinburgh, 66n, 88, 89n
Edinburgh Review, 37 and n, 47, 56n, 69n, 93n, 150, 179, 254; review of *Hours of Idleness*, 21 and n, 22 and n; review of Rogers's poems, 90 and n; attacked B., 158; B. doesn't want, 258; on Keats, 346
Edleston, John, 245 and n
Egypt, 29
Eigers, The, 131
Elba, 295
Eleanora, 186
Ellice, Edward, 41 and n, 188
Elphinstone, Margaret Mercer, 34n
Elwin, Malcolm, *Lord Byron's Family*, 197n
Encyclopaedia Britannica, 93n
England, B. glad to be away from, 24;

B. wishes to leave, 51; B. may come in spring, 136; B. does not wish to reside in, 142, 143; B. absent two and a half years, 178; divorce not so easy in, 200; reform in, 216; B. thought of returning to, 216, 224; might return on business, 222; B. glad he did not return to, 230, 231

English-Armenian Grammar, 147, 153

English language, 61, 153, 234, 252, 253 and n, 271, 299, 317

English Revolution, 271

Ephesus, 38, 39

Epicurus, 86

Epimenides, 299 and n

Epirus, 29 and n, 34, 35, 241

Erivan, Persia, 133

Erskine, Thomas, 1st Baron, 230n, 263, 304

Estramadure, 23

Eton, 309

Europe, 25, 35, 88, 179, 216, 266, 330

Eustathius, see Georgiou, Eustathius

Euxine, 84

Exeter 'Change, 84

Eywood, 86

Faenza, 218

Falcieri, Giovanni Battista (Tita), 237, 250

Falmouth, 23, 25

Falstaff, 102

Farebrother (Fairbrother), 193 and n

Farquhar, George, *The Beaux' Stratagem*, 175 and n; *The Recruiting Officer*, 194 and n

Farrell, Orson, 233

Fenice Theatre (Phoenix) 149, 157

Ferdinand, King of Naples, 242n

Ferrara, 159, 201, 202, 223, 352

Ferrara, Duchess of, 135

Fersen, Count, 148

Fielding, Henry, 185; Scott compared to, 239; *Jonathan Wild*, 230 and n, 279; *Joseph Andrews*, 102 and n; *Tom Jones*, 72 and n, 100, 193 and n; *Tom Thumb*, 23 and n, 218n

Finch, Col. Robert, 143 and n

Fiott, John, 46 and n

Fitzgerald, Col., 148

Fitzgerald, Lord Edward, 215 and n

Fitzgerald, William Thomas, 175 and n, 215 and n

Flahaut, Mme. (née Mercer) (*see also* Elphinstone, Margaret Mercer), 201

Fleet Street, 153n

Fletcher, William, 32, 33, 193, 250, 310n; in storm at sea, 32, 33, 40; dissatisfied, 33; sent home, 46; fat and facetious, 56; put B. to bed drunk, 76; married Ann Rood, 120n; in fear of banditti, 122; remained at Diodati, 126; and Margarita Cogni, 211; a breeding beast of burden, 217; on Hobhouse in Newgate, 230; dead commandant in his bed, 237; to copy Bacon's Apothegms, 240; disgusted by Eustathius, 332; "lamentations after beef and beer", 356

Fletcher, John, 328

Fletcher, John, and Massinger, Philip, *The Beggar's Bush*, 114 and n

Florence, 147, 159, 160, 161, 178, 185, 240n, 249, 253n, 292

Florida, ship, 319n

Ford, John, dramatist, 328

Fornarina (Fornaretta), *see* Cogni, Margarita

Forresti, George, 41 and n

Fortune (Goddess), 277

Foscolo, Ugo, 140n, 252–3; *Jacopo Ortis*, 190

Foster, John, 46 and n

Fox, Charles James, 172n, 176, 263

France, 25, 83n, 88, 165, 231, 268, 306 and n; language, 27, 129, 169, 268, 272, 297n; Revolution, 251 and n, 271

Franklin, Benjamin, 88

Frederick the Great, and Hell's torments, 284–5

French-Armenian professorship, 138

Frere, John Hookham, 141 and n, 165, 187, 189; "Whistlecraft", 169 and n, 227

Fribourg, Canton, 128, 132, 133

Friese, German servant, 22

Friuli, 60

Fry, Mrs. Elizabeth, 298, 302

Fusina, 177

Fyler, Capt., 226

Galignani's Messenger, 194n, 221

Galilee, 53

Gamba, Giulia, 317

Gamba, Laurina, 317

Gamba, Olimpia, 317

Gamba, Count Pietro, 240, 241, 314, 317; returns arms to B., 250; captured by the Turks, 310 and n, 311, 313 and n, 315; and purchase of red cloth, 314; *Narrative . . .*, 316n

Gamba, Count Ruggero, 225, 240, 317

Ganymede, 36

Garrick, David, and Colman the Younger, *The Clandestine Marriage*, 75 and n

Gay, John, *The Beggars' Opera*, 93

Gell, Sir William, *Topography of Troy, Itinerary in Greece*, 36 and n, 37

Geltrude, *see* Vicari, Geltrude

Geneva, 123, 125n, 136, 143, 155, 184, 224; Lake of, 128, 133

Genoa, 159, 294 and n, 295 and n

Genoa Gazette, 292

Gentiles, 53, 54

George III, 226

Georgiou, Eustathius, 42, 332

Germany, 252, 288, 294n; language, 129, 132, 169

Ghent, 122

Giavella, 297, 303

Gibbon, Edward, 105, 177

Gibraltar, 22, 24, 25, 28, 33, 47, 48, 50

Gifford, William, 157, 165, 171, 173, 237, 258, 335; and *Siege of Corinth*, 154; and B.'s praise of Pope, 167n; opinion of *Don Juan*, 212; and *Cain*, 281

Ginguené, Pierre Louis, *Histoire Littéraire de l'Italie*, 240 and n

Giordani, Pietro, 271 and n

Giraud, Nicolo, 42 and n, 332

Giulietta, 186

Glover, Mrs., 274

Glettenheimer, 186

Godwin, Mary (later Mrs. Shelley), 125n, 155, 182; and Shelley's hallucination, 195 and n; *Frankenstein*, 196

Godwin, William, 196

Godwin, Mrs. William, 182, 195

Goethe, Johann Wolfgang von, 288, 294 and n; *Faust*, 283

Goetz, Countess, 139 and n, 147

Goldoni, Carlo, 227, 241n

Goldsmith, Oliver, *Good Natured Man*, 111 and n, 191 and n; *She Stoops to Conquer*, 213 and n; *The Traveller*, 37 and n; *Vicar of Wakefield*, 42 and n, 49 and n, 158 and n, 310 and n

Gordon, Mr., wine merchant, 26

Gordon, Lord George, 229 and n

Gordon, Thomas, *History of the Greek Revolution*, 170 and n

Göttingen, 255

Graham, Sandford, 46 and n

Gramont, Philibert, Comte de, *Mémoires*, 77 and n

Grand Canal, 176, 177–8, 199, 204, 210, 224

Grattan, Henry, 263, 267

Great Britain, 200, 225

Greece, 33, 35, 46n, 48, 52, 82, 88, 90n, 128, 189, 258, 266, 296, 301, 302; ruled by Ali, 29n; "how I wrote there", 260; B. going to, 294; B. wanted to return to, 339; Government, 303, 304, 305, 306, 315, 318; language, 33, 46, 153, 172, 181, 272

Greek Loan, 303, 318 and n

Greeks, B.'s liking for, 36; state of women under, 241; dissentions among them, 296, 300, 302, 306; none know a problem from a poker, 309

Granada, Archbishop of, 217

Grenville, William Wyndham Grenville, Lord, 263

Grey, Charles, 2nd Earl of, 247, 263

Grey, Lady, 58 and n

Grey de Ruthyn, Henry Edward, 19th Lord, 28 and n

Grillparzer, Franz, 246

Grimm, Friedrich Melchior, *Correspondance Littéraire*, 69 and n

Grindelwald, 131

Guernsey, 259

Guiccioli, Count Alessandro, 192, 194, 204, 214 and n, 221, 224, 225

Guiccioli, Countess Teresa (née Gamba Ghiselli), 212, 223, 237; first meeting with B., 192 and n; fair as sunrise, 194; on B.'s jealousy, 203n; B. describes for Augusta, 204–5; in hysterics at Alfieri's play, 212; B. faithful to, 219; wrote Italian letter for B., 239, 240; to be given Scott seal, 244; on love in tragedy, 246; B. attached to her, 260; separated from her husband, 260; made B. promise to write no more of *Don Juan*, 262; arranged shipment of Allegra's body, 286; tearful at B.'s leaving, 339

Guilford, 4th Earl of, 159 and n

Holderness, Mary Doublet, Countess of, 276
Holland, 83 and n, 88
Holland, Henry Fox, 3rd Baron, 22 and n, 57, 93 and n, 240, 263, 270
Holland, Lady (née Elizabeth Vassall), 64, 78
Holland House, 93n, 348
Home, John, *Douglas*, 66 and n
Homer, 101, 175n, 243 and n, 296
Hone, William, 223n
Hope, Thomas, 103n, 159
Hope, Mrs. Thomas, 103 and n
Hoppner, Richard Belgrave, 173
Hoppner, Mrs., 224
Horace, 42 and n, 88 and n, 167; *Ars Poetica*, 174 and n, 285 and n
Horner, Francis, 159
Hornsey, 160
Horse Guards, 230n
Howard, Frederick, 50 and n
Hume, David, 54
Hungary, 61
Hunt, Henry ("Orator"), 229 and n, 230
Hunt, John, 292
Hunt, Leigh, B. on his character, 92; his Yahoo children, 289; and Murray, 289–90; B.'s relations with, 290–1; futility of trying to help him, 346; *The Feast of the Poets*, 115 and n; *Foliage*, 175 and n; *The Story of Rimini*, 117, 160, 175
Hussein Bey, 34 and n
Hyde Park, 204
Hydra, 296, 299
Hymettus, 45, 46

Ibraham Pasha, 29
Ida, Mount, 36
Illyria (Illyricum), 29, 35
Illissus, 35
Imola, 231
Inchbald, Mrs. Elizabeth, 171
Interlachen, 130, 132
Ionian Islands, 29n, 296, 300, 312n
Ipsara, 296
Ireland, 64 n, 148, 252
Irving, Washington, 255, 258; liked *Don Juan*, 282
Italy, morals and manners, 227–8; *poetry* of politics, 250; B. not tired of, 326; no government at all in, 351; opera, 333; language, 46, 49, 61, 135,

137, 144, 148, 161, 169, 190, 202, 219, 227, 240, 251, 272, 297n, 317
Ithaca, 296, 298, 300

Jackman, Isaac, *All the World's a Stage*, 213 and n
Jackson, John ("Gentleman"), 96, 156
Jamaica, 267
Janina (Yanina, Ioannina), 29 and n, 41n
Java Gazette, 247
Jeffrey, Francis, 56n, 151, 158
Jennings, Sam, 144
Jericho, 309
Jersey, George Childe-Villiers, 5th Earl of, 62, 85
Jersey, Lady (née Sarah Sophia Fane), 103, 137, 140
Jesus of Nazareth, 55
Jews, 54
Joao V, 25n
Job, the Arab Patriarch, 360
Johnson, Samuel, 92, 181n; *English Poets*, 214n; *Life of Savage*, 176; *London*, 187; *Vanity of Human Wishes*, 254 and n
Jones, Jacob, Commodore, 287
Jones, Rev., Thomas, 234
Josepha, Donna, 26 and n
Judaea, 53
Jugurtha, 340 and n
Jungfrau (Yung-frau), 130
Juno Lucina, 118
Junot, Andoche, 25n
Jura, 128, 133
Juvenal, Satires, 172n

Kalamos, 312 and n
Kean, Edmund, 103, 212, 274
Keats, John, and review on *Endymion*, 254; B.'s opinion of his poetry, 346–7; his attack on Pope, 347; *Hyperion*, 347
Kellam, William, 28n
Kelly, Frances Maria (Fanny), 142 and n
Kennedy, Dr. James, 308, 310n
Kennedy, Capt. Moses, 45
Keppel, Maria, 143
Kerr, Robert, 280n
Kidd, Capt., 22
Kilkenny, 61
King's College, Cambridge, 236

Ljubljana, 242n
Lo-Kristi, 122
London, 39, 48, 64, 83n, 101, 106, 108, 114, 234, 251n, 254n, 270, 287n, 306n; B. at 16 Piccadilly, 19n; compared to Cadiz, 26; B. just returned to, 112; Lady Byron left, 118; its weather compared to Ravenna's, 243; B. nostalgic for, 250; only place for fun, 335
London Greek Committee, 295, 296, 297, 302, 306, 307, 309, 318, 319
London, Plague of, 271
Long, Edward Noel, 233, 244 and n
Longman, Thomas Norton, publisher, 139
Lords, House of, 51n, 57n
Lotti, 186
Loughborough, 234
Loughborough, Alexander Wedderburn, 171
Loughnan, Son, and O'Brien, 318n
Louis XVIII, 231n
Louvel, Pierre-Louis, 231 and n
Lowe, Sir Hudson, 270
Lucifer, 280, 281
Lucretius, 86; *De Rerum Natura*, 24n, 180 and n
Luddites, 150
Ludlow, Gen. Edmund, 126
Ludwig, John Frederick, of Ratisbon, 25n
Lugano Gazette, 230
Luigi, Martini, 201, 353
Luigia, 186
Luriottis, Andreas, 318n, 319
Lusieri, Giovanni Battista, 42
Lutherans, 150
Lutzerode, Baron, 288 and n
Lyceum Theatre, 44n
Lycophron, Cassandra, 221 and n
Lyttelton, William Henry, 3rd Baron, 264 and n

Macdonalds, 151 and n
Macedonia, 29
Machiavelli, Niccolo, 249
Mackintosh, Sir James, 90, 91, 171
Macnamara, 233
Macri sisters, 38 and n
Macri, Mrs. Tarsia, 38n
Macri, Teresa, "Maid of Athens", 38n
Madrid, 27

Maestri, 177
Mafra, 25 and n
Magellan, Straits of, 217n
Magliabecchi, Antonio, 93 and n
Magnesia, 231
Mahmoud II, Sultan, 29n, 39, 41
Mahmout Pasha, 34 and n
Mahomet, 54, 171, 303, 316 and n
Mainote pirates, 45
Maitland, Sir Thomas, 36n, 300 and n
Malapiero, 150
Malcolm, 165n
Malone, Edmond, 169n
Malta, 22, 24, 28, 29, 33, 34, 36, 39, 40, 41n, 42, 47, 48, 272, 333
Malthus, Thomas Robert, 49, 55
Manchester, 220
Manicheism, 53
Mansel, William Lort, 19 and n, 237
Mansion House, 46
Mantua, 159
Marat, Jean-Paul, 229
Marathon, 35, 45
Marceau, Gen. François, 308
Margate, 159
Maria Theresa, Empress, 67
Marius, Caius, 231
Marmontel, Jean François, 148
Mary, The Virgin, 68
Massingberd, Mrs. Elizabeth, 19 and n, 110 and n
Massinger, Philip, 328; *A New Way to Pay Old Debts*, 206 and n, 212 and n
Matthews, Charles Skinner, 23n, 42, 53 and n, 232-7
Matthews, Henry, 236
Matta, Charles de Bourdeille, comte de, 78 and n
Maturin, Rev. Charles Robert, 159; *Bertram*, 164n, 273; *Manuel*, 164 and n
Mavrocordatos, Prince Alexander, 296, 299, 304, 306, 307, 312 and n, 319; with Greek fleet, 300; says B. will "electrify the troops", 310; to accompany B. to Salona, 318
Mawman, J., 281
Mechlin (Malines), 122, 123
Medea, 181-2, 209, 210
Mediterranean, 27, 37, 60, 116
Medwin, Thomas, *Conversations . . .* (ed. Lovell), 216 and n
Meillerie, 125, 195-6
Mekhitar, Peter, 137n

Melbourne, Lady (née Elizabeth Milbanke), 63, 66, 82, 86, 108n, 111
Meletius of Janina, Archbishop of Athens, 49n
Mengaldo, Cavalier Angelo, 177 and n, 201
Messina, 295
Metastasio, 67
Metaxa, Count Constantine, 298
Methodists, 310n
Meyler, Richard, 268 and n
Mezzofanti, Giuseppe, 271 and n, 272
Michelli, Countess, 194
Middleton, 62, 63, 70, 73, 85
Milan, 136, 139, 143n, 148, 185, 224
Milbanke, Annabella (Anne Isabella), B.'s opinion of her poems, 59 and n; requires all cardinal virtues, 61; B.'s tentative proposal refused, 63 and n; her "character" of B., 63 and n; the amiable Mathematician, 64; Princess of Parallelograms, 65; her requirements for a husband, 65 and n; patroness of Blacket, 67 and n; her letters to B., 71; melancholy letter to B., 73–4; proposal by Stratford Canning, 80 and n; a very superior woman, 92; wants to discuss religion with B., 102; B. sent her letter to Lady Melbourne, 103; has committed herself, 104; B.'s tentative proposal renewed, 107 and n; B.'s first visit to, 108 and n; very self-tormenting, 109; formed for B.'s destruction, 135; "that virtuous monster", 144; supposedly engaged to Eden, 340; a cold collation, 345
Milbanke, Lady Judith, 109, 111
Milbanke, Sir Ralph, 109, 111
Mildmay, Sir Henry, 269 and n
Millingen, Julius, *Memoirs . . .*, 306n
Milman, Rev. Henry Hart, *Fall of Jeruslem*, 281 and n
Milnes, Robert Pemberton, 233, 263
Milton, John, *Comus*, 39 and n, 244 and n; *Paradise Lost*, 100, 280
Mira, La, 224
Mirabeau, Honoré Gabriel de, 85n, 88, 263
Missolonghi, 32, 123n, 296, 297n, 298, 300, 302, 303, 306, 311 and n, 313 and n, 318n
Mitford, William, history of Greece, 239, 240, 241, 245, 246

Mocenigo, Palace, 178, 210
Modena, 159
Mont Blanc, 124, 125, 126
Montbovon, 127
Mont Davant, 127
Montgomery, Hugh, 73n
Montgomery, Mary Millicent, 73 and n, 79
Monthly Review, 157, 256n, 258
Montecchi, Castle of the, 139
Montenero, 288n
Monti, Vincenzo, 185 and n
Moore, Thomas, 94n, 117, 141, 171, 184, 249n, 258; attacked by *Edinburgh Review*, 22; his operatic farce, 54 and n; best of terms with B., 56 and n; a day with B. and Sheridan, 85; his talents, 87; mentioned in review of Rogers, 90 and n; on Lady Frances Webster, 113n; B.'s verses to, 149, 150, 157; visit to Ireland, 179 and n; Bermuda default, 180 and n; unpublished part of journal, 182 and n; "a degraded throne", 206; his financial trouble, 214; B. gave MS of Memoirs, 220 and n, 222 and n; in Venice with B., 220, 222, 224; married a pretty wife, 224; discussed at Java, 246–7; and Bowles, 255; sold B.'s Memoirs to Murray, 290; man of the world, 271; opinion of *Cain*, 283 and n; B.'s works in his hands, 282, 283; lives near the stove of society, 283; on Shelley's influence on B., 283 and n, 285n; B.'s friendship for, 291; and B.'s last letter, 316n; no affectations, 335; on a pretty wife, 340; attacked by Southey, 349; *Epistles, Odes, and Other Poems*, 245 and n; *The Fudge Family in Paris*, 174 and n, 252n; *Lalla Rookh*, 159, 167, 174, 220; *Life of Sheridan*, 176, 181; *Poetical Works of the Late Thomas Little*, 185, 220, 329
Moore, Doris Langley, *The Late Lord Byron*, 222n; *Lord Byron: Accounts Rendered*, 297n
Moore, Sir John, 36n
Moors, 28
Morat, 128, 133, 152
Morea (Peloponnesus), 29, 35, 43, 45, 84, 295, 296, 300, 307, 333
Moreau, Jean Victor Marie, 71 and n

Quarterly Review, 22n, 157, 165, 171n 212, 254, 258

Rabelais, François, 248n
Radcliffe, Mrs. Ann, 146
Radford, Miss, 98 and n
Rae, Alexander, 114, 142n
Ramsgate, 159
Rancliffe, Lady, 103 and n
Ransom, Messrs., 305, 314
Ravenna, 160, 192, 194, 195, 203, 204, 205, 214, 216, 219n, 225, 231, 232, 261, 280, 286n
Rawdons, 114
Reichenbach waterfall, 131
Rhine, 71n
Rhode, 233
Rialto, 176, 177, 179, 204
Richardson, Samuel, *Clarissa Harlow*, 65
Richmond, 274
Riley, Mr., creditor, 154 and n
Rimini, 160
Rizzato, 186
Rizzo-Paterol, Count Francesco, 185 and n
Roberts, Capt. Daniel, 289
Roberts, William, 218 and n
Robespierre, Maximilian François de, 229, 251n
Rocca, M. de, 165
Rochdale, 48, 51, 154, 163, 193, 220, 308, 309
Rogers, Samuel, 59, 158, 171, 252, 258; on Moore's aborted duel with B., 56 and n; a day with B. and Sheridan, 85; his fastidious elegance, 87; reviewed in *Edinburgh*, 90 and n; his gondola, 136; Tithonus of poetry, 159; on right poetic track, 167; "the black drop of his liver", 173; portrait by Denon, 347
Romagna, 197, 200, 227, 283
Romaic (modern Greek), 36, 46, 49, 304
Romanelli, 43
Rome, 46n, 88, 114, 147, 148, 160, 179, 220, 222, 239, 240n, 267, 280; B. going to, 158; B. returned from, 160; execution at, 161
Romilly, Sir Samuel, 184n, 215
Rood, Ann (Mrs. Fletcher), 120n
Rose Glacier, 131
Rose, William, 184

Rossini, Gioacchino Antonio, *Otello*, 174
Rousseau, Jean Jacques, 329; *La Nouvelle Héloise*, 127
Rubens, Peter Paul, 123
Rulhières, Claude de, 215–16
Rumelia, 302
Russia, 268; Czar of, 242n
Russians, 50
Rutland, Duke of, 200n

Saint-Germain, Mlle. de, 78n
St. Aubyn, J. H., 152, 163
St. Aubyn, Sir John, 163
St. Athanasius, 102
St. Clair, William, *That Greece Might Still Be Free*, 319n
St. Euphemia, 296, 297
St. Francis, 97 and n
St. George transport, 244
St. Gingo, 166, 196
St. Helena, 231, 270
St. James's Coffee House, 230
St. John, 213
St. John's College, Cambridge, 46n
St. Just, 88
St. Mark's, 139, 146, 186, 204, 270
St. Paul, 38, 308
St. Peter, 352
St. Ursula, 71 and n
Salamis, 303
Salfi, 240n
Sallust, 240
Salona, 318
Salora, 33
Samos, 297
San Benedetto Theatre, 184
San Lazzaro, 137n, 147
Santa, 186
Saranzo, 224
Sardinia, 28, 34, 39; king of, 28, 242
Sawbridge, 110
Scamander, 36, 116
Schadau, Chateau de, 129
Scheideck, 131
Schiller, Johann Christoff von, 129
Schlegel, August Wilhelm von, 166 and n
Scipio, 77
Scotland, 47
Scott, Alexander, 177, 202
Scott, John, Capt of *Hercules*, 295, 296, 302
Scott, Sir Walter, 101, 167, 175, 258;

Southey, Robert—*continued*
180, 182; ribald couplet on, 185 and
n; ribaldry on omitted, 187; fond of
applause of posterity, 189; and story
of incest, 196; B. will not attack
anonymously, 197; "a degraded
throne", 206; damned as a politician,
343; *Kehama*, 164 and n; his
"Vision", 349
Southwell, 21
Spain, 25–7, 34, 37, 39, 41, 50, 93n,
258, 279; language, 27, 135, 272;
Revolution, 271
Sparta, 172
Spence, Rev. Joseph, *Anecdotes of Books
and Men*, 240, 242; *Observations . . .*,
169 and n
Spencer, Dowager Lady, 264
Spencer, William Robert, 268n
Spetsas, 296
Spezia, 289
Spider, brig of war, 29
Spineda, Countess, 186
Spinozists, 53
Spooney, *see* Hanson, John
Staël, Albertine de (later Duchesse de
Broglie), 268
Staël-Holstein, Mme. Germaine de
(née Necker), 92, 197, 329; her anti-
suicide tract, 80; writes octavos, talks
folios, 85; reviewed by Mackintosh,
90 and n; flattered by note in *Bride*,
91 and n; her observations on B., 97;
"frightful as a precipice", 104;
Defended B., 125; lent B. *Glenarvon*,
138 and n; compared to Albrizzi,
140n; her letters, 163; quizzed by
Sheridan, 264; hated bores, 266;
mystified by Dandies, 268; *De
l'Allemagne*, 91n; *Considérations sur la
Révolution Française*, 165 and n;
Corinne, 219 and n
Stamboul, 159
Stanhope, Charles (later 4th Earl of
Harrington), 68 and n
Stanhope, Col. Leicester, 309, 316, 318
and n
Stanhope, Philip Henry, 4th Earl, 67
and n
Steevens's Coffee House, 216
Sterling, Charles, 294 and n
Sterling, James, British Consul, 308
Sterne, Laurence, *Tristram Shandy*, 72
and n

Stickles, John, 145 and n, 188
Stockholm, 148
Stockton, 83
Stoven, Sir Frederick, 312 and n
Strand, 237
Stranè, British Consul, 32 and n, 33,
41, 42
Strangford, Percy Clinton Smythe,
Viscount, 22
Stromboli, 295
Stuart, Sir Charles, 160 and n
Stuart, Charles Edward, 240n
Suetonius, 106
Suli, 32, 40
Suliotes, 29n, 297, 301, 303, 306, 310,
314 and n, 316
Sunium (Sunion, Sounion), 35, 45, 46n
Surrey Gaol, 175
Swedenborg, Emanuel, 55, 115
Swedish language, 272
Swift, Jonathan, 136, 195, 218 and n,
242, 249
Switzerland, 139, 154, 182, 260
Sylla (Sulla), 88, 277

Taaffe, John, 286
Tacitus, 106 and n
Tagus river, 24 and n, 25
Talavera, battle of, 27 and n
Tartar, 40
Tartars, 30
Taruscelli, Arpalice, 186 and n, 251
and n
Tasso, Torquato, 159, 169, 179, 202;
Gerusalemme Liberata, 203 and n
Tavernier, Jean Baptiste, 133
Taylor, John, 51n
Taylor (ed. of Pausanias), 123
Temple Bar, 270
Templeman, Giles, 110 and n
Tentora, 186
Tepelene (Tepaleen), 29 and n, 30–1,
35n
Terni, Fall of, 160
Terra Incognita, 53
Tetuan, 28
Thames, 230n, 271
Thebes, 35
Themistocles, 231
Theresina of Mazzurati, 186
Thirty Years War, 271
Thomas, usurer, 110
Thorwaldsen, Bertel, 228, 258 and n,
267

398

Thoun, 129, 132
Thucidides, 249
Tiberius, 54
Timbuctoo, 53
Tindall, Dr. 318 and n
Tip, Augusta's dog, 127 and n
Tithonus, 159
Tonson, Jacob, 226
Tooke, John Horne, 229
Tories, 22n, 191, 214
Torres Vedras, 25n
Trelawny, Edward John, 297n, 299, 305
Trieste, 214
Trinity College, Cambridge, 19, 20, 46n, 78, 233, 234, 237, 244
Tripolitza, 40, 299
Troad, 35, 36, 39, 45, 116, 296
Trojan War, 223
Troy, 36 and n, 242-3, 296
Tucker, surgeon, 48
Tully, Richard, *Tripoli*, 256 and n
Turin, 78n, 240n
Turkey, 23, 29, 30, 31, 34, 36, 39, 326, 357; Turks, 30, 31, 32, 33, 36, 47, 50, 172, 296, 300, 306, 316; advancing toward Missolonghi, 302; captured Gamba, 310 and n, 311, 312, 313; language, 36, 272
Tuscany, 185, 240; Grand Duke of, 93n, 242
Twiss, Horace, 139, 206, 268
Tyler, Wat, 229

United States, 287, 293, 301

Valsamachi, Capt., 313 and n
Vanbrugh, Sir John, *The Relapse*, 172 and n
Vaud, 129
Vega Carpio, Lope Felix de, 240
Veli Pasha (Velli), 29 and n, 40, 84; gave B. a horse, 41, 43, 46
Venetian dialect, 140
Venezuela, 217n, 222
Venice, 88, 138, 141, 147, 149, 160, 164, 174, 177, 204, 206n, 216, 219, 224, 225n, 231, 241 and n, 251n, 270, 271n, 272, 357, 358; greenest island, 136; B. likes, 152, 156; B. arrived in, 141; B.'s *heart*-quarters, 159; B.'s life in, 178-9; B. leaving, 195, 200; B. to return to, 202; B. in, 208; B.'s hatred of, 223; Patriarch of, 147

Verona, 136, 139, 147, 160
Vestri, Luigi, 241 and n
Vesuvius, 159, 160
Vevey, 126
Vicari, Geltrude, 205
Vicenza, 139, 160
Victor, Marshal Claude, Duc de Belluno, 27n
Vienna, 61, 270, 301
Vincy, Baron de, 133
Virgil, 159 and n
Viscillie (Basili, Vascillie), 31 and n, 42n
Voltaire, François Marie, Arouet de, 183, 185; epitaph on, 69 and n; *André des Couches à Siam*, 53 and n; *Candide*, 55 and n; *Histoire des Voyages de Scarmentado*, 232 and n, 326
Vorsberg, Countess, 199
Vostitza, 95, 332

Waite, dentist, 142 and n
Wakefield, Gilbert, 172 and n
Waldegrave, James, 2nd Earl, 257
Wales, 47
Wales, Prince of, 69
Wales, Princess of, 152
Walker, John, *Rhyming Dictionary*, 102
Walpole, Horace, 171
Walsh, William, 235 and n
Walworth, Sir William, 229
Ward, John William (later 1st Earl of Dudley and Ward), 55, 83, 91, 165, 170, 263
Warwick, 28n
Washington, George, 88, 279
Waterford, Lady, 99
Waterloo, 112, 138, 270
Waterpark, Richard Cavendish, 2nd Baron, 70 and n
Watier's Club, 268
Webb, Messrs., 305, 314
Webb and Barker, 308
Webster, James Wedderburn, B. on his character, 67-8; his philandering, 70; his claim of rights to women, 71-3; unaware of B.'s love for Lady Frances, 73; boasts of his success with women, 74; fooled by his wife, 99; B.'s loan to, 110-11; flirting with Caroline Lamb, 112-13 and n; judgment against Baldwin, 113n; replied to attack in *Quarterly*, 157; and Lady

Webster, James Wedderburn—*cont.*
Hardy, 291 and n; to theatre to see his wife cry, 345
Webster, Lady Frances, 179; in delicate health, 67–8; "very like Christ", 68; and her husband's jealousy, 68; pretty and intelligent, 70; made love with B. over billiards, 72; Platonism in some peril, 74; her caressing system, 77; stop at first tense of the verb "aimer", 97; her ingenious devices, 99; to name child after B., 111 and n; B. skeptical of her virtue, 113n; flirted with military officers, 113n; Moore on her character, 113–14n
Weimar, 294
Wellesley, Sir Arthur, 27n; (later Duke of Wellington), 113n
Wengen Alp, 130, 131
Wentworth, Thomas, 2nd Viscount, 111
West, William Edward, 287n
West Indies, 297
Westminster, 228–9, 230 and n
Westminster Abbey, 180
Westmorland, 10th Earl of, 28n
Westmorland, Countess of (née Jane Saunders), 28 and n
Wetterhorn, 131
Weybridge, Surrey, 266n
Whigs, 22n, 142, 176, 191, 214, 221, 230n
Whiston, John, 153n
Whiston, William, 153n
Whitbread, Samuel, 142n, 263
White, Lydia, 174 and n
White's Club, 268n
Wilberforce, William, 118 and n, 176, 263

Wilkes, John, 229
Williams, Edward Ellerker, 288–9
Wilmot, Robert John, 162 and n, 170
Wilmot, Mrs. (née Barbarina Ogle, later Lady Dacre), 164n
Wilson, Harriette, 268n
Wilson, John ("Christopher North"), 99n, 258
Winchester, Bishop of, 147
Windham, William, 263
Windsor, 286
Wolseley, Sir Charles, 7th Baronet, 216 and n
Wollstonecraft, Mary, 183, 196
Wordsworth, William, 167; in the *Poetic Mirror*, 99n; a "man-midwife", 101; Leigh Hunt on, 175; *The Excursion*, 115, 349; *Lyrical Ballads*, 115, 349; "we are seven", 41
Wright, Col., 315
Wright, Walter Rodwell, 44n

Xenophon, 239, 240
Xeres, 26

York and Albany, Duke of, 61, 95n, 266n
York, Duchess of, 266
Young, Edward, 242n
Yverdun, 133

Zaimes, Andreas, 317
Zambelli, Lega, 250
Zambieri, 186
Zantachi, Andreas, 42n
Zante, 297, 302, 303, 310n, 312 and n, 319n
Zitsa (Zitza), 29
Zograffo, Demetrius, 55 and n
Zoroastrians, 53